CHURCH MOTHER

THE OTHER VOICE IN EARLY MODERN EUROPE

A Series Edited by Margaret L. King and Albert Rabil Jr.

RECENT BOOKS IN THE SERIES

MARIA GAETANA AGNESI ET ALIA
*The Contest for Knowledge:
Debates over Women's Learning in
Eighteenth-Century Italy*
Edited and Translated by Rebecca Messbarger
and Paula Findlen

FRANCISCA DE LOS APÓSTOLES
*The Inquisition of Francisca: A
Sixteenth-Century Visionary on Trial*
Edited and Translated by
Gillian T.W. Ahlgren

LAURA BATTIFERRA DEGLI AMMANNATI
*Laura Battiferra and Her Literary Circle:
An Anthology*
Edited and Translated by Victoria Kirkham

GIULIA BIGOLINA
Urania: A Romance
Edited and Translated by Valeria Finucci

VITTORIA COLONNA
Sonnets for Michelangelo
Edited and Translated by Abigail Brundin

MARIE DENTIÈRE
*Epistle to Marguerite de Navarre and
Preface to a Sermon by John Calvin*
Edited and Translated by Mary B. McKinley

LOUISE LABÉ
*Complete Poetry and Prose: A Bilingual
Edition*
Edited with Introductions and Prose
Translations by Deborah Lesko Baker, with
Poetry Translations by Annie Finch

MADAME DE MAINTENON
Dialogues and Addresses
Edited and Translated by John J. Conley, S.J.

JOHANNA ELEONORA PETERSEN
*The Life of Lady Johanna Eleonora
Petersen, Written by Herself: Pietism and
Women's Autobiography in Seventeenth-
Century Germany*
Edited and Translated by Barbara Becker-
Cantarino

MADELEINE DE SCUDÉRY
*Selected Letters, Orations, and Rhetorical
Dialogues*
Edited and Translated by Jane Donawerth and
Julie Strongson

JUSTINE SIEGEMUND
The Court Midwife
Edited and Translated by Lynne Tatlock

MADAME DE VILLEDIEU
(Marie-Catherine Desjardins)
*Memoirs of the Life of Henriette-Sylvie de
Molière: A Novel*
Edited and Translated by Donna Kuizenga

Katharina Schütz Zell

CHURCH MOTHER

The Writings of a Protestant Reformer in Sixteenth-Century Germany

Edited and Translated by Elsie McKee

THE UNIVERSITY OF CHICAGO PRESS
Chicago & London

Katharina Schütz Zell, 1498–1562

Elsie McKee is professor of Reformation studies and history of worship at the Princeton Theological Seminary and author most recently of two volumes on Katharina Schütz Zell, *The Life and Thought of a Sixteenth-Century Reformer* and *The Writings: A Critical Edition* (1999). McKee is also the editor and translator of *John Calvin: Writings on Pastoral Piety* (2001).

The University of Chicago Press, Chicago 60637
The University of Chicago Press, Ltd., London
© 2006 by The University of Chicago
All rights reserved. Published 2006
Printed in the United States of America

15 14 13 12 11 10 09 08 07 06   1 2 3 4 5

ISBN: 0-226-97966-0 (cloth)
ISBN: 0-226-97967-9 (paper)

The University of Chicago Press gratefully acknowledges the generous support of James E. Rabil, in memory of Scottie W. Rabil, toward the publication of this book.

Library of Congress Cataloging-in-Publication Data
Zell, Katharina, 1497 or 8-1562.
[Selections. English. 2006]
Church mother: the writings of a Protestant reformer in sixteenth-century Germany/Katharina Schütz Zell; edited and translated by Elsie McKee.
   p. cm.—(The other voice in early modern Europe)
Includes bibliographical references (p.   ) and index.
ISBN 0-226-97966-0 (pbk.: alk. paper)—IBSN 0-226-97967-9 (cloth: alk. paper)
1. Reformation—France—Strasbourg. 2. Strasbourg (France)—Church history. 3. Christian women—Religious life. I. McKee, Elsie Anne. II. Title. III. Series.
BR372.S8Z45 2006
274.4′395406—dc22   2005029655

♾ The paper used in this publication meets the minimum requirements of the American National Standard for Information Sciences—Permanence of Paper for Printed Library Materials, ANSI Z39.48-1992.

CONTENTS

Acknowledgments vii
Series Editors' Introduction ix
Volume Editor's Introduction 1
Volume Editor's Bibliography 35
Note on Translation 39

I The Lay Reformer, Teacher, and Pastor 43

Introduction 43
Letter to the Suffering Women of the Community of Kentzingen 47
Introduction 47
Translation 50
Katharina Schütz's Apologia for Master Matthew Zell, Her Husband 56
Introduction 56
Translation 62
Some Christian and Comforting Songs of Praise about Jesus Christ Our Savior 82
Introduction 82
Translation 92
Lament and Exhortation of Katharina Zell to the People at the
Grave of Master Matthew Zell 96
Introduction 96
Translation 103
The Miserere Psalm Meditated, Prayed, and Paraphrased with King
David by Katharina Zell . . . , Sent to the Christian Man Sir Felix Armbruster 123
Introduction 123
Translation 129

II Autobiography and Polemic: A Lay Theologian Amid the Conflicts of Confessional Divisions 175

Introduction 175

To Sir Caspar Schwenckfeld 180

Introduction 180

Translation 186

A Letter to the Whole Citizenship of the City of Strasbourg from Katharina Zell, . . . concerning Mr. Ludwig Rabus 215

Introduction 215

Translation 222

Appendix: Letter of Ludwig Rabus to Katharina Schütz Zell (April 1557) 233

Series Editors' Bibliography 235

Index 251

ACKNOWLEDGMENTS

It is a pleasure to acknowledge the encouragement of colleagues, friends, students, and family who have looked forward "to hearing Katharina Schütz Zell speak English." My warm thanks to Professor Merry Wiesner-Hanks for suggesting that this lay reformer and theologian would be a good addition to the Other Voice series. I am especially grateful to Professors Albert Rabil and Margaret King for graciously welcoming Schütz Zell into their series and generously providing an ample stage for her as well as helpful editorial advice to me. Also I would like to recognize with thanks the invitation of Professor Thomas Kaufmann to share a seminar on Katharina Schütz Zell with him and his students when I was a guest professor at the University of Göttingen in the summer semester of 2004 and consultation with Dr. Ruth Jörg of Zurich on specific problems of translation. Discussion with these German-speaking friends of Schütz Zell has helped to make her debut in English flow more smoothly. Naturally, all the faults remain my own.

Special thanks is owed to the National Endowment for the Humanities for a grant that helped to provide financial support for a free semester and to Princeton Theological Seminary for granting the leave from teaching responsibilities. The generosity of both institutions has been very important in completing this project and also a significant encouragement to me.

Finally, I would like to dedicate this book to my mother and sisters, Mamu Ngolela, Mualakana, Mbongompeshi, and Tshitenga, and to the women of Witherspoon Street Presbyterian Church.

Elsie McKee, Tshimunyi wa Ngulumingi

THE OTHER VOICE IN EARLY MODERN EUROPE: INTRODUCTION TO THE SERIES

Margaret L. King and Albert Rabil Jr.

THE OLD VOICE AND THE OTHER VOICE

In western Europe and the United States, women are nearing equality in the professions, in business, and in politics. Most enjoy access to education, reproductive rights, and autonomy in financial affairs. Issues vital to women are on the public agenda: equal pay, child care, domestic abuse, breast cancer research, and curricular revision with an eye to the inclusion of women.

These recent achievements have their origins in things women (and some male supporters) said for the first time about six hundred years ago. Theirs is the "other voice," in contradistinction to the "first voice," the voice of the educated men who created Western culture. Coincident with a general reshaping of European culture in the period 1300–1700 (called the Renaissance or early modern period), questions of female equality and opportunity were raised that still resound and are still unresolved.

The other voice emerged against the backdrop of a three-thousand-year history of the derogation of women rooted in the civilizations related to Western culture: Hebrew, Greek, Roman, and Christian. Negative attitudes toward women inherited from these traditions pervaded the intellectual, medical, legal, religious, and social systems that developed during the European Middle Ages.

The following pages describe the traditional, overwhelmingly male views of women's nature inherited by early modern Europeans and the new tradition that the "other voice" called into being to begin to challenge reigning assumptions. This review should serve as a framework for understanding the texts published in the series the Other Voice in Early Modern Europe. Introductions specific to each text and author follow this essay in all the volumes of the series.

TRADITIONAL VIEWS OF WOMEN, 500 B.C.E.–1500 C.E.

Embedded in the philosophical and medical theories of the ancient Greeks were perceptions of the female as inferior to the male in both mind and body. Similarly, the structure of civil legislation inherited from the ancient Romans was biased against women, and the views on women developed by Christian thinkers out of the Hebrew Bible and the Christian New Testament were negative and disabling. Literary works composed in the vernacular of ordinary people, and widely recited or read, conveyed these negative assumptions. The social networks within which most women lived—those of the family and the institutions of the Roman Catholic Church—were shaped by this negative tradition and sharply limited the areas in which women might act in and upon the world.

GREEK PHILOSOPHY AND FEMALE NATURE. Greek biology assumed that women were inferior to men and defined them as merely childbearers and housekeepers. This view was authoritatively expressed in the works of the philosopher Aristotle.

Aristotle thought in dualities. He considered action superior to inaction, form (the inner design or structure of any object) superior to matter, completion to incompletion, possession to deprivation. In each of these dualities, he associated the male principle with the superior quality and the female with the inferior. "The male principle in nature," he argued, "is associated with active, formative and perfected characteristics, while the female is passive, material and deprived, desiring the male in order to become complete."[1] Men are always identified with virile qualities, such as judgment, courage, and stamina, and women with their opposites—irrationality, cowardice, and weakness.

The masculine principle was considered superior even in the womb. The man's semen, Aristotle believed, created the form of a new human creature, while the female body contributed only matter. (The existence of the ovum, and with it the other facts of human embryology, was not established until the seventeenth century.) Although the later Greek physician Galen believed there was a female component in generation, contributed by "female semen," the followers of both Aristotle and Galen saw the male role in human generation as more active and more important.

---

1. Aristotle, *Physics* 1.9.192a20–24, in *The Complete Works of Aristotle*, ed. Jonathan Barnes, rev. Oxford trans., 2 vols. (Princeton, 1984), 1: 328.

In the Aristotelian view, the male principle sought always to reproduce itself. The creation of a female was always a mistake, therefore, resulting from an imperfect act of generation. Every female born was considered a "defective" or "mutilated" male (as Aristotle's terminology has variously been translated), a "monstrosity" of nature.[2]

For Greek theorists, the biology of males and females was the key to their psychology. The female was softer and more docile, more apt to be despondent, querulous, and deceitful. Being incomplete, moreover, she craved sexual fulfillment in intercourse with a male. The male was intellectual, active, and in control of his passions.

These psychological polarities derived from the theory that the universe consisted of four elements (earth, fire, air, and water), expressed in human bodies as four "humors" (black bile, yellow bile, blood, and phlegm) considered, respectively, dry, hot, damp, and cold and corresponding to mental states ("melancholic," "choleric," "sanguine," "phlegmatic"). In this scheme the male, sharing the principles of earth and fire, was dry and hot; the female, sharing the principles of air and water, was cold and damp.

Female psychology was further affected by her dominant organ, the uterus (womb), *hystera* in Greek. The passions generated by the womb made women lustful, deceitful, talkative, irrational, indeed—when these affects were in excess—"hysterical." Aristotle's biology also had social and political consequences. If the male principle was superior and the female inferior, then in the household, as in the state, men should rule and women must be subordinate. That hierarchy did not rule out the companionship of husband and wife, whose cooperation was necessary for the welfare of children and the preservation of property. Such mutuality supported male preeminence.

Aristotle's teacher Plato suggested a different possibility: that men and women might possess the same virtues. The setting for this proposal is the imaginary and ideal Republic that Plato sketches in a dialogue of that name. Here, for a privileged elite capable of leading wisely, all distinctions of class and wealth dissolve, as, consequently, do those of gender. Without households or property, as Plato constructs his ideal society, there is no need for the subordination of women. Women may therefore be educated to the same level as men to assume leadership. Plato's Republic remained imaginary, however. In real societies, the subordination of women remained the norm and the prescription.

---

2. Aristotle, *Generation of Animals* 2.3.737a27–28, in *The Complete Works*, 1: 1144.

The views of women inherited from the Greek philosophical tradition became the basis for medieval thought. In the thirteenth century, the supreme Scholastic philosopher Thomas Aquinas, among others, still echoed Aristotle's views of human reproduction, of male and female personalities, and of the preeminent male role in the social hierarchy.

ROMAN LAW AND THE FEMALE CONDITION. Roman law, like Greek philosophy, underlay medieval thought and shaped medieval society. The ancient belief that adult property-owning men should administer households and make decisions affecting the community at large is the very fulcrum of Roman law.

About 450 B.C.E., during Rome's republican era, the community's customary law was recorded (legendarily) on twelve tablets erected in the city's central forum. It was later elaborated by professional jurists whose activity increased in the imperial era, when much new legislation was passed, especially on issues affecting family and inheritance. This growing, changing body of laws was eventually codified in the *Corpus of Civil Law* under the direction of the emperor Justinian, generations after the empire ceased to be ruled from Rome. That *Corpus*, read and commented on by medieval scholars from the eleventh century on, inspired the legal systems of most of the cities and kingdoms of Europe.

Laws regarding dowries, divorce, and inheritance pertain primarily to women. Since those laws aimed to maintain and preserve property, the women concerned were those from the property-owning minority. Their subordination to male family members points to the even greater subordination of lower-class and slave women, about whom the laws speak little.

In the early republic, the *paterfamilias*, or "father of the family," possessed *patria potestas*, "paternal power." The term *pater*, "father," in both these cases does not necessarily mean biological father but denotes the head of a household. The father was the person who owned the household's property and, indeed, its human members. The *paterfamilias* had absolute power—including the power, rarely exercised, of life or death—over his wife, his children, and his slaves, as much as his cattle.

Male children could be "emancipated," an act that granted legal autonomy and the right to own property. Those over fourteen could be emancipated by a special grant from the father or automatically by their father's death. But females could never be emancipated; instead, they passed from the authority of their father to that of a husband or, if widowed or orphaned while still unmarried, to a guardian or tutor.

Marriage in its traditional form placed the woman under her husband's authority, or *manus*. He could divorce her on grounds of adultery, drinking wine, or stealing from the household, but she could not divorce him. She could neither possess property in her own right nor bequeath any to her children upon her death. When her husband died, the household property passed not to her but to his male heirs. And when her father died, she had no claim to any family inheritance, which was directed to her brothers or more remote male relatives. The effect of these laws was to exclude women from civil society, itself based on property ownership.

In the later republican and imperial periods, these rules were significantly modified. Women rarely married according to the traditional form. The practice of "free" marriage allowed a woman to remain under her father's authority, to possess property given her by her father (most frequently the "dowry," recoverable from the husband's household on his death), and to inherit from her father. She could also bequeath property to her own children and divorce her husband, just as he could divorce her.

Despite this greater freedom, women still suffered enormous disability under Roman law. Heirs could belong only to the father's side, never the mother's. Moreover, although she could bequeath her property to her children, she could not establish a line of succession in doing so. A woman was "the beginning and end of her own family," said the jurist Ulpian. Moreover, women could play no public role. They could not hold public office, represent anyone in a legal case, or even witness a will. Women had only a private existence and no public personality.

The dowry system, the guardian, women's limited ability to transmit wealth, and total political disability are all features of Roman law adopted by the medieval communities of western Europe, although modified according to local customary laws.

CHRISTIAN DOCTRINE AND WOMEN'S PLACE. The Hebrew Bible and the Christian New Testament authorized later writers to limit women to the realm of the family and to burden them with the guilt of original sin. The passages most fruitful for this purpose were the creation narratives in Genesis and sentences from the Epistles defining women's role within the Christian family and community.

Each of the first two chapters of Genesis contains a creation narrative. In the first "God created man in his own image, in the image of God he created him; male and female he created them" (Gn 1:27). In the second, God created Eve from Adam's rib (2:21–23). Christian theologians relied principally on Genesis 2 for their understanding of the relation between man and woman, interpreting the creation of Eve from Adam as proof of her subordination to him.

The creation story in Genesis 2 leads to that of the temptations in Genesis 3: of Eve by the wily serpent and of Adam by Eve. As read by Christian theologians from Tertullian to Thomas Aquinas, the narrative made Eve responsible for the Fall and its consequences. She instigated the act; she deceived her husband; she suffered the greater punishment. Her disobedience made it necessary for Jesus to be incarnated and to die on the cross. From the pulpit, moralists and preachers for centuries conveyed to women the guilt that they bore for original sin.

The Epistles offered advice to early Christians on building communities of the faithful. Among the matters to be regulated was the place of women. Paul offered views favorable to women in Galatians 3:28: "There is neither Jew nor Greek, there is neither slave nor free, there is neither male nor female; for you are all one in Christ Jesus." Paul also referred to women as his coworkers and placed them on a par with himself and his male coworkers (Phlm 4:2–3; Rom 16:1–3; 1 Cor 16:19). Elsewhere, Paul limited women's possibilities: "But I want you to understand that the head of every man is Christ, the head of a woman is her husband, and the head of Christ is God" (1 Cor 11:3).

Biblical passages by later writers (although attributed to Paul) enjoined women to forgo jewels, expensive clothes, and elaborate coiffures; and they forbade women to "teach or have authority over men," telling them to "learn in silence with all submissiveness" as is proper for one responsible for sin, consoling them, however, with the thought that they will be saved through childbearing (1 Tm 2:9–15). Other texts among the later Epistles defined women as the weaker sex and emphasized their subordination to their husbands (1 Pt 3:7; Col 3:18; Eph 5:22–23).

These passages from the New Testament became the arsenal employed by theologians of the early church to transmit negative attitudes toward women to medieval Christian culture—above all, Tertullian (*On the Apparel of Women*), Jerome (*Against Jovinian*), and Augustine (*The Literal Meaning of Genesis*).

THE IMAGE OF WOMEN IN MEDIEVAL LITERATURE. The philosophical, legal, and religious traditions born in antiquity formed the basis of the medieval intellectual synthesis wrought by trained thinkers, mostly clerics, writing in Latin and based largely in universities. The vernacular literary tradition that developed alongside the learned tradition also spoke about female nature and women's roles. Medieval stories, poems, and epics also portrayed women negatively—as lustful and deceitful—while praising good housekeepers and loyal wives as replicas of the Virgin Mary or the female saints and martyrs.

There is an exception in the movement of "courtly love" that evolved in southern France from the twelfth century. Courtly love was the erotic love between a nobleman and noblewoman, the latter usually superior in social rank. It was always adulterous. From the conventions of courtly love derive modern Western notions of romantic love. The tradition has had an impact disproportionate to its size, for it affected only a tiny elite, and very few women. The exaltation of the female lover probably does not reflect a higher evaluation of women or a step toward their sexual liberation. More likely it gives expression to the social and sexual tensions besetting the knightly class at a specific historical juncture.

The literary fashion of courtly love was on the wane by the thirteenth century, when the widely read *Romance of the Rose* was composed in French by two authors of significantly different dispositions. Guillaume de Lorris composed the initial four thousand verses about 1235, and Jean de Meun added about seventeen thousand verses—more than four times the original—about 1265.

The fragment composed by Guillaume de Lorris stands squarely in the tradition of courtly love. Here the poet, in a dream, is admitted into a walled garden where he finds a magic fountain in which a rosebush is reflected. He longs to pick one rose, but the thorns prevent his doing so, even as he is wounded by arrows from the god of love, whose commands he agrees to obey. The rest of this part of the poem recounts the poet's unsuccessful efforts to pluck the rose.

The longer part of the *Romance* by Jean de Meun also describes a dream. But here allegorical characters give long didactic speeches, providing a social satire on a variety of themes, some pertaining to women. Love is an anxious and tormented state, the poem explains: women are greedy and manipulative, marriage is miserable, beautiful women are lustful, ugly ones cease to please, and a chaste woman is as rare as a black swan.

Shortly after Jean de Meun completed *The Romance of the Rose*, Mathéolus penned his *Lamentations*, a long Latin diatribe against marriage translated into French about a century later. The *Lamentations* sum up medieval attitudes toward women and provoked the important response by Christine de Pizan in her *Book of the City of Ladies*.

In 1355, Giovanni Boccaccio wrote *Il Corbaccio*, another antifeminist manifesto, although ironically by an author whose other works pioneered new directions in Renaissance thought. The former husband of his lover appears to Boccaccio, condemning his unmoderated lust and detailing the defects of women. Boccaccio concedes at the end "how much men naturally surpass women in nobility" and is cured of his desires.[3]

WOMEN'S ROLES: THE FAMILY. The negative perceptions of women expressed in the intellectual tradition are also implicit in the actual roles that women played in European society. Assigned to subordinate positions in the household and the church, they were barred from significant participation in public life.

Medieval European households, like those in antiquity and in non-Western civilizations, were headed by males. It was the male serf (or peasant), feudal lord, town merchant, or citizen who was polled or taxed or succeeded to an inheritance or had any acknowledged public role, although his wife or widow could stand as a temporary surrogate. From about 1100, the position of property-holding males was further enhanced: inheritance was confined to the male, or agnate, line—with depressing consequences for women.

A wife never fully belonged to her husband's family, nor was she a daughter to her father's family. She left her father's house young to marry whomever her parents chose. Her dowry was managed by her husband, and at her death it normally passed to her children by him.

A married woman's life was occupied nearly constantly with cycles of pregnancy, childbearing, and lactation. Women bore children through all the years of their fertility, and many died in childbirth. They were also responsible for raising young children up to six or seven. In the propertied classes that responsibility was shared, since it was common for a wet nurse to take over breast-feeding and for servants to perform other chores.

Women trained their daughters in the household duties appropriate to their status, nearly always tasks associated with textiles: spinning, weaving, sewing, embroidering. Their sons were sent out of the house as apprentices or students, or their training was assumed by fathers in later childhood and adolescence. On the death of her husband, a woman's children became the responsibility of his family. She generally did not take "his" children with her to a new marriage or back to her father's house, except sometimes in the artisan classes.

Women also worked. Rural peasants performed farm chores, merchant wives often practiced their husbands' trades, the unmarried daughters of the urban poor worked as servants or prostitutes. All wives produced or embel-

---

3. Giovanni Boccaccio, *The Corbaccio, or The Labyrinth of Love*, trans. and ed. Anthony K. Cassell, rev. ed. (Binghamton, N.Y., 1993), 71.

Series Editors' Introduction xvii

lished textiles and did the housekeeping, while wealthy ones managed servants. These labors were unpaid or poorly paid but often contributed substantially to family wealth.

WOMEN'S ROLES: THE CHURCH. Membership in a household, whether a father's or a husband's, meant for women a lifelong subordination to others. In western Europe, the Roman Catholic Church offered an alternative to the career of wife and mother. A woman could enter a convent, parallel in function to the monasteries for men that evolved in the early Christian centuries.

In the convent, a woman pledged herself to a celibate life, lived according to strict community rules, and worshiped daily. Often the convent offered training in Latin, allowing some women to become considerable scholars and authors as well as scribes, artists, and musicians. For women who chose the conventual life, the benefits could be enormous, but for numerous others placed in convents by paternal choice, the life could be restrictive and burdensome.

The conventual life declined as an alternative for women as the modern age approached. Reformed monastic institutions resisted responsibility for related female orders. The church increasingly restricted female institutional life by insisting on closer male supervision.

Women often sought other options. Some joined the communities of laywomen that sprang up spontaneously in the thirteenth century in the urban zones of western Europe, especially in Flanders and Italy. Some joined the heretical movements that flourished in late medieval Christendom, whose anticlerical and often antifamily positions particularly appealed to women. In these communities, some women were acclaimed as "holy women" or "saints," whereas others often were condemned as frauds or heretics.

In all, although the options offered to women by the church were sometimes less than satisfactory, they were sometimes richly rewarding. After 1520, the convent remained an option only in Roman Catholic territories. Protestantism engendered an ideal of marriage as a heroic endeavor and appeared to place husband and wife on a more equal footing. Sermons and treatises, however, still called for female subordination and obedience.

THE OTHER VOICE, 1300–1700

When the modern era opened, European culture was so firmly structured by a framework of negative attitudes toward women that to dismantle it was a monumental labor. The process began as part of a larger cultural movement that entailed the critical reexamination of ideas inherited from the ancient and medieval past. The humanists launched that critical reexamination.

THE HUMANIST FOUNDATION. Originating in Italy in the fourteenth century, humanism quickly became the dominant intellectual movement in Europe. Spreading in the sixteenth century from Italy to the rest of Europe, it fueled the literary, scientific, and philosophical movements of the era and laid the basis for the eighteenth-century Enlightenment.

Humanists regarded the Scholastic philosophy of medieval universities as out of touch with the realities of urban life. They found in the rhetorical discourse of classical Rome a language adapted to civic life and public speech. They learned to read, speak, and write classical Latin and, eventually, classical Greek. They founded schools to teach others to do so, establishing the pattern for elementary and secondary education for the next three hundred years.

In the service of complex government bureaucracies, humanists employed their skills to write eloquent letters, deliver public orations, and formulate public policy. They developed new scripts for copying manuscripts and used the new printing press to disseminate texts, for which they created methods of critical editing.

Humanism was a movement led by males who accepted the evaluation of women in ancient texts and generally shared the misogynist perceptions of their culture. (Female humanists, as we will see, did not.) Yet humanism also opened the door to a reevaluation of the nature and capacity of women. By calling authors, texts, and ideas into question, it made possible the fundamental rereading of the whole intellectual tradition that was required in order to free women from cultural prejudice and social subordination.

A DIFFERENT CITY. The other voice first appeared when, after so many centuries, the accumulation of misogynist concepts evoked a response from a capable female defender: Christine de Pizan (1365–1431). Introducing her *Book of the City of Ladies* (1405), she described how she was affected by reading Mathéolus's *Lamentations:* "Just the sight of this book . . . made me wonder how it happened that so many different men . . . are so inclined to express both in speaking and in their treatises and writings so many wicked insults about women and their behavior."[4] These statements

---

4. Christine de Pizan, *The Book of the City of Ladies,* trans. Earl Jeffrey Richards, foreword by Marina Warner (New York, 1982), 1.1.1, pp. 3–4.

impelled her to detest herself "and the entire feminine sex, as though we were monstrosities in nature."[5]

The rest of *The Book of the City of Ladies* presents a justification of the female sex and a vision of an ideal community of women. A pioneer, she has received the message of female inferiority and rejected it. From the fourteenth to the seventeenth century, a huge body of literature accumulated that responded to the dominant tradition.

The result was a literary explosion consisting of works by both men and women, in Latin and in the vernaculars: works enumerating the achievements of notable women; works rebutting the main accusations made against women; works arguing for the equal education of men and women; works defining and redefining women's proper role in the family, at court, in public; works describing women's lives and experiences. Recent monographs and articles have begun to hint at the great range of this movement, involving probably several thousand titles. The protofeminism of these "other voices" constitutes a significant fraction of the literary product of the early modern era.

THE CATALOGS. About 1365, the same Boccaccio whose *Corbaccio* rehearses the usual charges against female nature wrote another work, *Concerning Famous Women*. A humanist treatise drawing on classical texts, it praised 106 notable women: ninety-eight of them from pagan Greek and Roman antiquity, one (Eve) from the Bible, and seven from the medieval religious and cultural tradition; his book helped make all readers aware of a sex normally condemned or forgotten. Boccaccio's outlook nevertheless was unfriendly to women, for it singled out for praise those women who possessed the traditional virtues of chastity, silence, and obedience. Women who were active in the public realm—for example, rulers and warriors—were depicted as usually being lascivious and as suffering terrible punishments for entering the masculine sphere. Women were his subject, but Boccaccio's standard remained male.

Christine de Pizan's *Book of the City of Ladies* contains a second catalog, one responding specifically to Boccaccio's. Whereas Boccaccio portrays female virtue as exceptional, she depicts it as universal. Many women in history were leaders, or remained chaste despite the lascivious approaches of men, or were visionaries and brave martyrs.

The work of Boccaccio inspired a series of catalogs of illustrious women of the biblical, classical, Christian, and local pasts, among them

---

5. Ibid., 1.1.1–2, p. 5.

Filippo da Bergamo's *Of Illustrious Women*, Pierre de Brantôme's *Lives of Illustrious Women*, Pierre Le Moyne's *Gallerie of Heroic Women*, and Pietro Paolo de Ribera's *Immortal Triumphs and Heroic Enterprises of 845 Women*. Whatever their embedded prejudices, these works drove home to the public the possibility of female excellence.

THE DEBATE. At the same time, many questions remained: Could a woman be virtuous? Could she perform noteworthy deeds? Was she even, strictly speaking, of the same human species as men? These questions were debated over four centuries, in French, German, Italian, Spanish, and English, by authors male and female, among Catholics, Protestants, and Jews, in ponderous volumes and breezy pamphlets. The whole literary genre has been called the *querelle des femmes*, the "woman question."

The opening volley of this battle occurred in the first years of the fifteenth century, in a literary debate sparked by Christine de Pizan. She exchanged letters critical of Jean de Meun's contribution to *The Romance of the Rose* with two French royal secretaries, Jean de Montreuil and Gontier Col. When the matter became public, Jean Gerson, one of Europe's leading theologians, supported de Pizan's arguments against de Meun, for the moment silencing the opposition.

The debate resurfaced repeatedly over the next two hundred years. *The Triumph of Women* (1438) by Juan Rodríguez de la Camara (or Juan Rodríguez del Padron) struck a new note by presenting arguments for the superiority of women to men. *The Champion of Women* (1440–42) by Martin Le Franc addresses once again the negative views of women presented in *The Romance of the Rose* and offers counterevidence of female virtue and achievement.

A cameo of the debate on women is included in *The Courtier*, one of the most widely read books of the era, published by the Italian Baldassare Castiglione in 1528 and immediately translated into other European vernaculars. *The Courtier* depicts a series of evenings at the court of the duke of Urbino in which many men and some women of the highest social stratum amuse themselves by discussing a range of literary and social issues. The "woman question" is a pervasive theme throughout, and the third of its four books is devoted entirely to that issue.

In a verbal duel, Gasparo Pallavicino and Giuliano de' Medici present the main claims of the two traditions. Gasparo argues the innate inferiority of women and their inclination to vice. Only in bearing children do they profit the world. Giuliano counters that women share the same spiritual and mental capacities as men and may excel in wisdom and action. Men and women are of the same essence: just as no stone can be more perfectly a stone than another, so no human being can be more perfectly human than others, whether male or female. It was an astonishing assertion, boldly made to an audience as large as all Europe.

THE TREATISES. Humanism provided the materials for a positive counterconcept to the misogyny embedded in Scholastic philosophy and law and inherited from the Greek, Roman, and Christian pasts. A series of humanist treatises on marriage and family, on education and deportment, and on the nature of women helped construct these new perspectives.

The works by Francesco Barbaro and Leon Battista Alberti—*On Marriage* (1415) and *On the Family* (1434–37)—far from defending female equality, reasserted women's responsibility for rearing children and managing the housekeeping while being obedient, chaste, and silent. Nevertheless, they served the cause of reexamining the issue of women's nature by placing domestic issues at the center of scholarly concern and reopening the pertinent classical texts. In addition, Barbaro emphasized the companionate nature of marriage and the importance of a wife's spiritual and mental qualities for the well-being of the family.

These themes reappear in later humanist works on marriage and the education of women by Juan Luis Vives and Erasmus. Both were moderately sympathetic to the condition of women without reaching beyond the usual masculine prescriptions for female behavior.

An outlook more favorable to women characterizes the nearly unknown work *In Praise of Women* (ca. 1487) by the Italian humanist Bartolommeo Goggio. In addition to providing a catalog of illustrious women, Goggio argued that male and female are the same in essence, but that women (reworking the Adam and Eve narrative from quite a new angle) are actually superior. In the same vein, the Italian humanist Maria Equicola asserted the spiritual equality of men and women in *On Women* (1501). In 1525, Galeazzo Flavio Capra (or Capella) published his work *On the Excellence and Dignity of Women*. This humanist tradition of treatises defending the worthiness of women culminates in the work of Henricus Cornelius Agrippa *On the Nobility and Preeminence of the Female Sex*. No work by a male humanist more succinctly or explicitly presents the case for female dignity.

THE WITCH BOOKS. While humanists grappled with the issues pertaining to women and family, other learned men turned their attention to what they perceived as a very great problem: witches. Witch-hunting manuals, explorations of the witch phenomenon, and even defenses of witches are not at first glance pertinent to the tradition of the other voice. But they do relate in this way: most accused witches were women. The hostility aroused by supposed witch activity is comparable to the hostility aroused by women. The evil deeds the victims of the hunt were charged with were exaggerations of the vices to which, many believed, all women were prone.

The connection between the witch accusation and the hatred of women is explicit in the notorious witch-hunting manual *The Hammer of Witches* (1486) by two Dominican inquisitors, Heinrich Krämer and Jacob Sprenger. Here the inconstancy, deceitfulness, and lustfulness traditionally associated with women are depicted in exaggerated form as the core features of witch behavior. These traits inclined women to make a bargain with the devil—sealed by sexual intercourse—by which they acquired unholy powers. Such bizarre claims, far from being rejected by rational men, were broadcast by intellectuals. The German Ulrich Molitur, the Frenchman Nicolas Rémy, and the Italian Stefano Guazzo all coolly informed the public of sinister orgies and midnight pacts with the devil. The celebrated French jurist, historian, and political philosopher Jean Bodin argued that because women were especially prone to diabolism, regular legal procedures could properly be suspended in order to try those accused of this "exceptional crime."

A few experts such as the physician Johann Weyer, a student of Agrippa's, raised their voices in protest. In 1563, he explained the witch phenomenon thus, without discarding belief in diabolism: the devil deluded foolish old women afflicted by melancholia, causing them to believe they had magical powers. Weyer's rational skepticism, which had good credibility in the community of the learned, worked to revise the conventional views of women and witchcraft.

WOMEN'S WORKS. To the many categories of works produced on the question of women's worth must be added nearly all works written by women. A woman writing was in herself a statement of women's claim to dignity.

Only a few women wrote anything before the dawn of the modern era, for three reasons. First, they rarely received the education that would enable them to write. Second, they were not admitted to the public roles—as administrator, bureaucrat, lawyer or notary, or university professor—in which they might gain knowledge of the kinds of things the literate public thought worth writing about. Third, the culture imposed silence on women, considering speaking out a form of unchastity. Given these conditions, it is remarkable that any women wrote. Those who did before the fourteenth century were almost always nuns or religious women whose isolation made their pronouncements more acceptable.

From the fourteenth century on, the volume of women's writings rose. Women continued to write devotional literature, although not always as cloistered nuns. They also wrote diaries, often intended as keepsakes for their children; books of advice to their sons and daughters; letters to family members and friends; and family memoirs, in a few cases elaborate enough to be considered histories.

A few women wrote works directly concerning the "woman question," and some of these, such as the humanists Isotta Nogarola, Cassandra Fedele, Laura Cereta, and Olympia Morata, were highly trained. A few were professional writers, living by the income of their pens; the very first among them was Christine de Pizan, noteworthy in this context as in so many others. In addition to *The Book of the City of Ladies* and her critiques of *The Romance of the Rose*, she wrote *The Treasure of the City of Ladies* (a guide to social decorum for women), an advice book for her son, much courtly verse, and a full-scale history of the reign of King Charles V of France.

WOMEN PATRONS Women who did not themselves write but encouraged others to do so boosted the development of an alternative tradition. Highly placed women patrons supported authors, artists, musicians, poets, and learned men. Such patrons, drawn mostly from the Italian elites and the courts of northern Europe, figure disproportionately as the dedicatees of the important works of early feminism.

For a start, it might be noted that the catalogs of Boccaccio and Alvaro de Luna were dedicated to the Florentine noblewoman Andrea Acciaiuoli and to Doña María, first wife of King Juan II of Castile, while the French translation of Boccaccio's work was commissioned by Anne of Brittany, wife of King Charles VIII of France. The humanist treatises of Goggio, Equicola, Vives, and Agrippa were dedicated, respectively, to Eleanora of Aragon, wife of Ercole I d'Este, Duke of Ferrara; to Margherita Cantelma of Mantua; to Catherine of Aragon, wife of King Henry VIII of England; and to Margaret, Duchess of Austria and regent of the Netherlands. As late as 1696, Mary Astell's *Serious Proposal to the Ladies, for the Advancement of Their True and Greatest Interest* was dedicated to Princess Anne of Denmark.

These authors presumed that their efforts would be welcome to female patrons, or they may have written at the bidding of those patrons. Silent themselves, perhaps even unresponsive, these loftily placed women helped shape the tradition of the other voice.

THE ISSUES. The literary forms and patterns in which the tradition of the other voice presented itself have now been sketched. It remains to highlight the major issues around which this tradition crystallizes. In brief, there are four problems to which our authors return again and again, in plays and catalogs, in verse and letters, in treatises and dialogues, in every language: the problem of chastity, the problem of power, the problem of speech, and the problem of knowledge. Of these the greatest, preconditioning the others, is the problem of chastity.

THE PROBLEM OF CHASTITY. In traditional European culture, as in those of antiquity and others around the globe, chastity was perceived as woman's quintessential virtue—in contrast to courage, or generosity, or leadership, or rationality, seen as virtues characteristic of men. Opponents of women charged them with insatiable lust. Women themselves and their defenders—without disputing the validity of the standard—responded that women were capable of chastity.

The requirement of chastity kept women at home, silenced them, isolated them, left them in ignorance. It was the source of all other impediments. Why was it so important to the society of men, of whom chastity was not required, and who more often than not considered it their right to violate the chastity of any woman they encountered?

Female chastity ensured the continuity of the male-headed household. If a man's wife was not chaste, he could not be sure of the legitimacy of his offspring. If they were not his and they acquired his property, it was not his household, but some other man's, that had endured. If his daughter was not chaste, she could not be transferred to another man's household as his wife, and he was dishonored.

The whole system of the integrity of the household and the transmission of property was bound up in female chastity. Such a requirement pertained only to property-owning classes, of course. Poor women could not expect to maintain their chastity, least of all if they were in contact with high-status men to whom all women but those of their own household were prey.

In Catholic Europe, the requirement of chastity was further buttressed by moral and religious imperatives. Original sin was inextricably linked with the sexual act. Virginity was seen as heroic virtue, far more impressive than, say, the avoidance of idleness or greed. Monasticism, the cultural institution that dominated medieval Europe for centuries, was grounded in the renunciation of the flesh. The Catholic reform of the eleventh century imposed a similar standard on all the clergy and a heightened awareness of sexual requirements on all the laity. Although men were asked to be chaste, female unchastity was much worse: it led to the devil, as Eve had led mankind to sin.

To such requirements, women and their defenders protested their innocence. Furthermore, following the example of holy women who had escaped the requirements of family and sought the religious life, some women began to conceive of female communities as alternatives both to family and to the cloister. Christine de Pizan's city of ladies was such a community. Moderata Fonte and Mary Astell envisioned others. The luxurious salons of the French *précieuses* of the seventeenth century, or the comfortable English drawing rooms of the next, may have been born of the same impulse. Here women not only might escape, if briefly, the subordinate position that life in the family entailed but might also make claims to power, exercise their capacity for speech, and display their knowledge.

THE PROBLEM OF POWER. Women were excluded from power: the whole cultural tradition insisted on it. Only men were citizens, only men bore arms, only men could be chiefs or lords or kings. There were exceptions that did not disprove the rule, when wives or widows or mothers took the place of men, awaiting their return or the maturation of a male heir. A woman who attempted to rule in her own right was perceived as an anomaly, a monster, at once a deformed woman and an insufficient male, sexually confused and consequently unsafe.

The association of such images with women who held or sought power explains some otherwise odd features of early modern culture. Queen Elizabeth I of England, one of the few women to hold full regal authority in European history, played with such male/female images—positive ones, of course—in representing herself to her subjects. She was a prince, and manly, even though she was female. She was also (she claimed) virginal, a condition absolutely essential if she was to avoid the attacks of her opponents. Catherine de' Medici, who ruled France as widow and regent for her sons, also adopted such imagery in defining her position. She chose as one symbol the figure of Artemisia, an androgynous ancient warrior-heroine who combined a female persona with masculine powers.

Power in a woman, without such sexual imagery, seems to have been indigestible by the culture. A rare note was struck by the Englishman Sir Thomas Elyot in his *Defence of Good Women* (1540), justifying both women's participation in civic life and their prowess in arms. The old tune was sung by the Scots reformer John Knox in his *First Blast of the Trumpet against the Monstrous Regiment of Women* (1558); for him rule by women, defects in nature, was a hideous contradiction in terms.

The confused sexuality of the imagery of female potency was not reserved for rulers. Any woman who excelled was likely to be called an Amazon, recalling the self-mutilated warrior women of antiquity who repudiated all men, gave up their sons, and raised only their daughters. She was often said to have "exceeded her sex" or to have possessed "masculine virtue"—as the very fact of conspicuous excellence conferred masculinity even on the female subject. The catalogs of notable women often showed those female heroes dressed in armor, armed to the teeth, like men. Amazonian heroines romp through the epics of the age—Ariosto's *Orlando Furioso* (1532) and Spenser's *Faerie Queene* (1590–1609). Excellence in a woman was perceived as a claim for power, and power was reserved for the masculine realm. A woman who possessed either one was masculinized and lost title to her own female identity.

THE PROBLEM OF SPEECH. Just as power had a sexual dimension when it was claimed by women, so did speech. A good woman spoke little. Excessive speech was an indication of unchastity. By speech, women seduced men. Eve had lured Adam into sin by her speech. Accused witches were commonly accused of having spoken abusively, or irrationally, or simply too much. As enlightened a figure as Francesco Barbaro insisted on silence in a woman, which he linked to her perfect unanimity with her husband's will and her unblemished virtue (her chastity). Another Italian humanist, Leonardo Bruni, in advising a noblewoman on her studies, barred her not from speech but from public speaking. That was reserved for men.

Related to the problem of speech was that of costume—another, if silent, form of self-expression. Assigned the task of pleasing men as their primary occupation, elite women often tended toward elaborate costume, hairdressing, and the use of cosmetics. Clergy and secular moralists alike condemned these practices. The appropriate function of costume and adornment was to announce the status of a woman's husband or father. Any further indulgence in adornment was akin to unchastity.

THE PROBLEM OF KNOWLEDGE. When the Italian noblewoman Isotta Nogarola had begun to attain a reputation as a humanist, she was accused of incest—a telling instance of the association of learning in women with unchastity. That chilling association inclined any woman who was educated to deny that she was or to make exaggerated claims of heroic chastity.

If educated women were pursued with suspicions of sexual misconduct, women seeking an education faced an even more daunting obstacle: the assumption that women were by nature incapable of learning, that reasoning was a particularly masculine ability. Just as they proclaimed their chastity, women and their defenders insisted on their capacity for learning. The major work by a male writer on female education—that by Juan Luis Vives, *On the Education of a Christian Woman* (1523)—granted female capacity for intellection but still argued that a woman's whole education was to be shaped around the requirement of chastity and a future within the household. Female writers of the following generations—Marie de Gournay in France, Anna Maria van Schurman in Holland, and Mary Astell in England—began to envision other possibilities.

The pioneers of female education were the Italian women humanists who managed to attain a literacy in Latin and a knowledge of classical and Christian literature equivalent to that of prominent men. Their works implicitly and explicitly raise questions about women's social roles, defining problems that beset women attempting to break out of the cultural limits that had bound them. Like Christine de Pizan, who achieved an advanced education through her father's tutoring and her own devices, their bold questioning makes clear the importance of training. Only when women were educated to the same standard as male leaders would they be able to raise that other voice and insist on their dignity as human beings morally, intellectually, and legally equal to men.

THE OTHER VOICE. The other voice, a voice of protest, was mostly female, but it was also male. It spoke in the vernaculars and in Latin, in treatises and dialogues, in plays and poetry, in letters and diaries, and in pamphlets. It battered at the wall of prejudice that encircled women and raised a banner announcing its claims. The female was equal (or even superior) to the male in essential nature—moral, spiritual, and intellectual. Women were capable of higher education, of holding positions of power and influence in the public realm, and of speaking and writing persuasively. The last bastion of masculine supremacy, centered on the notions of a woman's primary domestic responsibility and the requirement of female chastity, was not as yet assaulted—although visions of productive female communities as alternatives to the family indicated an awareness of the problem.

During the period 1300–1700, the other voice remained only a voice, and one only dimly heard. It did not result—yet—in an alteration of social patterns. Indeed, to this day they have not entirely been altered. Yet the call for justice issued as long as six centuries ago by those writing in the tradition of the other voice must be recognized as the source and origin of the mature feminist tradition and of the realignment of social institutions accomplished in the modern age.

We thank the volume editors in this series, who responded with many suggestions to an earlier draft of this introduction, making it a collaborative enterprise. Many of their suggestions and criticisms have resulted in revisions of this introduction, although we remain responsible for the final product.

PROJECTED TITLES IN THE SERIES

Isabella Andreini, *Mirtilla*, edited and translated by Laura Stortoni

Tullia d'Aragona, *Complete Poems and Letters*, edited and translated by Julia Hairston

Tullia d'Aragona, *The Wretch, Otherwise Known as Guerrino*, edited and translated by Julia Hairston and John McLucas

Francesco Barbaro et al., *On Marriage and the Family*, edited and translated by Margaret L. King

Francesco Buoninsegni and Arcangela Tarabotti, *Menippean Satire: "Against Feminine Extravagance" and "Antisatire,"* edited and translated by Elissa Weaver

Rosalba Carriera, *Letters, Diaries, and Art*, edited and translated by Catherine M. Sama

Madame du Chatelet, *Selected Works*, edited by Judith Zinsser

Vittoria Colonna, Chiara Matraini, and Lucrezia Marinella, *Marian Writings*, edited and translated by Susan Haskins

Princess Elizabeth of Bohemia, *Correspondence with Descartes*, edited and translated by Lisa Shapiro

Isabella d'Este, *Selected Letters*, edited and translated by Deanna Shemek

Fairy-Tales by Seventeenth-Century French Women Writers, edited and translated by Lewis Seifert and Domna C. Stanton

Moderata Fonte, *Floridoro*, edited by Valeria Finucci and translated by Julia Kisacki

Moderata Fonte and Lucrezia Marinella, *Religious Narratives*, edited and translated by Virginia Cox

Catharina Regina von Greiffenberg, *Meditations on the Life of Christ*, edited and translated by Lynne Tatlock

In Praise of Women: Italian Fifteenth-Century Defenses of Women, edited and translated by Daniel Bornstein

Lucrezia Marinella, *L'Enrico, or Byzantium Conquered*, edited and translated by Virginia Cox

Lucrezia Marinella, *Happy Arcadia*, edited and translated by Susan Haskins and Letizia Panizza

Chiara Matraini, *Selected Poetry and Prose*, edited and translated by Elaine MacLachlan

Alessandro Piccolomini, *Rethinking Marriage in Sixteenth-Century Italy*, edited and translated by Letizia Panizza

Christine de Pizan, *Debate over the "Romance of the Rose,"* edited and translated by David F. Hult

Christine de Pizan, *Life of Charles V*, edited and translated by Nadia Margolis

Christine de Pizan, *The Long Road of Learning*, edited and translated by Andrea Tarnowski

Oliva Sabuco, *The New Philosophy: True Medicine*, edited and translated by Gianna Pomata

Margherita Sarrocchi, *La Scanderbeide*, edited and translated by Rinaldina Russell

Gabrielle Suchon, *"On Philosophy" and "On Morality,"* edited and translated by
Domna Stanton with Rebecca Wilkin

Sara Copio Sullam, *Sara Copio Sullam: Jewish Poet and Intellectual in Early Seventeenth-Century Venice*, edited and translated by Don Harrán

Arcangela Tarabotti, *Convent Life as Inferno: A Report*, introduction and notes by
Francesca Medioli, translated by Letizia Panizza

Laura Terracina, *Works*, edited and translated by Michael Sherberg

VOLUME EDITOR'S INTRODUCTION

THE OTHER VOICE

Katharina Schütz Zell was one of the most surprising—and, to modern eyes, appealing—women of sixteenth-century Europe. She was for many years a respected if unofficial "mother" of the established church in Strasbourg, in an age when ecclesiastical leadership was a male prerogative. She was a lifelong author who produced a significant literary corpus, in a time when the majority of people could not write their own names. She was a "commoner" who participated actively and effectively in public life, in a world dominated by nobles and aristocrats. She was an essentially equal partner in her marriage, in a society that required that the good wife be silent and obedient and in which women usually achieved some independence only as widows. As a lay reformer Schütz Zell proved that she could and would teach her new faith with intelligence and humor. As a writer of many different genres of religious texts she dared to challenge both male theologians and cultural conventions by speaking out publicly. As a social activist she organized relief for refugees and called the city government to account when welfare reform was needed. As one of the first and most daring models of "the pastor's wife" in the Protestant Reformation, she demonstrated that she could happily work together with her husband without losing the least part of her own identity.

Katharina Schütz, known to history by her married name as Katharine Zell, did not have the usual background on which a successful career could be founded.[1] Unlike most women of her day who are remembered, the

---

[1]. The present summary is based on part 1 of Elsie McKee, *Katharina Schütz Zell. Volume One: The Life and Thought of a Sixteenth-Century Reformer* (Leiden: E. J. Brill, 1999). Full documentation is found in that book; chapter 1 covers her youth; 2, the early Reformation; 3–4, the Zells' married life, children, and religious activities; 5, Matthew's death and the Interim; 6–7, Schütz

future reformer did not come from a family of high social rank, and she was never a member of a religious order, which were the two most common avenues to a public voice for a woman. Her parents, Jacob Schütz and Elisabeth Gerster of Strasbourg, were among the more comfortably established members of the "common people," that is, citizens of artisan rank,[2] and so were able to give their large family a healthy start in the ordinary life of a lively urban center. As was frequently the case in their milieu, the Schütz children received a good vernacular education. Katharina's later writings demonstrate not only a fluent command of her Alsatian German but also a well-formed hand. Her older brother "Meister Lux" may have attended university (perhaps in preparation for the priesthood), but she herself apparently never learned to read Latin, although she certainly memorized Latin prayers and understood and used a few key words and phrases of church Latin.[3] When Katharina was grown, one of her father's relatives would represent his guild in the lowest ranks of the city government, but

---

Zell's work as widow and controversies with Schwenckfeld and Rabus; and 8, her last days and death. The original German texts of her writings are found in Elsie McKee, *Katharina Schütz Zell. Volume Two: The Writings, a Critical Edition* (Leiden: E. J. Brill, 1999). Most of the material for Schütz Zell's life comes from her own writings, many of which appear in this present volume of translations. Fuller discussion of many points will be found in *Life and Thought* or *Writings*. Since her whole corpus is interconnected, cross references among her writings are often useful; for that purpose the translated texts are identified by short titles as "Women," "Apologia," "Hymnbook," "Lament," "Psalms/Prayer," "Schwenckfeld," and "Strasbourg Citizens," and the location may be given as page or footnote number.

2. There has been considerable discussion about who was described by the phrase "common man" (*gemeine Mann*) as used in the sixteenth century. Robert Scribner summarizes as follows: this phrase "often designated not the vast body of the disenfranchised but the citizen householder who was a legal member of the commune and was, we may surmise, most likely to have enjoyed elementary schooling and to have mastered at least some German book learning, if only in terms of the literature of practical and technical knowledge that formed a major part of the non-religious output of the printing press." See "Heterodoxy, Literacy, and Print," in *Religion and Culture in Germany (1500–1800)*, ed. Lyndal Roper (Leiden: E. J. Brill, 2001), 248. As Lyndal Roper points out, the term was not gender inclusive in its original usage; see "'the common man,' 'the common good,' 'common women': Gender and Meaning in the German Reformation Commune," *Social History* 12 (1987): 1–22. Here the term is applied more generally. This is the rank to which Schütz Zell's family belonged and which she often addressed; see below at nn. 4 and 31. However, it should be noted that she also had contact with rural peasants, although they formed a smaller percentage of her world and she did not usually address them in writing; cf. McKee, *Life and Thought*, 66–68, 337–38.

3. For Schütz Zell's formal education and limited knowledge of Latin, see McKee, *Life and Thought*, 7–10, esp. nn. 12ff. Examples of memorized prayers would be the seven penitential Psalms, which Schütz Zell cites by their Latin titles ("Psalms/Prayer," pp. 129, 133); in 1524 she tacitly admits she cannot read Latin ("Apologia" at n. 25), and the character of her knowledge is evident in the misspelling of the phrase *opus operatum* in 1553, although she uses the theological concept accurately ("Schwenckfeld" at n. 46).

the Schütz family clearly did not have a place in the circles of power. In fact, she herself later expressed a certain ambivalence about social status, criticizing the members of Strasbourg's wealthy aristocratic convents, whom she considered hypocritical, although she could also warmly praise those among the patricians and leading politicians who acted in accordance with her idea of integrity.[4]

The Schütz family was devout, and as a child Katharina dedicated herself to a holy life of virginity, to be lived in her own home. The choice to remain at home may have been influenced by the social and financial conditions of entry to a convent, which were out of her reach, but it also seems to have been an expression of her own familial piety. Some decades before Katharina's birth several women of the Gerster clan (to which her mother belonged) had followed this pattern, similar to the general beguine tradition, although Strasbourg's established beguines were more like its aristocratic nuns. There is more concrete evidence for the personal character of Katharina's choice, however. Besides her religious practices, the young girl prepared to contribute to her own support as a celibate woman by learning the rather exclusive craft of *Heidnischwerck*, which served some other independent women as a means of livelihood. *Heidnischwerck* was a kind of woven picture tapestry used in ecclesiastical furnishings or domestic decoration such as the pillow that Katharina made (and later willed to one of her nieces). Since this craft required a considerable investment of time and money, it is clear that the young girl made her decision to remain unmarried thoughtfully and early and that she had family support in fitting herself for a life of celibacy and good works in her own home. In effect, her birth, education, and proud consciousness of being an honest "ordinary" citizen (not one of the hypocritical social or religious elite) make Schütz Zell unique among those women of her day whose lives can be known in sufficient detail to set their voices in clear historical context.

Social origins were a matter of considerable importance in early modern Europe, but gifted individuals might make a mark on the larger world as Katharina Schütz Zell did by what she wrote and did. Unlike most lay writers of her day, whose pamphlets were focused on one or two topics and published in a single burst of activity in the early 1520s, Schütz Zell pro-

---

4. In the response to Rabus, Schütz Zell proudly contrasts her rough speech with the smoothness of "beguines, nuns, hypocrites, and the nobility." Cf. McKee, *Writings*, 221, n. 191. The inclusion of beguines here refers to the established groups of those women in Strasbourg, not necessarily the concept itself.

duced many genres of texts, which were printed over thirty-four years, almost her entire adult life.⁵ Like lay authors generally, the Strasbourg woman wrote about matters that were concretely, existentially significant to her and her community. She was, however, actively involved in her community in more different ways than most other laity of her rank, and thus the existential contexts of her publications provide a much more complex idea of women's—and "common" people's—voices than is available from any other single writer of her generation who was neither noble nor nun.

THE HISTORICAL CONTEXT

Early modern Strasbourg, the world into which Katharina Schütz was born, was a rich and complex place.⁶ Officially a part of the Holy Roman Empire, Strasbourg was in many ways a virtually autonomous state, and effectively the capital of Alsace; its population of about 20,000 made it also one of the largest cities in Germany. In addition, Strasbourg enjoyed a stable and prospering economic life; located strategically on the Rhine River at a major crossroads of trade, the city was the center of a diversified local market and complex guild system. Like the rest of western Europe, the Alsatian city was part of the universal church headed by Rome and thus had ties with the wider world through the immigration of clergy from outside the city and even other regions. Also like its neighbors, Strasbourg shared in the relatively new cultural, social, and economic influences of humanism and the printing industry, which were reshaping pedagogical ideals and resources and contributing to the reorganization of poor relief.

As a free imperial city, Strasbourg had gained the right to manage its own affairs, with a few general limitations. Essentially, this meant freedom in matters of internal government and the right to conduct foreign policy as it chose. The privy council of the XV handled domestic affairs, and the more powerful XIII controlled the external business of the city; these councils together with the Senate were the magistracy. Strasbourg was a

---

5. For a good picture of the variety of lay writers of all ranks, see Miriam Chrisman, *Conflicting Visions of Reform: German Lay Pamphlets, 1519–1530* (Atlantic Highlands, N.J.: Humanities Press, 1996). Schütz Zell began printing her writings in 1524 and published the last in 1558; the kinds of writings included pastoral, musical, homiletical, polemical, devotional, catechetical, and biblical-exegetical.

6. Strasbourg has been the focus of considerable research, and this section draws on a number of sources, especially Thomas A. Brady, Jr., *Ruling Class, Regime and Reformation at Strasbourg, 1520–1555* (Leiden: E. J. Brill, 1978); Miriam Chrisman, *Lay Culture, Learned Culture: Books and Social Change in Strasbourg, 1480–1599* (New Haven, Conn.: Yale University Press, 1982); and Lorna Jane Abray, *The People's Reformation: Magistrates, Clergy, and Commons in Strasbourg, 1500–1598* (Ithaca, N.Y.: Cornell University Press, 1985).

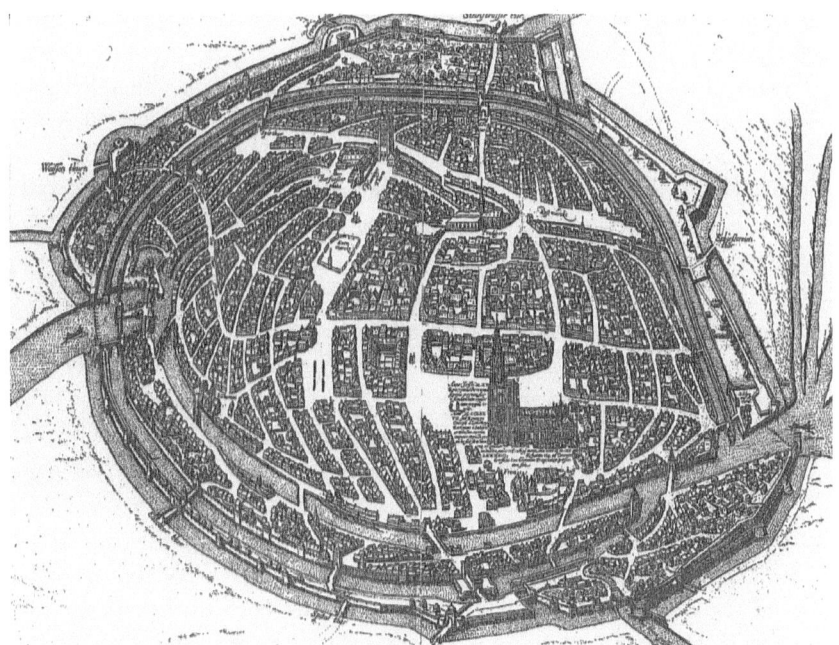

Figure 1 A scholar's reconstructed map from Emile Doumergue's *Jean Calvin: Les hommes et les choses de son temps. Tome second: Les premiers essais* (Lausanne: Georges Bridel and Cie, 1902), 300–301 of Strasbourg in the sixteenth century. The cathedral is prominent in the lower middle of the map. The Zell home was in the group of houses at the eastern end of the cathedral to the right. When the Protestant cathedral parish congregation was forced to give the cathedral to the reestablished Roman Catholic worship in 1550 at the introduction of the Interim, they moved to the Dominican church (Predigern, in the upper middle of the map). Photograph by Elsie McKee.

part of the Empire, however, which was a loose political entity made up of mostly autonomous princely territories and city-states, with an elected emperor. This meant that there were some constraints on its independence. The emperor's power was limited because he was not a hereditary ruler, but a strong leader could exercise a significant role through organs such as the Diets (legislative assemblies) or the Imperial Judicial Court in Speyer, especially by playing off the various princes and cities against each other.

A second political constraint on Strasbourg's government (shared with the whole of western Europe) was exercised by the ecclesiastical superstate of the Roman church. The clergy in Strasbourg were part of its society but independent of civil control, and the wealth of the church was not subject to taxation. In 1262, the Bishop of Strasbourg had been forced to move his residence out of the city, but nobles and patricians still made up the majority of the upper clergy in Strasbourg. The canons of the cathedral were younger sons of various imperial noble families; the canons of Saint Thomas and especially the women's convents were patricians of the city or regional aristocracy. As sons and daughters of the ruling class, these churchmen and women exercised a significant role in politics even when they did not hold citizenship or civil office.

The civil regime in pre-Reformation Strasbourg was a complex but relatively stable hierarchy of ranks. Over the course of the fourteenth and fifteenth centuries, the city had experienced a series of struggles between the traditional (more "feudal") structures of lordship and the growing power of the guilds. As a result, although an oligarchy of social and economic elites clearly dominated the city, by the early 1480s the guilds had gained certain roles within the system and a specific number of places in the Senate. The preponderance of power was held by an aristocracy composed of traditional nobility (often members of regional ruling families) and very rich merchants whose commercial interests linked them with the international network of trade and finance. The less wealthy merchants, next lower in social and economic rank and therefore also in power, were involved in the local and regional markets, but they were also closely tied to their richer colleagues by intermarriage as well as business. The representatives of the guilds who served in the Senate were the lowest echelons of organized power, but they could at times make their voices heard because of the sheer numbers of those who had elected them. It was to this artisan class that the Schütz family belonged; it was not until 1520 that one of the clan, Hans Schütz, Senior, could claim a place in the government, where he represented the shoemakers in the Senate. (During the early Reformation years he became a member of the XV council.[7]) As was true everywhere, some elements of society had no voice at all; below the guilds of gardeners, fishermen, and others, there were day laborers, servants, and vagrants.

The Reformation movement in Strasbourg both influenced and was shaped by the various conditions of its historical context. The most obvious effect that the new "Gospel" reforms had were to strain the political situation both within the city and in Strasbourg's relation to the larger Empire. Most of the earliest adherents of the new teaching came from the lower ranks, especially the guilds that had less power. It may not be a coincidence that they were responding to the preaching of one of their own. Matthew Zell, the priest hired by the noble cathedral clergy to handle the care of souls in that parish, had been born into a good artisan family in the neighboring city of Kaysersberg. Even though he had achieved a very respectable university career before coming to Strasbourg, Zell remained a man of the

---

7. For Hans Schütz, see Brady, *Ruling Class, Regime and Reformation*, 346–47.

people all his life, the most popular of the city's Protestant clergy. However, his message had a wider appeal. Despite their numbers, the artisans were not a sufficient political force to change the religious allegiance of Strasbourg, but they became so when combined with Zell's followers among the higher ranks. The latter were led by Claude Kniebis, a university-educated "rentier" (one who lived from rents, not trade), and others from the wealthy guilds, such as Martin Herlin, Daniel Mieg, and Jacob Meyer. Thomas Brady calls these enthusiastic Protestants the "Zealots," and certainly their zeal was an important factor in leading Strasbourg to break the long monopoly of the Roman church.[8]

The religious arguments divided the government; they also divided families. Andreas Drenss of the gardeners' guild, who later became a devoted Zealot, at first opposed his sister Margaret's marriage to the preacher Caspar Hedio as a terrible insult to the family's reputation. On the other hand, their powerful relative Claude Kniebis supported Margaret and her strong evangelical mother Agnes in this alliance. Despite arguments, the new teaching gained more adherents, and the evangelical clergy supported the role of the magistracy in reform by willingly renouncing clerical immunity and committing themselves to citizenship like other respectable burgers. Amid the growing unrest and riots (such as that against the Augustinian Conrad Treger in August 1524), the regime recognized the need for action. For the sake of civil peace, in 1525 they moved to accept the new religious teaching and suspend the practice of the Mass in all but four of the city's many churches.[9]

Although they had come to terms with their own internal crisis, the Strasbourg government still had to deal with the external political situation. When they voted to substitute the Gospel for the Mass, the city broke one of the major common bonds of the Empire. The emperor and many constituent members of the Empire considered the Roman church the only possible church; therefore, cities and princes who rejected the pope and the Mass could be prosecuted by their civil overlord as well as excommunicated by Rome. Happily for Strasbourg, there were princes like Frederick the Wise of Saxony

---

8. See Brady, *Ruling Class, Regime and Reformation*, 208–9 and passim. Schütz Zell had clear ties to the Zealots. She refers to Daniel Mieg's presence at the Zells' home when they hosted a gathering of reformers at the time of the Hagenau colloquy, claiming that he heard and approved what she did; see McKee, *Writings*, 244. Jacob Meyer was appointed Schütz Zell's guardian after Zell's death (since a woman was regarded as a minor); see McKee, *Life and Thought*, 220. For others with whom she hzd ties, see below at nn. 12, 15–16.

9. For Drenss, see Brady, *Ruling Class, Regime and Reformation*, 230–32, 269. For Treger, see introduction to "Apologia."

Figure 2 An engraving of the cathedral from *Souvenirs du vieux Strasbourg: cinquante planches avec texte explicatif* par Ad.S, ed. J. H. Strasbourg (Heitz and Mündel), 189?, folio page xxx, image no. 40. The Strasbourg cathedral was called "the eighth wonder of the world" because its amazing tower, completed in 1439, was the tallest in Europe. This engraving of the church, viewed here from the north, was made in 1630, but the scene had certainly not changed much in the intervening years since Katharina Schütz was born and lived in the tower's shadow. The large open plaza behind the cathedral (probably much more crowded than the artist suggests in this engraving) was used as a market from the thirteenth century. Photograph by Elsie McKee.

and Philip of Hesse, and cities like Augsburg, Nuremberg, and Constance, which also declared for the Gospel and broke with Rome. Throughout the 1520s these dissident members of the Empire made common cause and succeeded in avoiding the need to defend their new faith by force of arms. This political balancing act was possible in part because the emperor was distracted from prosecuting the "heretics" by the invasions of Ottoman Turks in eastern Europe, where his brother Ferdinand kept calling for military assistance. The siege of Vienna in 1529 was certainly a factor in assuring that Strasbourg's complete abolition of the Mass in that year escaped imperial retribution.

Strasbourg's decision to follow the Gospel had been a compromise, however, and there continued to be different opinions about the best way forward. For political and especially religious reasons, the Zealots led by Kniebis wanted to ally themselves with the Swiss, specifically with Zwinglian Zurich. This project led to a treaty concluded at the end of December 1529 and signed in early January 1530, to which Schütz Zell would later refer favorably. The defeat of the Swiss Protestants at Kappel in 1531, however, contributed to the demise of this Swiss-oriented policy. Strasbourg's premier diplomat, the aristocrat Jacob Sturm, leader of what Brady terms "the Politiques," then turned the city in the direction of an alliance with the (mostly Lutheran) princes and other Protestant cities of the Empire. Thus, in 1531 Strasbourg joined the Schmaldkald League.[10] Alongside this political reorientation there was a confessional shift, as Bucer continued his effort to bring Protestants closer together by moving from a "Zwinglian" toward a more "Lutheran" Eucharistic language. (This did not represent as great a change in the overall shape of Strasbourg's religious teaching as sometimes has been said, however, since other aspects, such as church discipline and perspectives on the Christian use of the law, remained clearly "Reformed" in orientation and Bucer's Supper doctrine itself never adopted the teaching on ubiquity characteristic of strict Lutherans.[11])

---

10. Brady, *Ruling Class, Regime and Reformation*, 236–45. For Schütz Zell's comment, see McKee, *Writings*, 301.

11. Abray, *The People's Reformation*, provides a helpful overview of the Reformation through the whole sixteenth century. However, her interpretation of Bucer's theology is somewhat skewed; she reads the Wittenberg Concord as Bucer's "personal submission to Luther" (41) and seems to accept Johann Marbach's view of Conrad Hubert who (with Johann Sturm and Girolamo Zanchi) "published old manuscripts of Bucer's, all written before 1536, all annulled by the Wittenberg Concord, and all misrepresenting Bucer as an unregenerate 'sacramentarian' " (128–29). This angle of vision falsifies the complexity of Bucer's thought and contributes to misunderstanding the religious heritage that led the Strasbourg magistracy to continue their openness to Calvinism even against the demands of the Lutheran clergy like Marbach (and Rabus). Abray emphasizes the political danger that encouraged Strasbourg's government to make common cause with Calvinists (93ff) but does not appreciate the kind of continuing

Supporting the Schmaldkald League was an expensive business, and by the early 1540s some Strasbourgers were not at all convinced that they were getting what they had paid for. The preachers, even Bucer who had worked most closely with the magistracy in the 1530s, had also now become disillusioned by what they regarded as the regime's unwillingness to take ecclesiastical discipline seriously. By the later 1540s, when Strasbourg was facing its second major religiopolitical crisis, its leaders and people were sharply divided. When Emperor Charles V defeated the Schmaldkald League definitively in the spring of 1547, both Strasbourg's autonomy and its confession were in danger. The Zealots wanted to defend their faith to the bitter end; the Politiques, led by Sturm, wanted "peace with honor" (meaning without sacrifice of their property, which, if they did not submit, would be judged fair game by the victorious emperor's Roman allies). Most of the lay Zealots came from the artisan guilds, although there were a few of high social rank, including representatives of the more powerful guilds like Schütz Zell's guardian Jacob Meyer, and a very few aristocrats like her friend Sir Felix Armbruster. The Politiques were essentially the wealthy elite, many of whom renounced citizenship to avoid risking their possessions. After the crisis, a considerable number of those who had fled returned and repurchased citizenship, and most reentered political life.[12] Despite the deep-seated regrets of the Zealots and their friends (including Schütz Zell), Strasbourg's future lay with Sturm's policy of increasingly close ties with the politically conservative Lutheran powers and with the Lutheran clergy who exerted increasing pressure against everyone who would not conform to the Augsburg Confession. By 1549, the clerical Zealots were exiled or dead and the new generation of ministers were even more Lutheran than Sturm and his friends desired, although the strict Lutherans did not achieve complete religious control until 1598.

Strasbourg's political story had a distinctive character, but the city was also affected by most of the significant social and cultural movements experienced by the rest of western Europe. One of the social challenges facing virtually every political entity was the expanding numbers and kinds of the poor.[13] There were the traditional and long acknowledged categories of

---

general "Reformed" ethos of part of the city that animated people like Schütz Zell, Hubert, and others. For a fuller discussion of Eucharistic doctrine, see "Psalms/Prayer" n. 158; "Schwenckfeld" at nn. 2, 45–47.

12. See Brady, *Ruling Class, Regime and Reformation*, 246–50, 259–89. For Armbruster, see introduction to "Psalms/Prayer."

13. The literature is extensive; for a general overview, see Lee Palmer Wandel, "Social Welfare," *The Oxford Encyclopedia of the Reformation*, ed. Hans Hillerbrand (New York: Oxford University Press, 1996), 4, 77–83.

poor: widows and orphans, the chronically ill, and the blind, lame, or otherwise handicapped. Alongside these permanently disabled, there were also many who were temporarily impoverished. These were especially people on the margins of economic survival, who had suffered sickness or crop failure or fire or other disasters that wiped out their always fragile means of supporting themselves and their families. Care for these "deserving" poor was recognized as right, even if it was more and more difficult in hard times. In addition, however, there were new categories of poor whose appearance not only burdened but also frightened early modern communities. These were the able-bodied who chose to beg as the easiest way to live. Some of these were wandering mercenaries dismissed far from home when the fighting was over and left with no means of support except begging or stealing. Others were an outgrowth of shifting patterns of labor, which contributed to uprooting significant numbers of rural people and adding many new individuals to the migrant population. Whatever their source, however, healthy beggars who practiced deceit (for example, feigning handicaps) in order to impose on the goodwill of the pious began to be distinguished clearly from the "deserving." The traditional charity was not sufficient to deal with the flood of beggars, and it was logical to exclude these "undeserving" and reserve alms for the helpless.

The social situation was not the only factor influencing how the poor were treated; religious perspectives on poverty also played a very important role. According to traditional Roman church teaching, voluntary poverty and almsgiving were virtues and no one should worry about regulating good deeds. Those who could give would do so, those who received alms would pray for their benefactors, those who wished to follow a particularly holy life would renounce their possessions and beg for their living. No one kept a record of the needy. Sometimes the wealthy would found endowments, administered by clergy, to do good to the poor: for example, a distribution of bread or pennies on the occasion of the anniversary Mass said for the founder's soul or a hospice to shelter pilgrims or lepers. Essentially, the object was doing good deeds and achieving salvation, not treating almsgiving like a rational business. However, not only did the huge increase of beggars in the later middle ages strain the traditional forms of charity, there were also growing doubts among many laypeople about the effectiveness or appropriateness of the means. Humanists objected to what they perceived as the haphazard (dis)organization of medieval charity, which wasted resources and made no effort to distinguish between the deserving and the deceivers.

Gradually, in the early sixteenth century, a reform of welfare was introduced across western Europe. In place after place, the poor were listed and organized in rational categories according to kind and degree of need. Usually, all the endowments and other funds for their care were centralized and fitted to a budget and laity often took over the management of the whole. Because the flood of vagrants was so large, each jurisdiction normally confined its welfare to citizens or recognized residents. The new system was introduced in northern Europe in the early 1520s, and Strasbourg in 1523 was among the first cities in the Empire to adopt the plan.[14] Its civic welfare system followed the common format, but Strasbourg also took into account the needy outside its bounds. In the crisis of the Peasants War, the clergy encouraged the city to admit the "innocent" refugees (ones who had not broken their oaths but who had been swept up in the confusion). Then the welfare administrator Lukas Hackfurt (also a devoted evangelical) and Katharina Schütz Zell organized kind-hearted citizens to set up a fund to feed these "outsiders," and the city offered a place to house them.[15]

Essentially, the organization of poor relief was similar across western Europe. However, there was one very controversial provision of the new welfare regulations: the attitude toward what constituted holy behavior or a problem with justifying the new measures. Although it involved several aspects of the welfare reform, including lay control, this controversy was focused on the practice of begging, which was received differently in different confessional traditions. Prohibiting begging was popular with all rulers but it could not be justified by Roman theology, which held that voluntary poverty and begging (by mendicant monks or friars) was a holy vocation and that giving alms was a good work, no matter who the recipient was. Protestants, however, believed that no one could contribute to his or her own salvation by doing good deeds like almsgiving. On the other hand, care for the deserving poor is part of the church's obligation, in which each Christian should participate but which the Christian prince or the diaconate (in Calvinist Reformed churches) manages. In addition, honest work in any calling that honors God and serves the neighbor is a holy service to God. Thus Protestants could readily justify theologically the idea that all the able-bodied should work and all the afflicted should receive the care

---

14. The authority on Strasbourg is Otto Winckelmann, *Das Fürsorgewesen der Stadt Strassburg*, 2 pts. (Leipzig: M. Heinsius Nachfolger, 1922).

15. For Schütz Zell's response to the Peasants War refugees, see McKee, *Life and Thought*, 67–68; McKee, *Writings*, 233–34. Here too one may see signs of the Zealots; Hackfurt was a very enthusiastic follower of the Gospel.

they need, in an orderly fashion. Certainly people like Schütz Zell clearly regarded the right administration of poor relief as a religious concern properly handled by lay Christians, and she visited the institutions that cared for the chronically sick, especially the one administered by Sebastian Erb, one of the Zealots. Years later, after Erb's death, when the Blatterhaus was being mismanaged and Erb's successor was helping himself to the resources, Schütz Zell considered it her obligation to intervene. She took the problem to the city government and demanded proper physical and pastoral care for the poor; there was an investigation and significant reform, even though not all her prescriptions were carried out.[16]

A dimension of common European cultural developments in which early modern Strasbourg shared even more visibly than the welfare reform was the new print culture. For some time, the growing urban centers of western Europe had been home to an increasing number of vernacular schools, intended primarily to serve merchants and others involved in the expanding commercial networks. More educated people meant a greater demand for reading material. The influence of humanism and its goal of getting "back to the sources" contributed to a new interest in publishing classics and textbooks, as well as the creation of better Latin schools for boys. One significant result of Strasbourg's importance as a regional market, and the development of a circle of humanists around Sebastian Brant and Jacob Wimpfeling, was that the new craft of printing expanded dramatically in Strasbourg.[17] Gutenberg had once lived and worked in the city, and Strasbourg had already established itself in the publishing business in the second half of the fifteenth century, particularly after 1480. By the beginning of the sixteenth century, this relatively innovative trade was expanding, as were the kinds of items being published. Religious texts were the most important between 1480 and 1520, including especially Latin liturgical or theological materials, and Latin or German devotional texts like the sermons of Strasbourg's famous preacher Dr. Geiler of Kaysersberg, edited by his secretary Jacob Otter. Beginning in 1490 there were also a number of writings by humanists aimed at the moral reform of church and society and presented as part of the new fashion of illustrated vernacular books for the laity. Two popular examples were Brant's brilliant and gently satirical

---

16. See McKee, *Life and Thought*, 188–93; for Erb as Zealot, see Brady, *Ruling Class, Regime and Reformation*, 261–62. Schütz Zell's letters to the city government are published in Winckelmann, *Fürsorgewesen der Stadt Strassburg*, 2: 72–76.

17. See Chrisman, *Lay Culture, Learned Culture*, esp. chaps. 4–5.

Ship of Fools and its more biting analog, *Narrenbeschwerung* (The Fools' Exorcism), by the imperial poet laureate Thomas Murner. A few years later Schütz Zell would refer to Murner and his books, and from her Protestant viewpoint both satires were worthy of censure. It is not clear how much of Murner's work she had actually read, but it is significant that she was acquainted with these popular writings.[18]

With the Protestant movement printing became a booming business, and in the early 1520s the number of texts published in Strasbourg soared to its highest point in the sixteenth century.[19] Even more notable, the majority of these publications were in German. Latin continued to be very important, but now vernacular pamphlets and books, especially polemic, overtook and often greatly surpassed the number of texts produced for the learned. Religious ideas, particularly as they were preached and discussed and argued in German, began to circulate in virtually all cities and at least a number of rural areas. With the appeal to the ordinary Christian to judge for herself or himself, Protestants gave a much greater scope to the reading lay public. Some books had been available to Katharina Schütz as a child, and she apparently had access to one of the German Bibles that Strasbourg presses produced. However, the explosion of broadsheet songs, pamphlets, booklets, and larger tomes coming off the presses in the early 1520s brought a (small) library within her reach. Now any literate person could acquire a pamphlet, a New Testament, a book of Psalms, an almanac, the latest thing in print. And laypeople could also contribute their part to this print explosion.[20]

LIFE AND WORKS

The life and writings of Katharina Schütz Zell can be summarized briefly— if one omits much fascinating detail. She was probably born early in 1498 and died on September 5, 1562, and lived all her life in Strasbourg, although she also traveled in Germany and Switzerland. Her life spans three generations of the most intense religious change in early modern Europe, and her writings provide a vivid window on that period, especially

---

18. See "Apologia" at n. 31. Schütz Zell was well acquainted with Otter, the pastor of Kentzingen who fled with his parishioners to Strasbourg in 1524; see McKee, *Life and Thought*, 56–57.

19. See Chrisman, *Lay Culture, Learned Culture*, chap. 7 and 287ff for graphs.

20. For Schütz Zell's Bible reading, see "Schwenckfeld" at n. 61. For her extensive reading of Reformation pamphlets, and the one extant remnant of her library (ten pamphlets against the Interim annotated in her distinctive hand), see McKee, *Life and Thought*, 288–93, 138–42.

the first generation of the Protestant reform and the beginning of institutionalized divisions among its followers.[21]

Katharina Schütz was reared as a faithful member of the church, in a city that manifested both the ecclesiastical problems and the reforming spirit of the late medieval and early modern world. By her own account (which no one who knew her as a young woman seems to have questioned), she was both actively devout and spiritually anxious. As an elderly widow, Schütz Zell would describe this period both privately and publicly, to two very different audiences, including people who had known her from childhood. The accounts vary in detail but not in substance, suggesting that however her memory and purpose may have influenced the emphases, the shape of the story was the same.[22] The young Katharina attended the sacraments, did good works, led other devout women in their common religious activities, and even read the Bible in German (which the clergy did not encourage!), but she could find no assurance of her salvation. Then she heard the teaching begun by Martin Luther and spread in Strasbourg by Matthew Zell and, probably late in 1521 or early 1522, she became convinced that she was saved by faith, by the grace of trusting in Christ alone, without her own works or the merit of anything created (including the sacraments).

This new teaching—"the Gospel" as it was called—did not turn Katharina Schütz away from the church. On the contrary, it gave new life to her commitment and transformed her understanding of the shape of her

---

21. Christians loyal to Rome are designated by the adjective "Roman" not (Roman) Catholic because the word "catholic" was not at this time a controversial one. The "Roman Catholic" identity as it is now used was shaped by the sixteenth-century conflicts; Luther and others can thus quite comfortably use the word "catholic" in its original meaning of "universal." The word "Protestant" is used here in the common connotation to designate those who broke with Rome and formed traditions that accepted established institutional form, usually with the support of civil governments. In the first generation "Lutheran" could be equivalent to "heretic," but here it is used in the more ordinary sense for the Lutheran confessional community that followed Luther and the Augsburg Confession. The only contemporaneous confessional term used here is "Anabaptist." Originally this was meant as an epithet for those who practiced believer's baptism—Schütz Zell always avoids this term and says "Baptists"—but now "Anabaptist" is normally used without negative connotation for those who broke with Rome but refused infant baptism (and normally also rejected the civil establishment that was traditional when civil and religious communities were identical). Those like Schwenckfeld who came to reject the need for outward structures of ministry and outward sacraments and preaching are often called "Spiritualists," although in the sixteenth century they could be included under the negative terms used for Anabaptists because all rejected infant baptism and civil establishment of religion.

22. Both accounts are translated below in chapter 2. A fuller examination of Schütz Zell's self-fashioning will be forthcoming.

religious vocation. Still dedicated to God, she no longer felt she had to earn God's approval: according to the newly understood teaching of scripture, God's acceptance is freely given to those who trust His Son alone, and that trust is God's gift, not human doing. Everyone who receives this faith is equally welcomed by God; no one needs any other human intercessor or ritual mediation. As a member of this priesthood of believers, the laywoman Katharina Schütz knew herself now called to be a "fisher of people." That meant that instead of worrying about herself she should tell other people how they could be saved, according to what she had learned from the Bible by the illumination of the Holy Spirit through the words of Luther, Zell, and others. She would say that they must trust only in Christ as their sole Savior and that their lives must be shaped by following God's word and that obedience itself was made possible by the gift of God's forgiveness and the Holy Spirit, although it also involved activity (which did not earn merit) on the part of those given this gift.

The outward life of Katharina Schütz soon changed as radically as the inward had: she married Matthew Zell on December 3, 1523. In Strasbourg the Protestant movement had begun to take hold seriously only a little more than a year earlier and it would not be secure for many months, so both Matthew and Katharina were putting themselves at significant risk. Clerical marriage was prohibited by canon law; for priests to marry was to court ecclesiastical condemnation, but Protestants saw it as a witness to the authority of the Bible over the "human-devised" teachings of the church's tradition. Clergy who determined to marry had to find women willing to be labeled immoral for living with priests, but the courage of these women has mostly been forgotten. Some priests married their housekeepers, regularizing long-term relationships; Katharina Schütz was (to her knowledge) the first respectable woman in Strasbourg to marry a priest. And Matthew Zell was not just any priest, but the one who was leading the Protestant "heresy," so Katharina soon felt the negative effects in scandalous rumors and slander. She was so confident of the rightness of her position that she wrote to Strasbourg's bishop defending clerical marriage on the basis of scripture. The first of Schütz Zell's known writings, this letter became a part of her second publication, an "Apologia for Matthew Zell on Clerical Marriage," which appeared early in September 1524. Besides the original letter to the bishop, and Schütz Zell's own privately circulated justification for exchanging her celibate holy life for a married holy life, this intriguing small text includes a very creative biblically based argument for a layperson, a woman, to speak out publicly.

Clerical marriage was far from being the only cause or manifestation of religious conflict, however. Schütz Zell's first printed pamphlet, which appeared in July 1524, was a letter of consolation and encouragement to the women of the town of Kentzingen where the community was suffering for their Protestant beliefs. Early in July, many of the men and their pastor, Jacob Otter, had been forced by their overlords, who were loyal to Rome, to leave Kentzingen; the women were under pressure, and the city secretary had been executed for possessing a German New Testament. The men took refuge in Strasbourg, the nearest city with Protestant sympathies, where the Zells welcomed eighty of the 150 into their large parsonage and helped feed them for four weeks. This was only the beginning of a lifelong practice of receiving travelers and refugees, a ministry dear to both Matthew and Katharina, which she would continue until her death. Besides looking after those who had fled, Schütz Zell was concerned about those who had been left behind. With her open "Letter of Consolation to the Suffering Women of Kentzingen" she began the published expression of her (equally) lifelong ministry of teaching and exhorting and consoling. Practical aid to the needy, and active work to teach, rebuke, and comfort her fellow Christians and citizens became the hallmarks of Schütz Zell's life.

The marriage of Matthew Zell and Katharina Schütz established one of the first Protestant parsonages, with important consequences for Schütz Zell as one of the first examples of that new female calling: the pastor's wife. The Roman church and its canon law taught that marriage is a sacrament, a mirror of the relationship between Christ and the church. Its primary purpose is procreation, and those who are sterile—"natural eunuchs"—cannot establish valid marriages. According to Roman teaching, marriage is also a means to prevent sexual sin and those who can do without this "concession" are considered more holy. Protestants clearly insisted that marriage is not a sacrament but a fellowship for the purpose of procreation and to avoid fornication. Martin Bucer, followed by much of the Reformed tradition and others, regarded marriage as a covenant; while keeping the other two justifications he subordinated them to a third reason for marriage, which was for him the chief one. For Bucer, "marriage is primarily a personal relationship embracing not only sexual but also and especially social and emotional elements . . . One can only speak of a marriage when, besides [the ceremony and living together], there is also a relationship of mutual love." Especially in Strasbourg where Bucer's ideas were first clearly known, the lives of the newly married priests and their wives were particularly visible models of that relationship of mutual love in the context of "holy households," which became the ideal pattern for families.²³

The social and cultural backgrounds of the new clergy couple in Strasbourg's cathedral parish were quite similar. Like Katharina, Matthew was an Alsatian from a substantial artisan family like the Schützes. Matthew's academic career, concluding with a year as rector of the University of Freiburg in 1517–18, and his ecclesiastical calling as priest to the most prominent parish in Strasbourg, expanded his contacts beyond those common for his social level. As an educated man and the most popular preacher in the city, as well as the first Protestant pastor, he became one of the leading figures of the church when Strasbourg adopted the Gospel. His wife also became more or less well acquainted with individuals from higher social ranks than those she had known as a girl—something that would not have been open to the housekeepers of earlier priests or even to a respectable citizen-wife of the "common people." As pastor of the cathedral parish, however, Matthew also knew the lower echelons of Strasbourg's inhabitants and these were very dear to him, as well as to Katharina, who had lived among them all her life. In effect, from being an obscure young woman known by name probably only in her family and the devout circles of woman and clergy in her home (cathedral) parish, Katharina Schütz became a recognized figure in the city of Strasbourg, where some continued to identify her by her old family name as a daughter of good citizens. She also became known beyond the bounds of Strasbourg, among Protestant associates of her husband in Germany and Switzerland, who called her Katharina Zell.²⁴

---

23. See Herman Selderhuis, *Marriage and Divorce in the Thought of Martin Bucer*, trans. J. Vriend and L. Bierma (Kirksville, Mo.: Sixteenth Century Studies, 1999), chap. 1 (canon law), chap. 5 "Marriage as Instituted by God," quotations 166. The phrase "holy households" has been made famous by Lyndal Roper in her study of Strasbourg's neighbor, Augsburg, where she argues that the claim that "the effects of the Reformation on women [were] largely beneficial ... is a profound misreading." See *The Holy Household: Women and Morals in Reformation Augsburg* (Oxford: Clarendon, 1989), 1. Roper's argument helps to make sense of some aspects of the increasingly patriarchal world around Schütz Zell. However, Schütz Zell herself is clearly an example of the beneficial effect of the Reformation's "positive evaluation of marriage and of women as wives, and the doctrine of the priesthood of believers" (Roper, 1) on some women of the first generation.

24. Often in Strasbourg records she is called "Meister Mathis' wife" or occasionally "Katharina Zellin," but writing after her death the chronicler Sébald Büheler can still identify her as "Catherine Schütz." In early modern Germany women often continued to be called by their father's names all their lives; in Schütz Zell's case it may have been a matter of pride for her to point to her honest burger roots. For a fuller outline of the naming issue, see McKee, *Life and Thought*, xii–xv.

Matthew Zell was certainly not the only married priest, nor Katharina Schütz Zell the only new pastor's wife, but the two seem to have been somewhat unusual. Despite the fact that he was twenty years older and Latin educated, Matthew regarded Katharina as a partner in faith from the beginning and, as the years passed, this regard increasingly extended to accepting her cooperation in his ministry as well. In her later writings his widow identifies three of Zell's "titles" for her; one is "wedded companion," another is "mother of the afflicted," and third is "assistant [minister]."[25] The first of these is an expression of the Protestant doctrine of marriage, the second is a natural extension of more traditional ideas about women's roles, but the third is definitely something more, as Matthew's clerical colleagues found to their dismay.

In fact, the Zells conducted their marriage as a kind of partnership in many ways, and Katharina herself saw her relationship with Matthew as one of mutual respect and shared ministry. It was the character of this "cooperative ministry" that exasperated critics. The Protestant pastors' wives of the first generation were often remarkable people in their own right, and both they and their husbands regarded their marriages as religious callings, but most couples expressed their sense of this vocation in more conventional ways than did the Zells. Wives were helpmeets in the home but usually not in the more visible sphere of public teaching to which Katharina aspired and in which Matthew at least acquiesced if he did not in fact encourage it. For example, Martin Bucer thought Katharina had undue influence over her husband when in the early 1530s she vigorously encouraged Matthew in his rejection of the custom of having godparents because it was not biblical. The point was not a fundamental issue and was resolved peaceably, but Bucer apparently felt that guiding Zell in the way he should go would be easier if Zell's wife (determined to exercise her biblical knowledge) were not pulling in the other direction. Despite their exasperation with her independence, however, the first-generation reformers never doubted the orthodoxy of Schütz Zell's faith and they consistently appreciated her service to the needy; it was the second-generation clergy who essentially shaped the negative view of Zell's widow.[26]

The exact character and degree of Matthew's openness may be difficult to interpret, but he was obviously more supportive of Katharina's expanded

---

25. See "Strasbourg Citizens," at n. 80.
26. For Protestant pastors' wives in Strasbourg and argument on godparents, cf. McKee, *Life and Thought*, 47–49, 53–56, 93–94; for contemporaries' views of Schütz Zell, 456–64.

version of "the pastor's wife" than his colleagues were.[27] However, there were also practical reasons that freed Katharina to work with him. The Zells' two children died very young, the first in 1528, the second probably in late 1532 or early 1533, and although her household included young relatives or students at various times, Katharina had more time to share her husband's work than did most of her fellow clergy wives. She deeply mourned the loss of her children, and their lives and then their memory no doubt contributed to her concern for other children. Probably before her second child died Schütz Zell had begun planning an exposition of the Lord's Prayer. Teaching the faith was a significant part of being a "fisher of people" as well as a mother, however, and even if her own children could not benefit, others could. When in 1532 she heard of the religious distress of two women in the neighboring city of Speyer, Schütz Zell decided to put her explanation of the Lord's Prayer down on paper. Speyer was a city loyal to Rome, but the fact that their story became known to the wife of a Protestant pastor in another city suggests that these women were not satisfied with the religious counsel they were receiving. Although the woman converted to the Gospel in Strasbourg did not know the women of Speyer in person, one might say she understood their complaint personally; they were worried about how "to live according to God's will" (an anxiety she remembered very well), and she believed that her exposition of the Lord's Prayer might help them.

It was not only distant women and children whom Schütz Zell felt called to teach through print, however; those at home might need it too. The Strasbourg of Katharina's childhood had known reforming preachers like Dr. Geiler, but the new perspective on biblical authority and justification by faith alone that Zell and his colleagues preached brought significant changes to the shape of belief and practice. Among the most visible signs of the new doctrines were the altered forms and language and character of

---

27. The statements about the Zells' "partnership" all come from Schütz Zell's pen (e.g., "Lament" after n. 81 and after nn. 94 and 95; "Schwenckfeld" at nn. 19–20 and after nn. 31f and 42; "Strasbourg Citizens" at n. 87), and the evidence for Zell's agreement is mostly circumstantial. However, her statements begin less than a year after their marriage (in 1524 with the "Apologia" at nn. 39f)—and so were clearly known to Zell—and there does not appear to be any objection on his part, much less denial. The circumstantial evidence is strong, also, for example, Bucer's witness to Schütz Zell's influence on her husband in 1533–34, the fact that she accompanied Zell on his extended travels to visit reformers in northern Germany in 1538, Löscher's approval of her speaking at Zell's burial in 1548. Perhaps most clear is the way contemporaries addressed her and treated her. The worst the first generation could do was complain about her for being so outspoken and friendly to everyone; if she had been defying her husband, it would have been common knowledge and caused scandal.

public worship. Like the Zells, many people welcomed the German services, which were shorn of the greater part of the traditional ceremonies and celebrated in more austere buildings with regular biblical preaching, corporate practice of the sacraments, and a voice in the prayers for everyone through song. However, although parishioners were now for the first time invited and encouraged to sing as a congregation, there were very few songs that met the standards of the new clergy. And that did not even touch the problem of what to sing or pray at home, since the old hymns to the saints were banned.

In this context, Schütz Zell produced her third printed work, an edition of the hymnbook of the Bohemian Brethren that had been translated into German in 1531. The Silesian nobleman Caspar Schwenckfeld, who had spent some time in Strasbourg (1529–33), including two years as the houseguest of the minister Wolfgang Capito, had probably brought Schütz Zell the book on one of his visits. Her chief contribution was a vivid little foreword, written in 1534 and published the following year in the first of the four booklets into which she divided the original hymnbook. Schütz Zell, or some assistant, also revised the music of the book, although she maintained the texts of the songs word for word as she found them. Now her friends in Strasbourg and its rural surroundings would have good, biblically based prayers for all kinds of occasions so that ordinary Christians could teach themselves and their households the new faith in an attractive and appropriate way. The songs of the Bohemian Brethren were generally acceptable in Strasbourg, but Schwenckfeld, probably seen as their sponsor, was not, and the book was never republished.

In the 1530s, Strasbourg was beginning to experience its own version of the religious tensions that were increasingly dividing people as the reaction against Rome moved toward the development of new church institutions. From being generally open to all who had broken with Rome, Strasbourg's leaders began to exclude by banishment those who did not accept the newly established Protestant forms of worship, although unlike many other territories they did not execute dissidents. The Zells, however, definitively shaped by the 1520s, continued to be friendly with and receive all kinds of people, against the wishes of some colleagues like Bucer, who was now Strasbourg's leading theologian, although Zell remained the most popular preacher.

The long-term tensions between Protestants and those loyal to Rome rose to new and more dangerous levels in the 1540s and finally to war in 1546. The Protestant Schmaldkald League was defeated in April 1547, and its spokesmen began negotiations with the victorious Emperor Charles V to work out terms of truce in what was called the Augsburg Interim. After several years of difficult diplomacy, when the provisions of the Interim took effect in February 1550 Strasbourg found itself once again a city where the Mass and other Roman sacraments were celebrated and Roman priests moved through the streets. The elderly Matthew Zell was one of the ministers who had strongly opposed compromise, but his fiery sermons ended with his death on January 10, 1548. Katharina was devastated to lose her beloved husband and pastor, especially at a time of such religious danger. When Zell was buried on January 11, his widow unexpectedly preached a sermon, recounting his life and death and urging his parishioners to hold faithfully to his teaching. Later she apparently wrote down the substance of what she had said (perhaps with additions), and friends preserved this in manuscript form. During the months following her husband's death, Katharina also privately wrote for herself a series of meditations on the book of Psalms, pouring out her grief over the loss of Matthew and the effects of the Interim on the Gospel and church to which they had devoted their lives.

Katharina Schütz Zell the widow continued to love and serve the church and people in Strasbourg, but in the 1550s she was living in a changed world. Almost all the first-generation church leaders with whom she had shared the early days of the reform were dead. Most of the city's new ministers were shaped by the increasing confessional divisions that pitted Protestants against each other, as well as against Rome and those like Schwenckfeld and the various Anabaptist groups who did not agree with any of the established churches. Although she acknowledged greater or lesser degrees of affinity with different ones, Schütz Zell herself steadfastly refused to take sides against any of those who had broken with Rome, as long as they held to the essential teachings of Christ as the sole savior and scripture as the sole authority. For Matthew's widow, not only Zell himself and Luther, but also Zwingli, Bucer, and Schwenckfeld were worthy teachers of the faith that she continued to understand in the form she had learned it in the early 1520s. She disagreed with the Anabaptists on some points but admired the ethical discipline that most of them demonstrated and thought they certainly should not be persecuted since, like Protestants, they rejected the wrong teaching of Rome and accepted the fundamental tenets of the Gospel.

In the 1550s Schütz Zell found herself defending her faith on two fronts, and the major writings of these years ably demonstrate how she argued for her integrity and autonomy as a lifelong servant of the Strasbourg church and faithful participant in its reform. One party was Schwenckfeld's circle of disciples in the city, who claimed Schütz Zell as one of themselves but criticized her for not conforming to their group. Schwenckfeld himself became involved in 1551 by publicly claiming Schütz Zell as his supporter, an act that apparently led to an estrangement between them. When Schwenckfeld then criticized his old acquaintance to his Strasbourg confidants late in 1553, she wrote him a long letter to explain her position and make clear both her appreciation for his gifts and her determination not to be claimed by his or any other party. In the process she also recounted her conversion and religious story as well as her position vis-à-vis each party that wanted to dominate her. Schütz Zell has been remembered as a "Schwenckfelder" not only because that party claimed her (against her expressed will) but also because the second generation of Protestant ministers in Strasbourg also considered her a disciple of Schwenckfeld despite her own objections. This was the other party against which she had to defend herself. The (Lutheran) clergy called her a "Schwenckfelder" as a term of opprobrium; Schwenckfeld's followers did so in praise, but neither side was willing to believe Schütz Zell when she insisted that she did not belong to any party and clearly pointed out her differences from both. She defended all who were maligned: Zwingli, Schwenckfeld, the Anabaptists, and especially her beloved husband, no matter who attacked them, but that did not make her the disciple of any of them—even of Zell; she would learn from anyone but follow only Christ.[28]

While her argument with the Schwenckfelders was not known beyond their circle (and apparently deliberately forgotten there), Schütz Zell's dispute with the Strasbourg clergy eventually became public. The central figures in the argument were Matthew Zell's two heirs, his widow Schütz Zell, and his successor, Ludwig Rabus, in what became a kind of controversy over the character of the first reform in Strasbourg and who could speak for it. Initially the conflict remained between the two of them, but owing to a number of circumstances, including Rabus's unauthorized departure from the city and his open criticism of Schütz Zell, the latter finally felt compelled to publish her correspondence with him to enable her fellow citizens and church members in Strasbourg to draw their own conclusions. Was she an apostate inspired by the devil who had always troubled her husband and the church, as Rabus said, or was she in fact a better representative and voice for the first-generation reformers than he was? This book, entitled

---

28. See introduction to chapter 2. Also Elsie McKee, "The Defense of Zwingli, Schwenckfeld, and the Baptists, by Katharina Schütz Zell," in *Reformiertes Erbe: Festschrift für Gottfried W. Locher zu seinem 80. Geburtstag*, ed. H. A. Oberman, E. Saxer, A. Schindler, and H. Stucki (Zurich: Theologischer Verlag Zurich, 1992), 1: 245–64; and McKee, *Life and Thought*, chs. 6–7.

"Letter to the Citizens of Strasbourg concerning Mr. Ludwig Rabus," printed at the end of December 1557, is a very full and detailed historical account. The dedicatory letter to Strasbourg Christians includes Schütz Zell's public account of her conversion and the character of her religious life. Naturally, the book infuriated Rabus and his friends, but it was received with considerable appreciation in Strasbourg, where the pastor who had abandoned them had not left a good reputation.

The last of Schütz Zell's publications was a composite work of devotion entitled "Meditation on Psalms and an Exposition of the Lord's Prayer for Sir Felix Armbruster," which appeared in mid-1558. Here the mature woman of faith prepared a printed form of the counsel she had been sharing for so many years, for those whom she could no longer easily reach in person. Included were some of her earlier writings, that is, the exposition of the Lord's Prayer from 1532 and some of her very personal private meditations on the Psalms from the time of terrible grief after Matthew's death and during the beginning of the Interim. Schütz Zell put these together with a letter of consolation and pastoral reflection for an elderly friend who was suffering with what was called "leprosy." In Sir Felix's isolation his old pastor's widow had been one of his very few visitors and had become his pastor. Now Schütz Zell was hindered by age and family burdens from doing as much as she once had so she wanted to give a more enduring shape to her words of consolation for both Sir Felix and others.

The last years of Katharina Schütz Zell's busy life carried on the same traditions of ministry that had always marked it. She cared for her extended family, especially a handicapped nephew for whom she had been responsible for many years. She helped the needy, both individually and by shaming the government into reforming the welfare institution that housed poor and sick Strasbourgers (where her nephew eventually lived). She continued to teach and comfort those who came to her and to insist on doing what she believed was right, no matter how controversial. In the months before her death, Schütz Zell actually preached at the burials of two women friends who were followers of Schwenckfeld because their families did not want the city clergy to castigate the dead as heretics. Controversy surrounded her own burial because the Strasbourg clergy considered Schütz Zell a Schwenckfelder, but her friends and family rallied around. Conrad Hubert, Bucer's secretary and the only remaining minister of the early years, reluctantly agreed to defy the ecclesiastical establishment by preaching for the service. Two hundred friends, relatives, and parishioners gathered to bid Katharina Schütz Zell an earthly farewell on Sunday afternoon, September 6, 1562, in the Strasbourg graveyard where her husband and children were buried.

THE TEXTS

The individual pieces of Katharina Schütz Zell's literary corpus were written over many years and take varied forms, but they are marked by common characteristics.[29]

One of the most obvious is the constant, explicit and implicit, appeal to scripture as *the* religious authority. Except in making creedal statements, Schütz Zell almost never piles up biblical phrases one upon the other (as some vernacular writers commonly did), but scriptural citations serve very aptly in her arguments and scriptural allusions are found everywhere. The Bible supplies both the authority and the logic of much of her thinking. A second common trait is the existential and practical nature of Schütz Zell's writings. Each one is called forth and shaped by a particular situation and has one or several consciously pursued goals. The contents are also very much down to earth, even when the subject is theology; Schütz Zell is writing for real people with real questions or needs, and along with the Bible she often appeals to common sense or folk proverbs—or humor.

A third, related characteristic of Schütz Zell's writings is her authorial confidence in her right and even duty to speak out. Often she feels obligated to make a case for writing, and usually this involves a combination of her religious convictions (based on scripture) with the particular circumstances. Never, however, does her "apologia" signify doubt about what she is saying or her right to say it; her voice is remarkably consistent in its assurance that she is acting appropriately. Almost never is there any sign of self-denigration as a woman, and the occasional instances that can be read that way are usually intended ironically (for example, references to opponents' views of her). Most of the language that modern readers might consider self-denigration is rather a mark of Schütz Zell's theology: her confession of sharing the sinfulness common to all human beings.

In fact, it is her theology that also gives Schütz Zell the confidence to speak out, and a fourth trait of her writings is the essentially religious nature of every part of her corpus. Perhaps this characteristic should be listed first, but it receives its full weight only when placed in the perspective of the authority of scripture, the existential call to write, and the confidence based on those two. In every text, Schütz Zell speaks with the assurance of a

---

29. Analysis of Schütz Zell's thought is found in part 2 of McKee, *Life and Thought*. Chapter 9 discusses her biblical theology; 10, her Protestant faith and creed; 11, her piety; 12, her historical and literary gifts; 13, her views of women, laity, and language; and 14, her self-understanding. Short articles dealing with specific points in Schütz Zell's thought will be noted as appropriate; otherwise the reader is referred to this volume.

member of the priesthood of believers who has studied the one source of religious knowledge, the Bible, with the help of learned teachers of the Gospel but also by herself.[30] In her own view, because she has been given faith and trust in Christ as her sole Savior, and diligently worked to know what the Bible teaches, she is qualified to help others. Whether they are still seeking assurance of their salvation or need to know the truth about some aspect of Christian practice or want help in making that truth a living reality in their everyday world, she has been there and can help. So throughout her writings, it is the Protestant woman and teacher who is speaking.

Schütz Zell's Protestantism, however, is defined by the early years of the reforming movement, before those who broke with Rome became divided among themselves. This makes "confessional" classification of her theology risky, but it is appropriate to note that the language and concepts of Strasbourg in the 1520s remained in many ways characteristic of what later came to be called the "Reformed" tradition. Ulrich Zwingli and John Calvin are usually considered the primary sources of the Reformed branch of Protestantism, but Martin Bucer, the most important theologian in the first generation of Strasbourg's reform, is now well recognized as one of the significant early Reformed leaders. So it is not surprising that while Schütz Zell's writings are not sharply confessional, when she does take a stance over against others who broke from Rome it can most often be identified as "Reformed."

A fifth characteristic of all Schütz Zell's work is her stance between clerical and lay Christians. This has several aspects; one is her fundamental interest in the view of lay Christians and great respect for their capacity to choose and act for themselves. As Schütz Zell understood it, one of her primary vocations as a learned lay Christian was to teach other laypeople, and she was able to do this in a way they could readily understand because she cared about the way things looked to them and listened to them before speaking. Sometimes these laity are people with a Latin-based education, but more often they are the "common people" who, like herself, were literate only in the vernacular.[31] Her listening is repeatedly evident in the way

---

30. The evidence is everywhere; specific statements are found in particular writings, for example, "Hymnbook" at n. 57; "Psalms/Prayer" at nn. 119f; "Schwenckfeld" at nn. 36f, 61ff; "Strasbourg Citizens" at nn. 91ff.

31. Twice Schütz Zell uses the phrase *gemeynen mann* herself, once in an autograph letter to Conrad Pellikan (January 4, 1549) speaking of those who mourn Zell's death with her, and once in the response to Rabus's accusations late in 1557; cf. McKee, Writings, 106, line 13; 269, line 31. Scribner indicates that polemical writings often identified the "'common man' as the most effective critic of the established system of religion and the surest guide to evangelical truth"; he goes on to point out that "the distinction between the 'learned' and the 'unlearned' (*litteratus/illiteratus*) turned not so much on the simple issue of literacy versus

she cites laypeople's questions and fears and suffering as her reason for writing and in the care she gives to responding. This is usually explicit, for example, in references to the issues raised by Strasbourg citizens in the "Apologia for Matthew Zell on Clerical Marriage" (1524), the two women in Speyer for whom she wrote the exposition of the Lord's Prayer (1532), her neighbors in the foreword to the hymnbook (1534), parishioners in the "Lament and Sermon at Matthew Zell's Grave" (1548), and letters to Ludwig Rabus and Sir Felix (1557, 1558). It could be implicit, as in her imagining the natural fears of the people of Kentzingen in the "Letter of Consolation to the Suffering Women of Kentzingen" (1524). Schütz Zell also addresses lay Christians as if they are capable of making their own judgments; one of the clearest examples of this is her dedicatory "Letter to the Citizens of Strasbourg concerning Mr. Ludwig Rabus" (1557) asking those who had been present with her from the beginning to consider whether she or the newcomer Rabus better represents the truth of Strasbourg's own first-generation reformers.

The other side of being a bridge between clerical and lay was the vocation of a lay colleague to speak the truth to ministers or other religious leaders, especially when they did not live up to what was expected of them. This rather daring role expresses Schütz Zell's confidence as a member of the priesthood of believers and her insistence on respect for the knowledge and integrity of lay Christians. The most obvious examples are her letters to Strasbourg's bishop (1524), to Schwenckfeld (1553), and to Rabus (1555–57), but other instances are found or alluded to in correspondence to or from or about her (for example, a lost letter to Luther to which his reply exists). A sense of equality in the faith is also implicit in Katharina's respectful claim to be Matthew's full partner in ministry and the colleague of his colleagues in reform (1557, in the context of defending herself against Rabus). While recognizing her exclusion from ordination, she does not appear to think that a biblically learned, faithful layperson should be excluded from anything else when the needs of the church call for her or his gifts. Thus all Schütz Zell's writings are marked by a great respect for and consciousness of lay Christian ability and responsibility—particularly her own. There is also warm appreciation for clergy in their different office,

---

illiteracy, as the distinction between Latin literacy and literacy merely in the vernacular." See "Heterodoxy, Literacy, and Print," 248, 249. Although clerical writers appeal to the "common people," Schütz Zell was particularly well situated to understand their concerns because she came from the same milieu. However, by her middle years, when she actually uses the term *gemeynen mann*, Schütz Zell seems to apply it primarily to her less well educated fellow citizens and sees a difference between herself and them in terms of religious knowledge.

along with an unwavering demand for integrity from both clerical and lay Christians and the assumption that they may expect it of each other.

A sixth characteristic common to many, though not all, of Schütz Zell's writings is a very strong historical sense. Whatever her training may have been, the Strasbourg citizen (at least as she grew older) became very much interested in contemporary history, and she was both observant and remarkably accurate in her observations. Her "Lament and Sermon at Matthew Zell's Grave" (1548), although it is mostly modeled on the popular accounts of Luther's deathbed, gives some idea of this historical sense. Some elements of Schütz Zell's historical work are also seen in the letter to Schwenckfeld (1553), but the fullest evidence is found in her book refuting Rabus's accusations ("Letter to the Citizens of Strasbourg concerning Mr. Ludwig Rabus," 1557). This large and detailed volume came eventually to be so highly regarded that in the mid-eighteenth century a Swiss historian reprinted it as part of his collection of sources for Reformation history.

Schütz Zell's historical sense is the twin of a seventh trait, which might be called an autobiographical orientation. The letters to Schwenckfeld (1553) and the citizens of Strasbourg (1557) give this explicit form. However, significant sections of her writings about her husband ("Apologia for Matthew Zell on Clerical Marriage," 1524, and "Lament and Sermon at Matthew Zell's Grave," 1548) also speak in the first person of Schütz Zell's life, as do some devotional writings and letters of consolation (ca. 1548–49, 1558), and elements of her story appear in every text. This autobiographical character is usually intended as a witness to her faith and integrity and/or as an expression of the common confession and experience that she shares with other Christians. It functions as both a very personal presence and as evidence of Schütz Zell's extremely strong awareness of, and her commitment to, participating fully in the common life of church and society with the real flesh and blood people she addresses.

A final point, which might be seen as another characteristic of her writing, is the difficulty of placing Schütz Zell among other lay authors. This may be an indication that the categories of lay pamphleteers are even more diffuse than has been thought, or it may be a genuinely distinctive aspect of the corpus of this "common" voice, which has few rivals for its breadth and variety. Because her writings span a much longer time than those of most laity, especially the lay pamphleteers who have been studied comparatively, it is not easy to "place" Schütz Zell exactly. However, it is possible to point out her somewhat anomalous location in relationship to the categories defined by Miriam Chrisman for German lay pamphlets between

1519 and 1530.³² Unsurprisingly, Schütz Zell's works do not resemble those of the nobility or knights, but she has affinities of various kinds with several other groups. However, she does not fit into any one category. There are themes that overlap with those of Chrisman's "angry men," such as the conflict between God and the devil, but these have a different flavor in Schütz Zell because they are related to the new ("Lutheran") ideas of justification and faith and spiritual life. The interest in theology and appreciation for the new reformers as interpreters of the Bible that are evident in Schütz Zell are identified by Chrisman as characteristics of the urban elite but not of the artisans. On the other hand, Schütz Zell's clear insistence on scripture as *the* authority—and her willingness, like the artisans, to take on herself the reforming task of teaching—links her closely with these "common" folk. Like the educated city secretaries who were much concerned for the "common good" (*gemeinen nutz*), Schütz Zell also knew this language and concept even if she seems to prefer the more biblical language of "brotherly love."³³ In effect, her writings seem most closely attuned to those of the artisans and educated laity of the city, bridging a wide spectrum of the "common people" and the social and intellectual leaders of Strasbourg.

Another trait that shows how Schütz Zell's writings bridge what was often a clerical-lay divide is her unusual combination of intense interest in theology and equally deep commitment to practical Christian witness. Bob Scribner maintains that the "main lay demands were pastoral not theological."³⁴ In arguing against Rome, however, Schütz Zell can clearly articulate the idea that doctrine is more vital than behavior, even if she also gives every indication that a wicked life is an indictment of the faith professed. On the other hand, like other laity and some clergy of the first generation, Schütz Zell was prepared to accept differences on secondary matters more readily than was true of most clergy, especially after divisions developed among those who broke with Rome. That is, the fundamental theological issues for Schütz Zell were articulated against the traditional Roman teaching, whether

---

32. Chrisman, *Conflicting Visions of Reform*, vii and passim, identifies and discusses various categories of pamphlet writers: "knights" as the first secular "propagandists" for Luther; "nobility" concerned with "Christian life and practice"; "angry men" attacking social injustice as the work of the devil; "urban elites" attracted to Luther's theology but focused particularly on monastic vows (especially because of family ties to wealthy convents); "artisans" intensely centered on "scripture and Christian practice"; "city secretaries and magistrates" most concerned for communal life.

33. For *gemeinen nutz* and "brotherly love" see "Apologia" at n. 28 and after nn. 15f and 21. See discussion in McKee, *Life and Thought*, 362–66.

34. Scribner, "Heterodoxy, Literacy, and Print," 257.

found in Rome itself or among second-generation Protestants like Rabus. Breaking with and correcting these false teachings must take precedence over moral questions. However, Schütz Zell certainly regarded the basic theological issues as pastoral as well as doctrinal concerns and put immense weight on the pastoral task of catechesis, education in the faith. The theological correction having been accomplished and brought home to every believer by good instruction at every level, she herself felt that all lesser doctrinal issues should be dealt with in the light of Christian love and tolerance. Knowledge and confession of true biblical teaching are fundamental, and they must be matched with lives that express right belief, but most doctrinal differences do not justify breaking fellowship.[35]

Thus, a distinctive characteristic of Schütz Zell's writing may be the significant evidence it provides for the ability of a woman from an artisan background with only a vernacular education to become a remarkably informed, articulate, and coherent voice for comprehensive religious reform in an age when that was one of the central issues.

THE INFLUENCE OF THE WRITER

Katharina Schütz Zell's various writings were received in different ways in her own lifetime. Since all appeared in German, their influence was restricted to German-speaking contexts until the later twentieth century. Sixteenth-century Alsatian gradually became less accessible even to Germans, and in addition the author was a woman publicly labeled as a heretic so many of Schütz Zell's writings were virtually forgotten after her death. In modern times, a combination of factors, including particularly an interest in women and dissidents, has given her work a new prominence.

Schütz Zell's "Letter of Consolation to the Suffering Women of Kentzingen" in July 1524 was welcomed and reprinted by other Protestants later that year; the fact that she addressed other women on a subject that was not controversial to Protestants contributed to the approval expressed by these contemporaries. Schütz Zell's "Apologia for Matthew Zell on Clerical

---

35. For Schütz Zell's view of the primacy of teaching in 1524 and how it is related to life, see "Apologia" at n. 24; later this idea is even more fully developed. For her awareness of differences among first-generation clergy (e.g., Capito's and Bucer's different views of Schwenckfeld), see "Schwenckfeld" at n. 48. Her insistence on education and not coercion is humorously demonstrated in Schütz Zell's lively conversation with one of Strasbourg's moderate Roman clergy, Jacques von Gottesheim, whom she invited to dinner one day in 1527 in order to dispute with him about theology—as he himself recorded in his diary. She also believed that this toleration should extend to Jews, who even if they were wrong should not be coerced. See McKee, *Life and Thought*, 77, 273–88, 321–27.

Marriage" in September 1524, which defended clerical marriage on the basis of scripture, was censured by the Strasbourg city government. Protestants would not have objected to the contents, but they were not pleased with a woman taking this public role, and the civil authorities were very much worried about being held accountable for libel. When the political tangle had been sorted out, the city gave three of Strasbourg's clergy permission to respond to Conrad Treger, whom Schütz Zell had intended her pamphlet to answer, so it is clear that what she did was not considered adequate and/or appropriate as a defense of scriptural authority. Both of her 1524 texts, printed under the name Katharina Schütz, were preserved in the library of Felicitas von Selmenitz. The latter was one of Luther's correspondents whom Schütz Zell did not know. It is probable, therefore, that the author sent her works to Dr. Luther and he passed them along, which suggests that the problem with this "Apologia for Matthew Zell on Clerical Marriage" was partly the timing and partly who said it, and not what was said.[36]

The hymnbook which Schütz Zell edited in 1534–36 was associated with Schwenckfeld's circle; that fact, plus the gradually increasing availability of other psalters and songbooks, may account for the fact that Schütz Zell's was not reprinted. (From this time on she signed herself Katharina Zell.) Comparison with similar texts suggests that her foreword would probably not have offended any of her Protestant contemporaries, and it was reprinted in a nineteenth-century collection of early modern hymnbook prefaces. Schütz Zell's sermon at her husband's grave in 1548 was appreciated by at least a number of those who heard it, including men, and was apparently preserved in copies made by relatives or friends. There was probably no question of printing it because the sharp anti-Roman polemic would have been unacceptable to the Strasbourg government, which was already walking a tightrope in negotiating the Interim. A manuscript form of the text in an early eighteenth-century hand is extant in the Zürich Zentralbibliothek collection and was reprinted in (not perfectly accurate) serial form in a nineteenth-century Alsatian journal.[37]

---

36. For discussion of censure and rationale for the possibility that Luther's copies came from Schütz Zell and were passed on to von Selminitz, see McKee, *Life and Thought*, 64–65.

37. For a reprint of her foreword, along with many others of the period, see Philip Wackernagel, *Bibliographie zur Geschichte des deutschen Kirchenlieds im XVI. Jahrhundert* (Hildesheim, 1961, reprint of 1855), 553–54. For a full study of her hymnbook, see Elsie McKee, *Reforming Popular Piety in Sixteenth-Century Strasbourg: Katharina Schütz Zell and Her Hymnbook* (Princeton: Princeton Theological Seminary, 1994). For the sermon, see W. Horning, "Das Leichenbegängniß des Reformators M. M. Zell in Straßburg," *Beiträge zur Kirchengeschichte des Elsasses* 7 (1887): 49–58, 75–80, 113–21.

Various pieces of Schütz Zell's correspondence are extant; all have been printed in the twentieth century. Two that are claimed to be hers are found in the publication of Schwenckfeld's correspondence. There are also some letters to the Strasbourg council about a city welfare institution, which are in Schütz Zell's own hand, which appear in a study of poor relief in Strasbourg.[38] Of the remaining five letters, all are addressed to individuals; three are autographs, two are later copies (eighteenth and nineteenth centuries), and all are published in the new critical edition.[39] Most of the letters to "important" people were preserved in their correspondence, and the ones about the welfare system were filed away in the official papers of the Strasbourg government. However, the longest and most significant of these letters is the autograph copy of one Schütz Zell sent to Schwenckfeld. Dated October 19, 1553, it is preserved in the Strasbourg city archives; exactly how it came to be there is not clear, but apparently one of Schütz Zell's relatives or friends kept this letter until it found its way into the archives. (One possibility is that her niece's husband, Simon Empfinger, who had risen from assistant city secretary in 1538 to hold that important office in his own right in 1554, put her letter with other documents in his care. Schütz Zell was very close to this niece and her family, and they shared her theological and political views, so it would be in character for Empfinger to value what she wrote.) This manuscript letter was virtually forgotten for centuries and was usually inaccurately described when it was mentioned in the second half of the twentieth century.[40] However, it constitutes one of the most interesting parts of Schütz Zell's literary corpus, both for its content and because it has now shed new light on an old controversy about her identity and the state of religious politics in Strasbourg in the 1550s.

The final publications by Schütz Zell are the two longest and most internally diverse. The correspondence with Rabus was probably the best known in her own day because it was very controversial and certainly the best known later because of its historical value. This "Letter to the Citizens of Strasbourg concerning Mr. Ludwig Rabus" became a source of some contro-

---

38. See *Corpus Schwenckfeldianorum*, vol. 8, no. 408, pp. 568ff; and vol. 9, no. 441, p. 93ff: these are part of a controversy with Johann Brenz; for discussion see Elsie McKee, "A Lay Voice in Sixteenth-Century 'Ecumenics': Katharina Schütz Zell in Dialogue with Johannes Brenz, Conrad Pellican, and Caspar Schwenckfeld," in *Adaptations of Calvinism in Reformation Europe: Essays in Honor of Brian G. Armstrong*, ed. Mack Holt (Aldershot, UK: Ashgate), forthcoming. For letters about poor relief, see Winckelmann, *Das Fürsorgewesen*, 2: 72–77 (nos. 33–34).

39. See McKee, *Writings*, 98–153.

40. See below, introduction to "Schwenckfeld" at n. 7 gives some modern (mis)citations. Also see Elsie McKee, "Katharina Schütz Zell and Caspar Schwenckfeld: A Reassessment of Their Relationship," *Archiv für Reformationsgeschichte* (forthcoming).

versy, and in late March 1558 the city government ordered Schütz Zell to hand over any remaining copies and to stop selling the book because Rabus was accusing the city of libel. The council had its own quarrel with their former pastor, however, and Zell's widow was very popular; many people agreed with her criticisms of Rabus (including probably some members of the council itself), so this censure was mostly a formality. The book was reprinted in 1753 with modernized orthography and with only a few minor—although interesting—changes, as a major source for the Strasbourg reformation.[41] The devotional book addressed to Sir Felix Armbruster was apparently welcomed by others of Schütz Zell's contemporaries. It is probably this book for which Ambrose Blaurer, one of the few surviving friends of the first generation, thanks Schütz Zell in a letter written from Biel, Switzerland, where he had found refuge after being driven out of Constance by the Interim. The copy of the "Meditations on Psalms and Exposition of the Lord's Prayer for Sir Felix" in the Zurich Zentralbibliothek was owned in 1579 by Benedict Stocker the elder, a member of a well-established Zurich family; its fine condition suggests that it was treasured by his descendants. In 1618 a Strasbourger, Oseas Schadaeus, included a reference to this book in his list of Strasbourg publications for 1558. Many German-language devotional books were beginning to be published in the later sixteenth and especially in the seventeenth century, however, so it is not surprising that Schütz Zell's "old-fashioned" one was not reprinted.

Any of Schütz Zell's writings that fellow citizens may have kept and deposited in the city's library were lost when that building burned in 1870 during the Franco-Prussian War. Thanks to the close ties between Protestants of south Germany and Switzerland that existed from the beginning of the Reformation, most of Schütz Zell's writings sooner or later made their way to Zurich, where they are now preserved in the Zentralbibliothek. Some other copies are found elsewhere in Europe. In 1999 a critical edition of her texts was published that includes all her corpus except those letters already available in twentieth-century editions; with a separate biographical and theological study, this edition forms the basic material on Katharina Schütz Zell.[42] The present volume is, however, the first collection of translations of her writings.

---

41. For responses to Rabus, including censure of Schütz Zell, see McKee, *Life and Thought*, 201–9. Reprint by J. C. Füsslin, *Briefwechsel Frauen Catharina Zellin von Strassburg und Herrn Ludwig Rabus: Superintendenten zu Ulm*, in *Beyträge zur Erläuterung der Kirchen-Reformations-Geschichte des Schweitzerlandes*. Part 5 (Zurich, 1753), 151–354. See "Strasbourg Citizens," n. 82, for one of the changes.

42. See McKee, *Writings* and *Life and Thought*.

VOLUME EDITOR'S BIBLIOGRAPHY

PRIMARY SOURCES

Füsslin, J. C. *Briefwechsel Frauen Catharina Zellin von Strassburg und Herrn Ludwig Rabus, Superintendenten zu Ulm*, in *Beyträge zur Erläuterung der Kirchen-Reformations-Geschichte des Schweitzerlandes.* Part 5. Zurich, 1753, 151–354.

Herminjard, Aimé Louis, ed. *Correspondance des réformateurs dans les pays de langue française.* Tome Premier: 1512–1526. Paris: Fischbacher, 1878.

Horning, W. "Das Leichenbegängniß des Reformators M. M. Zell in Straßburg." *Beiträge zur Kirchengeschichte des Elsasses* 7 (1887): 49–58, 75–80, 113–21.

McKee, Elsie Anne. *Katharina Schütz Zell. Volume Two: The Writings, a Critical Edition.* Studies in Medieval and Reformation Thought, no. 69: part 2. Leiden: E. J. Brill, 1999.

Rabus, Ludwig. *Historien der Martyrer: Erste Theil Darinn von den Heyligen / Ausserwölten Gottes Zeügen / Bekennern unnd Martyrern . . . Ander Theil . . .* Strassburg: Josiah Rihel, 1571, 1572.

Raemond, Florimond de. *L'histoire de la naissance, progrez et decadence de l'heresie.* Rouen: E. Veruel, 1622.

Schwenckfeld, Caspar. *Corpus Schwenckfeldianorum.* 19 vols. Leipzig: Breitkopf & Härtel, 1907–60.

Wackernagel, Philip. *Bibliographie zur Geschichte des deutschen Kirchenlieds im XVI. Jahrhundert.* Hildesheim, 1961: reprint of 1855, 553–54.

Winckelmann, Otto. *Das Fürsorgewesen der Stadt Strassburg.* Leipzig: M. Heinsius, 1922, 2: 72–77 (nos. 33–34).

Zell, Matthew. *Christeliche Verantwortung M. Matthes Zell . . . uber Artikel im vom Bischöfflichern Fiscal daselbs entgegengesetzt . . .* Strassburg: Wolffgang Köpffel, 1523.

SECONDARY SOURCES

Abray, Lorna Jane. *The People's Reformation. Magistrates, Clergy, and Commons in Strasbourg, 1500–1598.* Ithaca, N.Y.: Cornell University Press, 1985.

Bainton, Roland. "Katherine Zell." *Medievalia et Humanistica* n.s. 1 (1970): 143–68.

Brady, Thomas A, Jr. *Ruling Class, Regime and Reformation at Strasbourg, 1520–1555.* Studies in Medieval and Reformation Thought, 22. Leiden: E. J. Brill, 1978.

Volume Editor's Bibliography

Bynum, Carolyn Walker. "Jesus as Mother and the Abbot as Mother: Some Themes in Twelfth-Century Cisterian Writing." *Jesus as Mother: Studies of Spirituality in the High Middle Ages.* Berkeley: University of California Press, 1982.

Chrisman, Miriam U. *Conflicting Visions of Reform: German Lay Pamphlets, 1519–1530.* Atlantic Highlands, N.J.: Humanities Press, 1996.

———. *Lay Culture, Learned Culture. Books and Social Change in Strasbourg, 1480–1599.* New Haven, Conn.: Yale University Press, 1982.

———. "Women and the Reformation in Strasbourg." *Archiv für Reformationsgeschichte* 63 (1972): 143–68.

Davis, Natalie Zemon. "City Women and Religious Change." *Society and Culture in Early Modern France.* Stanford: Stanford University Press, 1975, 65–95.

———. *The Gift in Sixteenth-Century France.* Madison, Wis.: University of Wisconsin Press, 2000.

Douglass, Jane Dempsey. *Justification in Late Medieval Preaching: A Study of John Geiler of Keisersberg.* Studies in Medieval and Reformation Thought, 1. Leiden: Brill, 1966.

Dougmergue, Emile. *Jean Calvin: Les hommes et les choses de son temps. Tome second: Les premiers essais.* Lausanne: Georges Bridel and Cie, 1902, 300–301.

Ficker, Johannes. *Bildnesse der Strassburger Reformation.* Strassburg: K. J. Trübner, 1914, tafel 10.

Jancke, Gabrielle. "Publizistin-Pfarrfrau-Prophetin: Die Straaburger 'Kirchenmutter' Katharina Zell." In *Frauen Mischen Sich Ein,* edited by P. Freybe, pp. 55–80. Wittenberg: Ev. Predigerseminar, 1995.

Kaufmann, Thomas. "Pfarrfrau und Publizistin—Das reformatorische 'Amt' der Katharina Zell." *Zeitschrift für Historische Forschung* 23 (1996): 169–218.

Liebenau, Ulrike. *Catherine Zell: Une mère de l'église. Sa pensée à travers l'analyse de ses écrits. Mémoire de maîtrise.* Faculté de Théologie Protestante, Université des Sciences Humaines de Strasbourg. 1987.

Lienhard, Marc. "Catherine Zell, née Schütz." In *Bibliotheca Dissidentium: Répertoire des non-conformistes religieux des seizième et dix-septième siècles,* vol. 1, edited by A. Séguenny. Baden-Baden: Valentin Koerner, 1980, 97–125.

McKee, Elsie Anne. "The Defense of Zwingli, Schwenckfeld, and the Baptists, by Katharina Schütz Zell." In *Reformiertes Erbe: Festschrift für Gottfried W. Locher zu seinem 80. Geburtstag,* edited by H. A. Oberman, E. Saxer, A. Schindler, and H. Stucki. Zurich: Theologisher Verlag Zurich, 1992, 1: 245–64.

———. "Katharina Schütz Zell and Caspar Schwenckfeld: A Reassessment of Their Relationship." In *Archiv für Reformationsgeschichte,* forthcoming.

———. "John Calvin's Teaching on the Lord's Prayer." In *The Lord's Prayer: Perspectives for Reclaiming Christian Prayer,* edited by Daniel L. Migliore. Grand Rapids, Mich.: William B. Eerdmans Press, 1993, 88–106.

———. "Katharina Schütz Zell and the 'Our Father'." In *Oratio. Das Gebet in patristischer und reformatorischer Sicht* [Festschrift für Alfred Schindler], edited by Emidio Campi, L. Grane, and A. M. Ritter. Göttingen: Vandenhoeck & Ruprecht, 1999, 210–18.

———. *Katharina Schütz Zell. Volume One: The Life and Thought of a Sixteenth-Century Reformer.* Studies in Medieval and Reformation Thought, 69: 1. Leiden: E. J. Brill, 1999.

———. "A Lay Voice in Sixteenth-Century 'Ecumenics': Katharina Schütz Zell in Dialogue with Johannes Brenz, Conrad Pellican, and Caspar Schwenckfeld." In

Adaptations of Calvinism in Reformation Europe: Essays in Honor of Brian G. Armstrong, edited by Mack Holt. Aldershot, UK: Ashgate, forthcoming.

———. *Reforming Popular Piety in Sixteenth-Century Strasbourg: Katharina Schütz Zell and her Hymnbook.* Princeton: Princeton Theological Seminary, 1994.

———. "Speaking Out: Katharina Schütz Zell and the Command to Love One's Neighbor as an Apologia for Defending the Truth." In *Ordenlich und Fruchtbar: Festschrift für Willem van't Spijker*, edited by W. H. Neuser and H. J. Selderhuis. Leiden: J. J. Groen en Zoon, 1997, 9–22.

Reinburg, Virginia. "Liturgy and the Laity in Late Medieval and Reformation France." *Sixteenth Century Journal* 23 (1992): 526–46.

Reinis, Austra. *Reforming the Art of Dying: The ars moriendi in the German Reformation (1519–1528).* Ph.D. dissertation, Princeton Theological Seminary, 2003.

Roper, Lyndal. "'the common man,' 'the common good,' 'common women': Gender and Meaning in the German Reformation Commune." *Social History* 12 (1987): 1–22.

———. *The Holy Household: Women and Morals in Reformation Augsburg.* Oxford: Clarendon Press, 1989.

Scribner, Robert. "Heterodoxy, Literacy, and Print." In *Religion and Culture in Germany (1500–1800)*, edited by Lyndal Roper. Studies in Medieval and Reformation Thought, 81. Leiden: E. J. Brill, 2001, 235–58.

Selderhuis, Herman. *Marriage and Divorce in the Thought of Martin Bucer.* Translated by J. Vriend and L. Bierma. Kirksville, Mo.: Sixteenth Century Studies, 1999.

Souvenirs du vieux Strasbourg: cinquante planches avec texte explicatif par Ad. S. Strasbourg: J. H. Ed. Heitz (Heitz and Mündel), 189?, folio page xxx, image no. 40.

Wandel, Lee Palmer. "Social Welfare." In *The Oxford Encyclopedia of the Reformation*, edited by Hans Hillerbrand. New York: Oxford University Press, 1996, 4: 77–83.

Winckelmann, Otto. *Das Fürsorgewesen der Stadt Strassburg.* 2 parts. Leipzig: M. Heinsius Nachfolger, 1922.

Wolff, Anne. *Le recueil de cantiques de Catherine Zell, 1534–1536.* 2 vols. Mémoire de Maîtrise, Université des Sciences Humaines de Strasbourg, Institut d'Etudes Allemandes, 1986.

NOTE ON TRANSLATION

The texts presented here are translated from the German in the critical edition, published by McKee in 1999, and further details about the originals can be found there. The primary general rule of this translation is the choice to remain as close to the original as possible, consistent with clarity, in order to preserve Katharina Schütz Zell's own lively voice. The one exception to this rule is the decision to make slight alterations in certain formulations. Adjectival forms of the word *Mensch* are usually translated by "human" rather than the more common "man," and nominative forms are often rendered in the plural as "people." The purpose is not to transform Schütz Zell into a twenty-first-century woman but to exercise some linguistic liberty in cases that appear to express an inclusiveness implicit in her writing.

The main alterations in the translations as a whole are stylistic. The very long, sometimes run-on sentences have been divided into shorter units—although perhaps not often enough! Sixteenth-century German rarely used periods and had no commas or colons or semicolons of the modern kind; in fact, periods were not modern "full stop" marks either. The main form of punctuation was a breath mark usually printed as a bar (/), and each phrase between such marks refers both forward and backward. In translating, to break the flow into English sentences without breaking the linkage of ideas, it is sometimes necessary to repeat words. In the same way, the long passages of most texts, which often run for pages and pages without a break, have been divided into paragraphs. It should be remembered that these divisions also are largely editorial additions, and so the reader is well advised to read most texts, especially the shorter pamphlets, each as a single speech. Paragraphs printed here, therefore, do not begin with "topic" sentences, although every effort has been made to maintain a clear sense of the author's structure and make the transitions at the most logical shifts in the flow of ideas. References to God in the second person, when Schütz Zell is addressing God in prayer, are translated as "You," although she uses the equivalent of "Thou," since the more archaic form of the second person verb ("hast," "speakest," etc.) distances the prayer from the modern reader rather than increases the intimacy of the one praying to God as was intended. Also, pronouns for God (all three persons of the trinity) have been capitalized for clarity so that the reader will be able to distinguish when "He" means Father, Son, or Holy Spirit and when "he" refers to Zell or some other human being. Schütz Zell's writing can be rather dense at times; nouns have sometimes been substituted for pronouns, but more often capitalization is a simpler solution to indicate the referent. The occasional use of italics is an editorial addition for the purpose of clarification rather than emphasis.

To facilitate understanding, the translation is sometimes expanded slightly with bracketed names or other identification and separate notes are added only where more extensive explanation is needed. The individual introduction to each writing outlines its historical context and points out significant factors, but content notes are added to provide specific details needed to locate Schütz Zell in the contemporary argument. These also demonstrate how deeply engaged the Strasbourg lay theologian was in the debates of her day, illustrating how well she can serve as an introduction to what an intelligent member of the "common people" could know and how well such a "low-ranking reformer" could participate in a sphere dominated by learned men. Fuller notes are available in the critical edition. Biblical references and allusions are included in the translated texts in order to illustrate the character of Schütz Zell's knowledge and argument. (In addition, the latter can serve as a handy guide to answer specific questions if the reader who has a question about some point in the translation locates the corresponding place in the German by using the biblical references given in both texts.)

In the case of someone as prolific as Schütz Zell, it is necessary to make a selection of writings for translation. However, because she is in many ways a unique voice, it is also regrettable not to include texts that will remain virtually inaccessible in their original sixteenth-century Alsatian form. Here the decision has been made to provide not only Schütz Zell's shorter works, the "Letter of Consolation to the Suffering Women of Kentzingen" and "Foreword to the Hymnbook of the Bohemian Brethren," but also complete translations of the three medium-length ones, the "Apologia for Matthew Zell on Clerical Marriage," the "Lament and Sermon at Matthew Zell's Grave," and the "Letter to Caspar Schwenckfeld." Of the two longest texts, almost the whole of the devotional "Meditations on Psalms and an Exposition of the Lord's Prayer for Sir Felix" has been translated (an extended passage of proof texts has been omitted), but only the first and shortest segments of the "Letter to the Citizens of Strasbourg concerning Mr. Ludwig Rabus" are presented. Besides its great length, this last book is also rather repetitious, and although it is a gold mine of details about many aspects of the early reform in Strasbourg, it is less useful for the general reader. Therefore, from this book only Schütz Zell's letter to her fellow Christians and citizens is found here, plus (as an appendix) Rabus's brief note to her, to give an idea of his side of the argument.

These translations are arranged in two parts, which are essentially although not perfectly chronological. Chapter 1 includes all the writings between 1524 and ca. 1549, along with one from 1558 at the end. Since these are not presented in strictly chronological order (because the devotional work is a composite publication with sections dating from 1532 and 1548–49 as well as 1558), the table of contents gives dates so that those who wish can pursue Schütz Zell's intellectual development by a sequential reading. The texts in chapter 1 are generally characterized by the conflict between Rome and those who broke with Rome, so Schütz Zell is seen as a reformer and a teacher and pastor to Protestants. Chapter 2 is composed of writings from the 1550s, which include Schütz Zell's major autobiographical statements but also show her struggle to maintain her combination of independence and interdependence in the context of quarrels among second-generation parties. As a Protestant lay theologian she sets out her position in the sad situation of enmity among those who broke with Rome, even while insisting that she refuses all party divisions and is ready to hold out her hands to both Rabus and Schwenckfeld.

I

THE LAY REFORMER, TEACHER, AND PASTOR

INTRODUCTION

Most of the writings of Katharina Schütz Zell in the first generation of the Protestant movement can be characterized as the work of a reformer. The key focus is adapting the communication of "the Gospel" to the needs and level of lay Christians, calling them to a new understanding of faith, and supporting them in the break with Rome that she had already experienced and that now had reshaped her life.

Schütz Zell's first printed publication was a letter of consolation and encouragement to the women of Kentzingen in July 1524. Here she expresses both her commitment to the new teaching of the gospel of salvation by faith in Christ alone on the authority of scripture alone and her admiration for the women's witness to that faith against their Roman overlords. Building on traditional religious ideas such as spirit versus flesh, Schütz Zell leads her hearers—housewives—to reinterpret their apparent powerlessness (staying at home with the children) as active service to Christ in accord with His command. There is also an implicit claim and an explicit suggestion that women can use scripture to encourage and even teach themselves and others (including men—their husbands!) in spite of 1 Corinthians 14:34–35.

In early September 1524 Schütz Zell drew together several privately circulated manuscripts to form her second publication. This was an apologia for clerical marriage, an explanation of the new "heretical" idea of what constitutes a holy life, and a defense of scriptural authority. The teaching of the Gospel is cast into high relief by the way Schütz Zell guides her lay readers to see how they have been misled by the Roman clergy and traditional theology. It is not in the first place the "bad life" of the clergy and other leaders that is the problem: lay Christians can identify hypocrisy and sexual immorality for themselves. It is the "wrong teaching" of Rome undergirding the clergy's claims for holiness that is dangerous to salvation, and for that doctrinal instruction simple Christians need the kind of help their devout neighbor can offer. This fiery little book also presents a very creative argument for the right and obligation of any Christian—including a woman!—to speak out against unbiblical teaching for the sake of the truth and love of her neighbors.

The lay reformer's next text was an exposition of the Lord's Prayer, which Schütz Zell circulated privately in 1532. This was written to help those who, because of their rearing in Roman teaching, could not find peace of conscience and how to please God. The text provides a clear picture of her commitment to the orthodox, traditional creeds with their unhesitating affirmation of the trinity and to the Protestant reformers' conviction that right knowledge of God in His word is not an academic exercise but vital to pastoral care and peace of conscience. Schütz Zell's exposition also gives attention to specific Protestant teachings such as the significance of biblical preaching and the character of the ministers who preach and the people who hear them. Her treatment of the right way to celebrate the Lord's Supper and the relationship of the Supper to the Christian fellowship include distinctively "Reformed" notes. Besides the evidence for a woman teaching scripture, the preface to this exposition of the Prayer provides fascinating insight into the author's willingness to use feminine, especially maternal, imagery for Christ (and perhaps even for God the Father).

Two years later, in 1534, Schütz Zell wrote a foreword to the hymnbook of the Bohemian Brethren. This brief dense text expresses the central Protestant view of faith as the sole way to please God—no veneration of the saints—and especially develops the understanding of the priesthood of believers, including preeminently the "religious vocation" of women of faith and other laity (like peasant agriculturalists) in their most mundane domestic or daily chores. There are also pointed attacks on popular immorality and Roman monasticism. Clearly, in Schütz Zell's eyes it is not only the traditional clergy who need to change; lay Christians also need to reform their behavior and take proper responsibility for their households' religious education. Equally clear, however, is Schütz Zell's confidence in the capacity of "ordinary" Christians to take an active role in "preaching" their faith. If they have the help of a sister who knows somewhat more than they do, if they have a friend to direct and challenge them and provide them with ready-made "sermons in song," they can take charge of their lives by appropriating and passing on the good teaching offered to them.

Schütz Zell's sermon at her husband's burial in January 1548 is explicitly intended both as a witness to his faith and life and as a defiance of and guard against Roman teaching. She presents several summaries of Protestant teaching, especially insisting on the sole sufficiency of Christ as savior. This is coupled with a strong affirmation of the unique authority of scripture, interpreted though the early church creeds and the Chalcedonian definition of Christ's two natures, and explained by the Protestant reformers, as the basis of all belief and practice. There is an explicit picture of the Protestant rejection of Roman teachings such as trust in the Mass and in human merit and the belief in purgatory, as well as implicit criticism of Roman clerical behavior. The most significant thing about this sermon for women (or lay Christians) is not its content but its preacher, and yet the clarity and coherence of the contents in fact demonstrate the significant role that laity, reformers of the third or fourth or fifth rank, could and did play in adapting the new theology to "ordinary" people.

Over the course of the months following Matthew's death, Katharina expressed her grief partly through intensified Bible study. Her very private meditations on the Psalms give a glimpse of the pain and a sense of the sinfulness that were part of the traditional—and biblical—association of affliction with punishment for sin. Along with this there is also, however, the firm Protestant denial that human beings can do anything to save themselves, along with the frequently repeated affirmation of trust in God's mercy and forgiveness alone. The dynamic is often expressed as the struggle between belief and unbelief, faith and its opposite, a typically Protestant angle of vision on sin and salvation. This is evident in Schütz Zell's understanding of the work of the Holy Spirit in making known to the sinner the depth of the problem of sin and convincing the fearful that God's promises of grace can be trusted. So the one redeemed by grace can be and must be changed to act according to the pattern set out by God's word. Clearly, the role of the Holy Spirit is not to reveal further content; that the Spirit has already done in the Bible. But the Spirit makes the teaching alive in the believer and the believer alive in the teaching—a transformed life shaped by God's law, giving a "Reformed" inflection to a common Protestant theme. Here Schütz Zell includes a strong affirmation of the religious equality of women and men, high and low, married, single, or widowed, people of every condition, equality in sin and grace and Christian responsibility. The origin of these meditations in Schütz Zell's personal struggle with grief testifies to the way that the new faith could support and reshape individual devotional life.

The last of Schütz Zell's extant writings is the pastoral letter of consolation to Sir Felix Armbruster in July 1558. Here the same themes are heard again, including human sinfulness and God's mercy in Christ alone, the authority of scripture and the fellowship-creating, leveling experience of the priesthood of believers, and the different offices of the Holy Spirit and the human pastor-teacher. In this letter one hears the mature voice of confidence in God, Schütz Zell's expression of a faith that had been tested and tempered by adversity and come through to unshakeable trust. Again a woman teaches scripture publicly to a man, one of the "common people" to an aristocrat, with a wise and profound serenity. Or perhaps better: here Schütz Zell presents the record of two mature "ordinary" Christians giving and receiving encouragement in the understanding and practice of their faith as a model for those not yet so well taught or experienced in Christian life. In effect, this final text has moved beyond polemic to stand as a kind of testament to the lay reformer: believer, teacher, and pastor.

Figure 3 Title page of Katharina Schützin's "Den leyden." This comes from the second edition of Katharina Schütz Zell's *Letter to the Suffering Women of Kentzingen*, published in Augsburg in November 1524 by Philip Ulhart. The first edition appeared in Strasbourg at the end of July that year from the press of Wolfgang Köpffel. Note that in this pamphlet she signs her name using the feminine form of her father's name, Schützin; it was common in early modern Strasbourg for women to use the names of their family of origin even after marriage. Photograph courtesy of Zentralbibliothek, Zürich.

The Lay Reformer, Teacher, and Pastor

LETTER TO THE SUFFERING WOMEN OF THE COMMUNITY OF KENTZINGEN

Introduction

In July 1524, the first "public" text by Katharina Schütz Zell appeared in print, although other writings had previously circulated among selected recipients.[1] This letter of consolation and praise was directed to the women of the small city of Kentzingen who were suffering in the conflict between the Protestants of the town and their bishop and civil overlord, a vassal of the Habsburgs who were attacking "heretics" in all the areas they controlled. When trouble broke out, many of the men of Kentzingen accompanied their pastor into exile, but the women and families remained at home to face their angry rulers.

As a sister in the Christian faith, Schütz Zell felt compelled to write to the women left behind in Kentzingen where Protestants were being persecuted. Her letter combines consolation with admiration and encouragement based on exposition and personal appropriation of scripture. Far from considering the women pitiful, their Strasbourg sister praises their witness to their faith and even expresses a certain envy for their privilege of suffering for the Gospel, suffering that she assures them is evidence of their election by God as His children. Of all Schütz Zell's writings, this one is most like a tapestry of biblical quotations; these are not simply heaped up, however, but are woven into a pattern to form the substance of her argument. Besides drawing on New Testament passages such as the Sermon on the Mount and Old Testament texts of consolation in Isaiah, she gives particular attention to the biblical story of Abraham, Isaac son of Sarah, the heir of the promises, and Ishmael son of Hagar, the representative of the rejected children of the world.

Several aspects of Schütz Zell's argument are worth noting. One is theological, the expression of her Protestantism. A number of her themes, such as the contrast between the worldly and the holy, are quite traditional, but their treatment has a new orientation. The encouragement that Schütz Zell offers to the women of Kentzingen is not only intensely biblical, it is clearly a Protestant reading of scripture. This is often expressed somewhat indirectly, for example, by giving a gloss to interpret a passage that she is using in her argument. In treating the biblical contrast between the spirit and the flesh, Schütz Zell makes a traditional equation of the flesh with the world. She then, however, explicitly equates spirit with the gift of faith (". . . the spiritual, that is, the believing person . . .") rather than asceticism, which gives an

---

1. See "Apologia" nn. 15, 32, 39 and related texts.

unexpected twist to the argument—which she is directing to women "in the world," not their traditionally holy sisters in a convent. While it is certainly not stated in so many words, the conflict between the spirit and the flesh that echoes throughout this writing is defined primarily along confessional lines, Protestant versus Roman, faith versus the traditional idea of works. For example, Schütz Zell tells the women to pray the biblical prayer "Lord, help my unbelief" and so she indicates that the danger is really lack of trust in God, that is, the opposite of faith, not persecution. But the way God chooses to demonstrate their faith in Him to the women, that is, the very people who might doubt themselves, is through the obedience to His voice, His word. That is how He convinced Abraham of his own faith, by his willingness to sacrifice his son Isaac, and so the women can reassure themselves of their faith by their obedience to God's word in this suffering.[2]

By comparison with other texts of the period (including her own "Apologia for Matthew Zell on Clerical Marriage"), Schütz Zell's tone here is not explicitly polemical. Implicitly, however, she associates the Roman church with those who persecuted Christ because it is their Roman overlords who are persecuting the women of Kentzingen who "believe in Christ" (alone) for their salvation. When the women confess their faith publicly, they are following in Christ's steps and so, after suffering abuse for Him, they will also share in His glory. In this context, Schütz Zell even implicitly envisions the women as "preaching" to their husbands to encourage them by offering them quotations from Christ's own words.[3]

Another notable feature of Schütz Zell's text is the language and imagery of gender. This is found in her fascinating paraphrase of Christ's teaching about abandoning everything for His sake.

> So also to you, believing women beloved by God, Christ says, "Whoever does not want to leave father and mother, wife, husband, and child, and all that he has, for my sake and the Gospel's, that one is not worthy of me. Whoever, however, for my sake leaves father and mother, wife, husband, and child, farm and field, to that one I will return them a hundredfold here, and in the age to come eternal life".[4]

2. See below at nn. 9–10. The emphasis on faith is seen also in the paraphrase of Song of Songs 2:9, at n. 7. "Unbelief" is the chief sin and one of the primary objections to Rome (see "Schwenckfeld" at n. 69; "Lament" at n. 85), but here the context is pastoral concern and not exhortation to repentance or polemic.
3. For identification with Christ and preaching to husbands, see below at n. 6.
4. Cf. Mt 10:37, 19:29; Lk 14:26. See below, before n. 6.

The primary reference here is the two Matthean texts that list parents, children, siblings, and property; the Lukan parallel provides the "wife." However, Schütz Zell herself adds the word "husband," which does not appear in either gospel. Although this idea fits in one sense, as a parallel to a husband leaving his wife, it would not be considered "fitting" in Schütz Zell's own day when there was usually a strong prejudice against a woman leaving her husband for any reason, even for the Gospel. In effect, besides giving a somewhat free paraphrase of scripture, their Strasbourg sister is also reinterpreting the Kentzingen women's situation in a rather daring way. Despite the fact that the women of Kentzingen have stayed at home with the children, their female teacher has reversed the sign on that separation from their husbands from negative to positive. It is *because* they have stayed at home with the children, where they are actively suffering for the Gospel, that they can be said to have obeyed Christ's command and "left" their husbands for their faith; they, the women, are the ones who bear the immediate brunt of persecution, even while they are properly keeping house! Implicit here is the idea that this obedience should reassure the women of their faith, even as it witnesses to others.

Schütz Zell's language for men and women and her male and female imagery developed throughout her life; this first pamphlet shows only the earliest stages of that process. In the context of praising Abraham's faith in God as demonstrated in his acts, Schütz Zell exhorts her readers to share Abraham's "manly" courage, the only time in her entire corpus that she applies this kind of masculine language as an ideal for women. Later in the letter she balances this with feminine imagery for God and likens the God who loves and has chosen the women of Kentzingen to a nursing mother [Is 49:15].[5]

This open letter was printed in Strasbourg by Wolfgang Köpffel on July 22, although without the name of place or publisher. It apparently became known and appreciated over a fairly wide region of Germany and German Switzerland; it was reprinted by Philip Ulhart in Augsburg in November 1524 and received favorable comment in the chronicle by Johannes Kessler of Saint Gall. The author sent a copy to Martin Luther, which may be the one later owned by his correspondent Felicitas von Selmenitz.

---

5. For Schütz Zell's language about gender, see McKee, *Life and Thought*, chap. 13. For these examples, see below in the fifth and twelfth paragraphs.

LETTER TO THE SUFFERING WOMEN OF THE COMMUNITY OF KENTZINGEN, WHO BELIEVE IN CHRIST, SISTERS WITH ME IN JESUS CHRIST (1524)

May God, the Father of all mercy, send and grant you grace, peace, salvation, strength, and long-suffering patience [cf. 1 Tm 1:2] in overflowing fullness, through the merit of Jesus Christ, in your distressing suffering and trouble sent by God, O believing Christian women of the whole community at Kentzingen and my sisters especially beloved in God.

All of us, I, and those who are united with me in Christ, know and consider well with compassionate hearts the great distress that you suffer for Christ's sake. And yet we also rejoice with you because of it, with inward feelings of happiness when, because of this suffering, we hear and sense your God-given faith that you demonstrate in this trial [cf. Phil 1:29; 3 Jn 3–4]. With all of you I also ask God day and night [cf. Lk 2:37] that He may increase that same faith, as also Christ's disciples prayed: "Lord, increase our faith" [Lk 17:5]. By that faith I also exhort you with friendly request and exhortation, as your fellow sister in Christ Jesus, that you not let the invincible word of God go out of your heart, but always meditate on that word that you have had with you for so long and heard with all earnestness and faithfulness. And may you also receive these sufferings with great patience and thankfulness, as special fatherly gifts sent from God, which He does not give to any but His best loved children [cf. Heb 12:6–7; Lk 16:8].

For indeed to an unbeliever it would look strange that God should give such gifts to His children whom He loves! Such an unbeliever would much rather not be God's child but a child of the world, which does not treat its children that way: the world disciplines its children softly and tenderly. It is true, as Paul says, that faith is not everyone's thing [cf. Eph 2:8] and the worldly, that is, the carnal person cannot understand what is godly. But the spiritual, that is, the believing person [cf. Rm 8:5–8], understands that God deals marvelously, surprisingly, with His own, completely contrary to the world and its children. As also He says in the prophet Isaiah, chapter 55[:8]: "My thoughts (that is, His will) are not like your thoughts, and my way (that is, His ways of acting) are not like your ways." Therefore He says in another place in the prophet, "The one whom I want to make alive, that one I cause to die, the one whom I want to make well, that one I strike" [cf. Dt 32:39]. In sum, He wills that those whom He has eternally chosen and whom He has written as His children in the book of His heirs [cf. Rv 20:15; Eph 1:4] should also be won away from this world, and He wants to teach us to depend only on Him in one strong faith and not expect or take anything from anyone else but only from Him.

But the world's children He will not recompense, therefore He allows them to be given the world, honor, happiness, goods, and what the world has. That is their recompense and inheritance and with that He casts them out—just as Abraham, the man of great faith, cast out the illegitimate son Ishmael born of his maid Hagar with a gift of his goods and excluded him from his [Abraham's] inheritance [cf. Gn 16:15 with 25:6], when his legitimate wife Sarah spoke, "Drive out the maid with her son, for he should not inherit with my son Isaac" [Gn 21:10]. Truly this Ishmael signifies the children of the world, who will undoubtedly be excluded from the inheritance of the eternal Father, and they are established as rulers and owners of this world as also Ishmael was, for they must also have some recompense [cf. Gal 4:22ff]. But to Isaac, the legitimate son, Abraham gave nothing, but led him up to a mountain and wanted to kill him there with a sword and so sacrifice him to God; in the opinion of the world that was truly an unfatherly thing to do! But Abraham believed and knew that his heir was invisibly kept safe for him and that God could also bring him back to life [cf. Gn 22:1–19; Heb 11:19].

So I beg you, loyal believing women, also to do this: take on you the manly, Abraham-like courage while you too are in distress and while you are abused with all kinds of insult and suffering. When you may meet with imprisonment in towers, chains, drowning, banishment, and such like things; when your husbands and you yourselves may be killed, meditate then on strong Abraham, father of us all [cf. Rm 4:16]; struggle after him as a good child should follow his father in a faith like the father's. Do you not think that Abraham also suffered when God told him to kill his only son?! When He told Abraham to do it himself!—to kill the son in whom also the blessing of human beings was promised. Yes, indeed, he was very grieved, for he was also flesh and blood like all of us; but he knew (as the scripture says) that God could bring his son back to life [cf. Gn 22:1–2; Heb 11:17–19].

And so you also, when your husbands are killed, do you not know that Christ said, "I am the resurrection and the life, whoever believes in me, though he is already dead, yet he will live" [Jn 11:25]? And in the sixth chapter of John, He says that whoever eats His flesh and drinks His blood, that is, whoever truly believes that he is redeemed only through the death and shedding of blood of Christ, that one He will bring back to life on the last day [cf. Jn 6:54]. He says to His disciples, "If you know this, you are blessed" [Jn 13:17]. So also to you, believing women beloved by God,

Christ says, "Whoever does not want to leave father and mother, wife, husband, and child, and all that he has, for my sake and the Gospel's, that one is not worthy of me. Whoever, however, for my sake leaves father and mother, wife, husband, and child, farm and field, to that one I will return them a hundredfold here and in the age to come eternal life" [cf. Mt 10:37, 19:29; Lk 14:26].

Dear Christian women, if you know and do this, then you also are blessed, as Christ said [cf. Jn 13:17]. Trample your flesh under foot, lift up your spirit, and speak comfortingly to your husbands and also to yourselves the words that Christ Himself has said: "Do not fear those who can kill the body; I will show you one who can kill your body and soul and cast them in hell."[6] And shortly after that He says, "Therefore whoever confesses me before this adulterous and wicked generation, that one I will also confess before my Father and His angels. Whoever denies me, however, and is ashamed of me and my words, I will also deny him and be ashamed of him before my Father" [Lk 12:4–5, 8–9; cf. Mk 8:38]. In another place He also says, "The servant is not greater than his lord, the disciple is not more than his master. If they have persecuted me, they will also persecute you. If they have called the Father of the family Beelzebub, how much more will they call those of His household that. They will ban you and exclude you from their fellowship, and those who kill you will think they are doing God a service" [Mt 10:24, 25a; Jn 15:20, 16:2]. And He said to them, "Therefore I have told you that this would happen, so that when it happens you will not shrink back and fall away, because I have told you about it beforehand" [Jn 16:4, 1].

Therefore, dear sisters, I beg you to meditate diligently on these words, for the scripture must thus be fulfilled, as Christ said to the two disciples going to Emmaus: "You foolish and vexatious hearts, slow to believe all that the prophets have spoken! Must not the Christ suffer such things and so enter into His glory?" [Lk 24:25–26]. So you also, if you want to be Christians and to enter into His glory with Him, you must also suffer with Him, and for this you encounter abuse. Yes, even if you are put in chains for Christ's sake, how happy you are! [cf. Mt 5:11]. Would that God would

---

6. Schütz Zell audaciously tells the women to speak to their husbands using Christ's words—a kind of preaching that turns upside down the traditional idea that men are the teachers/preachers and women, especially wives, are subordinate. Schütz Zell says something similar about herself: she is using the words of God's Spirit through the scripture. Nowhere does she break the tie between the Holy Spirit and the Bible: the latter is *the* revelation of God's will; but she claims a place for untraditional speakers of that word, which loses none of its authority because of the sex/gender of those who proclaim it.

regard me with such grace and favor, and favor me with such great honor so that I should have gifts unlike yet also like yours, to suffer such things with His dearest Christ and with you. Then I would be more happy, proud, and glad than all the nobles at the Strasbourg fair in their golden chains and necklaces. Yes, I would be happier in that suffering than if I were the wife of the Holy Roman Emperor and sat in his highest imperial seat of majesty.

For I know and am certain, that such things [as persecution] are only signs of His fatherly love, and (indeed) the most trustworthy signs. For there is no doubt that above all He loved Christ, His Son and Eternal Word. (We have come into God's love by Christ, as Paul says to the Ephesians [1:6].) And God also allowed suffering to happen to Christ, and left His humanity uncomforted so that Christ also cried out, "My God, My God, why have You forsaken me?" [Mt 27:46]. As I have said before, God wants to discipline us and tear us away from the desires of this world so that we may learn to desire only Him. He also says through the prophet: "If my people sin against me, I will chastise them with rods but I will never take my mercy from them" [cf. 2 Sm 7:14–15]. His rod is temporal torment here, but His mercy is the eternal inheritance that He will not take from us, as He has sworn to our fathers Abraham, Isaac, and Jacob. Therefore David says, "The Lord has sworn and will never repent" [cf. Ps 110:4a; Lk 1:72–73].

Therefore, dear Christians, you should not receive God's rod and what He sends impatiently; as the wise man says, "My son, do not regard lightly the discipline of the Lord, and do not stop attending when you are chastised by Him, for the one whom the Lord loves He disciplines, He criticizes severely each son whom He accepts" [Prv 3:11–12]. And Paul says to the Hebrews in chapter 12[:7–8, 11] where he also cites these words: "If you endure the discipline, God takes you for His children. Where is a son whom the father does not chastise? If you do not experience chastisement, then you are bastards and not legitimate children. All discipline, when it is being experienced, is not regarded as a happy but as a sad thing; but afterwards it will give a peaceful fruit of righteousness to those who are exercised in it." Earlier in this chapter he also says, "Let us run with patience the struggle that is laid before us, and look to the ruler and perfecter of faith, Jesus, who for the joy set before Him endured the cross, despising the shame, and has sat down at the right hand of the throne of God. Consider Him, who endured such hostility toward Himself from sinners, that you may not weaken in your courage and become faint" [Heb 12:1b–3].

Therefore, dear Christian women, consider these words, which are not mine but are from the Spirit of God, and be thankful and welcome such gifts of God. Christ says, "The one who wants to follow after me, let him deny himself and take his cross upon him and follow after me" [Mk 16:24]. As it was for the dearest Son of God, so must it also be for those who want to inherit with Him [cf. Rm 8:17]. Christ says, "Holy Father, I want my servants also to be where I am" [Jn 17:24]; that is, He wants to have us with Him in suffering and in joy. Therefore, do not impatiently oppose Him. It has pleased God to leave you for a little, and also to test you a little, as sad widows without husbands, as He comfortingly shows in the prophet Isaiah in the fifty-fourth chapter, which place may well be applied to this and like matters. He says thus: "Fear not, for you will not be shamed. And do not be sad with thoughts of your widowhood, for the One who made you, that One will protect you, the Lord of Hosts is His name, and the Holy One of Israel is your redeemer; He is God of all the earth. The Lord has chosen thus that you should be a sad and abandoned wife. 'I have forgotten you for the blink of an eye, a little time, but I will gather you again in greater mercy; I have hidden My countenance from you for a little, but I will have mercy on you eternally, for I am your redeemer. Oh you poor thing, cast out in the storm without any comfort! My mercy and my covenant of peace are not divorced from you'" [cf. Is 54:4–8, 11a, 10b].

O you women, who are perfectly described in this chapter! Who would want a better description than this? Are you not now widows, called by God? All these things have happened to you for the sake of His word. Has He not hidden Himself from you for a little, so that you might think He had forgotten you? So that you could scarcely see Him through a window (that is, by faith), for He stands behind the wall, as also the lovesick soul wails in the Song of Songs in the second chapter [2:9a].[7] Are you not also insulted and left without comfort in the storm? Yes. Consider, however, what He says here: "Do not fear, you will not be shamed," and He says that His mercy and covenant of eternal peace will not be divorced from you in such a storm, for He will not divorce Himself from you as He does from the ungodly. As He [Christ] said to His disciples: "I will not abandon you as orphans, I am coming to you; a little while, and the world will not see me, but you will see me; because I live, you will also live" (John 14[:18–19]). These words are a reminder that He will not abandon you, nor forget you, as He also says in the prophet: "As little as a mother may forget her suckling

---

7. The identification of the Song of Songs or Song of Solomon as a dialogue between Christ and the soul was a long and popular tradition in Christian theology. What is remarkable here is the restraint of Schütz Zell's language, in what is one of her very rare instances of "bridal" language (see "Schwenckfeld" at n. 27). The parenthetical "by faith" is distinctively Protestant.

child, so little may I forget you; and if she does forget her child, still I will not forget you" [Is 49:15].

Therefore David says, "I will not fear what men do to me, and even if they set all their company and armor against me, still my heart will not fear" [cf. Ps 27:1–3]. For God does not want us to fear before humans, as He says through Isaiah in the fifty-third chapter, "Fear not, for I am with you," and before that He said three times to the believers, "Fear not, for I your God am with you. All those who fight against you will be shamed" [cf. Is 43:1, 5, 14, 44:2],[8] with yet many other glorious words. Are those not comforting golden words to a believer? That God, who may not lie, promises the believer His manifold help with the highest oath, that is, He swears by Himself that He will not leave him [cf. Heb 6:13, 18]. Therefore Paul says in 1 Corinthians 10[:13], "God is faithful, who will not let you be tried beyond your strength, for in the affliction He also gives an increase of grace so that you can bear it."

So, dear Christian sisters, trust God; He does not lay on you more to bear than is good and necessary for you. He will prove your faith as He did for Abraham, when He told him to kill his only son and yet had promised to bless the people through this same son. However, Abraham obeyed God, so God said, "Now I know that you fear me and believe me" [Gn 22:12, cf. 22:2, 17]. Not that God did not know beforehand, but He wanted to demonstrate Abraham's faith and make it certain to Abraham himself and to all of us; as Peter says, "The outward works of love make us certain that we believe" [cf. 1 Pt 1:6–7]. So also God wants to show you, and those who come after you, and all of us, that you believe and that He loves you.[9]

Dear sisters, even though sometimes your faith may be discouraged, and the flesh may fight against the spirit [cf. 1 Pt 2:11], do not therefore be frightened away. It is a holy struggle, it must be thus: faith that is not tempted is not faith. Therefore Job says, "Human life is a tournament" [cf. Job 7:1]. God will also not reckon what you do as impatience, if only the spirit does not remain under the flesh or the flesh overcome the spirit. Therefore you should constantly pray to the Father of those who are sick: "Lord, help my unbelief"

---

8. There is either a mistake or quite possibly a misprint of the chapter number, which gives "liii" instead of "xliii." The reprint made in Augsburg changed the Roman numerals to Arabic but did not correct the citation.

9. The paraphrase of 1 Peter 1:6–7 points to Schütz Zell's Protestant interpretation of "outward works" not as "good works" such as hearing Mass or giving alms but as obedience to God's command, which shows trust in God. Faith is the way to please God, and God gives those who may be discouraged a demonstration of their faith to reassure them (and witness to others) of two things: that those God has tried by suffering do trust Him and that He loves them because they have been disciplined as children and obeyed.

[Mk 9:24].¹⁰ Christ Himself was frightened when He considered the horrors of His (impending) death; He said, "Father, if it is possible, take this cup from me," but soon He said, "Not what I will but what You will" [Mt 26:39].

So, dear Christian women, I cannot comfort and exhort you more and better now than to counsel you to accept such suffering with right patience and spiritual joy, for these are fruits of the Spirit [cf. Gal 5:22]—so that God may be glorified in you above all others who are called, those who may not yet have been so greatly tried as you are. Consider the words of Christ, where He says, "Blessed are those who mourn here, for they will be comforted. Blessed are those who are persecuted for righteousness' sake, for the kingdom of heaven is theirs" [Mt 5:4, 10]. And He exhorts you and all His own to accept such things with patience and love; He says: "Love your enemies. Bless those who curse you. Do good to those who hate you. Pray for those who afflict and betray you, that you may be children of your Father in heaven." He concludes with, "If you love and do good to those who also do good to you, do not the unjust also do that? Therefore you should be perfect as your Father in heaven is perfect" [Lk 6:27–28; Mt 5:45, 47, 48]. No one can do this, however, unless he has the Spirit whom He will send to you according to His promise; He Himself wants to be your Comforter, trusted Guardian, and Protector [cf. Jn 14:16]. Amen.

Given Friday, Saint Mary Magdalene's Day, in the year one thousand five hundred twenty-four.¹¹

Katharina Schütz,
wife of Matthew Zell, preacher of the word of God to the Christian community in Strasbourg, your fellow sister in Christ

KATHARINA SCHÜTZ'S APOLOGIA FOR MASTER MATTHEW ZELL, HER HUSBAND

Introduction

From the beginning of her marriage to Strasbourg's popular priest Matthew Zell, Katharina Schütz was involved in writing about this event because it

---

10. This is the prayer of a man who had brought his epileptic son to Jesus's disciples, but they could not cure the boy. Jesus comes and the man asks Jesus to help "if He can." Jesus replies that everything is possible for someone who believes, and the man cries out this prayer. The plea to be able to trust Christ is answered by the healing of the boy; later Schütz Zell will point to unbelief as the chief sin ("Schwenckfeld" at n. 69). The point is not developed here, but clearly the women's main concern is not persecution but unbelief.

11. In the Strasbourg liturgical calendar Saint Mary Magdalene's day was July 22, which in 1524 fell on a Friday. Although Protestants rejected the veneration of the saints, most of the

represented a major and very controversial step in religious reform. In effect, she had two theological tasks: one was to prove that scripture teaches the rightness of clerical marriage, and the other was to disprove the superior holiness of celibacy as an invention of the church. In doing this she must also counter slander and prove her right to address these issues in the first place.

Clerical marriage raised the question of religious authority in the most pointed way. Protestants said that the authority of the Bible must be set above that of the church rather than subsumed under it and that the ideal of holiness must be changed to accord with scripture even against church teaching. In effect, no one questioned that the Bible is God's word, but it had long been understood that the written scriptures are not the only source of truth that must be believed and practiced in order to be saved. The Roman church, speaking through the clergy, believed itself to be the keeper of both biblical and unwritten traditions and that there was no distinction in value between the two sources. Those who broke with Rome, however, insisted that the Bible is the only source (*sola scriptura*) of knowledge about what must be believed for salvation and therefore the church must follow scripture alone and not add any further requirements to it. Most Protestants agreed that the church may properly decide such matters as the implementation of biblical instructions, but it cannot add to the scriptural teaching any content deemed to be necessary for salvation. The task of the church is to teach scripture and practice it, not control it.

The marriage of priests was one of the most graphic ways of asserting the primacy and sufficiency of biblical authority because it actively broke canon law. There might be disagreement about whether these men's preaching was "heresy," but there was no question that they had chosen to defy the church if they publicly married. Strasbourg clergy, including Matthew Zell, were among the first reformers to take this step. But a priest who wanted to marry had to find a wife, and so it must also be demonstrated to the satisfaction of laity that such marriages were honorable. Scriptural teaching that elevated the status of marriage as pleasing God as much as, or more than, celibacy would not only make marriage suitable for clergy. It would also vindicate the sanctity of the lifestyle of married (lay) people who were used to being regarded as not having a religious vocation, being less holy than their priests. However, despite this potential for improving their own religious status, laypeople had first to be convinced that clerical

---

first generation continued to use the traditional ways of naming days of the week, at least in the early years of the reform.

marriage is what the Bible teaches and that the church had been wrong, especially if they were to consent to marry their daughters to these (renegade) priests. Usually the focus of ecclesiastical attention was on the priests who defied their bishops, but naturally laypeople were often more interested in the women—members of their families—who would become the clergy's wives. Some priests married their housekeepers or concubines, regularizing unions that the church had previously not sanctioned, and many laity found this appropriate because it made "honest women" of their disreputable relatives. However, parishioners experienced a different kind of anxiety when a priest wanted to marry a respectable citizen; according to canon law, that woman was deliberately doing something immoral (almost equivalent to becoming a prostitute) and her "unconverted" family might object even if she did not. Further, some laity still worried about the quality of holiness their married priests could claim.

When Katharina Schütz became the first respectable woman in Strasbourg to marry a priest, Matthew Zell, on December 3, 1523, she was faced with several challenges from lay Christians as well as church authorities. Writing under the name by which she was known in Strasbourg even after her marriage—the name of good citizens who had dared to let their daughter marry a priest—in February 1524 Katharina Schütz addressed a letter to the bishop who had placed Zell and the other married clergy under discipline. In this private letter she defended clerical marriage on the basis of scripture, probably also attacking canon law regulations on celibacy and fornication. Apparently Matthew's young bride also circulated a private writing among her friends to explain why she had married because she had long been known for her dedication to a holy life as a virgin. She had to show that although she had previously understood following God's will to mean celibacy, she now knew it was right to marry a priest. Clear also is her conviction that marriage is a holy vocation, not a second-class Christian lifestyle. Furthermore, it was plain to Schütz Zell from observation that very few people are able to live virtuously when unmarried so everyone who could not be chaste should follow God's instructions and marry. Katharina thought that by marrying Matthew she could save him from temptation or immorality and affirm her belief in scripture. She could also encourage others to believe and act on that teaching and so save themselves from the false doctrines of clerical celibacy and the less holy status of marriage that they had been taught by the papal church.

Although the eager young wife of the priest had wanted to publish her letter to the bishop, when the city council ordered Zell to prevent that she accepted it. Some months later, however, when slanders about Matthew's behavior and the Zells' married life were circulating, Katharina decided that she had to do something to defend the biblical truth and act in love for her neighbors. Thus she put together an apologia for clerical marriage based on scripture, explained the grounds for the Zells' marriage, and refuted the lies. She absolves her husband of responsibility for her publication by saying that he knew nothing about it and did not even care about ill repute if he suffered it for the Gospel. The pamphlet has two major parts, each with several sections. Part 1, the more complex and interesting, includes two main sections. The first of these has two interwoven themes that demonstrate characteristics common to all of Schütz Zell's thought and make it well worth outlining this early pamphlet in detail.

One theme is a long explanation of Schütz Zell's obligation to speak out, based on scripture, and her confidence in her right to do this, also based on scripture. Although it serves as her defense for publishing, this discussion emerges as one of the most creative sixteenth-century examples of a layperson's argument for public speech. The presentation is somewhat loosely ordered; since this can obscure the clear argument, it is useful to summarize the latter briefly. Essentially, Schütz Zell believes that truth (faithfulness to "the Gospel") and love (of her neighbors) require her to speak out, and she proves this from scripture. On the basis of Christ's teaching and actions, she distinguishes between suffering for the sake of truth, which is right (Mt 5:11–12), and being silent in the face of falsehood, which is wrong because it seems to support the falsehood (Jn 18:22–23) and causes stumbling blocks for others (Lk 17:1–2). In effect, silently tolerating lies is contrary both to Christ's example and to His teaching. For Katharina, the falsehoods that need refuting are the lies about Matthew; these make people stumble by turning them away from the gospel he is preaching, which itself is the only way they can be saved (Rm 10:17). As she values her own salvation and knows that she must seek it in the Bible, and as the Bible has taught her to love her neighbors as herself (Lv 19:18; Mt 22:37–39), Katharina's obligation to the truth, and to love, is to speak out. One might think that her most important neighbor would be Matthew who is maligned by the lies, but in fact the lay reformer considers those who are being deceived by the lies and the deceivers who propagate these falsehoods to be the principal neighbors she must help.

A second theme is Schütz Zell's attention to the existential context which calls forth her writing and her ability to speak as both lay Christian and theologically informed teacher. Here as elsewhere, the lay theologian cites and responds to her neighbors' views as she perceives them (and perhaps even heard them); in a lively imagined dialogue she sets out the religious misunderstandings of the simple Christians who have been deceived by the lies against Zell. First his wife observes that the lies about Zell's morality are turning good simple Christians away from his biblical teaching. Then she draws what she considers the appropriate theological conclusions about their situation and her response. These good simple folk "stumble" because they think that Zell's marriage makes him unholy since they have been taught that celibacy is the real holiness and do not know that scripture teaches that priests can and should marry. For Schütz Zell, "stumbling" means that they return to their old (celibate) clergy, whose lives look (superficially) holy, and suffer the consequences. That is, when they reject Zell's biblical preaching about salvation through Christ's grace alone and adopt again the traditional doctrines of the Roman clergy, these simple Christians lose their salvation: the confusion about clerical holiness leads to following wrong teaching and so to damnation.

This contextual explanation for her need to speak out expresses clearly several aspects of Schütz Zell's thought. Besides taking her neighbors' questions seriously, the lay reformer understands that many ordinary people measure doctrine by life. She herself plainly sympathizes with this view. However, as a Protestant as well as a devout laywoman, she believes that the standard by which folk have traditionally determined the "holiness" of a life is wrong. The Bible shows what a holy life is and what leads to salvation, but that divine teaching has been displaced by the human teaching of the church, which is contrary to God's word and can only lead *away* from salvation. So Schütz Zell must vindicate Protestant teaching and life by demonstrating that her husband and others are following the authority of the Bible while the old clergy are following the devil. She begins with an expanded allegory-cum-biblical story to show her readers that their present location is life in the midst of a conflict between God and the devil. The devil has his hands on the church (by false clergy and their teaching) and God's preachers who teach His word are an invading army. The devil's messengers try to persuade simple folk that God's word is poison and God's messengers are immoral—but none of these lies can be proved from scripture. (Schütz Zell takes for granted that everyone believes the Bible is God's word and true.) This allegory is the pattern that she perceives in the biblical story of Joshua and Caleb and the other ten scouts who bring conflicting reports to the people of Israel about the promised land and God's ability to bring them into its fullness; so the allegory itself is given quasibiblical authority in the present situation. Schütz Zell implicitly identifies the Roman clergy with falsehood and the ten men who acted against God's will, while the Protestant clergy are like Joshua and Caleb, and the people she addresses can choose whom they want to follow.

This exploration of the simple Christians' need for right teaching, together with their obligation to choose among competing teachers, foreshadows and leads into the second section of part 1 of Schütz Zell's apologia. This is a defense of Protestant teaching (the Gospel) against three major Roman theologians. One, Johannes Cochlaeus, who was famous for his controversy with Luther, Schütz Zell knew only by his writings, but the other two, Thomas Murner and Conrad Treger, were active on the Strasbourg scene, although she almost certainly did not know either personally. Her mention of Cochlaeus's pamphlets here indicates that the Strasbourg lay theologian clearly saw the importance of the issue of justification by faith rather than by works, and elsewhere she gives the subject careful attention. However, this "Apologia" is directed especially to "simple" (literate but not learned) Christians, and so Schütz Zell's primary focus is another doctrine perhaps even more widely held among those who broke with Rome, that is, the sole authority of the Bible.[12] Besides answering her neighbors' questions directly, the young "fisher of people" wanted to show them how to argue against Roman theology—and, no doubt, to demonstrate her ability to take part in the current religious debates. She explicitly intended her biblical defense of clerical marriage as a response to a recent pamphlet by Conrad Treger, the most active Roman theologian in Strasbourg in 1524.

The second part of Schütz Zell's apologia for her husband also has two sections. Here she (at last!) comes to the stated purpose of her writing, dealing with the lies about Matthew Zell. In response to the question she hears someone asking, "Is this any of your business?" she promptly explains why she feels this matter concerns her. She is one of the people who acted on the biblical teaching of the rightness of clerical marriage. She, who had dedicated herself to celibacy, had changed her mind about its holiness and married a priest for the sake of defending scripture and dealing with clerical immorality in what she now saw was the way God intended. So Schütz Zell lists and refutes the lies about Matthew and herself and affirms that the basis of their marriage was a common commitment to their faith—a clear expression of the Protestant view of the primary purpose of marriage as fellowship in the life of faith. The Zells are willing to suffer for this faith—but not to be silent! In the final short section Schütz Zell poses and briefly answers three more challenges to her right to speak publicly that she antic-

---

12. For contemporary expression of her interest in justification by faith alone, see "Women," third paragraph; the explicit form is found in many other texts from later in Schütz Zell's life, for example, "Lament" at n. 84f, "Psalms/Prayer" at n. 125 and passim, and "Schwenckfeld" at nn. 69–70.

ipated (no doubt with some justification) would be addressed to her. In effect, although this section is usually read as her defense for writing,[13] it is essentially only a reply to her detractors; the positive argument had already been made in the first part of the booklet. Unlike most women and other laity, Katharina Schütz Zell did not found her claim to speak publicly on the grounds of being inspired by the Spirit, although she is happy to point out the biblical authorization for that position in order to contradict her detractors. She confidently based her argument, which she would defend and use all her life, on her knowledge of scripture and her determination to follow its teaching.

Schütz Zell's defense of clerical marriage was both remarkable and outrageous. It was printed in Strasbourg probably at the beginning of September 1524, by Wolfgang Köpffel, although no place or publisher was named. On September 10 the city council responded by confiscating the pamphlet and forbidding Schütz Zell to publish any more copies. Even if the author had not been a woman, the situation was too delicately balanced to have libelous attacks on Roman clergy circulating, but no doubt the sex of the writer compounded the offense.

KATHARINA SCHÜTZ'S APOLOGIA FOR MASTER MATTHEW ZELL, HER HUSBAND, WHO IS A PASTOR AND SERVANT OF THE WORD OF GOD IN STRASBOURG, BECAUSE OF THE GREAT LIES INVENTED ABOUT HIM

In this writing certain proud Sophists such as Dr. Murner, Dr. Johannes Cochlaeus, and Brother Conrad Treger, provincial of the Augustinian order, who has so recently undertaken to discredit the Christian preachers [of Strasbourg] with many lies, are "taken."

> What is weak before the world, that God has chosen so that He might put to shame what is strong.
>
> 1 Corinthians 1[:27][14]

---

13. For example, Miriam Chrisman, "Women and the Reformation in Strasbourg," *Archiv für Reformationsgeschichte* 63 (1972): 153; Gabrielle Jancke, "Publizistin-Pfarrfrau-Prophetin: Die Straßburger 'Kirchenmutter' Katharina Zell," in *Frauen Mischen Sich Ein*, ed. P. Freybe. Wittenberg: Ev. Predigerseminar, 1995, 55–80, at 58. Thomas Kaufmann, "Pfarrfrau und Publizistin—Das reformatorische 'Amt' der Katharina Zell," *Zeitschrift für Historische Forschung* 23 (1996): 169–218, at 202–4 and n. 116.

14. Frequently the scripture placed at the beginning of a text gives its theme; see "Hymnbook," title page; "Psalms/Prayer" at n. 113; "Strasbourg Citizens" at n. 83. Here Schütz Zell voices one of the common appeals used by women and lower social ranks, acknowledging her "weakness"

To all the elect who love the godly truth—I, Katharina Schütz, present my duty, respects, obedience, and willing service, with the offering of all the spiritual and material gifts of my honor, understanding, body, and life, together with my cries, groans, and prayers before God, with the heartfelt wish for grace, peace, and salvation from God our Father and the Lord Jesus Christ [cf. 2 Jn 1; 1 Tm 1:2].

I would have planned (if, according to the gifts God has given me, I wanted to permit something to be published)—I would have wanted to do something more useful and more necessary than what is done in this little book. For I have already produced many writings that I have sent to some persons,[15] writings that would perhaps be more useful and necessary to believers than this, writings that I have until now withheld on certain grounds, moved (as I hope) by brotherly love. However, I recognize that what I write here may perhaps not be very useful or necessary, for it concerns only my husband Matthew Zell, preacher of the word of God to the Christian community in Strasbourg: he who is now and has for a long time been maligned with such great lies.

Such lies, however, have moved me to write for the following reasons. Namely, I have considered the doubt and fear that many a simple, honest person receives from such untrue sayings, when he hears such unchristian things spoken with such great mischief and authority. The other reason is Zell's innocence. For every Christian is bound to defend his neighbor as his fellow member of the body in Christ and to stand by him when he suffers unjustly, as each would also want done for himself [cf. 1 Cor 12:27; Lk 6:31]. For God says in Deuteronomy 6, "Love your neighbor as yourself" [Lv 19:18].[16] Now if I were maligned with lies in a way that endangered the simple and I saw that these lies were harmful not only to me but also to other people, then how glad I would be to have someone defend me and

---

in the world's eyes but claiming that God is using her to correct the great ones of the world. This quotation of 1 Corinthians 1:27 and the citations Schütz Zell puts at the end of her pamphlet form a kind of parentheses; the final ones express her piety: forgiving her enemies and praying for them, but insisting that the liars have mocked God in His servants.

15. Besides the printed "Letter of Consolation to the Suffering Women of Kentzingen," Schütz Zell is referring to her letter to the bishop and a privately circulated explanation for her marriage; below at n. 32 and at n. 39.

16. In the Old Testament the two "great commandments" (Dt 6:5 for "love God" and Lv 19:18 for "love your neighbor") do not appear together, but the New Testament regularly cites them together, for example, Mt 22:37–39; Mk 12:29–31; Lk 10:27. Schütz Zell's mistake probably results from following Luther's New Testament marginalia, where Deuteronomy 6 alone appears in the margins of Matthew 22 and Luke 10 and only Mark 12 gives both Deuteronomy 6 and Leviticus 19.

prove my innocence! Oh, how then can I restrain myself, if I believe the word of God? How can I not do for my neighbor, Matthew Zell, what I would want my neighbor to do for me? Not because he is my husband, but only because he is my brother and fellow member of the body in Christ. Otherwise (if I defended him as my husband) I would not be acting according to the word of God but according to human love. For in God and Christ there is neither man/husband nor woman/wife, nor any partiality [cf. Jas 2:9; Rm 2:11], for the word of God concerns only spiritual kinship.[17]

What I say is true, although he [Zell] does not seek any defense and does not even know about this writing of mine. And I certainly believe that if he were to learn of it he would not allow me to do such a thing, for he bears in mind the words of Christ that he daily preaches, where He says in Mt 5[:11–12a], "Blessed are you when people insult and persecute and speak all kinds of evil against you, when they lie about you for my sake; rejoice and be glad, you will be well repaid in heaven." And in scripture God many times says, "Leave revenge to me; I am the avenger" [cf. Rm 12:19; Heb 10:30; Dt 32:35].[18]

Thus I cannot excuse myself and persuade my conscience that I should be silent about these very great devilish lies that have been said and published about me, as I have been silent until now. Yes, just as the commandment to love my neighbor does not allow me to excuse myself from acting, so also I cannot excuse myself for the following reason. That is, it is proper to (and part of) being a Christian to suffer, but it is not at all proper for him to be silent, for that silence is half a confession that the lies are true. And I have indeed seen what my excessive patience has done, namely, because I have not defended myself against the great lying insults done to me, both good people and bad have become suspicious, believing that I am guilty. If the good people have observed and considered my patience, they have

---

17. Although the Greek for Galatians 3:28 uses the words for "male" and "female," the German uses the words for man/husband and for woman/wife. It is clear that Schütz Zell knew that the intended meaning was man/woman, but the dual senses of the words in German give her an opportunity to make a play on the words. Because there is neither husband nor wife in Christ, she is not defending her husband but her fellow Christian.

18. Schütz Zell cleverly absolves her husband of responsibility for her writing. Zell had been ordered to prevent her publishing the letter to the bishop, and she had obeyed, but his wife does not believe her letter to the bishop is in question here (see at n. 32 where she names it as a separate document). This is a different text, addressed to a different audience. Zell would not want her to print this, a public defense of himself, because he is suffering for the Gospel. Schütz Zell clears herself of the charge of being disobedient to her husband by explaining that she acts for reasons that she implicitly affirms that Zell himself would approve if the person being defended were not himself.

indeed regarded it as if I act like a person being hanged, who says to the lord and the hangman, "I forgive all of you and will suffer this disgrace and death with patience, for I have deserved it." Good people have understood my patience as if it were a confession that I deserve what is said and because of that they have taken offense. "How the flesh clings," they have said to each other, and all of the most honest and learned among them have reflected to themselves, "Is this their Gospel? Does this follow from their preaching? If so, I will have nothing to do with them and hold to my old way." Has such a person not taken offense because of me? That is, has he not become worse? For "to take offense (*ergern*)" comes from "to offend (*argen*)," and "offensive (*arg*)" means "evil (*boß*)." For Christ says, "Woe to the one who causes an offense; it were better for him to have a millstone hung on his neck and to be thrown into the sea" [Lk 17:1–2].

Now I cannot say that I am innocent of this judgment, for I know of no more harmful stumbling block than one that turns people away from the faith: "For faith always comes from hearing, and hearing out of the word" [Rm 10:17].[19] For many an honest person comes to such an aversion toward those about whom this kind of lies are told—lies about those who are expositors and leaders of the Gospel!—so that such a person thinks and says, "Should I listen to the word of God from such people and learn from that to lead a Christian life, from those who act and live directly opposed to the word of God? God does not want that." Then that person turns to others [Roman clergy] who lead a spiritual life that is glittering—hypocritical (*gleyanerisch*)—but without God, and he wants to learn from their life itself how to serve God. And so he also arrives at the hypocrite's faith, for true faith must be received out of the word of God [Rm 10:17].[20]

However, as is proper for a Christian, I would suffer such insult and lies with patience, as Christ teaches [cf. Mt 5:39–42, 44ff], but along with that, for the sake of the simple, I would declare my innocence of such lies. "Dear

---

19. Schütz Zell demonstrates a very interesting lay perspective; as seen above at n. 16, she certainly knew and used Luther's New Testament (1522) and later she uses the Zurich translation (see "Psalms/Prayer" at n. 152), but here she follows the Vulgate. Luther and Zurich translate this as "faith comes from the sermon (*predigt*)," but Schütz Zell—the person in the pew—quotes Paul more accurately "from hearing (*gehörd*)."

20. The life of the celibate clergy is glittering (it looks holy) but hypocritical (perhaps partly because so many did not keep their vows of celibacy). Abuses, however, are not Schütz Zell's main focus; vows of celibacy are contrary to God's word and therefore those who follow them have a doctrine or faith "without God." Simple Christians can be seduced by the appearance of holiness because they have always been told that celibacy is more holy than marriage, and so they end up losing their salvation because that comes only from faith in the word of God, which Protestant clergy are preaching.

friend, I am guilty of all evil before God, as the prophet says [cf. Ps 51:3, 5]. However, in this outward work of sin you do me injustice, as God is my witness; but may God forgive you! [cf. Rm 1:9; Acts 7:60]. If you will not allow yourself to be instructed by the truth, I will patiently suffer such injustice with Christ, who teaches me not to resist evil and, when someone strikes me on one cheek, to offer the other and to let the overcoat go after the coat" [cf. Mt 5:39–40]. Then I could be excused before God and also happily, patiently live the word of God [Mt 5:11–12a]: "Blessed are you when people revile and persecute you and say all evil against you and lie [about you] for my name's sake; rejoice and be glad, your reward is great in heaven."[21]

Christ also did this when Ananias's servant hit Him in the face. He did not strike back, He did not flee, He did not resist the evil at all, as He had previously taught His disciples. However, He did not keep silent about it as if the servant acted rightly, but He said, "If I have spoken evil, give proof of it, but if not, why do you strike me?" [Jn 18:(22)–23]. For it is sufficient that we Christians suffer injustice; we should not say that injustice is justice. To keep silence is not patience; to suffer is patience. I should tell my innocence to the one who lies about me, and after that if he will not turn back from what he is doing then I should suffer his injustice. Otherwise by keeping silence I give him grounds to continue in his trumped up lies, and that, in my judgment, is against brotherly love. For I would be unwilling to be left in error and lies without instruction; why should I not also in turn correct the error and lies that my neighbor believes? Especially for the honest people who in every way seek the truth, so that they may be instructed.

This and similar reasons have moved me now to write as I otherwise would not have been willing to do. Therefore, then, I write here to good people and bad. To the good for use and love, so that they may be instructed in the truth and know how to protect themselves from such children of the devil [cf. Jn 8:44] and not to trust their words.

For these children of the devil are no other than the devil's messengers, whom he has sent out everywhere like a temporal lord whose land is invaded by the folk of a great lord who wants to conquer it. When that happens, the first lord must quickly warn and guard his authorized messengers everywhere, both where the invaders already are and in the places where he

---

21. Having put her simple neighbors' objections into words, Schütz Zell now answers them. She affirms freely that she is a sinner before God, but she is not guilty of the things the liars are saying about her. She will suffer what her neighbors can do but will not keep silent about the lies which are turning them away from Zell's preaching of the word, because telling them about the lies is showing her love for them and following the example of Christ.

fears that they will come afterwards. This is what the devil does. He sees that God is a lord with a strong army who are His servants who proclaim His word, which is so strong that it has created heaven and earth and all creatures and it is a two-edged sword, as Paul says in Hebrews chapter 4[:12; cf. Ps 103:21; Gn 1:1ff]. God has now stationed the word in all lands to win those who have for so long gone astray, like sheep without a shepherd [cf. Nm 27:17; Mt 9:36]. That causes the devil pain, and he does not want to allow it. Then he sends out his own messengers to warn the people that the enemies are poisonous and bad and they should not let them in. That is, with such great lies, which in fact have some semblance of truth, the devil wants to persuade folk everywhere that they should watch out and protect themselves well and not let in such a word as God's messengers bring. Then the devil's messengers malign the teaching of God's messengers, saying that it is dangerous, and also malign the way God's messengers live, saying how immoral and wicked it is. And yet these messengers of the devil are not themselves honest and learned enough to prove one of their lies from the Holy Biblical scripture (although they are still always referring to it). In fact, they *could* not prove them from the scripture.[22]

But God also has His messengers: the honest Joshua and Caleb [cf. Nm 13–14], who said to His people, "The people are good." They were seeking to lead the people of Israel out of the iron furnace of the severe imprisonment of Egypt into the good land, the promised land [cf. Dt 4:20; Ex 12:25], the eternal fatherland. That is the way it was then, in the time of Moses, when the ten false spies made the people afraid so that they did not want to enter the good land—the bad men were themselves also afraid of the things about which they spoke. But nonetheless the two, Joshua and Caleb, ceaselessly urged the people to enter there. When, however, the people did not follow them but followed the ten bad men, the wrath of God fell on the people and the bad men so that they never entered the place they would so much like to have been. So let all who are now called watch out that they do not (on account of these lying people [Roman clergy]) refuse to believe Him, so that hereafter, when they would very much like to enter [God's good land] He will no longer want them. Then Joshua and Caleb [probably Luther and Zell] will do their task of speaking the message that God commanded them, and thereafter they will enter into the good

---

22. Although the Roman clergy cite scripture, they do not know it well enough and are not honest enough in using it to be able to prove any of the lies they say about Zell and others. In fact, even if they knew the Bible better they could not prove clerical celibacy from scripture because it is not there.

land and receive it [cf. Nm 14:24, 30]. Also I have written (not only for the simple Christians here but) for all good-hearted people—not those in this city, who hear and know enough, but those in other lands where such fearful lies come, so that they may know how to take such lies.

I write this also for the wicked in this and other lands, to their shame because they have invented such unbecoming, farcical lies and have been found out as liars so that they must be ashamed of themselves. For Paul also commanded his disciple Timothy to punish publicly those who sin publicly so that the others may fear; so I also want to do, in case God may someday want to give grace to such stiff-necked people [cf. 1 Tm 5:20; Ex 32:9]. For they have spread such lies in all the land! So to be fair the truth also ought to be spread in every land to disgrace them so that their judgment may therefore be the more heavy and they may become the more hardened. Christ says, "If I had not come and spoken with them, they would have had no sin. But now they have no excuse" [Jn 15:22]. And the prophet Isaiah says in the sixth chapter, "Close your eyes and stop up your ears and blind your heart, that you may not see with the eyes nor hear with the ears, nor understand with the heart, and come that I should make you whole" [Is 6:10; cf. Mt 13:15]. And God says to Pharaoh, "Even for this have I raised you up, because I want to show my might in you" [Ex 9:16].

"To show His might" means to allow the godless to go on in their wickedness and become hardened, until at last they are at such a height that no human might can be enough against theirs. Then God comes and annihilates them, with His might and not a human power. Therefore He says, "I will manifest My power in you," as He also did then with Pharaoh, whom He left to persevere in his wickedness—and God's people in great suffering under him. They must also have feared Pharaoh so much, as if God did not want to shield them from him, until at last his power was at its height and he pursued the people with all his might and they knew of no further help. Then came God and broke Pharaoh's might. God will always do this. So long as the strength is small, so that it needs only small resistance, just so much as He has given to human beings and which they are able to use, He does not will to help, because the situation does not need more than human might. When, however, all human might and help give out and can no longer be expected, then God will use His might, as all the prophets say; and David repeats many times in the Psalter that one sees that God has kept back something for Himself [cf. Ps 41:2, 61:3, and passim]. So the one who believes in God must remain silent and be tested and strengthened in his faith.

The unbeliever also must be blinded in his wickedness if he thinks God will also be silent and not see his sins. As the prophet says in Ps 13 [Vulgate

(Vg.)]: "'The fool has said 'There is no god'" [Ps 14:1]; that is, he has behaved and led his life as if there were no God.[23] This is what our liars do now: they lie, dishonor, and revile God, His word, and all those who use it, as if there were no God who sees and hears it. But what else should such dragon mouths do than spew out fiery poison, since it is their nature? And how should devil's children be able to speak differently from their father, who has been a liar and murderer from the beginning? [cf. Jn 8:44]. Nonetheless, however, one must warn upright people so that they may not be destroyed by such poisonous fire belching and led away from the godly wholesome teaching. That is what I must now do here, that is, justify my husband Matthew Zell on account of the great lies invented about him, not for his sake alone but for the sake of many good-hearted people (as was said before).

Indeed an evil teaching is more dangerous than a wicked life. Teaching affects many others, but with a wicked life the greatest harm is to the self.[24] I must also say a little about the teaching, not only for my husband, but for the whole multitude of those who preach the Gospel, such as Luther, with all those who serve the Gospel with him, whose names are too many to count. I say then to the poison brewers, yes, to those who pour out all the worst kinds of poison, who are still in Strasbourg and in all the lands, whether they still wear gray hoods [Franciscans like Murner] or black hoods [Augustinians like Treger], or used to wear them, "If the teaching of Luther and his followers is false, why have you not shown its falsity and overcome it with clear godly scripture?" It is as if they [the Roman clergy] want to build beautiful houses and tall cathedrals with clay and straw, while the others [Luther and others] build them with good lime and stone [cf. Mt 7:24–27].

Among these who oppose Luther there is also one who carries on a very vehement and very candid argument against Luther, and his intelligence is obvious. As soon as I can, I want to admonish him in writing about his "wisdom" and take part in writing against him to see whether I may indeed learn something from him or answer him back. As the Queen of Sheba sought to hear the wisdom of Solomon [cf. 1 Kg 10:1], so I also seek

---

23. Here and below (after n. 42), Schütz Zell refers to the Psalms by their Vulgate numbers, which are (usually) one less than the Hebrew numbering soon adopted by Protestant Bibles. By the mid-1530s she had changed to the Hebrew/Protestant numbering; see scripture that prefaces the "Hymnbook" foreword, title page.

24. Here and above (at n. 19) Schütz Zell points to the danger of "evil teaching," something to which she will give much more explicit attention later (see "Lament" at nn. 84–86, 94, and passim). She insists that the only basis for identifying teaching as true or false is the Bible. She concludes that the Roman church builds with "clay and straw," that is, human-made church teachings, while Luther et al. build with the "lime and stone" of God's word.

to hear this Solomon—although I have already seen something of his wisdom, namely, two little books on faith and works, about which I will perhaps (if God gives me the grace) answer him a little. However, he used still greater wisdom in a Latin booklet; I will perhaps ask him to give it to me in the German language and so answer him.[25] However, in order that everyone may know of whom I speak—for, as I hope, he is not shy about his name—he is called Johannes Cochlaeus. I would almost have said "wooden [cooking] spoon (*kochleffel*)", for he acts just like a spoon that makes a lot of noise in an empty pot but is made out of such poor fir wood that one could not use it to stir a child's pap. There are also other things—more of the same. If I were better prepared than I am now, perhaps I would point them out in a summary. For Christ says in Matthew chapter 7[:18–19], "Protect yourself from false prophets who enter here in sheep's clothing but inwardly are rapacious wolves." So one must indeed know what they are.

Among these wolves there is one who is almost more dangerous than Cochlaeus: "Brother Conrad Treger, provincial of the Augustinian order in upper Germany," he calls himself on a little book that he published only after the beginning of the present Frankfurt fair, a book dedicated "to a praiseworthy [Swiss] Confederation."[26] In that booklet I and all Christians may call him a dog and evil worker who tramples God's vineyard with his feet and a rapacious wolf, yes, a father of all wolves, and a thief and murderer who comes to strangle and kill [cf. Phil 3:2; Jer 12:10; Jn 10:1, 10]. Therefore I warn not only an honorable Confederation about him, but all those who seek to be saved, for he is an enemy of the cross of Christ, whose end is damnation and whose god is his stomach; and his honor will be to dishonor. Paul often spoke of such people and finally with weeping to the

---

25. The person is Johannes Cochlaeus. Probably the texts are *Obe die Christen mögen durch iere guten wreck daz hymelreich verdienen* (Whether Christians Can Merit/Earn Heaven through Their Good Works) (October 1523) and *Der Leye. Obe der glaube allein selig mache* (To the Laity. Whether Faith Alone Saves) (January 1524), both in German; the Latin text might be *De Gratia Sacramentorum* (Concerning the Grace of the Sacraments), the first book Cochlaeus published against Luther in Strasbourg in December 1522. Schütz Zell has the audacity not only to claim she wants to answer Cochlaeus, but also to ask him to translate his Latin pamphlet into German so she (who evidently cannot read Latin) can respond!

26. Treger's first text, entitled *Ad reverendum in Christo . . . Episcopum paradoxa centum* (One Hundred Disputation Points), was in Latin and published in Strasbourg in March 1524. It was dedicated to the Bishop of Lausanne and ostensibly not intended for Strasbourg, but Protestants in the city thought it was an attack on them. One of Zell's colleagues, Wolfgang Capito, wrote a quick response to send to the spring Frankfurt fair (which was held twice a year, spring and fall, and was the largest and most important market of the new print culture). Treger wrote an answer to Capito in German, which is what Schütz Zell claims to answer; see n. 27.

Philippians in the third chapter [3:18–19]. And in the book of the Acts of the Apostles he says that he has proclaimed to us all the counsel of God; therefore we should pay heed to and take care of the community of God. For Paul knows that after his departure there will come bad wolves who will not spare the flock [cf. Acts 20:27–29].

Yes, Treger is not just a wolf like the monk among the Dominicans, called the Lector, who devours with his false teaching only those who come to him gladly and seek his teaching. But this one is much more: indeed he is the fourth beast that the prophet Daniel describes, that is, like a dragon and very fearful, who ate and crushed and trampled the rest with his feet [Dn 7:7]—this I want to communicate to him, himself, in writing, and answer this little book.[27] For he and his book are not worth bothering those [the Protestant clergy] who should be ceaselessly busy with the word of God, to give it to the lambs entrusted to them: they should not be hindered in that task by having to answer him [cf. Jn 21:15–17; Acts 6:2]. Their only reason for answering Treger would be that they are concerned for the common good (*gemeinen nutz*) and so want to refute such foolish calumny and shameless slander, which could not move any person of understanding but might lead astray and scandalize the simple.[28] Treger also has carefully kept his book back until this late time of the beginning of the Frankfurt book fair, so that this way it might be published and spread about the land but no refutation could be made because there would not be time.

---

27. When Treger's second booklet, *Vermanung . . . an ein lobliche gemeyne Eydgnossschafft vor der Böhemschen Ketsereg* (Warning . . . to an Honorable Confederacy against the Bohemian Heresy) was published in August 1524, a riot ensued and he and four Dominicans were arrested for their own safety. As Schütz Zell notes above, Treger timed his publication at the beginning of the autumn Frankfurt book fair; below she sees this as evidence that he wanted to present his accusations when no refutation could be available for the same Frankfurt fair, and it is this gap she wishes to fill so that Strasbourg's Protestant clergy do not have to interrupt their important preaching. In fact, in October 1524, the month after Schütz Zell's pamphlet appeared, Treger was tried and released (and he departed). At the same time, the city council gave the Strasbourg clergy permission to answer Treger's book, and Capito, Bucer, and Caspar Hedio immediately published replies. Apparently they thought that what Zell's wife had written was not only unauthorized but also inappropriate and inadequate; see McKee, *Life and Thought*, 58ff. For evidence that this pamphlet constitutes Schütz Zell's reply to Treger, see McKee, *Writings*, 48–54.

28. Schütz Zell uses a phrase characteristic of the pamphlets of the city secretaries and upper civil servants. Cf. Chrisman, *Conflicting Visions of Reform*, 222. She attributes the concern to the clergy, not herself, but since she also claims to fill their role she seems to share this perspective in some measure. The claim that Treger's book would not deceive any intelligent person but some simple folk might be scandalized (caused to stumble) is a common rhetorical strategy, but given Schütz Zell's concern about preventing stumbling blocks for the simple (see above at nn. 19ff), an answer is necessary.

Therefore I exhort all Christians, by the promise they made to God in their baptism, not to allow this poison spewer to corrupt them, but to choose to remain with the wholesome, life-giving teaching of Christ Jesus, who alone is our wisdom, righteousness, sanctification, and redemption, as Paul says in 1 Corinthians chapter 1[:30].[29] Indeed, He is the cornerstone of which Isaiah and Peter speak, one who is precious to believers but to unbelievers is a cornerstone of offense and a stone of stumbling. For they stumble against the word and do not believe in it [Him]. Therefore they would gladly put it [Him] out of the way, but He will fall on them and crush them [cf. Is 28:16, 8:14–16; 1 Pt 2:6–8; Mt 21:44]. If God grants me the grace, I want to deal with Treger gladly and from the heart. And I certainly hope for the help of God, which supported Judith against Holofernes, so that she cut off his head and saved God's people,[30] and which lent to Esther the grace to protect the people of God, and by which Haman himself was hanged on the gallows that he had prepared for Mordecai. For mightier is He who is with us than he who is in the world [cf. Jdt 13:6–8; Est 7:10; 1 Jn 4:4].

Next is one called Thomas Murner. I had well not dared to call his name, for he manifestly will not be seen as a sheep since he has too much allowed his fame to be heard so that now everyone knows him well. For his most important writings and poems have already appeared, that is, those about the *Gäuchmatt* (the pasture of fools) and fools' guild.[31] With that book

---

29. The reference to baptism was another important biblical counter to church tradition, although it does not receive much attention here. Protestants believed that clerical and monastic vows of celibacy, which the church had instituted, were unbiblical and a denigration of the biblically authorized vows taken by every Christian in baptism. Here Schütz Zell addresses lay Christians as Treger's equals because they share with him the only vows that matter. She knows that monks boasted of loyalty to their rules or vows so she emphasizes the importance of baptismal vows to encourage laity to be loyal to theirs.

30. Judith is the title of a book of the Apocrypha and the name of the main character, a devout Jewish widow who saves her people from an invading force by seducing the commander Holofernes and chopping off his head. This was a very popular story and often illustrated in art. The Apocrypha of the Old Testament are the writings found in the Greek version but not the Hebrew; since the Greek was the source of the Latin Vulgate all the Apocrypha were accepted as authoritative by Rome. Protestants generally regarded these additional books as not having the authority of the Hebrew ones; the first generations of Protestants translated the Apocrypha but printed these books in a separate part of the Bible (although later some Protestants omitted the books entirely). In 1524, there were no Protestant translations of the Old Testament so Schütz Zell might not have clearly understood the distinction. In fact, she refers to the Apocrypha only five or six times (Judith three times, 2 Maccabees once, Esdras once, see "Schwenckfeld" at n. 72, plus one of the additions to Daniel). Given her pervasive use of scripture, this virtual exclusion of the Apocrypha is a sign of her character as an educated Protestant.

31. The Franciscan Thomas Murner was made poet laureate by Emperor Maximilian in 1506. Murner's satires, the *Narrenbeschwerung* (Fools' Exorcism) (1512) and the *Gäuchmatt* (which

his praise has resounded so widely that many know well that he is the mayor and guild master of that same craft of fools. Since he is happy to be rich in fame, and very willing that his name be widely known, I must pay him according to his choice.

What else do all three these together do than fence with vain arguments of straw and devise many lies? With these they make big books and thus only deafen the people with their prattle, by which means they intend to keep their godless existence. They fight against the faith, by doing which they intend—not rightly but falsely—to maintain their own and not God's good work and holy service. From that [their own service] they have up to now gained wealth and sensual pleasure so they want to keep their stock in trade, which the Gospel would cut off from them—and that they cannot bear!

They also fight against clerical marriage, which has indeed clear and bright—not faint—grounds in godly scripture, in the Old and New Testaments, so that children and fools can read and understand, as I have shown and proved to the bishop of Strasbourg with a long writing. There I have compared marriage and harlotry with each other according to the teaching of godly scripture. Would to God that the bishop would finally become so angry with me that he would allow everyone to read this writing! However, the reason why (when I would talk about marriage) they remain adamant on this subject is that they [Roman clergy] intend to defy God and to put these scriptural teachings behind them again by force. For this, I must say, they have two reasons.[32]

---

plays on the word for fool or cuckold, known by 1514, published in 1519) were part of his pre-Protestant moral reform efforts. He began to attack Luther in 1520, although his most famous pamphlet, *Von dem grossen Lutherischen Narren* (About the Great Lutheran Fool), appeared in 1522. Schütz Zell concentrates on Murner's satires about immorality. In the foreword to the *Gaüchmatt* he calls himself their guild master. When she says he is not a sheep, Schütz Zell means his behavior contradicts the humility appropriate to one of Christ's flock.

32. Schütz Zell explains what she sees as objections to clerical marriage by church rulers and makes fun of the corrupt system that made clerical concubinage a kind of feudal practice, complete with its own "guild" structure. ("Harlotry" refers to organized patterns of extramarital sex, here specifically the concubinage system; Schütz Zell uses "harlots" for the priests as well as the women.) The presentation is somewhat repetitious, but the main ideas are clear. The church would lose money because unchastity would no longer be a source of revenue in the "taxes" paid by clergy for concubines and children, but Schütz Zell says that the church would rather have "celibate" clergy who break the law and can be fined than legally married clergy who are citizens who cannot be taxed by the church but only by the civil regime as citizens (which she believes is the biblical teaching). Church leaders would also be forced to rebuke unchastity instead of choosing to turn a blind eye in mutual tolerance, and priests themselves would have to accept the constraints of marriage, keeping to one wife and not engaging in promiscuity.

The first reason is that the pope and bishop and their servants, vicars and their fellows, do not raise so much tax money for harlotry from married people as from harlots and knaves. If a priest has a (legally married) wife, he behaves like any other honorable upright citizen and gives the bishop no tax for it [his married life] because God has given it to him freely. If priests (who are supposed to be celibate) have harlots, they must have their lords' permission and fairly pay them a tax for this permission since they are in feudal relationship to their lords the pope and bishops. Thus, yearly, they have their feudal tax made into steel traps, an obligation "as sure as taxes and death." Whether the priest is poor or rich, he must pay it; just like one who owes a feudal rent to another and pays his yearly tax for it, so the priests do also. Also the "harlotry guild's" own mayor or steward is set over these feudal taxes. He is called the Viscal; every year he collects the tax, from which also his wages are paid.

They protect and defend this shame and calumny against all teaching of godly scripture, in which the Holy Spirit strictly banishes harlots and shuts them out of the kingdom of God and forbids that one should either eat or drink with them. As Paul says in the first epistle to the Corinthians in chapters 5 and 6 and to the Ephesians in chapter 5 [1 Cor 5:1, 11 and 6:15, 18; Eph 5:3, 5; cf. Lev 20:10ff; Is 1:21]. But God implanted marriage in all people in the first creation, and no one is to be excused from it except the three kinds of people named in Matthew, chapter 19 [cf. Gn 2:18, 24; Mt 19:12].[33] And marriage also is plainly suitable for priests, as Paul says to Timothy and Titus in his epistles to them [1 Tm 3:2, 12; Tit 1:6]. But that which God wants to have, the Roman clergy want to condemn and, when they can bring priests who marry into their power, they make them suffer and be martyrs.

However, the unchaste "chastity" of celibacy, the sin-flowing harlotry of Sodom and Noah's age, they do not punish and have never punished, but instead they protect it. Indeed, temporal and spiritual authorities have made a covenant together about this to strive powerfully against God. Oh the blindness of the heads of society! How you conspire together! Those who ought to be inclined to all integrity and to give it a helping hand must allow

---

33. Matthew 19:12 speaks of those who are eunuchs from birth, those who have been made so by others, and those who have made themselves so for the sake of the Gospel. Since procreation was one of the main purposes of marriage (cf. Gn 1:28), sterility or castration was regarded as a valid impediment to marriage. However, Protestants generally regarded the third point of Matthew 19:12, the only "voluntary" kind of castration, as a very unusual situation in which the person was essentially untroubled by sexual desires. Apart from these three "exceptions," Schütz Zell indicates that everyone ought to marry.

it to be said of them that one has five, six harlots, another seven women in childbed at the same time and nevertheless a pretty prostitute at home and many such like things. It is indeed as Isaiah says, "There is no health from the soles of the feet to the head" [Is 1:6a]. O God, look on this! I know that You are silent so that Your wrath may increase.

Another reason they resist clerical marriage is that, should priests have (legal) wives, they would have to choose one and give up the others. They will not be able to behave as they do with the prostitutes: throwing out one, taking in another. For Paul says, "A bishop should be the husband of one wife" [1 Tm 3:2]. Therefore they must each live honorably, and if having the same woman does not please the man, he may not exchange her. For in marriage the couple must have and bear many griefs with each other (on which account these priests do not wish to be bound by marriage). Still, one often suffers more from a harlot—he would not suffer half of that from an honest (legal) wife!

However, if they wanted to treat clerical marriage honorably, they would then need to punish adultery in the pulpit more strictly. Otherwise how can they punish it when they are mixed up in it? In such a case (when they are mixed up in it also) the going thing is a mutual blind eye: "If you overlook my fault, I will overlook yours." If, however, a priest had a (legal) wife and then did evil, one would know how to punish him [because he would have a legal means of sexual expression and his violation of that would have no excuse—*trans.*]. But this way the clergy always have an excuse to say nothing else than, "You worldly folk can talk about this easily; you have your wives. So I also am a man; how can I behave like an angel?" and so forth. And that is also true. Oh, then why not leave things the way God made them?! "Let each one have his wife, on account of harlotry" [cf. 1 Cor 7:2]. Does God not know better than the devil what is good? For the prohibition of marriage comes only from the devil and marriage comes from God, says the Holy Spirit Himself in the epistle to Timothy [1 Tm 4:3].

Yes, it should be thus, but worldly people cannot bear it—people who have such fornicating priests among them (in their families).[34] When a married couple dies, their legitimate children take the inheritance. If the

---

34. "Worldly" or civil rulers also have financial and moral objections to clerical marriage. Many wealthy benefices were held by members of high-ranking families, in part because this was a good way to provide for younger children without having to divide family property. But if priests' bastards became legitimate heirs, the priests' original families would lose the financial benefits of their clerical members' wealth and could not pass the benefices on to other relatives. They would also no longer be able so easily to continue in their own immoral behavior if the clergy who rebuked them were of a character to make the rebukes stick.

children are not legitimate, the relations take the inheritance and throw out the bastards; what does it matter to them that the devil carries off the souls of the children? [This is what usually happens to the illegitimate households of fornicating priests, to the destruction of the souls of their children—*trans.*] However, it happens that some harlots and their children provide for themselves well. One sees daily that now a part of them comport themselves like the nobility [maintaining themselves in style on the priests' property—*trans.*], and it is fair that they do this.[35] Also, married priests would have to punish adultery in earnest. As John said, "It is not fitting for you to have seven women in childbed at one time, that is, to live in harlotry, and yet to help to rule the land and people." An adulterous ruler should be set on a gallows and not in a council and should have many stones thrown hard by him (close to him but just missing). Therefore a young fellow once said, when he was being punished for his harlotry, "Should I not do it? My father did it. If he wants to pay me for my harlotry, I would say to him that he should first punish himself."[36]

These are the prejudices of the worldly folk who are against clerical marriage. Part profit from prohibition of clerical marriage, and that comes from their offices and in many other ways.[37] Another part are the priests' friends, fathers, mothers, siblings, aunts, uncles, and so forth; these fear that legitimate wives and children will cut them off from the priests' property and the like. The third part are themselves involved in harlotry, and they fear they also will be seen to be in the game. Thus it was that finally Sodom and Gomorrah were together consumed in the sulfur and bitumen from heaven. O God, make an end soon! How long must the soul of the righteous Lot be distressed this way? Redeem the upright Lot, as You have spoken through your angel. You have set this biblical account as an example for those in the future who would be godless. For while the righteous person lives righteously among them, he must be distressed from day to day. You know how to redeem the blessed out of temptation but to keep the unrigh-

---

35. Without approving of immorality or luxurious living, Schütz Zell clearly expresses her sympathy for the women and children caught in the middle of the problem and considers it just that these families of priests be provided for, including by their own wits if church law does not make their households legitimate.

36. The "John" named here refers to John the Baptist and his rebuke of King Herod for having taken and married his brother's wife Herodias. The biblical account is much less colorful, but Schütz Zell sketches an imaginary formulation of it, shaped by contemporary stories of immorality. She indicates that this kind of promiscuous man is not fit for civil rule, but only an honorable priest could rebuke him effectively.

37. It is possible that "worldly" here may include clergy who behave in a "worldly" way, for example, tolerate, practice, and/or tax concubinage, as well as civil rulers.

The Lay Reformer, Teacher, and Pastor 77

teous for the day of judgment for punishment [Gn 6:4–5, 11–12, 19:4–5; Lk 17:27–30; 2 Pt 2:5–6].

There are still many more things that I will now omit, for people much more clever than I have written enough about them. Among these items is also the service of the saints, about which I must still someday write a little, as Paul bids us in Hebrews in the eleventh, twelfth, and thirteenth chapters to remember the saints.[38]

Should one say to me now, "This is an awkward long excursus; you have indeed quite interrupted and gotten away from your beginning." ANSWER: I know that; it is true. But perhaps it was not done without design. Do you mean that this matter is not my business? Then I say that I see how many souls already belong to the devil and continue so, which was also a reason that I have helped to raise up clerical marriage. With God's help I was also the first woman in Strasbourg who opened the way for clerical marriage, when I was then still not consenting or wishing to marry any man. However, since I saw the great fear and furious opposition to clerical marriage, and also the great harlotry of the clergy, I myself married a priest with the intention of encouraging and making a way for all Christians—as I hope has also happened. Therefore I also made a little book, in which I showed the foundation of my faith and reason for my marriage, because many people had been greatly amazed by my marriage. For no one had in any way been able to perceive in me, by word or deed, that I wanted to be married. Therefore it seemed necessary to me to set out for honest people my apologia and reason for so doing, as Peter teaches us [1 Pt 3:15].[39]

These reasons also moved my husband (so far as I have experience of him and I can still neither find nor sense anything else in him). He began such a marriage because he wanted very much to raise up God's honor, his own salvation, and that of all his brothers. For I can perceive in him no dishonorableness, no inclination toward lust or other such thing—for I am not gifted with either overwhelming beauty or riches or other virtue that might move one to

---

38. Schütz Zell refers to the wrong and right understanding of the saints; one must not pray to the saints or venerate them because Christ is the sole savior, but the book of Hebrews teaches what holiness is for "saints" (i.e., the people of God); below in her second answer to objections she repeats this idea. Although Schütz Zell did not return to this subject directly, her basic views are clearly expressed scattered through her writings, for example, see "Hymnbook" at nn. 53, 55, 63.

39. Schütz Zell explains her reasons for marriage, which (as was apparently well known) she had previously rejected. By marrying Zell, she wanted to counter first church opposition to clerical marriage because she believed the church to be wrong and clerical marriage to be biblical; and second, the immorality of the clergy by "making an honest man" of one and encouraging others to do the same.

seek me in marriage! Because of his [Zell's] behavior in teaching and life, he has borne such envy from the godless that it is as if his body and life were given over to the birds in the air and the worms on the earth—to say nothing about what people have done. And so I come again to my beginning, that is, to justify him. Such envy of him is so deeply rooted in the hearts of the godless that if they cannot discredit him in body, soul, and life, they do it through such great devilish lies invented and spoken about him and spread in all lands.

First, it is said that I ran away from him. That needs no reply. The liars must be ashamed of themselves, for I have never been out of Strasbourg for a single day. [That is, they have had me under their eyes all the time and seen that this is not true.—*trans.*]

Next, they have said that he has hanged himself for sorrow that he married me. That needs yet less answer. This lie was started perhaps by a disciple who grew away from him, who is so set against him. Indeed, they would give half their goods if this lie were true!

Third, because he would not be caught in these lies, they found others. They say he took a female citizen into a garden [seduced a woman of Strasbourg—*trans.*]. All that invention did not help them, and they were everywhere found out in their lies, so they have sought another way and invented devilish shameful lies and spread them and said them in all the city of Strasbourg and in the whole land. (1) They say that he treats me so badly, with blows and the like, and has often chased me out. (2) They have shamefully lied that I have found him with the maid, and when I would not tolerate that behavior, he struck me and chased me out of the house. (3) They say that I went weeping to the Ammeister [city official] and stayed away from him [Zell] eight days in my father's house. And more of the same, and still (other) different lies, so that what is said in one place is different from what is said in another. What else should I say about this than that they are children of the devil, who is a liar and works such lies in them [cf. Jn 8:44]. For without any grounds, only out of what the devil puts in them, they have invented such lies.

For God is my witness—no greater can I have—that I am not lying here. He [Zell] and I have never had a quarter of an hour, that is, in summary, no time at all when we have not been at one. Nor has there been any time when he has done me hurt, great or small, with words or deeds—and, I hope, I have not hurt him either. I know nothing else in this hour than that we would want to satisfy each other in all our intentions insofar as they are godly, and we do that. Also, with regard to the story about the maid: I have no maid, but only an honest little daughter [that is, a young child as a servant], still indeed young and not become cunning, who knows nothing at all of such things, to whom he [Zell] has never said four words so long as she has been in the house. Even if she were already old enough, yet I have found no such wantonness or mischievousness in him that I need have such cares. The servants of the antichrist give him so much to do that he would skip such a thing if it were still in him![40]

In summary, to close with a few words: I do not want to answer about how he kept house before I became his wife. He behaved then just as pope and bishop want: those who forbid the marriage that God commanded and permit harlots whom God forbade. That is also why I married him: having considered his life and that of others, I dared by God's grace and power to try to gain his soul and many others, as I hope I have done for God. But since I became his wife I want to defend him and risk my honor, body, and life for him. I attest that such liars forcibly struggle against him without any reason and lie about him; that these sayings about him that have gone out are altogether lying and invented without any basis in him; and that these lies are also against me and all people. For no one can truthfully chastise him [Zell] before the world; only God can judge the strength of the heart, it cannot be tested by human beings [cf. Acts 15:8 with Lk 24:25 or Rm 14:4].[41]

God grant that our marriage may thus endure, as it is now, until the end. So I hope it will and may be pleasing to God and useful to both of our souls and advantageous in soul and body to many people. And if it is not useful and pleasing to the antichrist and his servants, I cannot help that! And if that same antichrist is enraged and uses the princes of this world to help him, so that we are driven out and must suffer death for this whole business, well, we still have the consolation that Christ says, "You foolish and vexatious hearts, slow to believe all that the prophets have said! Must not the Christ suffer such things and thus come into His kingdom?" [cf. Lk 24:25–26]. And if we suffer, so Christ suffers in us, for we are His members [cf. 1 Cor 12:27; Eph 5:29–30]. What have the prophets said? Read David, the great prophet; in the psalm [2:1–2] he says, "The heathen have gnashed their teeth, and the peo-

---

40. Like many other Protestants, Schütz Zell identifies the pope or papacy with the biblical figure of the antichrist (1 Jn 2:18). The antichrist is normally understood as someone in the church, in Christ's place, whose behavior contradicts his public claim; see "Lament" at n. 86. Here Schütz Zell jokes that her husband does not have time for immorality because the Roman clergy keep him too busy defending his faith.

41. There is more than a hint here that Zell was not wholly chaste or at least was tempted to sexual sin before his marriage, but Schütz Zell says only that he behaved according to traditional clerical mores. It was to save him from temptation/sin that she married him. Zell's own marriage not only explicitly follows biblical teaching, but also provides an example of the efficacy of clerical marriage for dealing with the problem of abuses. In effect, Schütz Zell acknowledges that Zell is a sinner before God (as all people are), but no one in the world may judge him regarding the issues about which they slander him here (see above at n. 21).

ples have contemplated worthless things. The kings of the earth stood with each other and the princes gathered together against God and His anointed." Have our enemies not gathered together against God and His word now? That word in which Christ is proclaimed. Isaiah says the same thing in chapter 57[:1–2]: "How the righteous is here destroyed and no one remembers him! But peace will come to him." And all the prophets tell how the righteous will be destroyed and the godless will have the upper hand until the judgment of God is held.

Therefore we Christians should await the end in all patience; therefore have I placed myself and my husband in God's hand with a joyous heart: may His will be done in us! [cf. Ps. 31:5; Mt 6:10]. I know no greater honor we could experience than that we should die in disgrace with this world, and on the cross we would speak joyously to each other, he to me and I to him, to strengthen each other. Therefore, he and I want to accept such lies and all insults, yes, even death, with all patience, peace, and joy, the fruit of the Spirit [cf. Gal 5:22] and to say with the prophet Isaiah in chapter 41[:23], "Do good or evil, as you will," so we will speak together and fear no one. As God says many times in the prophet Isaiah, "Fear not, I am with you," and says again, "Why do you fear a mortal man? And the son of man, who withers like the grass/and have forgotten your creator, who is strong" [Is 41:10, 43:5, 51:12–13a].

He does not want us to fear human beings, as He also says in Matthew 10[:26, 28] and Luke 12[:4]. Equally little does He want us to trust in human beings and their help, and He cries in the prophet Isaiah in chapter 31, "Woe to those who trust in the great number and strength of human beings and not in the Holy One of Israel and who do not seek God." And He tells how He intends to send evil on them and not allow His word to be overcome and will rise up against the wicked and their help [Is 31:1, 2]. We have consolations enough in all the scripture, which we should have always before the eyes of our hearts. If, however, we are weak in our flesh [cf. Mt 26:41], we should always encourage each other with the word of God, by which we will be consoled through our faith that we share among ourselves, as Paul says to the Romans in chapter 1[:12].[42]

---

42. Schütz Zell articulates a very important stance of individual responsibility: neither to fear nor to trust any human being for salvation. The word of God in scripture is the means to this personal religious strength. However, it is clear that this strength or autonomy does not mean independence from the Christian community or any kind of individualism, but interdependence and a strong sense of corporate life. Scripture is the source of the consolation, which Christians receive from each other when they are weak; for one example, see "Schwenckfeld" at nn. 61–63.

That is why I have also allowed the publication of a letter of consolation that I wrote and sent to the unconsoled believing women in Kentzingen, when they were in greatest suffering and severe anxiety, and yet were forsaken and not consoled by all the world. They were in such a situation that they might well have said with David in Psalm 12 [Vg.], "Lord, how long will You forget us and turn Your face from us? How long shall our enemies be raised up over us?" [Ps 13:1, 26]. And in the Twenty-first [Vg.] Psalm: "We are disdained by human beings and cast off by all people. Many dogs have surrounded us, the counsel of the wicked has encircled us" [Ps 22:6, 16]. Someday (if God gives me the grace) I would perhaps like to write a little about these psalms for the comfort of the suffering, as I have allowed this letter (sent to the women of Kentzingen) to be published to comfort all who are also suffering. God grant that this letter and others may be useful and consoling to all believers. Amen.

Now in conclusion,[43] if anyone wants to say, "How then, does the flesh not understand better? Is that Christian? You have justified whom you wish and reviled and accused other people." ANSWER: No one can charge me here with any lies; I have fairly justified the innocent, and thereby I have also fairly pointed out the guilty. I have not reviled but only said the truth. Otherwise Christ and all the prophets and apostles would also be revilers, for in certain places they have even more sharply pointed out offenses and have called the wicked "devil's children," "snakes," "vipers," "dogs," and "burning brands" [cf. Jn 6:7, 8:44; Mt 3:7, 12:34, 13:33; Is 56:10,11; Phil 3:2; Amos 4:11; Zec 3:2]. If it is disgraceful to speak of offenses [as I follow Christ in doing—*trans.*], how much more disgraceful it is then to do them [as those I accuse do—*trans.*]!

If someone says, "This is none of your business: it belongs to other folk than you." ANSWER: A donkey once spoke and saw the angel whom the prophet did not want to see, (Numbers chapter 22[:23, 25, 27, 28–30]). Is it then a wonder if I speak the truth, since I am indeed a human being (*mensch*)?! And God says through the prophet Ezekiel in the twenty-second chapter, "You child of man (*kind des menschen*), will you not judge the city for its sins and point out to it all its accursed works?"[44] That chapter tells very

---

43. Schütz Zell takes up the objections she knows may be made to her publication. (1) She claims to object to evil speaking, but she accuses other people. REPLY: Those she accuses are lying, she is telling the truth and following Christ and the disciples. (2) Public speaking is not for her (here the indirect discourse has been translated as direct discourse). REPLY: Examples of speech by Balaam's donkey and Ezekiel's instructions to the "child of man" to judge the sinners. (3) The Ezekiel passage she cites is not addressed to a woman but only to (learned) men; scripture opposes women's speaking. REPLY: Citations of texts supporting women's speaking.

44. Schütz Zell cites Ezekiel's phrase as *"Du kind des menschen,"* while below her critic cites it as *"du sun des menschen."* Although she certainly did not know Hebrew herself, Schütz Zell was an

shockingly how the spiritual and the worldly are spilling innocent blood and how the princes do that in their lands; therefore God will send evil on them. And Ezekiel also points out how they despise His law and make no distinction between the holy people (saints) and the outlaws; therefore in the previous chapter he calls such a person a wicked, base leader of His people [cf. Ez 22:2, 4, 6, 12, 26, 21:25]. (On this matter, if God gives me the grace, I will also perhaps someday write what the saints are and what the outlaws are.)

If one wishes to say, "What is in the Ezekiel passage is 'You son of man' (*sun des menschen*)—that is not said to you but to learned men. Paul says that women should keep silent [1 Cor 14:34]." I answer, do you not know, however, that Paul also says in Galatians 3[:28], "In Christ there is neither man nor woman"? And God in the prophet Joel says in chapter 2[:28; cf. Acts 2:17], "I will pour out my Spirit over all flesh, and your sons and daughters will prophesy." And you know also that Zechariah became dumb, so that Elizabeth blessed the Virgin Mary [cf. Lk 1:22, 42–45]. So may you also receive me in good part. I do not seek to be heard as if I were Elizabeth, or John the Baptist, or Nathan the prophet who pointed out his sin to David, or as any of the prophets, but only as the donkey whom the false prophet Balaam heard [cf. Lk 1:42–45; Mt 3:7ff; 2 Sm 12:1ff; Nm 22:28, 30]. For I seek nothing other than that we may be saved together with each other. May God help us to do that, through Christ His beloved Son. Amen.

I forgive all people as I believe God also forgives me [cf. Mt 6:12].

O Lord, do not leave them to persist and perish in their blindness, and do not reckon their lies to them as sin (Acts 7[:60]).

Isaiah says, "You sons of the soothsayer, you seed of adultery and common unchastity, come here. Of whom have you made sport, about whom have you opened your mouth and put out your tongue? You are the seed of a liar" (Is 57[:3–4]).

SOME CHRISTIAN AND COMFORTING SONGS OF PRAISE ABOUT JESUS CHRIST OUR SAVIOR
Introduction

The early Protestant reformers in Strasbourg, as elsewhere, gave attention first to preaching, in order to persuade their hearers of the new under-

---

eager student of the Bible and attended preaching regularly; she could have learned from one of the Strasbourg clergy that the Hebrew did not require a masculine interpretation. A few years later Bucer would publish this idea in his 1529 commentary on the Psalms.

standing of the Gospel that they had come to know; then they began to change public worship and life to conform to the new theology.

In fact, although not necessarily in principle, the shape of public worship changed significantly for Protestants. In the medieval church the essential means of grace were the seven sacraments, and most of these could be administered only by ordained clergy. Every priest said the Mass daily. Laity usually attended on Sundays although normally only the priest and his assistant would commune, except at Easter when all were expected to do so. Preaching was desirable, and people often went to considerable lengths to hear sermons; however, preaching was not essential for salvation—the Mass was complete without it—and when sermons were offered the sources of sermon material included not only the Bible but all church teachings. Among Protestants, knowing God's grace in Christ and the work of the Holy Spirit was essential for trusting and being saved, and the only source for that knowledge was the Bible. Thus preaching what the Bible teaches became *the* primary focus of public worship and effectively one of the main, if not the only, means of grace. Sacraments (usually only baptism and the Lord's Supper) were also very important to most of those who broke with Rome, although in varying ways to different communities, but in no case were the sacraments sufficient without biblical preaching.

Related to these fundamental changes in theology and public worship were two doctrines which came to define and redefine being Christian; one was the teaching of justification by faith alone, the other the priesthood of believers. Justification by faith alone (*sola fide*), Luther's key idea that God forgives and accepts those who recognize themselves as sinners and trust in Christ's grace as their sole means of being set right with God, was quickly adopted by Schütz Zell and others in Strasbourg. A central corollary to this doctrine is the belief that by faith all Christians share a common religious status, "the priesthood of believers." This doctrine meant several things; first was a new way of seeing the relationship of individual believers to God and each other, and second was the character of holiness available to every Christian. Each of these points had significant consequences for changing the worship and daily lives of Protestants. All of these issues are explicit or implicit in Katharina Schütz Zell's foreword to the hymnbook of the Bohemian Brethren and thus need to be spelled out briefly in order to make sense of her rather dense text.

The foundation of the priesthood of believers is the affirmation that every believer can have immediate access to God in prayer through Christ the only mediator. In effect, no longer are specially ordained priests needed to intercede for the common people; everyone who trusts in Christ alone for salvation stands on an equal footing by God's gift of grace in the one mediator Christ. For Schütz Zell and her contemporaries there were two important consequences of this teaching for the practice of worship. One was essentially theological, a revision of what was regarded as appropriate purpose and content. Protestants insisted positively that the purpose of worship is to praise God and be edified by God's word, and thus common prayers and biblical preaching are essential. They also rejected much traditional piety as nonbiblical and a form of bargaining with God as if human beings could do something for God in order to receive something from Him. Such things as prayers to the saints, or the sacrifice of the Mass offered to God by the specially ordained priests, were now no longer acceptable on the grounds that there are no privileged intercessors except Christ and no other means to God's favor except to receive with thanksgiving what He offers in Christ.

The practical corollary of this new idea of the priesthood of believers was a change in the conception of what "participation" in worship meant. In the traditional medieval Mass, clergy and laity experienced worship in separate although (ideally) complementary ways. Although theoretically only the clergy were necessary to the rite, Virginia Reinburg points out that laity were understood to be socially necessary for the drama of the Mass.[45] A more common understanding of participation by the laity was that they offered God their devotions, which might be expressed in various ways such as saying their rosaries or reading books of hours or simply standing in quiet reverence. This conception of participation did not necessitate understanding what the clergy said because the laity were making their own offerings of prayers while the priest made the sacrifice of the Mass for them. Protestants advocated a new ideal of participation, however, based on the

---

45. "What we find in the [late medieval] laity's prayer books . . . is a notion of lay participation in the mass quite different from that on which the Protestant and Catholic reformers later insisted. Before the Reformation, the laity's participation was supposed to be less concerned with an intellectual grasp of eucharistic doctrine or scriptural teachings, than with assuming a proper role in the drama of the mass. While eucharistic theology taught that only the clerical celebrant had a sacramentally necessary role in the liturgy, lay prayer books presented the laity's role as equally necessary in a social sense." Virginia Reinburg, "Liturgy and the Laity in Late Medieval and Reformation France," *Sixteenth Century Journal* 23 (1992): 526–46, at 529–30. In a less ideal situation, laity individually said their memorized prayers or they were simply physically present in a devout attitude while the priest said Mass. A reformer like Geiler von Kaysersberg recognized the difficulty for laity who did not understand Latin, but his solution was to counsel them to stand quietly, knowing that God was being praised; cf. Jane Dempsey Douglass, *Justification in Late Medieval Preaching: A Study of John Geiler of Keisersberg* (Leiden: Brill, 1966), at 67. Roman Catholic reformers also were concerned for all people to understand the worship, and they introduced preaching; but the purpose of the liturgy continued to be the traditional idea of the sacrifice of the Mass carried out by the clergy for the people.

The Lay Reformer, Teacher, and Pastor 85

idea that an important part of worship is listening to what God teaches in His word and receiving edification; thus it was essential that the content of the liturgy be intelligible to every person present. Equally clearly, every person must be engaged in the same form because it is dishonor to God to pay no attention to His word when it is proclaimed and dishonor to the body of Christ to attend to one's individual devotions instead of sharing in the corporate praise and prayers. Therefore, first Protestants introduced biblical preaching at every Sunday service, and in most cities at weekday services as well, depending on the availability of preachers. Then, as soon as people were persuaded of "the Gospel" by preaching, the new clergy began to prepare vernacular liturgies aimed at making all worship "common" in the sense that it could be clearly understood and used together by all the people present as one worshiping body. Translation was the first step, but with this went a series of (sometimes radical) transformations of the content of liturgies to make them appropriately biblical worship.

Besides creating vernacular liturgies, one of the most exciting liturgical changes that most Protestants[46] made was the introduction into public worship of regular singing by laity—including women!—since one of the purposes of worship was the common praise of God by the whole priesthood of believers. Singing in medieval liturgies had been almost exclusively Latin texts performed by clergy for the people; sometimes there were simple sung responses by the laity, but these were the (usually rare) exception rather than the custom. One consequence of this was that virtually the only time women's voices were heard in worship was in convent chapels (not strictly speaking "public" worship, even if laity might attend). The Protestant inclusion of women in the common priesthood and thus in the vocal prayers sung by all the faithful was therefore an innovation, which pleased many but could also shock others who did not accept the idea of women sharing

---

46. Not all who broke with Rome agreed on the rightness of corporate singing. Zwingli, the most talented musician among the Protestant reformers, rejected corporate song mainly because he feared the distraction of beautiful music, although he wanted choral recitation by the congregation. Some Anabaptists rejected corporate song because they thought scripture required that only someone moved by the Spirit should sing or that Christians should sing only in the heart (not audibly). Most Protestants, including those in Strasbourg, welcomed congregational singing, although they differed on whether one should sing only actual biblical texts such as the Psalms or whether the criterion for faithfulness was biblical content. All the music, however, had to be simple enough for everyone to sing and must be subordinated to the words in order to ensure understanding of what was being sung. Usually in public worship all sang in unison, with one note to one syllable so that the teaching would be completely clear, although Lutheran choirs might sing harmony, and Reformed allowed harmony in singing the Psalms outside public worship.

in public religious leadership.[47] The fact that regular corporate congregational singing had been practiced only by "heretical" groups such as the Bohemian Brethren may have contributed to the fact that it had not been considered desirable in the eyes of the Roman church leadership.

Protestants generally agreed that congregational singing was a vital expression of corporate praise, but it was not easy to implement because at first there were few songs that were both accessible to ordinary people and appropriate in content. Medieval liturgical music was often polyphonic and very complex so that even those who knew Latin could find it difficult to understand, much less sing. Paraliturgical religious songs existed, both in Latin and in the vernaculars. These might be sponsored by clergy, but they were not necessarily officially sanctioned and thus ranged from the pious to the ribald. Late medieval moral reformers were indignant about the "bad" songs that (less than devout) parishioners mingled with their popular prayers to the saints.[48] Protestant reformers rejected prayers to the saints entirely and considered many other church-approved songs unbiblical or idolatrous. Altogether this meant that when Protestants wanted to express the common priesthood of the faithful by congregational singing, there were at first very few songs in German or other vernaculars that were regarded as musically feasible and theologically fitting for good followers of the Gospel. This was one of the issues Schütz Zell would address.

---

47. While not a major point of controversy, singing by women could produce opposite reactions among sixteenth-century Christians. Gérard Roussel, one of a group of reformers within the French church who did not finally break with Rome, had to take refuge temporarily in Strasbourg in 1525 during a reaction against reform in France. One of his letters comments very favorably on the beauty of hearing men and women's voices together in worship (obviously an innovation to him). Cf. Aimé Louis Herminjard, ed., *Correspondance des réformateurs dans les pays de langue française*. Tome Premier: 1512–1526 (Paris: Fischbacher, 1878), 1: 411–12. However, sharp Roman criticism of women singing in public worship was also possible, for example, in the attack of Florimond de Raemond on Calvin and the Reformed tradition: "Was the practice of the ancient and wise Christianity like the young and foolish Calvinism, which allows women to sing in church? 'Let her keep silent,' says Paul; 'let her sing,' says Calvin. They say that according to St. Paul, there is no distinction between man and woman. This is the same passage which some heretics of the early centuries produced to prove that women could and should preach, the same as men. But these old and new [heretics] do not consider that St. Paul is not speaking in this place of praying or preaching, but only that all, both the one and the other sex, are equally called to Christian faith and life eternal . . . It seems that St. Jerome accuses them, and in raising his voice against Pelagius he speaks to Calvin. 'It is not enough,' says this good father, 'that you have given women the scriptures in their hands, but you also want to have the pleasure of hearing them sing. You say that it is legitimate for them to sing the Psalms, but this singing should be in their closets and not in the presence of men.'" *L'histoire de la naissance, progrez et decadence de l'heresie* (Rouen: E. Vereul, 1622), book 8, chap. 10, 1010.

48. The songs set to music by Carl Orff in *Carmina Burana* might serve as examples.

A second aspect of the priesthood of believers is what faith in Christ alone implies about the nature of holiness. That is, if all believers stand on an equal footing before God by the gift of faith, that has consequences not only for public worship but also for every other aspect of life. If there are no longer privileged intercessors, then there are also no longer privileged holy persons or times or places or things. For Protestants, what makes a person, place, thing, or time holy is not ecclesiastical status (for example, as priest or sanctuary, relic or saint's day), but the relationship to God in the context of ordinary life in God's created world. Schütz Zell and those around her had been reared to believe that the calling to separate themselves from the cares of marriage and the "worldly" life by becoming monks or nuns or priests was *the* religious vocation and that laypeople's families and work "in the world" were a secondary rank of Christian life. Now that changed; now the criterion of a religious vocation would be determined by the believer's faith in God or lack of it. Any calling could be a religious vocation and holy for any persons who trusted in Christ's grace alone (*sola gratia*) for their holiness and lived their daily work as dedicated to God and the good of their neighbors. Any time or place could be holy if it was dedicated to God and used in accordance with God's teaching in the Bible. Thus, from the viewpoint of laypeople, the belief in the equality of all the faithful meant that their lives as well as their prayers should be considered as holy as those of the clergy. In fact the new Protestant clergy shared this view and put it into practice not only in vernacular liturgies and congregational singing, but also by renouncing the traditional clerical immunity and becoming citizens like their parishioners so that all Christians would be subject to a common civic order.[49]

One might ask, Why would Protestants have clergy at all? To affirm that all believers' prayers and lives can be equally holy and acceptable to God, that is, to have only one rank of holiness is not to say that everyone does the same thing in the same way. All the priesthood of believers have the right and duty to pray for each other and themselves and to love and

---

49. Regardless of his personal knowledge or piety, a properly ordained Roman priest had the power to carry out the sacraments because of his "indelible character" received in the sacrament of ordination. By law he also had "clerical immunity," which meant that he could be judged only by a church court, and this often led to clergy receiving lighter sentences than laity who had to face a civil court. Protestants gave high honor to the ministry of the church but insisted that pastors have no intrinsic clerical character or immunity to civil prosecution; ministers are members of the priesthood of believers and citizens as well as servants of God called to special duties. For her fullest exposition of the Protestant view of ministry, see "Psalms/Prayer" after n. 153; "Schwenckfeld" introduction and at nn. 62–63, and n. 54 for standards of clerical behavior.

serve God and each other. Since the word of God is the only criterion of what is holy and pleasing to God, every member of the priesthood of believers must also learn and proclaim what the Bible teaches. Some reformers, often called "Anabaptists," generally held that the only requirement for reading the Bible is faith and/or the inspiration of the Spirit. However, while they were convinced of the need for the Holy Spirit and the gift of faith in order to understand God's word rightly, most Protestants believed that God also intended people to use His "ordinary" gifts of intelligence and human education to interpret His word. That included learning what the Bible meant when it was written, either through personal or second-hand acquaintance with the original biblical languages and with a breadth of knowledge not usually available to every believer.[50] Thus some people are better able to understand and teach God's word than others; that is not a special status but an office or calling and gift. (Protestants considered the preaching *office* a special ministry because the knowledge of the word of God is the means to salvation, but clergy as people are no more holy than any other members of the priesthood of believers.) Schütz Zell believed that it is incumbent upon every Christian to study the Bible as much as possible and teach the faith at least to her or his own household, but she did not assume that everyone is equally able to explain the faith. In fact, even memorization of scripture is not enough to make a good preacher. Real understanding, based on study of the Bible and the basic creeds (Nicene, apostles') along with the assistance of the best interpreters (that is, early Protestant reformers), is essential. Thus trained teachers and prepared materials (such as biblical hymns) are still needed, but everyone can use these texts to praise God and proclaim His grace—even the most simple folk can and should sing their faith as they go about their daily lives of faith and service.[51]

The foreword to her edition of the hymnbook of the Bohemian Brethren was Katharina Schütz Zell's most important articulation of the priesthood of believers, both with regard to the worship of the faithful and

---

50. For Schütz Zell's view of the Christian office of love, see "Psalms/Prayer" at n. 107; for her sense that prayer for the community is always needed (and expected of everyone), see "Schwenckfeld" after n. 35. For her rejection of special revelation or inspiration by the Holy Spirit as the source of knowledge and her insistence on education and description of ministerial qualifications, see "Schwenckfeld" at nn. 26, 67. For reference to the "humanist" concern to interpret scripture as the human writer understood it, see "Psalms/Prayer" at n. 136.

51. The present hymnbook is evidence of Schütz Zell's insistence that everyone must learn and teach as well as possible, even if the texts are "prepared sermons in song." For objection to rote memorization, see "Schwenckfeld" at n. 56; for discussion of the authority of the Bible and creeds and the role of early Protestant reformers, see McKee, *Life and Thought*, 233–64, 288–94.

to their vocations as holy people living in the world. As with her other publications, this one responded to the situation in Strasbourg. Like most laity, Schütz Zell welcomed worship and singing in her own language. Perhaps better than the clergy, however, she recognized that many of her neighbors were not satisfied with the extremely limited repertoire of songs available for them to sing. Some people (including Strasbourgers, whose complaints she cites) were also unhappy with the new clergy's desire to outlaw much of what was familiar and popular in their ordinary devotional lives; those old songs to the saints were staples of their daily prayers, and they missed them. Furthermore, in the early reform of the liturgy the Strasbourg clergy had also eliminated the practice of the traditional liturgical year, with its feasts of Christ as well as those of the saints, and focused only on Sunday and daily worship without any of the old "holidays." That situation would change in the later 1530s, as Christmas and other Christological feasts were gradually reintroduced as "holy days," but at the time Schütz Zell prepared her hymnbook many laypeople were upset by the loss of these Christological feasts as well as the saints' days. While she agreed with the clergy in her rejection of prayers to the saints—the Protestant lay reformer understood the category of "saints" as witnesses for God, not people who can grant petitions in their own right—she nevertheless sympathized with the laity who missed the Christological celebrations.

The learned laywoman therefore played an important role as both a Christian neighbor and a colleague of the clergy; as her little songbook demonstrates, she shared the theology of the clergy and the concerns of the laity regarding worship and especially music.[52] In 1531, the hymnbook of the Bohemian Brethren (those "heretics" who practiced congregational singing) had been translated from Czech into German by Michael Weisse. The book included songs of praise for many different Christological feast days and other situations of daily life, such as prayers at meals or different hours of the day, teaching songs about the sacraments, or consolation for bereavement. Someone, probably Caspar Schwenckfeld, gave Schütz Zell a copy, and it delighted her so much that she promptly decided to republish it herself. Her work was the first new edition of Weisse's translation and the only one to appear in Strasbourg, although four printings of his original form were published in Ulm between 1538 and 1540 and later Brethren naturally continued to use and modify their hymns.

---

52. For Schütz Zell's views on song in the context of analyzing her hymnbook, see McKee, *Reforming Popular Piety*, 19–23, 26–34.

As a Christian and a Protestant, Schütz Zell welcomed these songs with their biblical content as exactly the right thing to replace the "bad" songs that people had been singing, to their moral harm and the loss of their eternal salvation.[53] The lay theologian was sure that the Strasbourg ban on the traditional practice of the liturgical year did not signify that remembering the biblical feasts of Christ was inappropriate; anything taught in the Bible is true and acceptable. Schütz Zell's confidence in her own knowledge of scripture—which she felt permitted her to judge the biblical character of these songs—is evident in her foreword. As a layperson, she was very conscious of the need for more material for daily devotion than was supplied by the currently available Protestant liturgical books. Furthermore, she was fully convinced of the priesthood of believers, that all who have faith in Christ alone are equal in God's sight. Both women and men are called to the praise of God and active religious lives right where they are, in the world, and they not only can but should teach their faith to their households—but they must be taught!

And so Katharina Schütz Zell decided to supply her neighbors—all members of the priesthood of believers—with the proper instruction to do this home-style "lay preaching" by making available good biblical songs with attractive music. She presents Weisse's translation of the Bohemian Brethren's hymns, along with her own foreword and selection of tunes and annotations. The hymn texts were copied word for word, using Strasbourg orthography. Schütz Zell (and/or an assistant) chose the music, which she thought should be "pretty" so that people would be drawn to sing "enthusiastically." All but one of the tunes in her book came from religious sources, but the latter were quite varied: liturgical music and popular hymns, Weisse's own volume of Bohemian Brethren songs, and some quite good melodies that were apparently original in Schütz Zell's circle. (The one secular tune had already been used for a hymn to the Virgin Mary in the previous century, so it could be counted as a religious tune also.) Many of the texts were

---

53. Reform of immoral popular songs was a common goal of many theologians who remained in communion with Rome and ones who broke with Rome. Reform of veneration of the saints or other aspects of official teaching or popular piety that Protestants believed contradicted the Bible was critically important to Schütz Zell as to her fellow Protestants. The two issues must be distinguished: Roman clergy promoted the veneration of the saints even if they criticized some expressions of popular piety. Protestants usually attacked both aspects, working to eliminate piety that they considered theologically wrong as well as what was morally unacceptable. One example: in February 1528 the Strasbourg City Council reprimanded the orphans who sang for alms and their guardians because the children were singing prayers to the Virgin Mary: "Remind them again for the third time to stop singing such things and to learn the right honoring of the Mother of the Lord and the saints." See McKee, *Reforming Popular Piety*, 10–11.

printed with musical notes, although often the melody could be indicated by giving the title of another hymn ("to be sung to the tune '———'").[54] A few of Weisse's songs had been prefaced with theological annotations. Schütz Zell kept these but also added her own comments to almost every song, especially the ones in the fourth booklet, which covered a wide range of topics and needed more explanation than the hymns about Christ's life. The lay pastor was deliberately providing "study aids" to make the hymns into a kind of teach-yourself catechism, thus contributing further to her neighbors' capacity to understand and communicate their faith. These annotations express, more clearly than the foreword, Protestant views such as objections to the veneration of the saints, including the most important, the Virgin Mary.[55]

With her usual attention to the powerless, Schütz Zell remembered that many of her neighbors who particularly needed instruction and wanted devotional materials were young or poor or both, so she wished to make her publication inexpensive and easy to handle. She divided Weisse's fat little book into four sections costing a few pennies each so that even a child or the poorest household might buy at least one booklet. The pagination of the sections was consecutive, however, so that anyone who bought all four could bind them again into one book. Schütz Zell's foreword, dated 1534, served as a preface to the first of the four booklets and was actually printed in Strasbourg in 1535 by Jacob Frölich; the second booklet of hymns came out later that year, and the third and fourth in 1536.

The foreword to the hymnbook is Schütz Zell's shortest writing published in her lifetime and one of the most dense and sharp in its polemic. First she uses biblical examples to justify the appropriateness of Christians singing and

---

54. Schütz Zell's hymnbook was published at the point in musical history when the modal music of the Middle Ages was shifting toward the tonic form characteristic of modern music. A comparison of her book with Weisse's original reveals that more of the music Schütz Zell published followed the modern orientation. A full musicological examination of the music is found in Anne Wolff, *Le recueil de cantiques de Catherine Zell, 1534–1536*, 2 vols. (Université des Sciences Humaines de Strasbourg, Institut d'Etudes Allemandes, 1986).

55. For her insistence that these are "teaching" songs, see below at nn. 58, 65. The titles of the hymns and a transcription of Schütz Zell's comments on each are found in McKee, *Reforming Popular Piety*, 69–80. One example of Schütz Zell's care to honor the biblical saints but never to allow them to usurp Christ's role as savior is found in an annotation in her fourth booklet. Weisse had written, "About Mary the Mother of Christ," and Schütz Zell adds, "How she, from the race of Jesse, bore Christ through the Holy Spirit, and how all the saints have built on Christ and not on Mary" (*Reforming Popular Piety*, 54, 80). Mary was the chief saint, and medieval Christians sometimes prayed to her as mediatrix or comediator with her Son, so it is notable that Schütz Zell rarely mentions Mary and that when she speaks of her it is very restrained (see "Schwenckfeld" before n. 67).

explains her practical decisions about dividing the text and pricing the booklets. Then she makes a sharp distinction between "bad" and "good" songs and emphasizes the importance of "lay preaching" by parents and others. It is clear that she has in mind ordinary households, the rank and file of the priesthood of believers; not only does she name common labors of artisans and peasants but she also gives particular attention to women's domestic activities.[56] In the context of encouraging laypeople to practice the musical prayers, praises, and teachings she is offering, Schütz Zell ranks "ordinary" Christians above the monks and nuns who had always been held up to them as the "more holy" people. However, it is plain that she does not mean a simple elevation of lay above clerical: the criterion of a Christian life is faith, not works; laity and clergy are all the same in God's eyes, and a mother's task (which she has just praised) is not more holy than a nun's if it is not done in faith. The brief text ends with a sharp challenge to the readers to choose between good and evil, right and wrong, the most pointed such exhortation in all Schütz Zell's corpus.

SOME CHRISTIAN AND COMFORTING SONGS OF PRAISE ABOUT JESUS CHRIST OUR SAVIOR, HIS INCARNATION, BIRTH, CIRCUMCISION, ETC., OUT OF A VERY FINE SONGBOOK ABOUT WHICH MORE WILL BE SAID IN THE FOREWORD

Sing to the Lord a new song, for He has done wonders.
Psalm 98[:1a]

Sing joyously to God, who is our strength.
Psalm 81[:1a]

I will praise the Lord during my life, I will sing praise to my God while I live.
Psalm 146[:2]

Foreword

Out of special love and friendship a songbook was given to me to read. It was printed in Bohemia and sent to good people in Landskron [Bohemia] and Fullneck [Moravia] by a God-fearing man, indeed, a man who knows God. His name is Michael Weisse. I do not know him personally, but as the

---

56. The reference to peasant labor is fairly stereotypical, and this kind of appeal to semiliterate folk as readers of the Bible was a rhetorical commonplace (e.g., the most famous example being Erasmus's *Paraclesis* or preface to his Greek New Testament). Schütz Zell's specific examples of women's work are, however, unusual, because most exhortations to popular Bible reading were written by men.

The Lay Reformer, Teacher, and Pastor 93

Lord says, "By their fruits you shall know them" [cf. Mt 12:33]. When I read this book, I had to conclude that, so far as I understand the scriptures, this man [Weisse] has the whole Bible wide open in his heart. Indeed, he has the same knowledge and experience as the two dear men Joshua and Caleb had of the promised land when they had faithfully visited and walked through it by the command of the Lord given through Moses [cf. Nm 13:2–3 and chaps. 13–14].[57]

I found such an understanding of the work of God in this songbook that I want all people to understand it. Indeed, I ought much rather to call it a teaching, prayer, and praise book than a songbook.[58] However, the little word "song" is well and properly spoken, for the greatest praise of God is expressed in song, as when Moses sang a glorious song of praise to God when the Lord brought him and his people through the sea (Exodus 15[:1–18]). And the holy Hannah the same way sang thanks and praise to God the Lord when He had given her Samuel (1 Kings 2 [1 Sm 2:1–10]). As also David made so many glorious psalm songs and often used the expression, "We should sing to the Lord," and such like [see quotations above and also Ps 33:2; 57:7, 9; 59:17; 104:33]. From that have also come all the songs of the church, where they have been kept in the right way and with the right heart, as they were by the first singers.[59]

Now, however, so many scandalous songs are sung by men and women and also children throughout the world, songs in which all slander,

---

57. Schütz Zell praises Weisse for his knowledge of the Bible, which she (rather audaciously) claims to know well enough herself that she can judge his work.

58. It is possible that this care to distinguish her work from a "songbook" reflects a certain critique of the popular songs that circulated both orally and in print. Here and elsewhere Schütz Zell clearly states that hers is a teaching book (see after n. 64; "Lament" before n. 105), and her annotations support the claim. For a woman to teach theology was a significant challenge to the clergy, but Schütz Zell's instrument of a songbook—not labeled as a catechism but functioning as such, and one expressly intended for other women and the simplest people (peasants)—was a clever means to circumvent criticism.

59. Schütz Zell here demonstrates from scripture that singing in worship is good when it is rightly done. The last point is critical: not just any singing is approved, but it must be in accord with the Bible and faith. Implied here is a view of history common to humanists and Protestants, that the earliest church was the model of right understanding of scripture and later changes were corruptions. Schütz Zell uses Old Testament passages as proofs; it was characteristic of Protestants, especially those who came to be called "Reformed," to regard both Testaments as equally authoritative. (Some Anabaptists regarded only the New Testament as definitive and rejected proofs from the Old.) Schütz Zell uses the Vulgate name for the books of Samuel, which together with the books of Kings were known as the four books of Kings. In texts written in the 1550s she adopts the newer Protestant nomenclature of "Samuel"; cf. "Psalms/Prayer" at n. 130 (although at n. 142 in her exposition of the Lord's Prayer from 1532 she still has "Kings").

coquetry, and other scandalous things are spread through the world by young and old—and the world likes to have such things sung! So it seemed to me a very good and useful thing to do as this man has done, that is, to convey the whole business of Christ and our salvation in song, so that people may enthusiastically and with clear voices be exhorted regarding their salvation and the devil with his songs may not have any place in them. So that good parents may also say to their children, "Up till now we have all sung bad songs, to the scandal of our souls and our neighbors' souls [but now we will not do that anymore—*trans.*]." But in order that you may not complain, "So may we never sing? Must we become like sticks and stones?"[60] Therefore now let us sing these songs, which express so admirably God's love toward us and exhort us so faithfully not to neglect the salvation offered to us. Wherefore also Saint Paul teaches us in Ephesians 5[:3–4, 18–19] and Col 3[:16], that we should not allow anyone to hear us use avaricious, insulting words, raillery, or such foolish things; we should not be full of wine but full of the Spirit, and we should exhort one another with psalms and hymns and spiritual songs.

And Saint James says, in chapter 5[:13], "Whoever is anxious should pray, and whoever is in good spirits should sing psalms (that is, all kinds of praise of God)." As also this man of God [Weisse] has divided up the songs in his book into eighteen groups of songs about the works of God.[61] This book was a concern to me: there were too many songs to be printed all together; that would be too expensive for people to buy. So I took the book in hand, for the use and service of children and the poor, and divided it into several small booklets costing two, three, and four pennies. However, in the first booklet I put a little index of the order and titles of all the songs of the whole book, and in the next booklet I indicated what follows in the other, so that if anyone wanted to buy all of them and put them together in order in one book (until perhaps it is complete, as it has been printed), that would be possible.

For here there are to be found many attractive songs about the feast days: the coming and the work of Christ, such as the angels' salutation, Christmas,

---

60. This is the first of two specific objections Schütz Zell believes laypeople are making to the liturgical changes in Strasbourg. Here they complain that the clergy have taken away all the songs people are accustomed to sing, as if they want to prevent people singing at all. In fact, Schütz Zell herself agrees with the clerical objections to the songs the people have been using, but she agrees with the laypeople that they need more good songs to sing. To justify both the rejection of some songs and the appropriateness of others, Schütz Zell cites the New Testament texts that were commonly used to support congregational singing.

61. The citation of James 5:13 is intended as a kind of biblical evidence that Christians can sing hymns on a variety of topics, apparently to explain why she kept the eighteen categories into which Weisse's book divided the hymns.

Easter, Ascension, Pentecost, and so on and about the true dear saints—so that many good people may not complain, "The holy remembrances themselves will all be forgotten, if no one ever celebrates the feasts of Christ and the saints."[62] Therefore, dear Christian, whoever you are, since you have until now allowed your children and relatives to sing false scandalous songs at the country dances and elsewhere, and even much more on the feasts of Christ and the saints! As on Saint John the Baptist's day, when it would be more fitting for all Christians to be sorrowful that things were in such bad shape in the world then—and are still so—that one who spoke and taught the truth as John the Baptist did had to die for doing so. So now (in response to this clear call that God makes to the world) encourage your children and relatives to sing godly songs in which they are exhorted to seek knowledge of their salvation.[63]

And teach them to know that they do not serve human beings but God, when they faithfully (in the faith) keep house, obey, cook, wash dishes, wipe up and tend children, and such like work that serves human life and that (while doing this very work) they can also turn toward God with the voice of song. And teach them that in doing this, they please God much better than any priest, monk, or nun in their incomprehensible choir song, as they lifted up some foolish devotion of useless lullaby to the organ. A poor mother would so gladly sleep, but at midnight she must rock the wailing baby and sing it a song about godly things. That is called, and it is, the right lullaby (provided it is done in the faith)—that pleases God. Not the organ or the organist—He is no child, and you may not silence Him with piping and singing! But silence yourself: He requires something else.[64]

---

62. Here is the second objection the laity raise: the holy days will be forgotten if there are no songs for them (which also suggests how important devotional singing was for religious education). Schütz Zell's response is sympathetic but critical; one tiny example may be the way she cites what would normally be called "the Annunciation" or "the Conception," one of the most important Marian feasts. Giving it a biblical description ("the angel's salutation," Lk 1:28) could serve to make readers think more about the source and perhaps distance them from the adoration of Mary (cf. above nn. 53 and 55). Schütz Zell may also have intended to disarm clerical criticism by citing simple laity and emphasizing the biblical character of both the songs and feasts, since she is defending publishing hymns on the basis of the traditional liturgical year, which the city no longer practiced.

63. Schütz Zell's objections to the practices traditionally associated with many feast days are much the same as those voiced by other reformers: the ways people behave and what they sing are both immoral and theologically wrong. She gives the example of the riotous behavior on Saint John's Eve, which was celebrated at midsummer with a huge bonfire, and contrasts this with a biblically appropriate way to remember John the Baptist by following his witness for truth. Now that God has called people (her readers) by sending the Gospel out into the world, they can follow the Baptist's example by using these biblical hymns to know and preach the truth.

64. The priesthood of believers, the primacy of faith, and the holiness of serving God and neighbors "in the world" are clearly expressed here. Schütz Zell compares the "incomprehensible" Latin

But the seven holy times, Mass, vespers, and matins, will be sung thus: the artisan at his work, the maidservant at her dishwashing, the farmer and vine dresser on the farm, and the mother with the wailing child in the cradle—they use such praise, prayer, and teaching songs, psalms or other such like things, provided it all is done in the faith and the knowledge of Christ, and provided they devoutly direct their whole lives with all faithfulness and patience toward everyone.[65] These faithful artisans, servants, farmers, mothers will also praise God, with and in Christ the everlasting priest, with His angels, before God's throne [cf. Heb 5:6; Rv 7:9–12]. But the others—who only use scandalous knavish songs and rotten, wanton sayings and so forth, and have let their children and relatives be taught these and sing and say them—they will have to weep, wail, and gnash their teeth forever with the devil [cf. Mt 8:12].[66]

Here let each one choose which one he wants; he will receive final judgment according to that choice. But I wish for all people knowledge of the good and everlasting salvation. Amen.

LAMENT AND EXHORTATION OF KATHARINA ZELL TO THE PEOPLE AT THE GRAVE OF MASTER MATTHEW ZELL

Introduction

Matthew and Katharina Zell had been partners in life and ministry in Strasbourg for a little more than twenty-four years when he died early on

---

songs sung in a monastic chapel to useless lullabies sung to an insensate organ and elevates instead the useful vernacular biblical lullabies a faith-filled mother sings to a fretful baby. She sharply insists that God does not want the kind of "noise" monks and nuns make, but instead wants people to keep silence—listen to Him, not invent their own ways to please Him.

65. Schütz Zell names the three most common times when laity could attend daily worship; Mass was said daily by clergy, usually early in the morning; matins and vespers were two of the "seven holy times" (i.e., the regular monastic services), which laity might be able to attend before or after work. Keeping the full monastic schedule was both the traditional ideal of holiness and impossible for most laypeople, who (if they were devout) often envied nuns and monks their freedom to come closer to God by such dedication to prayer. Schütz Zell clearly knows this longing but she also has a new Protestant perspective on how a holy life can be lived in the world. One does not need to abandon one's occupation in order to pray regularly, but faithful prayer to God can accompany every hour of daily life while those praying fulfill their mundane responsibilities to their families and neighbors. There are no set-apart holy times or places, anymore than set-apart people; daily life wherever the believer is can be dedicated to God with prayer. Also, in the section of hymns on Christ's Passion, the "seven holy times" are identified with specific events in His betrayal and death, which gives these traditional monastic hours a Christological character.

66. Here Schütz Zell demarcates the saved and the damned more starkly than any other place in her writings. She does not name those in the Roman communion as the damned, however,

the morning of January 10, 1548, at the age of seventy. Always the most popular preacher in Strasbourg, in his last years Matthew had become if anything more fiery, particularly in face of the military defeats which he and other Protestants feared would threaten the continued existence of the faith to which they had given their lives.

After suffering reverses for many months, in April 1547 the forces of the Protestant Schmaldkald League were definitively defeated and their leaders imprisoned by the victorious Emperor Charles V. Ongoing negotiations were being held in the city of Augsburg to set the terms the Protestant cities and territories would have to accept in the new political and religious settlement known as the Augsburg Interim. (This was not intended to be a final solution to the confessional struggle in the Holy Roman Empire because each side still hoped for something better, hence the name.) It was clear that the emperor would reintroduce Roman clergy, worship, and practices in conquered territories, but the details varied from one city or land to another, depending on what terms each defeated party could negotiate. Strasbourg did not learn of its own fate until the beginning of January 1549, but the previous two years had seen the citizens split into parties, some wanting to resist the return of Roman worship and stick to their confession to the death, others determined to work out the best deal possible even if it meant making religious concessions to maintain as much autonomy as they could. The latter party would eventually gain the upper hand, and in February 1550 Strasbourg would see the Roman Catholic sacraments and clergy reestablished in about half of the churches, including the cathedral, while the Protestant people of those parishes had to move to other quarters.

It was in the context of Strasbourg's fluctuating fears and defiance regarding the impending Interim that its first reformer came to the end of his long life. Despite his failing health, Matthew Zell had continued to preach strongly against the traditional (Roman) theology and compromise with the pope. Although he was quite old by the standards of the day, his death on Tuesday January 10 was a great shock and sorrow to his wife and partner, who was twenty years younger and still very active. The next afternoon, one hour after noon, many people of Strasbourg, both citizens and refugees, formed a long procession to accompany Zell's body to the graveyard outside the city

---

but points generally to those who follow wickedness. For the saved it is obvious that faith plays the central role. For the damned, the emphasis seems to fall on behavior but teaching is not missed; the rest of the foreword and her annotations on the hymns demonstrate that the "scandalous" songs included those that are immoral and theologically wrong.

walls. There the city's chief theologian, Martin Bucer, preached in both German and Latin (for foreigners who did not know the local vernacular).

Then Matthew's widow stood up and spoke to the gathered company. Although some later historians doubted the fact and/or argued about who was present for the sermon, Schütz Zell's action itself is attested by two contemporaries who mention her speech with approval. Abraham Löscher, a Strasbourg humanist and teacher who was present at the burial, published a long Latin poem in praise of Zell within months of the latter's death. This eulogy includes words of approval for his widow's account of Zell's devout life and her grief and the way she consoled herself with her faith. As far as who the hearers were, Löscher's words suggest that some of the crowd had left before Schütz Zell spoke. A generation later (1587) Daniel Specklin, a Strasbourg chronicler who might have been present as a boy but probably heard the story from others, also praises the "beautiful sermon of Katharina Schütz, Master Mathis' wife" and identifies her audience as women. It is apparent that at least some Strasbourgers, both at the time and later (after Schütz Zell had been dubbed a heretic by the Lutheran clergy), considered both the words and the action of their first pastor's widow to be perfectly appropriate and praiseworthy. Some modern authors (several writing before the text of the sermon had been recovered) rejected the tradition that Schütz Zell had spoken, but others agreed that this was the meaning of Löscher's words, while leaving open the question of her audience.[67]

Examination of the rediscovered text makes it clear that the sermon was indeed the work of Katharina Schütz Zell. The contents show that Matthew's widow intended to address the whole community, although she gave particular attention to the young people of his parish. It would be natural if most of the rest of the hearers were women, but certainly at least some men were present. It is most probable that Schütz Zell herself later wrote down the substance of what she had said, no doubt with some retouching and perhaps additions, and circulated it among friends.[68]

---

67. For the debate, quotations of poem and chronicle, and specific references, see McKee, *Writings*, 66–67, nn. 2–6.

68. The nineteenth-century editor doubted that the speech was given in its present form, especially because of the considerable length; cf. Horning, "Das Leichenbegängniß des Reformators M. M. Zell in Straßburg," 50. The fact that the orthography is characteristic of the early eighteenth century, the date of the one extant copy, is not an issue, since even those who copied a text in the sixteenth century changed the spelling to reflect local usage (for example, in the two printings of the "Letter of Consolation to the Suffering Women of Kentzingen," both made in 1524 but in different cities). More serious is the fact that the copyist expanded the text by adding more verses to the burial hymn, as discussed more fully below in note 105. However, the flow of the text is clearly sixteenth century in its linguistic form and

The Lay Reformer, Teacher, and Pastor 99

The content of the lament is primarily an account of Zell's life and teaching, for the purpose of reminding his beloved parishioners and fellow citizens of the Gospel that he had preached and for which he had suffered. After a brief introduction that includes a few words to justify her speaking as the outpouring of her own grief and her concern for all those whom he had left behind, Katharina describes the character of Matthew's life and gives a summary of his teaching. The note of polemic here implicitly contrasts Zell's life with that of the Roman clergy, and the presentation of his teaching is simple but solidly orthodox: an extended series of biblical allusions and references to basic points of the early Christian creeds. After this Schütz Zell sets out in detail the last days of her husband's life and his deathbed, which he consciously modeled on that of Martin Luther. Her expression of her own grief and submission to God's will round out this account of Pastor Zell's good death.

Setting aside temporarily her personal sorrow, the widow then exhorts Zell's parishioners to stand firm in their faith in face of the impending Interim, the religious changes that threatened all of Strasbourg. The rest of the sermon is a vigorous reminder about what is at stake and a renewed exposition of the basics of the faith that Zell and his colleagues had taught, given point by the sharp anti-Roman polemic, which explicitly contrasts the Roman and Protestant theologies.[69] To justify her teaching, Katharina claims to be standing *in* Matthew's place but *alongside* all Christians, including her listeners, to confess the essentials of the faith. She likens herself to Mary Magdalene announcing Christ's resurrection to His disciples, a messenger caught up in God's work willingly but unexpectedly, with words put into her mouth by someone else's authority. In effect, Zell's widow leads his congregation to

---

includes words that would have been unusual in the eighteenth century. Also, even if it is conceivable (although not proven) that the copyist might have made occasional alterations of specific words in order to modernize them for his readers, the character of the content and the style of writing are overwhelmingly consistent with all the rest of Schütz Zell's corpus. Even in the sixteenth century, clarification by substituting one word for another was unremarkable; in the Augsburg printing of the "Letter of Praise to the Suffering Women of Kentzingen" the word *verieichen* of the Strasbourg first edition was replaced with the locally more familiar synonym *vertreyben*. Thus, despite the possibility of some verbal alterations, the present text can be regarded as faithful to what Schütz Zell wrote.

69. As Schütz Zell had said earlier ("Apologia" at n. 24), bad teaching is more dangerous than a bad life. Zell's good life could be expressed as an implicit contrast to the well-known behavior of the traditional clergy, but Schütz Zell apparently thought that what she repeatedly called "false teaching" (see below at n. 84) was both a greater danger and more likely to deceive ordinary lay folk, so the differences needed to be made explicit. She may also have reflected that many of her hearers were young enough to have grown up as Protestants and might not be sufficiently armed to recognize and avoid the errors of the Roman teaching that would soon be reintroduced.

reaffirm what their pastor had taught by reciting the common teaching that each and every Christian should be able to tell. Schütz Zell concludes by turning back to her personal grief; she expresses her trust in God and the resurrection of the faithful with a prayer and a verse from one of the hymns in the book of the Bohemian Brethren, which she had edited.

To understand Schütz Zell's sermon and account of her husband's death it is important to set it in historical context. By long tradition, the way a person died was understood to indicate whether she or he was saved or damned. Books (called *ars moriendi*, the art of dying), which explained how to make a "good death," were very popular in the late middle ages and were frequently printed and widely circulated in Schütz Zell's day. According to these texts a good death included any or all of the following: dealing with attacks or temptations by the devil and with fears of damnation by means of various prayers and other formulae supplied by the books, calling on God and the saints, making a good (full, sincere) confession and receiving the sacraments, especially extreme unction, meditating on Christ's Passion (perhaps with a crucifix or cross held up by one of the family and friends who always attended a dying person), and dying peacefully.[70] A "bad death" naturally was one lacking these signs, where the dying person was defiant, impenitent, or terrified and did not die peacefully.

Behind these deathbed practices of the medieval church were three theological ideas, which can be summarized briefly. First, each person is obligated to do as much as she or he is able in order to contribute to his or her salvation; second, apart from special revelation no one can be completely sure of salvation until he or she dies; and third, every person has the free will to make choices, even if the choice is only to confess his or her sins and hope for God's forgiveness. Some writers of *ars moriendi* emphasized that having done what one could and trusted in Christ and the saints and sacraments, the dying person should feel assured of salvation. Others tended to weight the equation in the other direction, insisting on more attention to one's own failures than Christ's grace.[71] Thus, how one died became the last

---

70. For a recent summary of the various aspects of a "good death" and preparation for it, see Austra Reinis, *Reforming the Art of Dying: The ars moriendi in the German Reformation (1519–1528)* (Ph.D. dissertation, Princeton Theological Seminary, 2003), chap. 2.

71. Reinis cites these three teachings from a discussion of late medieval *ars moriendi* by Sven Grosse in the final chapter of his book, *Heilsungewißheit und Scrupulositas im späten Mittelalter: Studien zu Johannes Gerson und Gattungen der Frömmigkeitstheologie seiner Zeit* (Tübingen: J.C.B. Mohr/Paul Siebeck, 1994), esp. 225ff. Reinis then adds her own analysis of several other texts, including one by Stephan von Landskron (*Die Himelstrasz*, Augsburg, 1484), which illustrates the more severe attitude of focus on the dying person's sins, and the anonymous *Versehung leib, sel, er und*

and most important sign of one's eternal fate: whether one would be damned or saved (in the latter case normally going first to purgatory to complete the penance for the sins one had confessed and finally to heaven and everlasting bliss).

Deathbeds remained very significant occasions for Protestants, but the new teaching made some distinctive changes in the conception of a good death. Some of these were obvious differences of practice: there were no prayers to the saints for their intercession because Christ is the sole mediator; there was no obligation to confess every sin because forgiveness is not measured mechanically; there was no sacrament of extreme unction or communion with a reserved host because grace is not a function of a holy ritual or holy object; and there was little attention to the devil. Less obvious but equally or more important were changes in the theology. Christ is the sole savior and only through faith in Christ can a sinner be justified (accounted as acceptable) before God. However, since such faith is God's gift, which humans do not and cannot earn—they do not have free will—it also cannot be lost because one does not die peacefully. Because human beings cannot contribute to their salvation—to claim that would dishonor Christ by implying that His work was not sufficient and God's forgiveness was not complete—there is also no purgatory.[72] On the other hand, right knowledge and trust in God and lifelong faith and Christian practice are the important things and if these are evident in the person's life, even a death troubled by doubts does not reverse them. The new emphasis in a good death included recognition of sinfulness, but the main focus was prayers confessing faith and trust in Christ's grace and confidence in the certainty of salvation. There also continued to be an association of a peaceful death with that assurance of salvation by faith alone.[73]

---

gutt (Nuremberg, 1489), which seeks to reassure the dying person without actually promising salvation. See Reinis, *Reforming the Art of Dying*, 37ff.

72. Although the contrast between medieval teaching and Protestant views must not be stated too sharply, there are clear differences in anthropology, that is, free will and human capacity. For Protestants like Luther, Zell, and others, there is no human free will in matters of salvation and no ability to contribute to one's salvation either by earthly action or after death. Humans can make choices about earthly matters, but they cannot even effectively recognize, much less choose to turn their backs on, their sin and trust in themselves. Only the work of the Holy Spirit can make them know their sin and trust that the God who could condemn them actually means His promises of forgiveness. For Schütz Zell's own formulation, see below ("lead us not into temptation") and ("forgive our debts"), after n. 103. "Psalms/Prayer" in Psalm 51:1a and Psalm 51:6, after n. 124 and n. 126; "Schwenckfeld" at nn. 66, 70; for her rejection of the teaching on purgatory, see n. 95 below.

73. Reinis, *Reforming the Art of Dying*, examines the earliest Protestant version of books teaching about dying, especially focusing on Luther's 1519 *Sermon on Preparing to Die* and its influence.

Protestant leaders did not discount the propaganda value of a peaceful death, especially because any other kind would be interpreted by most Christians—including many of their followers as well as their Roman opponents—as a sign of condemnation of their (Protestant) faith. (In fact, spurious accounts of dreadful deaths of major reformers like Luther and Calvin were an important form of Roman propaganda.) For this reason, accounts of deathbeds of Protestant clergy were particularly important and popular publications. In the eyes of ordinary people—whom Schütz Zell always had in view—the outline of her husband's life and death was as much a defense of his/their faith as the actual teaching she recites and undoubtedly played a vital role in the way her sermon was received. Here was a model of a faithful Christian's story, demonstrating that his life and his death were of a piece and both reflected his biblical teaching. The way his wife expressed her grief and her trust also confirmed her own faith.

The "Lament for Matthew Zell" probably circulated in manuscript form among those who loved the Zells, and it may have been particularly popular with those who, like the Zells, had resisted the Interim. It may be inferred that it was passed on as a living witness to the faith. At the end of the sermon Schütz Zell says she will conclude with one verse of a favorite hymn, but the only extant copy of the sermon, in an eighteenth-century hand, gives all seven verses of the hymn in the form that the copyist apparently knew in his own day. This raises the question of the trustworthiness of the manuscript. However, it is probable that a deliberate forgery would have smoothed out this contradiction, while someone transcribing a text for the edification of devout readers would be likely only to try to make the piece as intelligible as possible for his audience.[74] This logic would also explain the scope of any possible alterations in Schütz Zell's original. If the copyist changed anything in the text, it would probably only be an occasional archaic word brought up

---

Her study, which covers 1519–28, hints at the beginning of diversity on this issue among those who broke with Rome but does not see marked evidence of it. Schütz Zell's outline of her husband's death is somewhat simpler than Luther's early prescriptions and, despite being modeled on accounts of Luther's own death, it may illustrate a different orientation; for example, there is no mention of the sacraments for the dying person, a point on which Lutheran and Reformed traditions developed somewhat different views. As Schütz Zell saw it, Zell approached death without fear and lived his deathbed with prayerful trust, to a quiet peaceful end without any ritual or fanfare (see below at nn. 87, 102). For some of her own trustful reflections on death, see "Psalms/Prayer" at nn. 121, 165; for the seriousness of the deathbed, see "Schwenckfeld" at n. 58.

74. It is possible that a copyist might want to alter aspects of a text that did not seem edifying to his age, but the tenor of this whole piece is so consistent with the rest of Schütz Zell's work that any significant changes are improbable here.

to date. Internal evidence from the language and argumentation (some of which is identical with references to Zell's death found in writings his widow published in print) makes it nearly certain that only the final hymn represents a significant alteration in the text. That pious addition tends to confirm, however, the edifying purpose of those who preserved Schütz Zell's sermon. Apart from these devout readers, her sermon was "lost" or forgotten for several centuries; it was printed in a somewhat inaccurate form in the later nineteenth century and then critically edited in 1999.[75]

LAMENT AND EXHORTATION OF KATHARINA ZELL TO THE PEOPLE AT THE GRAVE OF MASTER MATTHEW ZELL, MINISTER AT THE CATHEDRAL IN STRASBOURG, HER UPRIGHT HUSBAND, OVER HIS DEAD BODY, THE 11TH OF JANUARY 1548

Dear friends: Although this burial and sad occasion most closely concern me, namely, to bury the body of my dear and upright husband after his departure from this temporal life (as all people must depart), still, out of the overflow of my grieved heart, yes, which the Lord has grieved, I must say something about it to you, something I cannot hold back [cf. Lam 1:12b, 20a; Lk 6:45]. I thank all of you with my whole heart for the love and faithfulness that you have now all shown to my dear husband and the diligent way you have followed him, your upright, simple, but faithful shepherd. I see that today the thoughts of the hearts are revealed [cf. Lk 2:35] and love that was hidden for a time now breaks forth. Where I also can serve all of you in your needs and each one individually, I will gladly do that according to the measure of my ability.

Second, I cannot fail further to exhort you who are here present (for my heart is full). Yes, I cannot fail to remind you and myself of the teaching and life that my good husband led and exhort all of us not to disregard the witness of his death or forget his teaching; as the Lord laments in the prophet Isaiah and says, "The upright will be taken away and no one takes that seriously, or pays attention" [Is 57:1]. God does not measure things that way at all; for He also says in the psalm how faithful and valuable before Him is the death of His great saints [Ps 116:15]. You have now heard an exhortation and prayer from Mr. Martin Bucer (do not forget it!). These

---

75. For the nineteenth-century printing, see Horning, "Das Leichenbegängniß des Reformators M. M. Zell in Straßburg," and the critical edition in McKee, *Writings*, 93–94, n. 116 for details about the hymn.

preachers will be taken away for their good and profit to rest in their Lord Christ, but for us their departure is our great chastisement.[76]

But first I ask you not to take it wrongly and not to be irritated with me for what I am doing, as if I now wanted to place myself in the office of preachers and apostles: not at all! But it is only as the dear Mary Magdalene without any prior thought became an apostle and was charged by the Lord Himself to tell His disciples that the Christ was risen and was ascending to His Father and our Father [cf. Jn 20:14–18]. So I also now speak, without any prior intention; when I went out of my house I had not thought to be able thus to say something but only planned to follow to the grave this, my dearest treasure on earth, with silent but great pain—as also the mother of Jesus together with the others from Galilee performed their love to the Lord Christ and followed Him to the cross and grave [cf. Jn 19:25b–27; Mt 27:55–57, 61]. Now, however, without my prior knowledge and consideration, my heart and mouth have opened to all of you and I cannot restrain myself.[77]

This my upright husband was seventy years old, in his thirtieth year as pastor in the cathedral here in Strasbourg, a servant of his Lord Jesus Christ. He was simple, faithful, and truthful; he believed the holy scriptures, taught them and held to them purely as to the word of God ordained through the Holy Spirit for our light on this pilgrimage [cf. Ps 119:105].[78] He was not

---

76. It may be inferred from Löscher's poem that the text of Bucer's sermon was the passage from Isaiah quoted by Schütz Zell, and she may have cited it to link her words to what the people had just heard. She also had reason to fear the loss of other preachers besides Zell, even though at this moment the future was still unclear. Schütz Zell thought that God's punishment on Strasbourg for compromising with Charles V would take the form of loss of its clergy: probably by death, but in fact exile and death were both coming. The Italian Protestant theologian Peter Martyr Vermigli, who had been teaching in Strasbourg, had already left at the end of 1547. In the spring of 1549, Bucer and Paul Fagius, the two most vocal clerical opponents of the Interim, would be exiled—and in fact spent their last days in Strasbourg hidden in Schütz Zell's home. By 1552, all the significant first-generation preachers were dead.

77. In John's Gospel, Mary Magdalene sees the resurrected Jesus Christ and is commissioned by Him to tell the disciples that He has risen. One version of the medieval book of saints' stories, *The Golden Legend*, quotes the church father Ambrose's description of Mary Magdalene as an "apostle to the apostles." Schütz Zell's repeated emphasis on "no prior thought" is a rather different introduction from her usual justifications for speaking out. It is likely therefore that she states this partly to exculpate herself because a woman preaching in public would be shocking. Her grief would be an acceptable explanation for speaking of her husband, and the fact that she also speaks of theology could be allowed as simply repeating Zell's words. Given the careful consideration with which she normally approached publication or public speech, it is also very likely her sermon was a surprise to herself, even if she might well have meditated during Zell's last days about how she would defend his work after his death.

78. Zell was born in 1477 and came to Strasbourg as priest of the cathedral parish in the summer of 1518. Thus in January 1548 he was some months past his seventieth birthday but had

The Lay Reformer, Teacher, and Pastor 105

involved in worldly matters and practiced no hypocrisy in his spiritual office, nor could he have done so; therefore I could well say of him as it is written of the holy Job, "There was a man in the land, simple and upright and fearing God" [Job 1:1]. Yes, he loved and feared God and behaved according to the simplicity and faithfulness of his means and ability. He was ready to serve everyone and highly valued love; he was quick to forgive the sins of his neighbors and gladly covered them (so long as they were not public sins against God and His Spirit [cf. Mt 18:15–18]).[79] Anything he failed to do was not out of wickedness or unfaithfulness or laziness but from inability and simplicity. He ordered his household without pride or arrogance or other faults and led a simple and quiet and austere life; indeed he disciplined his body in all things. He was frugal in his use of food and drink but opened his home and gladly kept a free table for all refugees (foreigners), the poor, and good friends in the faith.[80]

It is well known how he began to preach the holy Gospel of Christ our crucified and resurrected Lord here in Strasbourg, after the blessed (*selig*)

---

not yet completed his thirtieth year in Strasbourg. Schütz Zell's carefulness with numbers demonstrates her interest in history; here it reminds his people how impressive Zell's service to the city was: he had been their pastor for more than a generation. "Simple" is a word of praise.

79. Schütz Zell's description of her husband implicitly contrasts him with the traditional clergy who were often accused of being involved in worldly matters and hypocritical in their work. One form of hypocrisy in view here is the abuse of excommunication for money; one of the great complaints against the late medieval church was the practice of excommunicating people for debt. Some clergy also wanted to reform this, and in fact, before his preaching became "heretical" Zell was already in trouble with Strasbourg's bishop for absolving penitents without charging the regular fees. The statement that he was ready to forgive sins quickly and cover them as long as they were not public sins against God probably indicates both Zell's refusal to make excommunication a means of enforcing payment and his rejection of the traditional view of obligatory private confession to a priest (the sacrament of Penance). Protestants understood Matthew 18:15–18 to mean that if a person who wronged another confessed to that other and was forgiven, the matter was closed and no priest needed to be involved. If the sinner would not acknowledge the fault, then he or she was confronted by several fellow Christians, and only if she or he then refused to repent was the matter made public. For the first two stages there was no obligation to confess to a minister, although that might be done by personal choice for pastoral counsel. Only if a sin was publicly known were public confession and rebuke needed because leaving known scandal undisciplined dishonored God and allowed a kind of *lèse majesté*. See "Strasbourg Citizens" at n. 98.

80. One further point was a contrast between Zell's behavior and monastic claims to be especially holy. Zell lived a frugal, disciplined (ascetic) life and fed laypeople instead of begging food from them as mendicant monks did. In fact, the Zells ran something of an open house. The refugees from Kentzingen (the husbands of the women she addressed in her letter) were only the first among the foreigners, and Schütz Zell would later say that she and Matthew welcomed everyone who shared the confession of Christ as sole savior, even if some guests differed on secondary points. Among the good friends in the faith were Ulrich Zwingli and Johannes Oecolampadius, who stayed with the Zells on their way to the colloquy at Marburg in 1529.

dear Dr. Luther had also preached and fought and sent out his writings in all the lands. He [Zell] also learned from him [Luther] how to teach rightly, and, as soon as he [Zell] knew it, he preached and taught the truth of God eminently and happily, with great effort and in danger of his life. He also diligently protected those who came to him in his field of work.[81] It is now twenty-four years since he and I took each other in marriage, in the Lord and in His word, without any evil motivation (God knows), acting against the wicked pope's lying and devil-spawned prohibition of marriage [cf. 1 Tm 4:1, 3]. In these years I have been his [Zell's] helper according to my means and ability: in his house and also in his office and service. He and I have received much insult and infamy for the sake of the Lord Jesus; in that experience, however, he was always happy and patient, despising the abuse [cf. Heb 12:2]. This was not the less so when he was brought before the court by the bishop and much insulted; as many who are still alive know, he conspicuously carried on teaching the truth.[82]

And, from the beginning to his death, his teaching was that the eternal word of God became flesh, and now through such flesh He took away the curse of our father Adam (which had come upon us all); that He paid for our sins in His body, and washed us in His own blood; that He lifted up on the cross the written accusation of our sins and the law of our damnation. He Himself became the true Easter lamb that was appointed by the Father from eternity for our sins, as was testified about Him in the prophets and psalms. After He was killed in the flesh and made alive in the Spirit, He went down to prison [hell] and took prisoner the whole prison and led the prisoners out with Him and rose alive again [cf. Jn 1:14; Rm 5:12, 14–15;

---

81. The "blessed [selig] Luther" would be translated as "the late Luther" in more secular times, but throughout this book it is consciously used as Schütz Zell apparently meant it, to describe one taken into heaven—which is also an implicit denial of the doctrine of purgatory. She does not use *selig* indiscriminately; it is only applied to Luther, Zell, Capito, or some other of the first generation whom she knew personally. Zell was the first established priest in Strasbourg to begin preaching what the reformers called "the Gospel," ca. 1521 by his own calculations (see below at n. 90), and both Matthew and Katharina looked up to Martin Luther as the one who had taught them this gospel. Zell did more than preach; he also helped others do this, even when that was risky. In the summer of 1523, when Zell was in trouble with the bishop for what he was saying but had not yet broken canon law by marrying, he nevertheless welcomed Martin Bucer and his wife Elisabeth Silbereisen, a former monk and priest married to a former nun, and even opened his home to them and his pulpit to Bucer.

82. Schütz Zell again gives exact times. The bishop of Strasbourg called Zell to account for his preaching in 1523, and he answered with his *Christeliche Verantwortung* (Christian Response) and continued preaching. For the slanders see "Apologia" after n. 39; for a fuller expression of the claim to be Zell's partner in ministry, see "Schwenckfeld" at nn. 19–20 and after n. 31; "Strasbourg Citizens" at nn. 86–87.

Gal 3:13; 1 Pt 2:24, 1:19, 3:18–19; 1 Jn 1:7; Col 2:14; 1 Cor 5:7; Acts 2:23; Is 42:7]. After He thus laid down His life as a guilt offering, and took it back again to Himself by His own power, He obtained all of us from His Father as the spoil He deserved, as the prophet Isaiah witnessed [Is 53:10]. Thus He won the victory and triumph over the enemy, death, and hell for us all and with divine power drove the devil out chained at the neck and swallowed up death in life. Then He set Himself at the right hand of God His Father until all His enemies are made into footstools for His feet, according to the word of the Father, who gave Him a name above all names, that in the name of Jesus all knees in heaven and hell should bow and all tongues should confess that Jesus Christ alone is God. In His name repentance and forgiveness of sins should and must be preached, for He has obtained the seat, lordship, power, and might in heaven and earth, since He is now our Lord and Christ [cf. Jn 10:18, Phil 2:9–11; Lk 24:47; Mt 28:18; Ps 110:1], true God and true Man (*mensch*) in one person, of the same power and being with the Father and the Holy Spirit.[83]

Christ has power to save us from sins, death, and hell and to give us eternal life. In Him is all salvation, and in no other creature or work in heaven and earth, for no one comes to the Father, or dares to think of coming to Him, except through this living Son of God, who should be honored as the Father is. The one who has Him has everything; He is the way, the truth, and the life [cf. Jn 14:6, 5:23]. The one who does not have Him has nothing but distress and error, lies and eternal damnation. So He alone is the savior of all flesh that believe in Him, and there is no other name (I repeat) by which one may be saved, but all who believe in Him have the power to become children of God [cf. Acts 4:15; Jn 1:12]. That is the sum of the teaching and preaching of my upright and now blessed husband, which all of you have heard from him up to his death, teaching against all sanctification by works and false worship.[84] That is why for long years he so greatly applied himself in all his doing and speaking, for he wanted to make known to the world this Lord Jesus of

---

83. The final sentence refers to the fifth-century Chalcedonian definition, which defined the relationship of the two natures in Christ as true God and true Man in one Person, and the fourth-century Nicene Creed, which defined the three Persons of the trinity as one God. The intent here is to affirm how completely orthodox Zell's confession of faith was, according to both Bible and creed.

84. This statement intends to assert that only Christ is the mediator: no creature (e.g., saint or consecrated host of the Mass) or work (e.g., purchase of indulgences, pilgrimage) can contribute to human salvation. Repeatedly, the word "teaching" echoes through this sermon; Schütz Zell explicitly contrasts Zell's teaching and faith with the "false teaching/worship" and

Nazareth (to whom Moses and all the prophets have testified), to make known that God the Father has made Him Lord and Christ [cf. Acts 2:36]. On this account, my good husband acknowledged this throne of grace [Christ], and from that acknowledgment came a great confession. With great zeal, like a forerunner of Christ, he opposed and cast out of the way everything that set itself up against this Lord and Christ (whom the Father anointed and on Mount Zion gave to His church as a head) [cf. Heb 4:16; Mt 3:3; Ps 2:6; Eph 1:22; Col 1:18]. All such things did he oppose and cast out of the way, namely and especially, the wicked pope with his whole kingdom and all who follow him with false teaching and wicked action, secretly and openly.

His [Zell's] own light and action, however, were always entirely open and sincere, through and through, up to the end, against all the wicked crowd (whether they made an outcry or behaved quietly). God compelled him with His zeal [cf. Jn 2:17], as [you know] happened and as you heard from him. Also now in many—no, all—of his last sermons he could do almost nothing else or more than confess his faith in this, His Christ, so well that (from the beginning of his teaching until the end) the saying in the psalm was fulfilled in him: "I have believed and therefore have I spoken" [Ps 116:10; cf. 2 Cor 4:13]. Indeed, he also spoke in such a way that he might say with Saint Paul, "I have not withheld anything from you, but have proclaimed to you all the counsel of God that He has revealed to me" [Acts. 20:27]. He also always demonstrated the unbelief of the pope and all his followers and so sincerely warned you away from it that once again the saying of Saint Paul lived in him: he believed with the heart and confessed with the mouth in an eminent and manly way to his own salvation and that of every one [cf. Rm 10:10].[85]

"unbelief" of the pope and his followers. The chief concern is theological, and the life of the believer (who knows and trusts) must be coherent with what is taught and confessed. Below, after note 101, this is summed up in Schütz Zell's prayer: "You [God] have also allowed him [Zell] to confess and preach Christ among Your people and to confirm and testify this with his life."

85. When Protestants accused the Roman church of "unbelief" (here and below after n. 86) they meant that Rome did not recognize that all people are totally dependent on Christ alone "to justify" them or put them right with God. "Unbelief," the opposite of faith, was for Schütz Zell the chief sin (cf. "Schwenckfeld" at n. 69; also "Psalms/Prayer," Psalm 51:1b at n. 125; in "Women" at n. 10 and "Psalms/Prayer" at n. 163 Schütz Zell expresses a Protestant prayer not to be unbelieving). For Rome to teach that people can contribute to their own salvation meant to Protestants not only denigration of the completeness of Christ's work but also a dangerous deception to people who would be lulled by this idea into false security. Schütz Zell sums this up below in her confession, after n. 94, as those who "do not allow the Lord Jesus to be the sole shepherd and savior in Israel . . . but come in some other way [which they find for themselves—trans.]."

As also he happily left his house last Sunday morning, the eighth of this month January, to magnify the name of Jesus his Lord [cf. Mal 1:11]. Yes, his purpose was the same: to confess his faith to the people to the last (as also some people heard him say that), to comfort his people, and to warn them against false teaching and godless acts of all the abomination that might soon be promoted and set up again, as he had always warned against and greatly opposed the pope and all those who wanted to follow him. These he opposed: even if indeed all the mighty (no one on earth excepted) wanted to reestablish this antichrist of sins here in the place and temple of God, which are the hearts of people! This is the antichrist's work, whatever fine appearance and form it wants to take.[86] For he [Zell] was much concerned for his people, to whom he had hitherto taught the truth through the inspiration and teaching of the Holy Spirit, that after his death these same people might not be seduced through the inspiration and teaching of the devil, who has possessed the man of sin and who still carries on his business in the children of unbelief [cf. Eph 5:6]. But the Lord will make an end of him (the man of sin) at His coming: that day will be horrifying, a great and terrible day to the unbelievers [2 Thes 2:3, 8].

On that Sunday the eighth [Zell's] zeal and distress in his sermon on the Lord Christ became so great that he could no longer really speak for weeping, and it was hard on his heart. Yes, in this and other sermons, such ardor came from his heart and disfigured him that some people judged that he was expressing an inappropriate furious rage. However, he could in good truth have said to the Father with his Lord Christ, "The zeal for Your house has eaten me up" [Jn 2:17; cf. Ps 69:9]. As the same zeal brought Christ to the cross, so I might well say, the zeal for the house of God has also eaten up my dear husband and brought him to this sickness and death—so eagerly and greatly did the only savior compel him to speak against the teaching of the false apostles, who would not allow Christ to be the sole savior. They indeed confess Him with their mouths, but they deny His power and disown Him [by their actions], as Saint Paul laments [Tit 1:6].

---

86. For the pope as antichrist, see "Apologia" at n. 40. The idea is expressed concretely just below: Zell opposed "the teaching of the false apostles, who would not allow Christ to be the sole savior. They indeed confess Him with their mouths, but they deny His power and disown Him [by their actions]." The words "all the mighty" refer to Charles V, the civil power assisting the antichrist. The "abomination" is another Protestant epithet for the Mass, drawing on Jesus's quotation (Mk 13:14–23) of Daniel 9:27 warning of an "abomination" to be set up in the temple, which Protestants identified with the emperor's plan to reestablish Roman worship in defeated territories.

After his last sermon, he was again alert that day; he went to a good friend and had a good conversation about godly matters and death. Also that night he was able to go to sleep without any special pain. In the night, however, he had so much pain in his chest that he got up from bed and suffered greatly during the night, so that about two or three in the morning he and I prepared ourselves for his death. Then he began to confess his sins before God and prayed the Lord's Prayer and then said, "I think indeed that this is Martin Luther's [last] illness."[87] And then he said, "O God, let me not see any abomination against You and Your word. As I think that You will take me hence like him [Luther], so I say with him that You have revealed Your dear Son Christ to me, and You have used me along with others as a witness to preach to the spiritual ones of the world. That I have done faithfully. Still I confess Christ against the gates of hell, I love and honor Him also for my own Lord, savior, and God. Again I pray, let me not see any abomination against Him, You, and Your word. I seek to come to You through Him and in Him, with whom You are well pleased" [cf. Mt 24:15, 16:18; Jn 20:28, 14:6; Mt 3:17].

Thus he continued with many other words and prayers until four in the morning. Then he felt completely well again, sought his bed, and lay down and slept peacefully and well until into the day. Monday he appeared well and happy, had much conversation with dear friends, read and wrote until into the night. His last writing was the text of his sermon on John [8:51] where Christ says, "Truly I say to you, whoever keeps my word will never see death." That night he ate dinner happily, lay down to sleep and thanked God that it was well with him; he hoped to sleep well and did so until eleven. Then the pain in the chest came on him again, he quickly got up, dressed himself, went into his study, and experienced great distress; he fell down on his knees, weeping and praying to God. And he said to me, "I know this is the illness of our dear Martin Luther; my end will be like his and I will accept my death as he did."

---

87. Zell's approach to death is not anxious; he visits a friend to talk about "godly matters and death" and carries on his ordinary work. When he comes to his deathbed there is no reference to saints but only prayer to God and confession of sin and repeated expressions of his faith and trust in God, all in the presence of his wife (no traditional priest). Much of this experience is modeled on accounts of Martin Luther's "good death," which had been quickly published and were very popular with Protestants. (Copying Luther does not imply any insincerity, but simply shows that his story served many Protestants as the old *ars moriendi* had served late medieval Christians.) Particular points of Luther's deathbed, such as his thanks for his calling, his prayers for his "sheep," committing his soul into God's hands (Ps 31:5), and the use of John 8:51 as a last testament, are echoed in Zell's prayers and actions recorded by his wife. For references, see McKee, *Writings*, 78–79, nn. 40, 43.

Then he began to repeat his first prayer and said: "O my dear Lord and God Jesus Christ, I have faithfully preached and proclaimed what You have done for us and taught us. Miserable as I am, let me also experience what I have preached and do not leave me behind; grant me a good ending and let Your people who have believed through my preaching be commended to You. Love them and give them again a man who will love them as I have loved them; do not set over Your inheritance a coward or someone who will suborn them, so that the building that I have built on You may not be destroyed again. Oh, remain Yourself the chief shepherd over them! [cf. Mt 16:18; 1 Pt 5:4]. I give up my office and entrust to You my spirit" [cf. Ps 31:5]. Then he sat down in his armchair, soon became silent, closed his eyes and mouth himself with all quietness. Thus with my words of lament and confession of faith, he expired in my arms between one and two in the morning.

Then in my great anguish, fear, and pain of heart, I cried to our God from my heart to receive His servant and receive his spirit into the number of His prophets and apostles and give him communion with all the elect in Zion; to bless his going forth from this perishable body, lay His hand over him, and let the going forth of his spirit be fruitful and happy, that he might lay aside the mortal and perishable and put on the immortal and imperishable kingdom and eternal life [cf. 1 Cor 15:53]. I also thanked the Lord that he died in my arms and did not fall into the hands of the godless, so that they could not enjoy mocking him as they did the Lord Christ and others [cf. Mt 26:67–68, 27:28–30; Jn 18:22, 19:2–3; Acts 7:54ff, 23:2]. Indeed, I still give thanks on account of him and his great age, that he was not afflicted with shame, but that the saying in the Thirty-first Psalm was fulfilled in him: "You will hide him secretly from everyone's arrogance" [Ps 31:20].

But with what great pain of heart I lose our companionship! and lament to God that He has exacted this of me so quickly and made me an afflicted widow! [My husband's] death is so unbearable to me, speaking from the viewpoint of my flesh: I will mourn it to my grave. And I ask, in the name of Jesus Christ, that God may be merciful to me and graciously forgive me where I have hurt this His devout servant and when I have not rightly served or helped him. For I know that he loved me and gladly forgave me everything before I asked and as much as it lay in him showed me friendly and Christian fellowship. And so, without God's help, I cannot bear and endure this parting and loss of our housefather (whom many a distressed person visited for counsel and protection).

In the meanwhile, however, I also see this wicked time and distress in the whole land, and it is also before our door [the Interim]. So I once more thank God my Lord with my whole heart (according to my inner being), that He has brought him [Zell] to the rest that he long sought and, as the prophet said, has taken him away from calamity [Is 57:1] and received him in the number of his many brothers who had gone before him in the same confession of Christ. I also thank our most dear God for all the gifts and good deeds that He granted to him in many ways and that He let him come to a fine and honorable age (though with many weaknesses that he had in his old age, and now with great pain of his flesh he has paid the highest price of the serpent, the debt of earthly death) [cf. Rm 6:23; Gn 3:1ff].[88] That is what I wanted to exhort you about, dear friends, that you should not so quickly forget this your faithful shepherd. Not for the sake of his body (which will now be committed to the earth), but because of his teaching that he so faithfully preached to you and because he was so zealous for your salvation, that the abomination and idolatry might not come again (like a bad weed) into his work and field through the enemy (the devil) [cf. Mt 24:15, 13:25], that his work in you might not be muddied and trampled down—the way a reckless blockhead tramples on the grain in the field and muddies it, right when people are supposed to be harvesting it.

O dear friends, what a great concern this man had for the honor of Christ and the salvation of the poor little sheep! For he heard from foreigners in several places that again the false worship has begun, to the shame of Christ and His word; because of that many honest people, preachers, and servants have died for sadness.[89] (What God will allow to happen to us we do not yet know!) Such things in the midst of God and His word caused him [Zell] such pain day and night that he could well have said with the psalmist, "The insults of Your house, with which they insulted You, break my heart," and with Jeremiah in the book of the prophets, "I am an afflicted man, who sees now the rod of Your wrath" [cf. Ps 69:9, 20a; Lam 3:1a].

---

88. Schütz Zell repeats her gratitude that Zell has been freed of the burdens of earth (not experiencing the persecution that would have come if he had been alive when the Interim was implemented) and her confidence that he has entered into heaven. Death was commonly understood as the final penalty of the Fall, which was caused by the serpent tempting Eve and Adam, and now that this debt is paid Zell is free: no purgatory; see "Psalms/Prayer," at n. 131.

89. Even before the final defeat in April 1547, the negative consequences of earlier ones had already been implemented in some places; news of the Protestants' problems in Ulm was circulating by February 1547, and Bishop Hermann von Wied, whom Bucer had helped to reform his diocese of Cologne, had been deposed in the spring of 1547. Peter Martyr Vermigli, who had already been forced to leave his homeland for his faith, did not wait for the Interim to be implemented in Strasbourg; in December 1547 he went to England at the invitation of Archbishop Cranmer.

Yes, it broke his [Zell's] heart and brought on his death, so great were the care and pains that he bore for the honor of Christ and the salvation of all of us. As a faithful shepherd he also sought to give all that he had, even his life, for his teaching and his little sheep, and he never buried his pound as the lazy and bad servant did. He taught the sole salvation in Christ like a faithful householder and wise scribe, for the feeding of all the hungry [cf. Jn 10:11, Lk 19:20; Mt 24:45], and strove earnestly against the enemies of Christ for that. For more than twenty-five years now he has with great earnestness steadfastly worked to keep himself and us pure in faith in his Lord Christ (faith that alone purifies the heart), as also Paul requires [cf. Rm 10:8ff].[90] Yes, God knows and I also, what great work he had day and night, and how bitter and hard his studies, preaching, and all became to him in his old age. He wanted to lead us all and keep us in all truth through the Spirit of God [cf. Jn 16:13] so that he could well have said, as did Christ the Lord, "With what great earnestness have I sought to gather you before the face of the enemy, as a hen gathers her chicks before the kite, but you would not have it" [Mt 23:37].[91]

Our dear apostle Dr. Martin Luther has for long years gathered Germany, taught and indeed warned. In his day he had peace: what has followed his death we see now. This my upright husband has long taught here in Strasbourg and warned everyone in the temple of Jerusalem: what will follow his death, we will now see. For Moses and Joshua are dead, their hands are lowered, so that they cannot still pray for us. The king of Assyria has come before the gates of Jerusalem so that he can lead the people away from their God [cf. Ex 17:11–12; 2 Kgs 15:29, 17:5, 18:11]. That is why he [Zell] bore such care day and night. How often did he say to me, "As the Gospel began here with me, I worry that it will also cease with me."[92]

---

90. Schütz Zell refers here to the parable of the 10 pounds, which she will develop elsewhere (below at n. 93 and "Schwenckfeld" at n. 16). In the Lukan parable each of ten servants is given 1 pound with which to trade; when the time for accounting comes, one has a profit of 10 pounds, one of 5, but a third has none because he hid the pound rather than trading with it. Schütz Zell affirms that her husband was a good steward of what had been entrusted to him, that is, the teaching of "sole salvation in Christ." Her reference to Zell's preaching the Gospel "more than twenty-five years" may indicate that it was some time in 1522 when a layperson would have noticed that what he said was different from earlier reform-minded Roman preachers. In his preface to the 1534 publication of Bucer's catechism, Zell himself claimed to have begun to preach "the Gospel" in 1521.

91. Schütz Zell's paraphrase suggests a glimpse of local daily life; the biblical text does not name the threat to the chicks, but the paraphrase makes the Bible very down-to-earth by adding "kites," a danger that threatened Alsatian chicks.

92. Luther's predictions of the religious troubles that would follow his death were well known; cf. McKee, *Writings*, 82, n. 56. Here Schütz Zell likens Zell to Luther in this prediction also.

But now, all of you who have gladly heard the teaching of this your faithful shepherd and believed it, and who have shown your love to him today in his burial, such a great crowd! I exhort and beg you with great earnestness, as upright little sheep, to honor your shepherd by keeping his teaching and acting according to it, that you never allow it to be torn from your hearts but rather allow your life to be taken instead. [The enemy can do no more than take your life—they cannot take your salvation unless you give up the true teaching—*trans.*] So that on the great judgment day of the Lord, when the chief shepherd Christ will appear, he [Zell] may also lay his pound there before Christ with great profit. So that he may joyfully bring [the fruit of] what he has sown here with great effort and faithfulness, that is, the fleeces (of his flock), the fruit that we (his flock) are, and may pay them over to the Householder Christ [cf. 1 Pt 5:4; Lk 8:12, 19:16–19; Jn 4:26], so that, as the apostle Paul also says, we may be his honor, joy, and crown [1 Thes 2:19–20].[93] Consider and hold on to his [Zell's] last teaching, what he taught with the dear John, that is "guard yourselves from idolatry" [1 Jn 5:21], a text that the whole papacy cites and yet partially manipulates against the sole redemption and salvation of Christ our Lord. My good husband openly rejected that papacy and died as an enemy to it, but as a zealous confessor and friend of the Lord Jesus Christ and of all who believe in Him.[94]

And so I stand here today by the holy body of my husband and confess with him and all believers the forgiveness of our sins only through the blood of our Lord Jesus Christ the spotless Lamb, who was with the Father

---

Moses and Joshua led Israel out of Egypt, as Luther and Zell led the people out of Roman bondage. The Israelites won their battle as long as Moses held up his arms, but when he lowered them the army faltered. Now both Luther and Zell are gone (hands lowered), and the "King of Assyria" Charles V threatens the Protestants of Jerusalem with deportation from their faith. When Moses's hands fell from exhaustion he sat on a rock and Aaron and Hur stood on either side of him to hold up his hands, so Israel won the battle, but Schütz Zell does not have that positive ending here; she concludes with Protestant Israel's loss of its Moses and fear for the destruction of the Gospel.

93. Schütz Zell mixes parables and metaphors here, but her point is clear. Zell has used his pound well and gained more money with it; the pound is the Gospel, and the profit is the people he has brought to faith in it, who are the fruit of his tree or profit of his work. This increase of souls he will give to Christ as evidence that he has worked well with what was entrusted to him.

94. Protestants considered Roman worship and teaching idolatry because Christ was not *treated* as the sole mediator (whatever might be said about Him); cf. above n. 86. Rome did not see prayers to the saints or the mechanical grace of the sacraments (*opus operatum*) as idolatry or denigration of Christ, but Protestants did. Schütz Zell's following confession emphasizes salvation by faith versus the teaching of those who "do not allow the Lord Jesus to be the sole Shepherd . . . but by their works, unbelief, and false teaching they insult His Passion . . ."

from eternity and was killed in the flesh for us. Likewise I confess the only righteousness that counts before God: our inheritance of eternal life through the resurrection of our Lord Jesus Christ from the dead [cf. 1 Pt 1:19–20, 3:18; 1 Cor 1:30; Mt 19:29b; Rm 6:4]. And so I say today, with and in the place of my dear husband, with Mary Magdalene, "The Lord is truly risen and lives for us all!" [cf. Jn 20:18]. And on the contrary the devil and eternal death have died and are dead to us all and have no further power over all those who are in Christ Jesus [cf. Rm 6:9].

And so, with my devout husband I reject and disavow the pope with his followers and kingdom and worship as the living devil. Those who will not recognize or learn this likeness [of pope and devil] do not allow the Lord Jesus to be the sole shepherd and savior in Israel, but by their works, unbelief, and false teaching they insult His Passion, death, and the righteousness of His resurrection. Yes, again I reject and proclaim to all those who will not let the Lord Christ be the sole Christ and the one who takes away sin, death, and eternal destruction, that they will die in their sins as thieves and murderers—those people who (in spite of the fact that they bawl the name of Jesus) do not go in through the right door but come in some other way [cf. Jn 8:21, 24, 10:1; Mt 7:21–23]. He is none other than a savior who wills to save His people from their sins: He Himself, and not by any creaturely work. But only those will be saved who receive the Lord Jesus as their sole righteousness, recognizing that He is the true shepherd and Son of the living God, also the sole sanctifier and minister of whom Moses, David, and all the prophets spoke and whose name "Jesus" the angel foretold [cf. Mt 1:21, 16:16; Jn 10:11]. He is the sustainer and savior of all those who enter through the right door and believe that no one comes to the Father but through Him: all who receive and accept this will find in Him good pasture, as Christ Himself says in John 10[:7, 9; 14:6].

And in John 5[:24] He says that those who honor Him will not come into any judgment but will pass from death to life.[95] That is what this my devout husband has done, believed, and taught, and the kingdom of heaven, which must suffer force, he has drawn to himself with force, as Christ said [Mt 11:12]. Therefore I know that he [Zell] has not come into any judgment, but he lives in and with Christ and sees His glory, according to the word of the Lord Jesus to Martha, "Have I not told you? If you

---

95. Here and below Schütz Zell rejects the doctrine of purgatory. Zell now "lives in and with Christ," and below she is "sure" of the same hope of eternal life after this earthly "sorrowful" one because of forgiveness through Christ's blood—not through any work of her own, including suffering in purgatory.

believe you will see the glory of God" [Jn 11:40]. How this man believed and confessed is well attested this day by such a crowd, more than six thousand people.[96] I hope that this testimony here stands before God and may be a foretaste of the last day, when his little sheep will also stand around him [Zell] and with him acknowledge Christ, the chief shepherd, and they will enjoy together the eternal pasture that they have received from that same Christ [cf. 1 Pt 5:4]. Meanwhile, I was with him [Zell] from the beginning in a confession of Christ like his and still hope for a blessedness like his with him after this sorrowful life, in spite of all my sins and misdeeds, which will all be washed away by the blood of Jesus Christ, whom I confess with sure hope.

I want to stand by that confession through the grace of our God, and I will, with force under the cross, draw to myself the kingdom of heaven, which must suffer force. Let there come pope or devil, the prince of darkness [cf. Rv 1:5; Mt 11:12], also all the powers of earth! I should never, I hope, be driven away from the pure knowledge of the Lord Christ that I heard and learned from my devout and God-sanctified husband and that he as an apostle and servant of the Lord Jesus received and learned from the Holy Spirit Himself. Let this stance cost me body, honor, or goods, in fire or water [cf. Ps 66:12], whatever God the Lord wants to send me—or (if God chooses for me) the same quiet death as my dear husband. Whatever it may be, I want to hold to his knowledge and confession that we at Strasbourg have so long heard from him, through the one who can strengthen me and who did strengthen him [cf. Phil 4:13].

For the sake of this confession now there is all the distress on earth, and all the opposition to the holy Jesus Christ, as Simeon prophesied [cf. Lk 2:34].[97] As you have indeed heard this same thing from my devout husband in past days: that everyone dashes his head against this target, the Lord

---

96. Schütz Zell gives the number of the crowd as six thousand; other contemporaries say "thousands," "over three thousand," and "many thousands," and one later writer says five thousand. Estimates of crowds are often inaccurate in this period, but in a city of around twenty thousand, even three thousand would have been a large gathering. (For example, when a very important member of the government, Mathis Pfarrer, was buried in 1568, the funeral cortege was counted as 2,500.) Löscher's poem says the crowd included youth, city notables, Zell's relatives, and many citizens and others from the surroundings. For specific references, see citations in note 67 above and McKee, *Life and Thought*, 127, n. 31.

97. The distress is the Interim; like Schütz Zell, most if not all Protestants identified this opposition to their faith with opposition to Christ, as the citation of Simeon's words to Mary when Jesus was presented in the temple demonstrates ("This child is set . . . for a sign that is spoken against . . ."). In Strasbourg are preserved ten Protestant pamphlets against the Interim with annotations by Schütz Zell; her comments on what others said—mostly approving—illustrate her place among her contemporaries, cf. McKee, *Life and Thought*, 138–42.

Jesus Christ. Even if the world should be senseless, on the last day they will have to confess that they have to do with this Jesus of Nazareth, that He alone should be the shepherd and Christ. He will be established and preached as the sole savior, against all their teaching and doing, and that they do not want and cannot endure. Because of their anger all of us will be judged before the godless crowd for the sake of the confession of Christ and the hope of the resurrection in Jesus [cf. Acts 23:6], on account of which we suffer everything, as those who went before us also suffered.

With my husband and all believers, I hope to obtain that costly resurrection of Jesus, through the resurrection of Jesus Christ, who could not experience corruption. We must experience corruption [cf. Acts 2:27, 31], but we will not remain in it. For the Spirit of God will bring our flesh and bones together again, signal the dawn, and make us alive, as the prophets Ezekiel and Daniel and also our holy Christ Himself have testified: that the hour will come when the dead who are in the grave will hear the voice of the Lamb of God and go forth. Saint Paul also says this [Ezek 37:7–10; Dn 12:2; Jn 5:25, 28–29; 1 Cor 15:52]. I hope to obtain and see that resurrection with my dear husband, along with our dear children. (Together we had two, and they lie in this place.) It is now in the twenty-first year since—with great pain!—we carried out our first child and trod this place with him; he was the first person buried in this graveyard, where with such fitting earnestness he [Zell] so often longed to come. Therefore just as he desired to be buried in this place with his and my children, so I hope that this place will also be my abiding place until the trumpet [1 Cor 15:52] and voice come: "Rise up, you dead, for the judgment." Then my good husband and all the believing dead will hear the happy voice of our worthy Lord Jesus Christ: "Come here, you blessed, into the kingdom that was prepared for you from the beginning; you have fed me, sheltered me, given me drink, clothed me, and comforted me." But to the godless He will say, "Go hence into the eternal fire that is prepared for the devil and his angels; you did not feed me, shelter me, or comfort me." Then they will all say, "When have we seen You thus?" He will answer, "What you did to the least of mine, you did to me" [Mt 25:34–45]. My husband has taught, and demonstrated in action, works of the faith like these and not the pope's hypocritical works.[98] Dear friends, may you maintain and do such things, to honor him and for your own salvation.

---

98. The text says "God has taught . . . ," but the sense requires "my husband has taught . . ." Schütz Zell contrasts two kinds of works: biblical ones like those cited in the parable of sheep and goats in Matthew 25 and "the pope's hypocritical works" taught by the church, such as not eating meat in Lent. Zell has taught and done the biblical and not the papal ones. For her own contrasting lists, see "Psalms/Prayer," Psalm 51:19 (at n. 134).

And you youths, who today have seen this amazing burial—the like as has never been seen in Strasbourg, so that I remember and must cite once more what the prophet said, "His righteousness will break forth like the morning star" [cf. Is 58:8; Rv 22:16] and again where it is written, "His burial will be honorable" [Is 53:9b]. These things were written about Christ, who was honorably buried, and His righteousness broke forth in His resurrection. However, it is also nonetheless prophesied to us about His members, to whom He gives all that was His [cf. 1 Cor 12:27; Jn 17:8, 14, 22]. For who would have thought that the honor of my dear husband and the love of the people would break forth this way! And that his burial would have happened in such a way, that so many sheep have followed their shepherd with earnestness and tears for the sake of the wholesome pasture that they have received from him. I hope that today many of you will beat your hearts and chests [cf. Lk 23:48], repent, and say, "This one has taught rightly." But God grant that his death may not bring along with it the saying of Zechariah, "I will strike the shepherd and the sheep must be scattered" [Zec 13:7b], because that was fulfilled in the Lord Christ.

Let all you who have now followed him [Zell] take this to heart. Many of you stand there weeping, and many tears were poured out over him, today and yesterday, with kissing his dead body. Along with those signs, however, love and honor him above all in this way: keep his teaching and act on it, that teaching that you—also you young people here present—received from him in his very diligent catechism classes. Hold onto that, devote yourself to it, and learn to bear the Lord's yoke from youth on [cf. Mt 11:29–30]. Also, henceforth love and honor the other remaining leaders whom you have (who knows for how long!). Listen to them, follow them insofar as they teach and offer you God's word, so that all of us too may come to a blessed end and be found in the confession of our God and His Son Jesus Christ. That confession the Holy Spirit (the third Person of the godhead) must teach us, and He will lead us in all truth—He, and not the abomination at Rome [cf. Jn 16:13; Mt 24:15], whom today we want to deny and oppose as the worst enemy of our Lord Jesus Christ. And we want to confess our God, in three Persons but in one eternal divine being, and want also to say and confess that "we all believe in one God, Father, the Almighty, Creator of heaven and earth . . ."[99]

---

99. Schütz Zell probably recited the Nicene Creed, which affirms the three Persons of the trinity in one God. This creed had been commonly used in the Mass; most Protestants preferred the Apostles' Creed for general use (Schütz Zell recites it in her devotional book, see "Psalms/Prayer" at n. 147), but the Nicene is more detailed, especially on the character of the Holy Spirit and the trinity, which she discusses more below.

This is the sum of our faith, which we have received from our elders the apostles, that there is one God, who has made everything by His word; and one Christ, His eternal Son, who redeemed all through His blood; and one Spirit, who makes all alive through His power. Through the same Spirit a church and communion of the believing will be gathered, and in this church He gives and works love and fellowship in the blood of Jesus Christ, forgiveness of sins through the key of David, who is Christ, who opens and no one can close, where He closes, however, no one can open. The same way we believe in the resurrection of the flesh, where the perishable will put on the imperishable and the mortal will put on the immortal, and the flesh will also have life eternal in the one and only divine being God when God will be all in all. For the sake of that we suffer, do, and hope everything here [cf. Rv 3:7; 1 Cor 15:53, 28, 30]. We want to call upon that same only true God, to seek from Him everything that we need, and to pray in the name of our Lord Jesus Christ His dear Son [cf. Jn 14:13–14, 15:16], who has taught us to pray thus, "Our Father, who art in heaven, Your name be hallowed" [cf. Mt 6:9–13].[100] Here I will once again thank God, and also explain the Our Father a little, and then want to go hence.

O almighty eternal God, You who have now set on me this my great cross—on account of my sins You have so quickly incited Your Spirit and allowed Your rebuke to fall on me. You have taken this man so quickly from me just as You did Elijah in the fiery chariot, ones of whom I and the world were not worthy. But Your judgment and deed are just and right [cf. 2 Kgs 2:11; Heb 11:38; Rv 15:3–4]: no one can or may reproach You. I, a poor, submissive, miserable person,[101] stand now before You over this dead body of Your servant, who in his zeal for Your honor and people was a successor of Moses and Elijah, with John the Baptist and the preaching about Christ (the Lamb who bears the sins of the world [cf. Jn 1:29]). I praise and thank You from my inner being that You have created him [Zell] according to Your image and have adorned him with many good gifts [cf. Eph 3:16; Gn 1:27; Ps 8:5]. You have also allowed him to confess and preach Christ among Your people and to confirm and testify this with his life. You have made him proof against everyone, when the [ecclesiastical] authorities cast

---

100. Schütz Zell probably recited the Lord's Prayer and then went on to explain it, as she had done with the Creed. Between reciting the Prayer and paraphrasing an exposition, however, she offers her own prayer about her husband and her loss.

101. As was common in her time (and before and after!), Schütz Zell interpreted suffering as punishment for sin; cf. her "Psalms/Prayer," especially Psalm 51. Her description of herself as *armer mensch* can be polyvalent: poor, submissive, miserable; in this context probably all the meanings apply.

off those who confessed the Lord Christ; You have given him a sense of peace up to the end. Finally also now You have called and taken him away to Your grace even as he was praying and confessing Your name. You have not allowed him to fall into the hands and insults of the revilers, that he also should not see any abomination against You and Your Son—as he had asked You [cf. Jn 9:22; Ps 69:6]. You have now reclaimed him from all his work and released him from his sorrows and will keep him eternally with You in the fellowship of Your Son and all the elect.

Yes, I thank You from my heart for all the love that You have shown him and that You have made him worthy to bear Your name before Your people and also to bear abuse from unbelievers for Your name [cf. Acts 5:41]. You have also called him to death in a special way, as You commanded Moses to do. Moses was to call the people and bless them, then he went up on the mountain and so died alone, without all the people being present [cf. Dt 33:1ff, 34:1, 5–6]. Did You not also say to this man [Zell], "Call your people, bless them in the name of Jesus, go hence, sit in the armchair and die without all the people, alone with only your poor wife"?[102] He obeyed You in that; right after his prayer to You he closed his eyes—not as if dying but as if in a healthy sleep—and his spirit went to You and Your will was done. But my flesh, O Lord, my inner being, cannot understand that or endure it because of great sorrow and pain of heart! [cf. Ps 31:5; Mt 6:10, Eph 3:16]. But I beg You, through Your dear Son Jesus Christ, that You may make me submissive through Your Spirit, so that I may humble myself under Your mighty hand—which no one can resist, and its action is always just [cf. 1 Pt 5:6; Acts 11:17; Rv 15:3].

Through *Your name*, O holy Father in heaven, also now in this work may Your will *be hallowed*, known, and magnified, that in it we may know and praise You.[103] May *Your kingdom* of the knowledge of Christ *come* to us poor people in our hearts—that kingdom You have now bent down and favored him [Zell] with; in Christ You have called and drawn him to Yourself. And do not let us come again to the kingdom, abuse, and prison of Egypt and the Assyrians. Give us also a good will, which (with Christ on the Mount

---

102. Zell's death is likened to Moses's: blessing their people, then alone with God, in contrast to the late medieval tradition of having a crowd of relatives and friends present. Schütz Zell emphasizes the peaceful nature of Zell's death: prayer, closing his eyes, appearing to fall asleep.

103. In the paraphrase of the Lord's Prayer italics are added for clarity. Note allusions to the Interim in the contrast between the knowledge of Christ and the threat of the "Assyrians." This short form may well be compared with the longer text written in 1532 ("Psalms/Prayer," after n. 149; there are also significant similarities to the private journal of Psalms that Schütz Zell probably began shortly after this sermon ("Psalms/Prayer," before n. 117 and after n. 124).

of Olives) may make itself submissive to *Your will,* which should always fully and rightly come off victorious in heaven and on earth—the good will that the angel from heaven wished us [cf. Ex 1:8–14; 2 Kgs 17:5–6; Acts 7:39; Mt 26:39; Lk 2:14].

And *give us today our daily bread,* peace, comfort, and joy of our consciences, battle weary before You—yes, give us the living bread and word, Your Son, whom I now need so much, O God! [cf. Jn 6:35, 48]. You have grasped me in my sins and afflicted me severely; You have chastised and struck not only my body but also my whole heart and conscience, and You know how I suffer. Just Father, feed me and give me drink now with Your comfort and peace, in my great cross, through Your Holy Spirit; also with right teaching and wisdom keep me henceforth according to Your will.

And *forgive us our faults, as we also forgive the faults against us.* O God, we never forgive rightly! Yet do not look at us but at Your dear Son Jesus Christ, who forgave His enemies from the heart and on the cross prayed to You for them; and so He fulfilled everything for us [cf. Lk 23:34; Jn 19:30]. O God, let the repentance and goodness effected by Christ be mine, and graciously forgive all my sins. Also forgive my sins against this Your servant whom You commended to me. He was also so dear to me—You know that!—but even so, through my lack of understanding I did not honor or serve him or do as I ought and was obliged to do. O God and Father, You will forgive me all and cause all this to be forgotten, and You will comfort me, for I have no doubt of Your grace. You also forgave him everything that he in his flesh did against Your commands and prohibitions, forgiveness through the blood of Jesus Christ Your child, the blood in which he believed. So also, dear God, forgive those who seek forgiveness of You, through Him [Christ] who took all our sickness upon Himself [cf. Is 53:4].

And *lead us not into temptation.* Do not let me, a poor miserable (*armen*) person, become fainthearted toward You in my great affliction or forget Your promises. Do not take away from me and from us all the knowledge of You and Your dear Son Jesus Christ [cf. Ps 51:11]; that loss would bring us to eternal *evil*. From that protect us! *For the kingdom, the power, and the glory are Yours alone.* They do not belong to the devil, the pope, the antichrist, or all false teachers—because the kingdom, power, and glory are spiritual, but the devil, the pope, the antichrist are carnal [cf. 1 Jn 2:18, 22; Rm 8:5]. The kingdom, power, and glory are Yours, You good and faithful God. To that let us all say "Amen!"

Now then, dear friends, I keep you all too long. Do not be irritated with me: my heart is entirely full of great trouble—the mouth speaks what overflows from the heart [cf. Lk 6:45]. I still had much to say, but you yourselves have known him [Zell] and heard his teaching; keep it, and follow his teaching and faith. He was faithful, upright, true, and simple. He troubled no one but was much troubled by others, which he quickly forgave. He gladly helped everyone, including many of those present; and there, with tears, stand some poor orphans who were supported by him and who, having lost him as a good patron, now have trouble. For the Lord Christ has said that He will not leave us orphans but will come to us again to comfort us and take us to Himself [cf. Jn 14:18, 3]; let us go home relying on that same help and grace. We commend the body of my good husband to the earth from which it came, from which, with all honorable and angelic glory he will rise again in the general resurrection to eternal life, as I also commended his spirit to Him from whom he came (that is God [cf. Gn 3:19; Mk 12:25; Lk 20:36; Eccl 12:7]).[104] Yes, he himself commended himself to the Lord Jesus, who will bring his flesh and spirit together again and make him alive with His Spirit [cf. Ps 31:5; Ezek 37:7–10], so that he and we may say with the dear Job, "in my flesh and with my eyes I will see God, my sustainer" [Job 19:25–26]. May God strengthen us all in such faith and hope, with love [cf. 1 Cor 13:13; Col 1:11]! And may He help me, a poor miserable (*armen*) person, as I now make my way home: the hard way of the cross. My offering, O God, is my husband, the highest and best treasure that I have on earth (humanly speaking), whom I received from You and now leave behind me. Lord Jesus Christ, make him alive again in Your coming; You have said that You are the resurrection and the life, that whoever believes in You will live even though he dies. You are the eternal truth: grant that I may believe You [cf. Jn 11:25, 14:6].

Now then, dear friends, let us finally close with a little saying out of a booklet that was dear to my good husband, a booklet in which are many fine songs, teachings, and prayers. Among others is this one about how we should commend the dead to the Lord. (To use the whole thing would be much too long here; the one who wrote it tells the story from the beginning of man and to the end of his life.) From all this let us take the last verse, which is this,[105]

---

104. Here Schütz Zell affirms the "resurrection of the body" of the creed as well as the life of the spirit, which is already with Christ. Her confidence in Zell's salvation is clear: he does not need anything more from her (e.g., no Masses for the dead!).

105. The manuscript gives seven verses, not just the last. The copyist apparently used a form of the hymn from his own day, when in fact various versions of this hymn were circulating. The final verse from Schütz Zell's own hymnbook (Bb5 verso) reads as follows: "Now let us leave him here to sleep and all go our own ways And order our lives with all diligence for death comes to us all in like fashion."

Now let us bury the body, about which we have no doubt that
It will at the last day arise, and go forth immortal.

It is from the earth and must return to earth again,
But from the earth will rise again when God's trumpet goes forth.

His soul lives eternally in God. He was here by His grace
From all sins and misdeeds purified through His blood.

His work, trouble, and exile have come to a good end,
He has borne his Lord Christ's yoke. He has died here and yet lives there.

The soul lives in God without any lament, the body sleeps until the last day.
Then God will glorify it and keep it safe with eternal joy.

Here he was in great affliction, there he should have profit from that,
In eternal joy and dwelling to shine like the stars and sun.

So now we want to leave him here and go our ways,
And order our lives with all diligence, for death comes to us all in like fashion.

With that, she went hence from the grave, and said, "O God, You who are gracious to all flesh who come before You in prayer, have mercy also on me, take me under Your protection and grant that I may be one of those widows who will receive their own loved ones again from the dead on the day of resurrection" [cf. Ps 86:5, 51:1; Heb 11:35].

THE MISERERE PSALM MEDITATED, PRAYED, AND PARAPHRASED WITH KING DAVID BY KATHARINA ZELL, . . . , SENT TO THE CHRISTIAN MAN SIR FELIX ARMBRUSTER

Introduction

Throughout her life Katharina Schütz Zell was engaged in personal prayer and study of the Bible and in teaching what she knew. Nearly all the private devotion was naturally hidden from view, and most of the time the teaching was also informal. Toward the end of her life, in mid-1558, however, Schütz Zell drew together some of her most intimate meditations on the Psalms and an exposition of the Lord's Prayer that had circulated earlier in manuscript form and published these with an open letter to an elderly friend as a source of comfort for troubled souls. This devotional book, the second longest of her writings, offers striking insight into both the depths of her personal spiritual wrestling and the mature pastoral heart of a wise and practical woman.

The first section of the book, which was actually the last to be written, is the letter of dedication to Sir Felix Armbruster. This elderly patrician had been an important member of the Strasbourg government, where he was one of the few highly placed citizens to resist the imposition of the Augsburg Interim, a stance appreciated by those like Schütz Zell who shared this view. When in the early 1550s Armbruster became ill with what was known as "leprosy" he was obliged to withdraw from society and live in a house outside the city. His wife had died, and his daughter did not want to associate with him, probably for fear of contagion. The widowed Schütz Zell was one of his very few visitors, but she remained a faithful pastor to the old man whom virtually all others had abandoned. When age and responsibility for a handicapped nephew whom she had adopted made visiting her sick friend increasingly difficult, his elderly but indomitable counselor decided to send Sir Felix an open letter with some of her devotional writings.

As she usually does, Schütz Zell includes in this letter an explanation of her reason for writing. Although it was not too surprising for a woman to publish a devotional book—after all, the young Katharina Schütz's first printed text in this genre had won considerable favor—it was still not common for a layperson to produce an instructional religious text for the public, presented in the voice of a pastor. As her grounds for addressing him, Zell's elderly widow claims long acquaintance with this high-ranking man she had probably first come to know through her husband and speaks especially of Sir Felix's illness and his grateful response to her visits. She goes on to quote his own words with an almost reverent appreciation for the honesty and faith of this remarkable man. Her words are sincere but also astute. She presents Sir Felix as a model of the way a faithful Christian should deal with affliction, as an example for the others whom she addresses: people with troubled consciences who need to hear the teaching she is offering. For Schütz Zell, Sir Felix is both friend and patron; dedicating her book to him helps to give her an entrée to other readers. While her concern for Sir Felix is obviously quite real and she did not look for any practical help from him, Zell's widow was prepared to use the name of this patrician "parishioner" to reach others in need as well as to remind those who had forgotten him that he was their equal in God's sight—and perhaps outranked them in faith! Her use of the tradition of gift giving and dedications illustrates another facet of the education this woman of artisan background had

The Lay Reformer, Teacher, and Pastor   125

absorbed over the years. It also demonstrates how she shaped the tradition for her own purposes—and in the process reveals something of her unusual confidence as a "pastor" who was also a woman.[106]

After presenting this Sir Felix, an exemplary Christian, Schütz Zell gives explicit attention to two issues. One is the relationship between the divine and human roles in consolation. Acknowledging that the only true comfort is that provided by the Holy Spirit, Matthew's partner in ministry affirms the subordinate but biblically authorized role of the human comforter—equally subordinate whether male or female! It is the office of the Holy Spirit to speak to the heart, but it is the office of human beings—the obligation of love—to speak to the outward ears of their neighbors.[107] The second point Schütz Zell discusses is her own experience of suffering and of God's consolation in that situation, which fits her to console others. Thus the lay pastor has biblical authority for this duty of love, and—unlike the "Letter to the Women of Kentzingen" where Matthew's young bride plainly acknowledges her own lack of any experience like that of those she addresses—here she can also claim the existential justification of a fellow sufferer to authorize her speaking.

Schütz Zell's sober yet confident explanation for this open letter is part of the remarkable character of her "voice" in this last of her extant writings. The degree of maturity in faith manifested here is notable as compared with the

---

106. For the best recent study of gift-giving traditions in the sixteenth century, see Natalie Zemon Davis, *The Gift in Sixteenth-Century France* (Madison, Wis.: University of Wisconsin, 2000). Books were "the present most readily circulated among learned friends, sometimes with a dedication . . . with the courteous language of benefits and gratitude, but also . . . mutual teasing, barbed comments about enemies, praise for other scholars, and requests for favors . . ." They "also addressed the contents of the book" (36). "Women's dedications in printed books, few in number though they are in the sixteenth century, can suggest general attitudes among educated women. . . What was on the dedicators' minds was their authority as women speaking in public" (77). Ones addressed to men usually expressed "the traditional commonplaces of female unworthiness" in "ornate and convoluted" terms, but those dedicated to other women (as was more commonly the case for women writers) were often very different, using "direct and feeling prose" (77). Comparing Schütz Zell with these contemporary French men and women reveals similarities and differences of her practice. Her work clearly fits the category of a present among learned friends, if one grants that the learning in question is Christian maturity. The tone and language are rather distinctive; Schütz Zell addresses Sir Felix without the usual claims of unworthiness as a woman—her words are inadequate by comparison with the Holy Spirit's, not a man's! See below at n. 120 and "Strasbourg Citizens" at n. 79.

107. The language of "office" may sound strange to modern ears, but it was a very important religious concept, which Protestants developed in specific ways; see "Hymnbook" after n. 49. "Office" for Protestants had to do with role or function, not ontology or essence. Fully convinced of the Holy Spirit's divine being, Schütz Zell is nevertheless more interested in the Spirit's work and the role or function that people are to fulfill (cf. below at n. 116). Later (below in Ps 51:1a) she refers to God's "office" of forgiveness: God's trustworthy character in responding to repentance, not an ontological discussion of God's nature.

letter addressed to the women of Kentzingen thirty-four years earlier. This is natural and appropriate as the fruit of her life's journey. It is also, however, rare to be able to observe the spiritual development of a member of the "common people" over the course of a lifetime of religious devotion and suffering and teaching. Also worth observing in this letter is the quality of the author's interchange with Sir Felix, who was not only a man but a person of much higher birth and estate than the woman who addressed him. Schütz Zell had dedicated most of her earlier published writings to women or to corporate bodies of which she was clearly a part, such as the parish and the city. Although she certainly did not hesitate to speak directly to men of any rank, normally that was done in private. Here, however, she writes publicly, as a pastor and sister in the faith to a man of the highest rank in Strasbourg society, addressing him with respect but also a certain friendly warmth. It is apparent that in the face of common suffering for their faith (opposing the Interim) and submission to God's will (in personal or family illness), the priesthood of believers had taken on an existential character for Schütz Zell and Sir Felix; status had become less important than mutual support in Christian fellowship. The patrician to whom the lay theologian dedicates her work is not only its patron to commend it to others, but also her brother in Christ. In keeping with the maturity and profound simplicity of the faith they shared, what the pastor offered her friend was anything but superficial. In the context of Sir Felix's swiftly approaching death, and her awareness that her own was not too far off, Schütz Zell also expresses her trust in God and her own lack of fear in the face of that usually dreaded event. These thoughts, coupled with some reflections written earlier but included in this book, give another glimpse of a Protestant "good death," which rounds out her earlier description of her husband's last days.[108]

The second section of the book invites Sir Felix and other readers into Katharina's most private place of prayer. In effect, to comfort her friends, Matthew's widow took out the booklets in which she had prayed, wept, and lamented her way through the book of Psalms at a time of deepest desolation, probably the months following Zell's death. From these she chose two of the seven Penitential Psalms, numbers 51 and 130, traditionally known by the first word(s) of their Latin form as the Miserere and De profundis. The Penitential Psalms had long been the favored prayers of the afflicted, expressing the common religious conviction that sin brought suffering on the sinner and that the way to healing was through repentance. Though her words may strike the modern reader as extreme self-castigation, that tone was quite normal in Schütz Zell's world and for centuries before and long

---

108. See below at nn. 121, 165. "Lament" at nn. 70 ff.

after her time. Some turns of her thought are distinctive, such as the way she applies Psalm 51:18 to the situation of Strasbourg in the Augsburg Interim, but her providential vision of the interconnection of sin, suffering, repentance, and forgiveness would be completely familiar to her readers.

Yet it is also clear that the writer is Protestant: not Roman or Anabaptist or Schwenckfelder; the emphasis on the Holy Spirit as God's active power—not a source of further information—is particularly significant. Schütz Zell clearly expresses her sense of having no free will to seek salvation; as a human being she is powerless in the face of sin, something she can recognize only by the work of the Holy Spirit. She speaks of her knowledge of and trust in God's forgiveness and acceptance ("justification") by faith and grace alone through Christ's life, death, and resurrection—effected in her by the action of the Holy Spirit. She firmly states her conviction that a transformed life should follow God's teaching in the Bible but is itself God's gift, again by the power of the Holy Spirit: it is never perfect or acceptable in itself; there is no human merit but there is Spirit-enabled action. Here there is also an indication that her Protestantism has a Reformed flavor as the lay theologian speaks positively of the role of God's law in guiding the Christian life. The commentary appended to the fuller version of Psalm 51 also gives a glimpse of Schütz Zell's sensitivity to the intellectual issues of biblical interpretation. Her expressed concern not to misrepresent the historical author's intent is the only hint of a "humanist" interest in her corpus, but it provides evidence that she was paying careful attention to the clerical exegetes who were teaching Protestants how to read—and how not to read—the Bible.[109]

For Schütz Zell, sharing her personal, intimate meditations was a way of offering others both words for their prayers and her own witness to the efficacy of trust in God. The second, literarily more interesting form of Psalm 51 suggests that the writer was trying to express the interplay of "voices" in prayer: Speech or Narrative (telling God how things are), Confession and Lament (recognizing sin and repenting), and Prayer (seeking help but also trusting God to hear and respond). (These headings, which were marginalia in the original, are inserted into the text here.) Helping those who felt God had rejected them, or who sought a way "to get right with God," was something this woman teacher had been doing since her youth. It was also typical of her down-to-earth pastoral sense to show the way by her own example, speaking as one of the priesthood of believers who could offer God's comfort because she herself had received it.

---

109. See below, after n. 124 for the longer version of Psalm 51; for the humanist ideal see at n. 136.

The third section of Schütz Zell's book, the exposition of the Lord's Prayer, might be something of a surprise to modern readers. In a collection intended to console, the meditations on the Psalms seem natural, even though their piety may be rather foreign to modern sensibilities. By contrast the somewhat didactic treatment of the Lord's Prayer sounds more familiar in content but is less immediately recognizable as "consoling." Like the clerical reformers, however, Schütz Zell believed that wrong teaching (which placed the intolerable burden of earning their salvation at least in part on themselves) was the crucial cause of people's despair; it was certainly a feeling she herself had known as a child. Thus the basic source of consolation for sick souls is true teaching: that Christians are made right with God solely by Christ's grace—justification/acceptance as a free gift—not by their own works or sacraments and that God *wants* to give them this free gift. This teaching they learn from scripture and the ancient creeds. They are able to trust the teaching because of the work of the Holy Spirit, who also guides them in following God's will, but God uses human messengers to teach them scripture. And implicitly Schütz Zell knows herself to be one of those teachers. Therefore, because of the importance of right knowledge for trusting and being consoled, their unknown sister in Strasbourg wrote an exposition of the Lord's Prayer for two women in the city of Speyer when she heard that they were distressed because they did not know how to please God. In the course of treating the section on "daily bread" Schütz Zell discusses the Lord's Supper, which means celebrating the "living memorial and communion in Jesus Christ with [their] fellow believers." Here she insists that discerning Christ's body means discerning the people of God (not focusing on the elements). Both the language and the ethical emphasis suggest the Reformed orientation of her Protestantism.[110] In 1558, when the lay pastor-teacher was assembling the counsel she wanted to offer to those in spiritual distress, she included her earlier exposition of *the* key biblical prayer as right teaching that truly consoles.

It is notable that before the exposition of the Lord's Prayer Schütz Zell sets two pieces as an introduction. First in importance although second in order is the Apostles' Creed, the primary statement used by Protestants in teaching the basics of the faith, since those who pray should know to whom they pray; it is accompanied by a didactic prayer. More intriguing is the preface placed first in order, an extended reflection on the initial words of the Prayer, "Our Father." This little introduction provides a very appealing

---

110. For creed, see below at n. 147; for Supper, at nn. 158 and 160 (quotation just after n. 158). Repeatedly Schütz Zell insists that faith includes right knowing; for example, "Lament" esp. at nn. 85–87; "Schwenckfeld" at nn. 61–62 (also at n. 28); "Strasbourg Citizens" at n. 92.

meditation on the character of God and the Christians who address Him as "Father," the children of God for whom Christ is their brother and the Holy Spirit is the one who makes them all able to be a family and say "our" together. In this context Schütz Zell also refers to the women at the tomb who proclaimed the resurrection, seeing what they did as a kind of preaching. More intriguing than the rich familial imagery, however, is the feminine language for Christ. Here Katharina the mother, probably only recently bereaved of her own babies at the time she composed this text, reflects vividly on the maternal work of Christ in the salvation of those who are His children as well as His brothers (for example, Jn 19:34).[111]

This book of devotional meditations, Katharina Schütz Zell's last publication, was printed in August 1558, probably in Strasbourg, although no name of place or publisher is given. It was fairly uncontroversial in content—unless the thinly veiled reference in Psalm 51:18 to the government's failure to resist the Interim made it unwelcome to those in power.[112] However, the author herself was controversial and her patron Sir Felix no longer had any real power. The book was probably received with both gladness and disdain, depending on the reader's view of the old pastor's outspoken widow and their respect for a "has been" like Sir Felix whose primary influence now was his Christian character.

THE MISERERE PSALM MEDITATED, PRAYED, AND PARAPHRASED WITH KING DAVID BY KATHARINA ZELL, THE BLESSED MATTHEW ZELL'S WIDOW, TOGETHER WITH THE OUR FATHER WITH ITS EXPLANATION, SENT TO THE CHRISTIAN MAN SIR FELIX ARMBRUSTER FOR COMFORT IN HIS ILLNESS, AND PUBLISHED FOR THE SAKE OF AFFLICTED CONSCIENCES THAT ARE TROUBLED BY SINS. SOME SAYINGS FROM THE PSALMS AND PROPHETS[113]

I cry with my voice to God, to God I cry and He hears me; in the time of my need I seek the Lord, and I hold out my hands to Him the whole night,

---

111. See at nn. 141ff. For a fuller discussion, see Elsie McKee, "Katharina Schütz Zell and the 'Our Father'," in *Oratio. Das Gebet in patristischer und reformatorischen Sicht* [Festschrift für Alfred Schindler], ed. Emidio Campi, L. Grane, and A. M. Ritter (Göttingen: Vandenhoeck and Ruprecht, 1999), 210–18.

112. See below, at n. 133, and "Lament," introduction, for the Strasbourg situation in 1548–49 when the Psalms were written and the introduction to chapter two for the 1550s when the letter to Sir Felix was written and the whole was published.

113. For Schütz Zell, as for many of her contemporaries, biblical quotations were both the appropriate way to begin and part of the argument, not simply pious window dressing; see

for my soul cannot be comforted; and I am very anxious that my sins be forgiven.

                Psalm 77[:1–2] and 38[:18]

Lord, turn toward me and be gracious, for the distress of my heart is great; rescue me from my trouble and forgive all my sins.

                     Psalm 25[:16–18]

When I am in distress I call on the Lord and cry to my God.

                         Psalm 18[:6a]

I will not keep silent; my mouth shall speak of the distress of my heart and the affliction of my soul.

                            Job 7[:11]

When I would keep silent my strength dries up.

                         Psalm 32[:3a]

Therefore I will confess my sins to the Lord; so forgive me, Lord, and protect me in my distress.

                        Psalm 32[:5, 7a]

I have taken you by the hand and hold you, says God, and I will protect you.

                     Isaiah 42[:6a], 49[:8b]

Why are you afflicted, my soul, and why are you so disquieted in me? Attend to God; I will yet thank Him for helping me.

                      Psalm 42[:5], 43[:5]

At the same time you will say: I thank You, Lord, that You were angry with me but that Your wrath has turned away and now You comfort me.

                           Isaiah 12[:1]

[LETTER TO SIR FELIX ARMBRUSTER]

Grace and mercy from God the Father, and from His only natural (*eingeboren*)[114] Son Jesus Christ, together with His love, through which He hum-

---

"Apologia" at n. 14; "Hymnbook," title page; "Strasbourg Citizens" at n. 83). The texts here summarize her piety and that of her age: prayer and petition to a God she knows through faith and scripture, a pattern of recognizing and confessing her sin, and trusting in and giving thanks for God's forgiveness.

114. Here and throughout the text the German originals for words referring to conception and birth are usually included, in order to illustrate Schütz Zell's development of

bled Himself, putting aside His divinity, became Man (*mensch*), and was given over to death on the cross for us miserable people (*armen menschen*); and the sanctification of the Spirit of God, who awoke Jesus again from the dead for our justification and eternal life. For this work the Father loved the Son, exalted Him above all the heavens, and set Him at His right hand. He gave Him the judgment and iron scepter: that is, the Father made the Son equal to Himself in all divine power, honor, and glory of divinity; through that we now have peace and access to God [cf. Phil 2:7–9; Ps 110:1, 2:9; Mt 28:18; Eph 3:12]. I wish you with my whole heart the peace, joy, comfort, and confirmation of your conscience before God in the Holy Spirit, to eternal life, Sir Felix, beloved of God, whom I know to believe in the Lord Jesus.

Since we have known each other for a long time—yes, almost thirty years—I have been moved to visit you at home in your long and now endless, very distressing illness. You received my visits with great thanks, comfort, and joy, and I promised to visit you now and again. However, although I cannot come to you as much as I would gladly do because of my poor, indeed pitiful sick boy, for whom God has laid on me great labor, still I am always with you in heart.[115] And I pray God to dwell with you all the time, with comfort and patience though His Spirit, whose proper office it is to gather the afflicted and seek out the abandoned, to comfort them in their affliction and to hold His dear conversation with them in their hearts [Jn 14:16ff]. The Spirit's visiting is above all human visiting, conversation, and comfort. For the latter is only human, outward, and not lasting, and sometimes it is also hypocritical, weak, and only goes in the outer ear. The visiting of the Holy Spirit, however, is divine, inward, enduring, truthful, strong, and mighty; it pierces the heart so that the person willingly entrusts his body in obedience to Christ on the cross, accepts discipline and the wholesome rod [cf. Job 15:2ff; Heb 12:5–6], and so he commends soul and spirit eternally to God in Christ and thanks Him.[116]

---

the traditional language; here it is of course a traditional echo of the creeds (both Nicene and Apostles').

115. By referring to their long acquaintance, Schütz Zell offers one justification for speaking to Sir Felix, although this factual detail also expresses her historical sense. The sick boy she mentions is her handicapped nephew Lux Schütz, son of her younger brother Jacob whom she had effectively adopted (probably after his parents' death). Care for Lux occupied her very fully, at least from the early 1550s until her death, and one of the main concerns of her will was to make provision for his care; see "Schwenckfeld" at n. 21.

116. Schütz Zell contrasts the value and effectiveness of the comfort of the Holy Spirit with that of human beings. She clearly insists that the former is always better, but in the following paragraph she goes on to state that the comfort of human beings is also important because

And yet we ought to exercise and practice toward each other our office (commended to us by God), the office of care and love, as also the Lord Christ will say at the last judgment, "You have visited and comforted me in sickness and in prison, enter into the kingdom of my Father" [Mt 25:36, 34]. And the holy apostle says, "Comfort each other now," and further: "God has not made us for wrath but to inherit salvation through our Lord Jesus Christ, who died and rose for us. Therefore admonish each other, and let each one build up the others; comfort the fainthearted, bear the weak in love" [1 Thes 4:18, 5:9–10, 14]. He speaks in another place, "The Father of mercy, a God of all comfort, comforts us in all trouble, so that we may also be able to comfort those who are in all kinds of trouble, with the comfort with which God has comforted us" [2 Cor 1:3b–5]. For, just as much suffering comes upon us because of Christ, so also much comfort comes to us through Christ. Yes, the whole Holy Scripture teaches us to love and serve our neighbors as the members of one body help each other bear evil [cf. Lv 19:18, Mt 19:19, 22:39; Rm 13:9; Gal 5:14; Jas 2:8]. But the head must sway all the members and give the whole body life, force, strength, and everything [cf. 1 Cor 12:25; Eph 4:15–16]. So also the Spirit of God must come to help our speaking, praying, comforting, and everything, to give force, breath, and life, if our actions are to serve and be useful to people.

Since then, my dear Sir Felix, you and I have talked together in many conversations about the way things stand between God and ourselves and how He has so severely visited you, humbled and cut you off—like a string—from the nobility (to which you belong), from office, government, friends, wife, and all joys and fellowship of this world, and, by an illness that horrifies everyone, has caused you to be left alone and abandoned. However, you [Sir Felix] have said to me and confessed that you thank God for this and confess that He does not treat you or anyone unjustly. You bow the knees of your heart before Him [cf. Phil 2:10], humble yourself, and say, "Lord, I know that You have done this out of fatherly love, for Your honor and my soul's salvation, to remind me of my sins and of Your great love and goodness, that I may learn foremost rightly to know and strive after the cross of Christ and be directed in true faith and enjoy His power." Since I heard such things from you, I have

---

God has commanded it as an expression (office) of love and care for the neighbor. It has its effectiveness only by the power of the Holy Spirit. See above, n. 107. Repeatedly Schütz Zell distinguishes carefully between the offices of God and human beings; both are valued as God's will and both have effect through the Spirit, but they may not be confused; see "Schwenckfeld" at nn. 65–66.

diligently thanked God the Father and the Lord Christ for that and have never forgotten you for a single day.

Also I have thought about the words you spoke to me, how for a while it became so bitter for you to tear yourself out of affliction, until God helped you and gave you patience. Besides, however, I know how your illness is a daily unending pain up to the end and into the grave; and that pain would easily stir up and call forth many afflictions and impatience. Human beings are weak, and, when the cross weighs him down so much, a person thinks about and bewails the cross more than the sins that earned it and brought it upon him. So I sought in my reflections some way to be present with you for comfort and in part to help bear your cross—spiritually if not physically—or to lighten it with as much spiritual comfort as God has given to me when, in my need, He has also admonished and comforted me about my acts [cf. Gal 6:2; 2 Cor 1:4]. So I sought out some of my old booklets that I wrote years ago for myself, in which I worked through the whole Psalter with lament, prayer, and thanks. Out of these I have taken one, namely the Miserere (Ps 51), in which the dear David shows the right way to lament and confess sin, when God through the prophet Nathan pointed out his sin and horrified him by showing the punishment. This same Miserere psalm (which David made as a prayer of one troubled and anguished in heart) I also meditated on once alone before God, when I was in great affliction and distress. I prayed and paraphrased this psalm when my heart and conscience were tortured, together with Psalm 130, the De Profundis, when I was torn apart inside between the wrath and the grace of God. Yet the Lord comforted me in such a fatherly way.

Since I have experienced so many afflictions in myself and in others, and also God has given me again much comfort, I have thought about your affliction and the word of Paul where he says, "God afflicts us that we may believe the afflicted, and He comforts us again so that we can comfort the afflicted out of our experience" [cf. 2 Cor 1:4].[117] So I wanted to share these two psalms

---

117. The citation of 2 Corinthians 1:4 here is very slightly different from that above ("The Father of mercy . . . comforts us in all trouble, so that we may also be able to comfort those who are in all kinds of trouble, with the comfort with which God has comforted us"). Here she paraphrases slightly, adding a phrase based on ideas found in other biblical texts combined with her own perception; 2 Corinthians 1:4 itself does not say that God afflicts the believer, although that idea is quite clear in many passages such as 2 Samuel 11-12, which Schütz Zell, like her predecessors and contemporaries, believed was the context for Psalm 51. It is a Christian tradition that God uses affliction for positive purposes, most frequently vindication of God's truth or turning the sinner to repentance, as the quotation of Sir Felix above indicates. Here Schütz Zell identifies the purpose of affliction as a means of developing love; those who are not afflicted may not believe the reality of other people's suffering, so they must also

with you in writing. While I hope that God will give you more teaching and comfort in bearing your cross than I can do here, nevertheless love does not cease to be concerned for others: like the [love of] the dear Mary's, who wanted to anoint the Lord after He was already risen and had no more wounds [Mk 16:1, 9]. May the Lord Christ grant that your pain may all be healed by the grace of God and you may be happy and comforted, without any wounds in your conscience, and you may be already resurrected in God! But still I hope that God and you will not take amiss my work of love, this booklet.[118]

Besides my concern for you, Sir Felix, I was also prompted to publish this book because of the many troubled people who have for a long time sought me out with great weeping and afflictions, and still do so. These people bewail with great cries not their physical problems, but the spiritual distress and illness of their consciences, and—throwing up their hands—they have said to me, "Oh, no bodily illness is so great that I would not gladly bear it, indeed would not complain about it, if God would take away this distress of my heart and tell me that He is gracious to me and forgives my sins." I have held many and great conversations with these people about the high, inexpressible, eternal merit of Christ the Son of God, that same strangled and murdered Lamb who alone is worthy to open the book with the seven seals, that Lamb who is able and willing to save all races of people who fall down and worship before Him [cf. Rv 5:1, 6, 9, 14]. Along with my thought for you, Sir Felix, I have published my prayer and conversation with love for troubled hearts like these who still lack the right knowledge of Christ.[119] Also following these psalms you will find an exposition of the Lord's Prayer,

---

suffer in order to be able both to believe and to comfort others with the comfort that God has given them. The practice of interpreting one text by another is common, but Schütz Zell's paraphrase is particularly apt for her argument.

118. In the Gospels, the women come to the tomb early Sunday morning (the first day of the week) after His crucifixion to anoint Jesus's body with the spices that were part of the traditional Jewish burial practice, but they arrive only after He has already risen. Schütz Zell hopes that Sir Felix will have such healing ("teaching and comforting") from God that he will not need her book but she offers it as an act of the love prescribed by scripture, since (as her next words imply) others may not be as mature in faith as he. The dedication to an important figure who has clearly progressed from bitterness to trusting God in his affliction may encourage others who need it to read her book.

119. Traditionally, many people were afraid of not being able to atone for their sins and gain forgiveness, a fear the young Katharina herself had known and which was particularly sharp on one's deathbed (see "Lament" at nn. 70 ff; "Schwenckfeld" at n. 58). Schütz Zell's answer is to trust only in the merit of Christ, who has atoned for every person who believes in Him, and this knowledge is their comfort (see above before n. 110). This insistence on biblical teaching about Christ as vital for pastoral care was more characteristic of Protestant clergy than laity—evidence of Schütz Zell's "bridging" role between the two.

The Lay Reformer, Teacher, and Pastor   135

which I once wrote for two women in Speyer who lamented that they could not live according to God's will. When I heard of them, I chose the Lord's Prayer to explain to them and pray with them in the simplest way.

This, my simple short conversation that I have had with God in good times and bad, I ask you please to accept favorably from me, a poor disregarded woman, as a greeting and conversation although I am not physically present with you. I have noted down still many other things about the more than forty years of conversations between God and me; if I thought that these would be of some use and comfort to you or others, I would gladly share them also.[120] Now I am conscious of my age and its weakness; indeed I see coming soon the time of my release from this life. I rejoice in and welcome it and know that to die here will be my gain: to lay aside the mortal and perishable and put on the everlasting immortal and imperishable [cf. 2 Tm 4:6; Phil 1:21; 1 Cor 15:53]. I am now sixty years old, and I have walked before God in fear of Him and despising of the world for fifty years so that I could say with Saint Ambrose, "I have lived so that I am not ashamed to continue to live among the faithful, but I also am not afraid to die, for I am certain that in Christ I will live again and that in Him I have a gracious God forever."[121]

Please now receive my conversation and speech favorably and with a friendly heart, my very dear Sir Felix, as I mean it and have written it from the heart. With this, I commend you to the love of God the Father, and of His true Son Jesus Christ, together with the sanctification and comfort of God the Holy Spirit, who comes forth from the Father and the Son and gathers together the saints: may He fulfill this also in you and me and in all who seek it. Amen.[122]

---

120. Schütz Zell indicates that her own life of prayer—"conversations with God"—has been very long. Below she gives her age as sixty, so the claim of "more than forty years" points to a beginning of this intimate relationship with God in her teens. "Forty years" is also a biblical number for a very long time (e.g., the time the Israelites wandered in the wilderness), and Schütz Zell probably intends to convey more than simple numbers. The phrase "poor disregarded woman" probably refers to the way Schütz Zell was being treated by Rabus; see "Strasbourg Citizens" at n. 98 and appendix at nn. 1f. As with virtually all self-deprecating language focused on gender (not human sinfulness), Schütz Zell's words here reflect irony or sarcasm, not any sense of her unworthiness as a woman per se; see above at n. 106.

121. Schütz Zell indicates that she dedicated herself to God and renounced the world when she was ten years old; this point had been further developed in her autobiographical writings (see "Schwenckfeld" at n. 37; "Strasbourg Citizens" at n. 91). The story of Saint Ambrose, the fourth-century Bishop of Milan and the church father, was told in the popular medieval collection of saints lives called the *Golden Legend*. Schütz Zell probably read the story in the Alsatian version of the book; see McKee, *Writings*, 316, n. 19. Although her main authority was scripture and the second was the early reformers like Luther, Schütz Zell also occasionally cited church fathers, primarily as stories and always as secondary to the Bible; see McKee, *Life and Thought*, 291–94.

122. Note the Trinitarian emphasis and echoes of the Nicene Creed's description of the Holy Spirit "who proceeds from the Father and the Son . . ."

Dated on the day of Margaret the Virgin, of whom (and of her companion Agnetha) it is sung, "The riches and desires of this world have I left, so that I might depend upon Christ my spouse and follow Him above all."[123] May God grant this to us also. Amen.

Katharina Zell,
your longtime acquaintance and fellow companion in the faith of the Lord Jesus

Now Follows the Miserere Psalm [51]

A Little Exhortation about the Miserere Psalm:

The sin of King David could not be seen in his flesh. He was a prophet and knew that it was sin and done against God's command [cf. Ex 20:13–14; Dt 5:17–18]—the command he was to maintain in its power and glory because (as king) he was something more than others and had received it from God. But David did not see his sin until God worked with him. God had to show David that He had not given him this power for destruction but for improvement [2 Cor 10:8]. God does that more to someone who foolishly does not want to see what is right and what he should do: that one must be made to see by rebuke and gnawing worm. Through His Spirit God says to people in the psalm, "Because I kept silent about your deeds you have thought that I did not see them and that you were right; however, I will rebuke you and set your fault before your eyes" [Ps 50:21]. God does that in the heart, and through the voice of people. So He did to David, so He does still to many.[124] As David behaved, so each person ought to behave; what David obtained, each one who does what David did will also obtain.

---

123. In medieval Strasbourg, Saint Margaret's Day was July 15. Identifying the other saint is difficult, however; Strasbourg's calendar included three virgin martyrs named Saint Margaret, Saint Agnes, and Saint Agatha. It is possible that Agnetha is an error for Agatha, but it is also possible that Agnes was intended. There was a double Dominican convent in Strasbourg known in Schütz Zell's day as Saints Margaret and Agnes. The liturgical song cited here, which apparently joins the two virgins' names, may have been sung there for both patron saints, and the devout young Katharina could have heard it if she visited in the convent. Although Schütz Zell calls these traditional holy women "saints," it is clear that she honors them because they witnessed to and followed Christ: she does not see them as patron saints to be petitioned in their own right. For treatment of saints, see "Hymnbook" at nn. 55, 63. For language about Christ as the bridegroom see "Schwenckfeld" at n. 27.

124. Schütz Zell indicates the reason for affliction: unwillingness to see what is right without rebuke. Here and often she points to the coordination of God's inward speaking by the Holy Spirit and God's use of human instruments. See below in Psalm 51:15, "Schwenckfeld" at nn. 65–66. Also see the reference to inner and outer punishment below in Psalm 51:4a.

The Lay Reformer, Teacher, and Pastor 137

The one who humbles himself and confesses his sins before God and fears Him, one who believes in the name of Jesus, that He is the anointed Christ and sin bearer who offered His back and countenance to rebuke—that one will obtain forgiveness [Is 53:12b, 50:6].

The Speech of an Afflicted and Believing Sinner

[51:1a] When the reckoning and knowledge of sin became great, and my sins stood in a great heap before my inward eyes and I saw no help at all—neither the (ability to) work nor the repentance are in myself—then (as was fitting) I spoke these words:

O God, be gracious to me according to Your goodness, and deal with me according to Your grace, which cannot be bought or obtained by any (human) work or goods; but goodness and grace are Your own essential way and office. [51:1b] Wash out my sins according to Your great mercy; take them from me, that they may not be eternally reckoned in Your wrath and judgment. [51:2] Wash me well from my misdeeds, O Lord, that my behavior may not be so shameful, bad, foolish, and worthless as up till now. Because of that behavior I have come under Your wrath, rebuke, and such affliction. Cleanse me from my sin of unbelief, which I have committed till now: I have cast off Your working (control), I would not suffer Your hand, I would not wait for Your help. I wanted to carry out my own desire according to my will, which still sticks in me, and will remain if You, O God, do not cleanse it and destroy the reign of sin in me and reign in me Yourself.[125]

[51:3-4a] I know and confess my misdeeds: how all my acts in thoughts, words, and deeds have been so dull and not according to Your word. My sins are continually before me, with the chastising, terrifying appearance of Your judgment, so that I now see against whom I have sinned: not only have I sinned against the people to whom I have done evil, but [51:4a] I have sinned against You Yourself. I have done evil before You; I have broken Your commands (not human ones). I have been at fault and have sinned against these commands and not noticed that You have seen it all, that You have exhorted and chastised me: sometimes in my heart and also with outward acts done before my eyes. Still I have not feared You with pure fear, but with stiff-necked wicked self-will I have behaved according to my carnal Adam's sense and carried on with disobedient

---

125. Note that the sin confessed here is "unbelief," and Schütz Zell insists that of herself she is powerless to turn from sin—again signs of the Protestant character of the theology. Usually the sin associated with Psalm 51 had a moral character, like the adultery or murder of David; Schütz Zell gives this a place, but the chief sin is unbelief; see "Schwenckfeld" at n. 69 and "Lament" at n. 85. A Protestant use of this, a petition to be saved from "unbelief," is found below at n. 163, also in "Women" at n. 10.

wicked behavior against Your word and prohibition [cf. Gn 3:17, 1 Cor 15:46]. [51:4b] Therefore, You would be justified in punishing me, and no one who saw what You said or did against my sin and misdeeds would judge that You were unjust to me. And I myself know (as I have already seen) that Your word is true and Your judgment is right [cf. Jn 17:17, 5:30].

And yet, O Lord, be gracious to me now, and forgive my sins according to Your own innate favor and mercy. Remit my punishment, keep me in rightly directed faith, according to Your promise to forgive the sins of one who groans and never to remember them [cf. Ezek 18:27]. So You may have the honor and the glory that You are the most righteous one of all because You have mercy; You are the most steadfast of all because You carry out Your promises and condemn those who still will not repent after all Your long-suffering mercy. You must be seen and confessed as the most worthy of all, and I as wicked and deceitful. [51:5] However, what should, what can I now say except, O Lord, have patience with me! I was begotten (*gezeuget*) from unclean sinful seed—from where then could I have righteousness? My mother also conceived (*empfangen*) me in sin since in my conception she did not have the image of the first created human being who was pure, but the shape of the fallen nature with its carnal desire. From such impure seed I came forth and grew up as bad fruit; therefore as a prisoner to sin by inheritance, I can do nothing but allow the insolent wicked desire to overcome me and then cover that same sin with wicked lies and hypocritical pretense.[126]

[51:6] But You desire truth, which is hidden and secret in Your wisdom. That You have also now permitted me to know, since You have recognized my helplessness, that I can do nothing but follow my sinful conception (*empfengnus*) and birth. So You have given me another birth that should purify me through Your word that You send to me. In accordance with Your long-standing grace, You show me my sins and teach me what lies hidden in You: how people were corrupted in the root and there is nothing good in them but worthless sin and wrath, which, however, no one can confess or in truth understand without Your Spirit [cf. Jn 3:3; 1 Pt 2:22–23; Rm 7:18]. This is a great human stupidity: people always want to be and do something according to their former (car-

---

126. Schütz Zell contrasts the "pure" human nature as God created it with fallen "carnal" human nature. Although she shares the common view that "original sin" is inherited and refers to her parents, she does not focus on sexual sin as primary. It is the fallen nature inherited by every person that is the problem, not the sexual act of begetting or conceiving. Above she spoke of unbelief and self-will; referring here to disobedience, lies, and hypocrisy, she has in mind the story of Adam and Eve, who disobeyed God's command not to eat the fruit of one specific tree and then tried to cover up their sin by hiding from God and blaming others. Note that she speaks of being both "begotten" (*gezeuget*) and "conceived" (*empfangen*); this linguistic distinction seems deliberate and significant; see below at nn. 144–146.

nal) birth, the thing that You hate as lies and hypocrisy. Therefore it is a great wisdom in Your eyes (but hidden to the sight of many) for a person to recognize and confess Your true righteousness and his true sin. Ah, to do that is the real truth that You love, and You desire such truth, which is intimate and hidden with You. You give it to those You choose, and You reprimand the haughty who are not willing to confess the truth of their powerlessness [1 Cor 2:7; Ps 119:21]. But I confess that my life began in sin and has brought forth such bad fruit in me. I cannot hide that from You, for You know it; all my inward self is known to You, for Your hand made and formed me. Therefore I pray and weep before You with my whole heart and ask You to be gracious to me according to Your word, which You have spoken—that same word abides continually eternally in heaven! [Ps 139:1ff, 13ff].[127]

[51:7] O Lord, help me! Sprinkle me with hyssop (in the truth) as happened (in figure and shadow) to Your people Israel, who were purified from sins with hyssop in the blood of animals by Moses Your servant. But for me the washing is with the cross of Christ Your child, in His blood.[128] Wash me so I will be pure and white from my sins before You, and then You will heed my prayer and remember Your word, in which You have permitted and instructed me to hope [Ex 12:22, 24:18; Lv 14:6–7; Nm 19:18–19; Heb 9:19ff; Ps 119:49]. [51:8] Ah, God, allow me to hear and receive that in my heart, so I may have such joy and gladness and may become true, so that I may be in Your grace again, and my bones and inward strength—which, in Your wrath over my sins You have torn in two by many painful thoughts, anxieties, and sadness—may be comforted. [51:9] Ah, Lord, forget those things, turn Your face away from my sins, do not take them to heart, act toward me as if You did not know or see them, but turn toward me and wipe out all my misdeeds. Do not reckon them to me in judgment. Remember whence I have come: from people of disobedience, who have begotten (*bezeuget*) their offspring in unholy and wicked desire.

[51:10] But, O God, give me another, a pure heart! a new, steadfast, sure spirit that may teach and direct me to behave and do according to Your

---

127. Note emphasis on knowledge of sin as a gift of grace by the Holy Spirit, knowledge which Schütz Zell implicitly claims because she confesses her sin; see below in Psalm 51:15, before n. 136 and at n. 138). "Word" here means both Christ and the Bible/Gospel.

128. The reference is to the tenth plague in Egypt and God's command to Moses on how to save the people of Israel. Each household was to kill a lamb and sprinkle its blood on the doorpost with a bit of hyssop plant so that the angel of death who was sent to kill the firstborn of the Egyptians would pass over the homes of the Israelites and not kill anyone. The Passover was naturally the most important Old Testament prefiguring of Christ's work as the Lamb who was killed to save those who believed in Him by washing in His blood.

will and command in order that I may not waste my strength in senseless things and fall further into Your wrath. (That way one sin would be the punishment for others and finally destruction would come upon me.) Ah, dear Lord, how much I need the wisdom of Your Holy Spirit to know how to behave in all my afflictions and griefs! Therefore, let me experience Your mercy, for I am so terrified before You that my flesh and skin tremble for anxiety of heart when I consider Your judgment [Ps 119:77a; Job. 4:14–15].

[51:11a] But I beg You, do not cast me away from Your face: do not allow me to go completely out of Your care and teaching, as if You had not looked upon me in the first place. For indeed You formed me in Your foreknowledge when You still had favor and honor for people, when You made them according to Your image in the creation of Your glory [Ps 139:16; Is 43:1; cf. Gn 1:26–27].[129] [15:11b–12] And take not Your Holy Spirit from me, the Spirit whom You once gave me to make it possible for me to know You. I beg You with great weeping before Your face: do not let that knowledge cease in me, so that I may not despair and say, Who is my help? Where is my God? [cf. Ps 42:2–3]; so that in my downfall I may not be cast away from You. But deal with me according to Your grace, comfort me with Your aid and support, and may Your excellent joyous Spirit preserve me henceforth in all my afflictions and desires so that they may not overcome me or crush me [Ps 119:133], but that I may live rightly. Let me not be brought to shame before You because of my hope.

[51:13] So then, as one who has experienced Your goodness, I will be able and will want to teach others who are in sins and afflictions to turn back to You and how they can come to You. So I may bring them to You because they see Your grace in me, that You have not left me without help or cast me away because of my sins. Therefore they also will properly trust in You and come to You when they see that the word of Your promise abides (and can be trusted).

[51:14a] O God, save me also from sins of bloodguilt that have fallen upon me, that I have destroyed the blood and life of the innocent [cf. 2 Sm 11:14–17].[130] Oh how great and hard is this sin in many ways and encom-

---

129. The words imply Schütz Zell's belief in election, that God foreknew His chosen ones before the fall (cf. Eph 1:4). Elsewhere the idea of election (not just foreknowledge) is expressed explicitly; see "Schwenckfeld" at n. 70. Following this, Schütz Zell again affirms the work of the Holy Spirit: to know God, be upheld by Him, and enabled to live rightly.

130. Schütz Zell puts "2 Samm. 11" (sic) in the margin, and here she most clearly takes on the persona of David, who committed adultery with Bathsheba who then became pregnant. Since Bathsheba's husband Uriah was out in the field with David's army, it would be obvious that her child was not Uriah's and there would be public scandal when the pregnancy became known. David arranged to have Uriah set in the most dangerous place and killed in battle and then

The Lay Reformer, Teacher, and Pastor 141

passed with many vices! You who are my God, may You will to declare me free from such guilt, which I have indeed brought upon myself. O God, God of my salvation, You can destroy me or preserve me, You and no one else! For the deed was done with wicked blows in secret (unknown to people), but to You it is entirely manifest, before and in the act. For it was already known to You before I had decided to do it: You already knew the evil in me before I knew it. Your law states that the one who kills shall be killed [Lv 24:17]; that is why You had Nathan say to me that the sword should not cease from my house, since I did not fear You but carried out secretly the sin of unholy shame and through the murder of Uriah caused Your name to be slandered among Your enemies. Although I acted in secret You saw it all; will You punish me publicly before all Israel? [cf. 2 Sm 12:10–14].

Oh how grievously have I fallen into this bloodguilt before You! Oh how great must be Your grace that You redeem me again from it: to forgive the sin of bloodguilt that I committed and redeem me from the penance and punishment of blood and death, and also to turn the sword of my bloodthirsty enemy away from my house. No work, no sacrifice, no human means can be enough to make amends for this sin, because no one can redeem his sin or reconcile himself to You, Lord, with anything except with what is Your own [cf. Ps 49:7]. Your grace and mercy alone must pay You and help me out of this guilt; therefore turn to me and be wholly gracious to me, as You have promised to do with those who still love and fear Your name.[131]

[51:14b] Do this, O Lord, so that my tongue may praise Your righteousness, which according to its nature and promise surpasses my unrighteousness and covers my shame. Do this so that, quickly and without any work of penance of mine, through Your forgiveness of my sins, I may obtain favor, grace, and eternal righteousness before You. [51:15] But open my lips (otherwise I can do nothing), so that my lips may praise You and my mouth may proclaim Your glory. Your glory is that You deal honorably and do not break Your covenant and pledge to me on account of my shameful breach of that covenant and my rebellion. But You remember Your

---

married Bathsheba. The prophet Nathan accused David of his sin, saying that God had decreed that David's family would be torn by bloodshed and the baby Bathsheba bore would die. David repented and confessed, but the child died as punishment for David's sin.

131. Here forgiveness and salvation by grace alone are clearly expressed. Schütz Zell next insists that she does not need any lengthy time or work of penance (e.g., purgatory) to gain forgiveness. All she can do is praise God for keeping His covenant despite her rebellion, praise which only God Himself by the Holy Spirit and grace makes possible; see below in Psalm 51:18a and 51:19.

word, which You have sworn, regardless of all my wrongdoing [cf. Ezek 16:59ff], and You seek to concern Yourself only with faith. Therefore You now send me Your admonitions through people and in my heart, that I may humble myself and bewail my sins [cf. 2 Sm 12:1, 13], that I may search into Your word, awake faith, and show forth that You help me without any work (of mine): that is the way to salvation which You point out.

[51:16] For You do not desire sacrifice: otherwise I would gladly give You what I have. Also burnt offerings do not please You: otherwise I would give not calves but my body; I would discipline, rack, and beat my own body, which committed such evil. But You, O Lord, do not want all that. [51:17] The sacrifices that please You, O God, are an afflicted spirit and a wounded, broken heart, which confess sin and what is done against You with pain and stillness; such a spirit, such a heart is not haughty in despising its sins, but acknowledges You, humbles itself, is shamefaced and timid before You. That, O God, You will not despise. Still I know (despite my faintheartedness), that You will also not cast me away, miserable as I am, with others of Your miserable sinners because I have transgressed and sinned against You. But You will forgive me and enroll me again (as Yours), for You love those who fear You and who, although full of sin, nevertheless trust in Your mercy.[132]

[51:18a] Ah, God, do not do any less good to Zion, according to Your good will toward those who still believe You, who entrust themselves to Your discipline and chastisement with a gentle spirit, who do not drive Your prophets away but listen to You in them and believe Your word. Ah, where there are such in Zion (that is, among Your people) I also want to join myself to them, to listen to and take hold of the prophets, to become a gentle quiet soul. I want henceforth never to be like the godless, to follow their worthless, capricious, murderous desires and works, but I want to walk with the kind, suffering Zion and henceforth praise You so long as I am here. So I will hide myself among Zion-like people (who are Your Christian church) until Your wrath passes over me. Zion receives much favor and good from You, but not because she deserves any: it is only from Your good will—which is that You love those who can do nothing for You, who can give You nothing, those who can only receive Your gifts from You with thanks. And

---

132. Here the value of the humble confession to God and trust in God is preferred over ascetic practices (such as were common for monastics). In the following paragraph similar ideas are expressed for the corporate body of Zion: God gives unmerited grace to Zion/the church purely of His good will and love for the powerless, who recognize their situation and receive His forgiveness with thanks. Although much of her meditation is personal, it is not individualistic; Schütz Zell is intensely conscious of being part of the body of Christ.

The Lay Reformer, Teacher, and Pastor   143

You wish her well because of Your good will, which is her treasure, wealth, and pledge, yes, her promised inheritance. May You also allow me, miserable as I am, together with the same Zion-like believing company, Your people, to experience and enjoy this; and allow me again to come into Your love and fellowship, forgiveness of sins, and the following resurrection to life in You.

[51:18b] And may You also will to build the walls of Jerusalem, for Zion cannot stand when she does not have Jerusalem, and Jerusalem cannot stand when she does not have walls.[133] Ah, God, Zion must have the holy teaching of God, faithful, kind, true teachers and preachers, who are fittingly called "Jerusalem" because out of Jerusalem should come the wisdom and rule of God [cf. Mi 4:2b]. Jerusalem, however, must have walls against His enemies: faithful, wise, God-fearing kings and government who protect Jerusalem. Jerusalem, however, teaches Zion with holy teaching, but if the king has become a worthless adulterer, how can he then endure spiritual and right teaching? If he has become a killer and murderer, how can he protect Jerusalem with His prophets, when he should be the wall and (yet) has fallen so disgracefully? If the city no longer has any protection, then enemies rush in and destroy her; if the city is destroyed, then she can no longer help or teach poor Zion; if Zion has no help or teaching, then she lacks wisdom; if she has no sacrifice or righteousness anymore, then she goes astray and is imprisoned and weeps in exile as she did in the imprisonment in Babylon [Ps 137:1].

O God, how great will be the punishment, however, of the king who is guilty of all this! Therefore he rightly prays to You heartily and unceasingly and waters his prayers with tears. He prays that You may be gracious to him according to Your ancient favor and great mercy, which alone can help in this evil; that You may again allow Your countenance to shine upon him [Ps 6:6, 2, 4; cf. Nm 6:25]; that You may cease from Your wrath and do

---

133. Comparing this verse with her "Lament for Matthew Zell" and other writings of the late 1540s and early 1550s makes it clear that the reflections here are not abstract metaphors. The allegorical interpretation of Zion, Jerusalem, and its walls has a concrete application: Schütz Zell implicitly contrasts Protestants (who follow "the Gospel") with the Roman church and criticizes the civil rulers of Strasbourg for the compromises they have made or are making for the Interim. "Zion" or the followers of the Gospel have received God's grace without any merit of their own. Zion cannot stand without its capital Jerusalem, the ministers who preach the Gospel, and Jerusalem cannot stand without its walls, the civil rulers who are supposed to protect the preachers. When Protestant cities and territories like Strasbourg agreed to readmit Roman clergy and worship as a condition of the Interim, Schütz Zell believed that the civil leaders (walls) had failed to defend the preaching of the Gospel (Jerusalem). In fact, Bucer and Fagius, the most outspoken ministers, were exiled, and Zion was in serious trouble.

good to Zion according to Your good will (not according to these evil deeds) and thus build up again the walls of Jerusalem; that You may again give to the king Your Holy Spirit (whom You have previously given to him to prophesy and keep holy teaching); that You may not cast away him whom You previously loved, whom You freed of guilt, and of whom You said that he was according to Your heart. O God, take away the sin and shamefacedness; let him return again into Your grace, let him keep Your justice and rejoice before You and Your ark and henceforth walk in Your command with wisdom [cf. 1 Sm 16:13, 13:14; 2 Sm 6:12ff].

[51:19] Then the sacrifices of righteousness, burnt offerings, and whole offerings will please You; then they will lay bulls on Your altar. Ah, Lord, until You cleanse me nothing that I do will please You: everything I do is still worthless sin offerings. You have ordained offerings for sins [1 Sm 15:22–23]), but if I make many sacrifices all I do is witness to my sins here before Your face. But if You take away the sin, if by Your great mercy You forgive me and never again reckon my sins against me, if You cleanse my heart and conscience and give me assurance by Your good Spirit, if You open my mouth to extol Your righteousness and show me how to praise You for Your great grace (I who have been guilty of death and the sword!)—then the willing sacrifice of my mouth (the confession of Your righteousness) will be pleasing to You [cf. Rm 6:12ff; Gal 5:3ff]. The same is true also for burnt offerings, prayers, fasts, sufferings, yes all the disciplining and slaying of my body along with each offering: yes, then what I do will not be so small. Then everything: all honor and service to You and to the neighbor, when it comes out of such a purified heart (purified by You), will please You. Then You would continuously teach me Your justice so that I might offer You the complete sacrifice of all my inward strength and thoughts, all my outward deeds, what I do and do not do: yes, body, soul, and spirit [cf. Ps 139:1ff].[134]

---

134. Schütz Zell contrasts the kinds of outward discipline that the Old Testament teaches and that Protestants thought Rome wrongly continued with the main points that most Protestants considered primary: service to God and neighbor made possible by God's forgiveness and not her own merits. She goes on to explain this in detail, indicating what kinds of "sacrifices" believers can make and on what grounds and what their value is. (1) The Bible/law teaches the acts of obedience that please God: here the law is "spiritualized" (see below after n. 136 and at n. 137). Note the positive reference to the law, which is characteristic of the Reformed teaching that the biblical law is the model for the Christian life (unlike the generally negative connotation of law typical of Luther and many of his followers). (2) Christ's grace is the only basis for her acts to be accepted (just as it is the only basis on which she herself is accepted).

The Lay Reformer, Teacher, and Pastor   145

I will not offer doves, kids, or other small animals of the little, vain human works, works that need to be treated with indulgence. But I will offer calves and bulls, strong animals of the important, right, useful works of God, the works that Your law and Your command require. Your law and command will be the outward altar on which I lay my offerings so that they may all be pleasing and acceptable to You, as they are indeed sacrifices and works according to Your Word and command. Besides this, I would also lay my offerings on Your spiritual and holy altar, that is, Your dear Son Jesus Christ who, as the faithful priest, completed the sacrifice of His flesh in His blood on the altar of the cross. He was a holy sweet fragrance to You, pure and honest; He took away all sins, entered to You through the sanctuary, and still always stands for us before Your face and sanctifies all that is given to Him [cf. Heb 9:11ff, 24ff]. To the same one, You, my Lord Jesus Christ, the sole right sacrifice and sacrificer,[135] to You I cry from my heart: teach me, cleanse and direct me in all my life, occupations, and afflictions, through the Holy Spirit whom You have promised to give to all who love you [cf. Jn 16:7]: may He henceforth rule my inward and outward person with His holy gifts, wisdom, counsel, leading, and understanding of all that is fitting! Amen.

Now then I hope that this exposition and prayer on this psalm Miserere (in which I have reflected on David's sin, my own, and that of us all) may not be contrary to the meaning of David and of his thoughts that he had about his sins when he made and prayed this psalm. That was when God sent Nathan to him to point out his sin and set it before his eyes [2 Sm 12:1ff]. Also, I hope each one who is afflicted because of his sins may pray thus, even if he has not done any adultery or murder of the body and hand in outward works, as David did, for no one is innocent before God in his heart, thoughts, and desires, even if his sin is not consciously known to him. So let him pray with David for the secret sins that are in him and that he himself does not know (but before God they stand in the light) [Ps 19:12, 90:8].[136]

---

135. Christ is identified as both the Sacrifice that He offers to God and the priest who offers that sacrifice (His own body on the cross). This was a traditional idea, but in Protestant fashion Schütz Zell very clearly counters any idea that a human being could be a priest to offer Christ to God (as the Roman priest was understood to do in the "sacrifice of the Mass"). Protestants disagreed on how Christ was present in the Lord's Supper, but they all firmly agreed that the sacrament is not a sacrifice; Christ's death on the cross was the unique sacrifice for salvation.

136. Schütz Zell expresses her concern that scripture be interpreted as the writer intended, not simply used as a basis for an edifying meaning. This marks the closest she comes to a "humanist" note shared by virtually all Protestants (although not necessarily by Anabaptists).

To these secret sins belong many murders done without hands that may indeed happen when a person allows someone to die in his bed. There are many kinds of murder: prejudice, lack, need for food, drink, clothing, warmth, and so on: many and all bodily needs—if one snatches away all of these or omits to do them it is murder. The same is true also for spiritual things, if one fails to give to each as he has need: counsel, comfort, help, cause for gladness, and so on; each one should act according to his ability and God's law. It is the same also with the opposites: it is murder to despise, afflict, mistreat, irritate, insult, abuse, revile, blame people, to make them go astray and be unhappy, it is murder to do all things by which one harms someone's soul and makes him weak in bodily and spiritual comfort. Who can recount all these sins and murders, much less know them, without Christ the Lord who knows and teaches us to know them [Mt 5:21ff]?

Also adultery does not consist only in acts of the body but in the heart and thoughts, as also the Lord says in Matthew chapter 5[:28], "To look on a woman or man with lust is already to be an adulterer."[137] Adultery also consists in much capriciousness and superfluity in many things, yes, in making occasion for each other to fall by how one eats, drinks, dresses, speaks, gestures; all the examples of that behavior cannot be enumerated, including examples among all the most spiritual people and those who fear God.

In the third place are all kinds of unfaithfulness. Let each one look in himself and consider what great lacks there are in his marriage, how husband and wife condemn, act with impropriety, despise, afflict, hate, show wrath, and mistreat each other, so that the love that God commanded and planted is wounded. Part of this happens from lack of understanding, the other part from wickedness. The dear prophet Malachi also laments and

---

The new intellectual studies of humanism aimed at getting back to the original sources (*ad fontes*) and reading these in context. Most medieval exegetes, relying on the church as the final authority, had looked for "spiritual" teachings in scripture and were not troubled if these edifying interpretations were only loosely related to the text at hand, but Protestants (and others) rejected this method. Having attended to David as such—the meaning of Psalm 51 in its (traditionally accepted) historical context—Schütz Zell then explicitly turns to broaden the definitions of murder and adultery from the acts themselves, to other behaviors that cause death or lust, to a spiritualized idea of harm done to others or a spouse from ill will or ignorance. Expanding the scope of a commandment was a common practice of Protestant theologians (again with humanist antecedents); it was understood not as changing the meaning but as carrying the intent of the original writer to its logical spiritual conclusion as Christ had done with the law in Matthew 5:28 (which Schütz Zell quotes below).

137. Schütz Zell adds "man" to the text; here as earlier ("Women" at n. 4), she slightly paraphrases scripture to make women as well as men explicitly present, this time in a negative sense (i.e., a woman who looks on a man with lust is just as culpable as the reverse). In effect, the same standards hold for men and women!

The Lay Reformer, Teacher, and Pastor   147

punishes this in his book of prophesy; he says of the wicked husbands and afflicted wives, "What an abomination to God are your offering and all that you do." For this reason also divorce itself shows why he did not consider these right marriages [cf. Mal 2:13–16]. Also this is true when a couple indeed have great love for each other and think they are doing exactly the right thing and yet do not understand what either marriage or adultery means before God. Ah, in all these things, who would not say with the dear David, "Who can know how often he fails? Lord, do not remember the sins of my youth and ignorance. Cleanse me from my secret sins. God alone knows what is secret in the heart" [cf. Ps 19:12, 25:7; 51:2 6; 44:21]. And Isaiah says, "You are a transgressor from your mother's womb on." And God Himself says, "The human heart is inclined toward wickedness from youth on" [Is 48:8b; Gn 8:21b].

Therefore let no one consider himself pure from murder and adultery, whether he be man or woman, high or low, clerical or lay, married, widowed, or virgin, and so forth. That must be known and confessed not hypocritically in words, but in truth before God and ourselves because it is the truth before God. Therefore David also said, "No living person will be found just before Your judgment." Similarly Job also laments, "From one time to another [it is impossible to answer God—*trans.*]" [cf. Ps 143:2; Job 9:2]. The one to whom God grants to know what sin rightly is, and for whom God sets sin before his eyes, that one has little joy and carries more crosses in his heart than he can describe with written letters. Each one can only say with David, "My sins are more than the hairs on my head and sand in the sea; they have piled up over me before I could know and see them" [Ps 40:12; cf. Gn 20:17]. There is no better way a person can come before God than to let himself be proved to be under sin, so that God may have mercy on him [cf. Rm 11:32; Gal 3:22].[138]

[Here follows a long passage of proof texts justifying why, as she says, Schütz Zell "concludes the psalm with Jesus Christ" (pp. 329–37 of the critical edition, McKee, *Writings*; C8r–D7v in the original pagination). Essentially, this is an explanation for the common Christian tradition of reading the Old Testament in general and the Psalms in particular as being about Jesus Christ. Schütz Zell probably put this

---

138. Everyone without exception: both sexes and every civil or ecclesiastical or social rank, all are equally involved in sin; sin is the condition, not just the acts of sinful behavior. Only by divine grace can this situation be known, and although painful, that knowledge is also the best way to salvation.

series of proof texts together from other sources[139] (it is not typical of the way she ordinarily uses scripture texts), and it may have been added specifically for this publication—*trans.*]

Now Follows the Hundred and Thirtieth Psalm Paraphrased

[130:1] O God, out of the depths of my heart, of all the most inward and spiritually rich power in me, I cry to You now in my great distress. [130:2] Hear my voice, let Your ears be open to me. Take to heart, give heed to, and receive my plea to You, which I make with earnest sighing and weeping. [130:3] If You should regard sins, to reckon and chastise them and therefore not listen to prayers, who could stand before You, or dare to pray for something, much less hope to obtain it?

Refusing to forgive would be contrary to Your accustomed way of acting, which has come down to us from of old, contrary to Your faithfulness and goodness, which have been experienced and known. [130:4] For with You there is much forgiveness, and You never weary in doing good, if only a person fears You and does not despise Your faithfulness and goodness, but builds on them. This truth You have granted me to know; this truth I confess with thanks because I know it and have experienced it in my many afflictions.

[130:5] So I wish now to keep watch for You; yes, my soul should keep watch for what You will to do—with such watching that I may hope in You with my whole heart through the word of Your promise. [130:6a] Yes, indeed, my soul should keep watch in such a way that You will say to her that You are still my God [cf. Ps 42:5–6, 11; 43:5]. [130:6b] This is so, even if indeed the watching goes on from one morning watch to another, from one time to another, from one affliction to another, from one promise to another, from one body to another, yes, from one life to another, and even if we still find the time long. [130:7a] Yes, whoever can believe thus will appropriately be called "Israel," one who overcomes God [cf. Gn 32:28], because he took God at His word: therefore he may hope and will not be put to shame before his enemies.[140]

[130:7b] For with the Lord alone is grace and many and varied ways to redemption in many difficult and secret afflictions, beyond all human knowledge and understanding. [130:8] And He will redeem Israel (the seed

---

139. Schütz Zell may have modeled this on a book by her acquaintance Urbanus Rhegius (ostensibly for his long-suffering wife) to expound Luke 24:27, the point at which the risen Christ explains the (Old Testament) scriptures about His suffering, death, and resurrection.

140. When Jacob was returning to his homeland, an angel came to him one night and wrestled with him until morning; then the angel acknowledged that Jacob had won and gave him a new name, "Israel," which means "he who strives with God" (and prevails). Usually the angel was interpreted as a representation of God and so Schütz Zell concludes that those who keep watch through every trial, trusting in God, will "overcome" God by taking Him at His word.

of Abraham), the guilty, afflicted, distressed, believing sinner, from all his sins, which are a cause, foundation, and power of all afflictions. Amen.

Another Miserere Psalm: In Meditation on Sins

Prayer [51:1–2] O God, be gracious to me according to Your goodness, wipe out and forgive my sins according to Your great mercy. O God, wash me now again and purify me from my sins through the blood of Jesus Christ Your little Lamb. *Lament* [51:3–4a] For I recognize again my misdeeds, and my sin is ever unceasingly before my inward eyes. I cannot forget it, because I have sinned against You Yourself and I have done evil before You (from whom nothing is hidden). *Speech-Narration* [51:4b] Therefore You would also be just in the word of Your law, which You have given and which I have not kept. You may also not be rebuked even if You have tested and judged our thoughts (and see) how gladly we always seek an escape and want to excuse ourselves. *Lament and Confession* So I must confess that You are faithful and I am wicked and lying. [51:5] See, Lord, how could it be otherwise? Indeed I was begotten (*gezeuget*) from sinful seed and my mother also conceived (*empfangen*) me in sin. That sin, however, I, O Lord, have allowed to reign in me—that sin which I could well have killed through Your grace (gift) of the free Spirit. Therefore I am wholly guilty of capriciousness and wantonness before You, for by force I have extinguished Your light, which You have often kindled in me; I have lit my own wit and pleasure in the obstinacy of my wicked desires, and I have walked in that way. *Confession* Therefore it is fair that I have appropriately been abandoned by You and have come into such gnawing worms, suffering, and anguish of my heart, since I did not pay attention to Your law and speech but became their master.

Lament [51:6] O my God! I have gotten myself into this mess, but I can never get out of it without You! But since You, Lord, desire truth, and since (besides that) by Your special mercy You allow me to know that same secret truth, so that I should confess in truth before You and pray to You to forgive my sins—*Prayer* so I, a miserable person, ask You, my Lord and God, from my whole heart and longing, with all the might that You have given to me: turn Your mercy toward me and for the sake of Your reputation do not allow me to lack Your former well-known goodness. Have mercy on me, O God, have mercy on me! *Lament* How completely I have tangled myself up in shameful sins and so shamed myself! *Prayer* But help me, miserable as I am! [51:7] Purify me again, O God, and forgive me again, and wash me from my sins. Cleanse me again through that fully adequate hyssop, the blood of Jesus Christ, Your obedient one in whom You are well pleased [cf. Mt 3:17]. May I enjoy that washing in the blood. Remember the offering that was accomplished by Him on the cross—the offering to You, but for me—for payment and reconciliation.

[51:8] O dear Lord, grant that I may know such joy in my conscience before I go to the grave, where faith will cease and there is no more hope of help [cf. Ps 88:5, 11–12]. *Speech-Narration* While I live here in the flesh, O Lord, I want to give myself over to Your discipline, chastisement, and penance in body and heart and gladly walk before You and myself, shamefaced, fearful, and humbled.

Prayer But, O God, help me! When soul and spirit part company and the flesh shall complete the goal of penance in the suffering of death, may I then have joy and comfort in Your crucified and resurrected Christ. May my sins be wiped out, forgotten, and overcome: before You through Your grace and before me through my faith (which You teach me here under the cross). So then my bones and inward strength, which now are torn apart because of my sins, will be happy. [51:9–12] O dear Lord and God, turn Your countenance away from my sins, but be gracious to me and wipe out all my wickedness. Create in me besides, O God, a clean heart, and give me at last a new and assured spirit. Do not cast me away from Your countenance, do not allow me again to become more godless. Do not take Your Spirit entirely from me because of my sins, but let Him chastise those sins in me and keep me in quiet and repentance, and (so far as it may serve Your honor) let Him also sometimes give me words of comfort. [51:14, 16–17] O God, You are my God and savior. Save me indeed from my sins of bloodguilt, which You know are in me and which I now confess before You.

Speech-Narration I would gladly free myself from them before You, with payment and offering of my body and life as sacrifice. Since, however, that does not please You and is not enough to pay for sins, so I know nothing to bring to You except a broken and quiet heart, a heart that is sad and sorrowful before You because it has so provoked You. *Prayer* So be gracious to me, O Lord, only for the sake of Your good will, Your great name and Your fatherly mercy, in Jesus Christ the holy, innocent, living sacrifice who redeems me from eternal anguish and fear. Amen.

Now follows the Our Father, written in 1532 for two dear God-fearing women of Speyer, namely, Barbara Semler, the wife of Master Hans the Leser, and Elizabeth Bomer, the wife of Gregory the Pfennigmaister. (Both of these men are members of the Imperial Chamber Court in Speyer.)[141]

---

141. Since the emperor of the Holy Roman Empire was elected and did not have the same personal authority there as in his hereditary lands, he had to negotiate with the princes and free imperial cities of the Empire. The context for this negotiation was the imperial chamber court, which dealt with major legal matters of the Empire. One of the most difficult issues facing the court in the first generation of the Protestant Reformation was the conflict between the princes and cities loyal to Rome, with the Emperor Charles V at their head, and those—like Strasbourg!—which had broken or were breaking with Rome. The women Schütz Zell addresses are wives of two of the lesser functionaries of the court, identified here by their administrative titles: Leser (archives) and Pfennigmaister (finances).

With this exposition of the Our Father I sent a letter of consolation, which is too long to include here.

Foreword

I have—as I thought I ought to do—put the confession of faith at the beginning of this Our Father. It was and is right to acknowledge and confess the one to whom one prays and whom one wishes to petition, and I have also used that way and rule here. It is followed by a short address and simple little exposition of the creed: why Christ died and rose for us and will judge us. Also, I briefly explain the Holy Spirit, the church, the communion of the saints, and forgiveness of sins, etc.: all that comes to pass through Christ's work. However, I have not wanted to write this with artfulness and difficulty but only in a completely simple, short, and childlike fashion, as also I was prompted to this writing by children, for whose sake too I wanted to summarize it all together in such a childlike and simple way.

But I ask you please to take to heart one little word, a word that belongs to all devout children: that is the word "Father." What a friendly, pleasant word that is, yes, the most gracious and most comforting that has ever come on earth: it welcomes all requests, makes all friendship, turns aside all punishment, yes, softens all hearts. When this voice cries, the ears quickly hear, as everyone knows who has experienced it. Yes, this also strengthens a person to suffer all afflictions in all patience, as one also sees sometimes among children. When one strikes the other, the one who was struck says, "I will tell my father"—with great hope that his father will take the matter to heart and avenge it. There are many such examples, which God has used also in the prophets and Christ in the Gospel.

Because of His great love, He has wanted to be called a "Father" but especially first through Jesus Christ [cf. Jn 14:6]. For among His former folk [Israel] He did not often call Himself "Father"; indeed it was rare. He called Himself their Lord and God, and His might went before them. When, however, His love broke through and was manifested through His child Jesus, then He wanted to have another name, as He also wanted to have another people. He had previously spoken of this in the prophet: "In that time I want to make another covenant with them, not as I did with their fathers, but I will write My law in their hearts" [cf. Jer 31:31–33]. And in the second book of Kings: "I will be a Father to him and he shall be My son; if he indeed sins, I will beat him with the rod I use for children but I will not take My mercy from him" [2 Sm 7:14–15]. All that is now said about the new people who will be under Christ; to them He has called Himself a Father, by and on account of Christ.¹⁴² Therefore Moses and all the prophets have only said, "The Lord your God," [Ex 20:2]; that name is lordly and fearsome, and so the people should fear and be in awe of Him.

But since Jesus Christ came He has brought the name "Father" from heaven with Him, along with the work of a Father, which is His love, as John says, "God so loved the world that He gave His Son for it" [Jn 3:16]. Therefore, throughout the Gospel Christ always called God "Father," also "our Father" and us His children. Also in the last address at the Supper [cf. Jn 13, 14–17] when He talked a lot about the Father to comfort them all, He called them also "children." "You dear children," He said and told them that they also were God's children; so He said to them, "In my Father's house there are many dwellings, and I go hence to prepare a place for you. I am going to my God and your God, to my Father and your Father" [Jn 14:2, 20:17b]. He has also taught them and us to pray: "Our Father in heaven" [Mt 6:9] and not our "God" or "Lord." By that He wanted to strengthen and increase our trust and certainty in prayer.

For no lord with his servant and no woman with her maid is so quick and kindly to listen and attend as the father and the mother do with their child, as the proverb says, "What does not come *from* the heart also does not come *to* the heart." A woman who has never had a child, never experienced or felt the pain of birth and the love of feeding a nursling, cannot understand. Who would love, treat kindly, and have compassion for helpless children as the true mother can and does? So also God: with His former folk [Israel] He did not want to be called a "Father" but a God and Lord, because He created us in His image intending for us to obey and serve Him and be of like mind with Himself. But we fell away, we disobeyed Him but obeyed the serpent [cf. Gn 1:26–27, 3:1ff]. So all God could show us was wrath and punishment as a Lord and zealous God. For He did not experience the bitter and hard labor of a mother, He created us by His word without work, created us pure, in obedience to Him, to honor Him, and therefore He could have no pity on us.¹⁴³ For after Adam's fall, He was no longer so

---

142. Repeatedly in this section, Schütz Zell contrasts the situation of God's people in the Old Testament with the more favored ones in the New. Evidence that this text was not revised for publication is found in the citation of 2 Samuel as "2 Kings" here, something Schütz Zell was still doing in the early 1530s (see "Hymnbook" at n. 59). In discussing Psalm 51, where she explains the context of David's sin with Bathsheba, Schütz Zell names the book 2 Samuel, a change she apparently made in the late 1540s (see above n. 130).

143. Schütz Zell contrasts the first creation by God's word in Genesis with the new birth by Christ's labor on the cross; she sees the former as easier (an interesting touch by a woman who had borne children) and also as less intimate.

kindly toward us, but He was a God who punished transgressions, for He is not like us: He is God without any imperfection. That is why He could not accept Adam's excuse but cast him out of paradise as punishment [Gn 1:26–27, 3:23–24].

But the grace of God through Jesus Christ is the true mother, that Christ who is in God and God in Him [Jn 14:11]. Christ became a human being (*des menschen son*) like us, and therefore He is also called Emmanuel, God with us [Is 7:14, Mt 1:23], for He has come to us in our flesh. With great anguish He bore (*geboren*) us in grace or brought us back to grace, such anguish that He also poured out bloody sweat over the effort, when He said, "My soul is troubled even to death, and I must be baptized" [Lk 22:44, 12:50; Mt 26:38], that is, "I must go to the cross: oh, what I anguish I feel!" He also demonstrated that anguish in Jn 12[:27] and said, "Now my soul shrinks back! What should I say? 'Father, help me out of this hour'? But I am come to this hour for this purpose." And He gives the analogy of bitter labor and says, "A woman when she bears a child has anguish and sorrow" [Jn 16:21], and He applies all of this to His suffering, in which He bore (*geboren*) us with such effort and pain, nourished us and made us alive, gave us to drink from His breast and side with water and blood, as a mother nurses her child [cf. Jn 19:34].[144]

He has also known our timidity and borne our suffering, for He emptied Himself of His divinity, humbled Himself and took on the form of a servant [Phil 2:6–8], in which He was tempted by the devil and various kinds of harm. Therefore the apostle also says, "We do not have a high priest who cannot have compassion for our weakness but one who has been tempted in every way like us but without sin. Therefore let us approach with confidence the throne of grace," that is, Christ Jesus, who is the true throne of grace and mediator [Heb 4:15–16; cf. 1 Tm 2:5] and the only Son born (*eingeboren*) of God whom the Father loves, and God loves us in Him. For through the Beloved we are all beloved, for through the Son God has

---

144. This section explores the metaphor of Christ as the mother of believers. Maternal language and imagery for Christ were not uncommon in some medieval piety; Cisterians could call Jesus (and their abbots) "mother." The image of Christ feeding Christians with the blood and water flowing from His side (Jn 19:34) was often visually represented as a reference to the sacrament of the Mass, and sometimes the blood could be interpreted as milk. Most medieval allusions to Jesus as mother were gentle in tone, however, and did not give much attention to the pains of labor in John 16:21 (as Schütz Zell does). See Carolyn Walker Bynum, "Jesus as Mother and the Abbot as Mother: Some Themes in Twelfth-Century Cisterian Writing," in *Jesus as Mother: Studies of Spirituality in the High Middle Ages* (Berkeley: University of California Press, 1982), 113, 115, 120ff, 132f. For Schütz Zell's use, see McKee, "Katharina Schütz Zell and the 'Our Father.'"

given us birth (*geboren*) again and given the Son birth (*geboren*) from eternity [cf. Jn 3:3; 14:21].

It is like the way a grandfather loves the child of his child and also the father and the child are his heirs because the child is born (*geboren*) of his child.[145] So also God is our Father, yes, our grandfather, and we are His heirs through Jesus Christ His Son, through whom we are given birth (*geboren*) again by God as new people [cf. Jn 3:3; 2 Cor 5:17]. And so we dare confidently to cry out and say, "Abba, dear Father," through the adopting Spirit whom we have received from Christ, the Spirit who assures us that we are God's children and fellow heirs of God with Christ, as the apostle has clearly taught in his letter to the Romans and all his letters [cf. Rm 8:15–17; Gal 4:6, 3:26; Eph 1:11; Phil 2:15; Col 1:12]. As also all the other apostles have taught [cf. Jas 2:5]. And John in all his writings always calls God our Father and us His beloved little children [cf. Jn 1:12; 1 Jn 3:1, 2, 9; 5:1–2].

In summary, Christ Himself teaches us and says that God is our Father and we are His children through Him [Christ], therefore He also wants to be called our brother—and this is said explicitly three times in the scriptures. The first is in the law; Moses says, "God will raise up one of your brethren; to Him should you hearken" [Dt 18:15]. The next time is in the Psalms; David says in the Spirit of Christ, "I will make Your name known to my brethren" [Ps 22:22a]. The third is in the Gospel; when He was resurrected, Christ said to the women, "Go hence and tell it to my brothers" [Mt 28:10]. For in the law there is terror and curse; the people fled from the mountain and did not want to hear the voice of God or look at the face of Moses, for he bore the law. As also the people said to Moses, "You hearken to the Lord and tell us, that we may not die" [Ex 20:18–19; cf. 34:29–30]. Therefore God sent His Son, through whom He spoke with us. The Son bears truth and grace; He put Himself under the law in order to fulfill it and to free us from under it and to lead us out. He took our flesh on Himself and thus became our brother, that He might lead us through Himself to God so that we might hearken to Him [cf. Jn 3:16, 1:14; Gal 4:4–5; Mt 17:5].

For in Him there is no terror or curse, but comfort and access [to God]. Therefore the Spirit of Christ rightly and truly says in the psalm, "'I will proclaim Your name (that is, Your honor and might, Your favor, grace, and peace) to my brothers' [Ps 22:22]. I, Christ, I and not Moses am a brother

---

145. The image of God as grandfather because Christ is the believer's "mother" would appeal to a child. Despite the central focus on Christ's work, however, it is clear that the whole trinity is necessarily involved in the believer's salvation.

who calls and gathers in kindly fashion; Moses is a judge who drives and hastens on. Moses threw down the tables of the law in great anger; I lift them up on the cross with great patience. Moses struck and killed many thousands and judged sin with punishment; I, however, was struck and killed, and I give my blood for many, and so I bear away and pay the punishment of sin" [cf. Ex 2:14, 32:19, 27–29; Acts 7:27, 35; Nm 25:5ff; Mt 26:28]. Thus Christ is a true faithful brother, as He Himself says, "Greater faithfulness and love has no one than to give his life for his friend" [Jn 15:13]—as He did! Therefore, He is appropriately proclaimed and called a "brother" in the law and Psalms. Of that He also wanted to make us more certain, now a third time, when He said to the women at the grave, "Fear not; go hence and announce to my brothers that I am resurrected and live, and that I am going to my Father and your Father" [cf. Mt 28:10; Jn 20:17].

What else is this? When Christ made peace for us with God the Father through Himself, when He suffered to do that and rose again alive and announced that to us through the women who saw Him, by doing that He gave to them and us a pledge that He is our brother. He announced to us the will and name of His Father and promised us His Father's kingdom, which He also won for us through His death and confirmed and made that victory strong with His mighty resurrection. For us He brought forth in lordly fashion the victory and triumph over sin, death, the devil, and hell and showed Himself to His own for forty days. Henceforth He also called us His brothers, and His Father our Father, that we may have part and inheritance with Him in God's kingdom. So we remain in His love, and God will give us what we ask the Father in His name [cf. Acts 1:3; Rm 8:17; Jn 14:13]. Thus, being comforted and happy, we should pray and call out, "Our Father in heaven . . ." [Mt 6:9], for He loves us and knows what we need before we ask, as Christ says, "I do not say to you that I will pray for you, for the Father Himself loves you because you have loved me and believed that I came from God" [Jn 16:26–27]. So I ask you indeed to take this very comforting word to heart. Never let it go out of your heart; build and place all your prayers on it (like a house built on a rock). Pray with confidence and faith as a child calls on his father, so He cannot and will not turn His countenance away from you [cf. Mt 7:24–25; Ps 27:9]. As He Himself says in the prophet, "As little as the mother forgets her suckling child, so little can I forget you; and if she indeed forgets her child, so can I not forget you" [Is 49:15].

Further, let us also take to heart the [second] little word [implied here] "children." If He is our Father, then we must also be His children, for He says there, "I will be a Father to him," and immediately afterwards He says, "And he will be my son" [2 Sm 7:14]. What does it mean to be a son and child? Clearly it means to be begotten (*erzeuget*) or born (*geboren*) of Him[146] and to behave in accordance with that birth: obeying the Father's will and pleasure, remaining in His house, not following bad company, acting with all honesty, faithfulness, and honorableness, and not spending the Father's goods uselessly or capriciously but faithfully keeping the other children together and providing for them in their need.

And now we take the third little word [after the pair "Father" and "children"]; He says "Our" and not "My" Father. What faithfulness, love, fellowship, peace, forgiveness, and all that siblings should have with each other ought to come from such a spiritual reflection! Clearly you should be led onward by the working of the Holy Spirit, to direct your life, and live and behave with other people so that you may be beloved children of God. And so you may receive the unfading inheritance with Jesus Christ from the Father of all comfort in the assurance of His Holy Spirit. Amen.

Here follows the confession of faith, which is a root of prayer and precedes it:

I believe in one God, the Father Almighty, Creator of heaven and earth. And in Jesus Christ His (only) natural (*eingeboren*) Son, our Lord, who was conceived (*empfanngen*) by the Holy Spirit, born (*geboren*) of the Virgin Mary, suffered under the judge Pontius Pilate, was crucified, dead, and buried and descended to hell; on the third day He rose again from the dead, ascended into heaven, sitting on the right hand of God His Father the Almighty; from thence He will come again here to judge the living and the dead. I believe in God the Holy Spirit, one holy Christian (*Christliche*) church,[147] the communion of the saints, the forgiveness and pardon of sins, the resurrection of all flesh, and eternal life.

Now a prayer based on this confession:

Almighty eternal God and Father of all mercy [cf. 2 Cor 1:3], whom we have now confessed by the knowledge that Your Holy Spirit has worked in us: You, O God, who are by Your own power, strength, and might, without beginning or end, with no other above or beside You. There is no other from whom help or comfort may be sought, but our faith, fear, love, honor, service, and all are in Your name alone. You are also the Father of Your holy word in eternal birth, through whom You made us and everything, He who

---

146. Note that Schütz Zell uses both "masculine" and "feminine" words for the way God is Father to believers.

147. This was the normal translation in German, not a peculiarly Protestant note. The intended sense of "catholic" is "universal," and at this time the church centered in Rome was not specifically called "Roman Catholic" but (as in this book) Protestants usually said "Roman" or "papal."

is with You and who with You is eternal, through whom and for whose sake also our fathers received from You life, food and drink, clothing and everything. You care for us and save us from temporal and eternal evil. You are also almighty: of Your (own) eternal and divine strength, might, eternally undefeatable power, foresight, and holy counsel You are Creator and beginning of all things, who made fast the heavens, founded the earth, and divided it from the water, who created the birds of the heaven, the fish in the water, and living animals in the field. You also made man (*den Menschen*) in Your likeness and set him as ruler over all this [cf. Gn 1:6ff, 20ff]—an order that no one can break against Your will and none can maintain without Your help and will. But by means of everything that is visible, everyone should learn to know You, to love and serve You and adhere to You.

We have also confessed Jesus Christ: He is the only natural (*eingeborner*) Son and the same Word who was in the beginning with and in You, through whom everything was made, and in Him is life. He is our Lord and anointed king, pioneer and Prince of Faith [cf. Jn 3:3, 1:1–4; Heb 12:2]. He was promised to us by You in the prophets and given and came from You into the body of the virgin without any man's (*männlichen*) will, only through the work of the pure Holy Spirit and her obedience to Your word. This was hidden from human understanding but pleasing before Your eyes. There He became true flesh and blood from her purified and sanctified flesh, according to the promise of David and Abraham, and without any harm to her virginity He was born of her into this (earthly) exile to serve and help us [cf. Jn 1:13–14]. He was tested with many sufferings and troubles but held firm in Your will and also proclaimed that to us to the end. After our fall and merited death, He brought us again to life by the sacrifice of His blood, which He brought to You for us on the wood (tree) of the cross, and He became the curse for us—since it was on the wood (tree) that our first father Adam disobeyed You and sinned against You because he wanted to live and to know as God does, a disobedience that has continued up to us [cf. Gal 3:13; Gn 3:1ff].[148]

---

148. According to 1 Corinthians 15:45, the created Adam who sinned was "the first Adam," and Christ who came to reverse the effects of sin is "the second Adam." The play on the "wood" of the forbidden tree and the "wood" of the cross was a common tradition. It is worth noting, however, that Schütz Zell never mentions the very common topos of Eve-and-Mary (that is, the one "causing" the Fall, the other "reversing" it); she focuses on Adam for the Fall, and Christ for the Redemption. Here Schütz Zell, like many other first-generation Protestants, follows the tradition that Mary remained perpetually a virgin and follows tradition in reading John 1:13 as "the will of man" (*männlichen*, meaning male person), although the Greek is not gender specific.

But our second Adam [Christ] was obedient to You and reconciled us to You on the wood. He humbled Himself and died as a man (*mensch*); He also bore penance for us and suffered in the body that You had prepared for Him. Through that He freed us from the prison of the hellish bond of sins and justified us in His resurrection and brought us to living resurrection and overcame eternal death. He also opened the closed-up heaven of Your favor and grace and set Himself as the first at Your right hand to prepare a place for us. And He will come again to gather us there, yes, all those who give themselves to Him and remain in Him, and to punish and show His power in those who have torn themselves from Him and have not remained in His life [cf. 1 Cor 15:20; Jn 14:2–3; Rm 9:22ff].

We have also confessed God the Holy Spirit who is Your strength and breath, who proceeds from You and Your Son to make alive everything that You have created.[149] Through Him also all are won to know You and Your Son Christ and to live according to Your will, driven and led by the ardent fire of love. He is also a teacher and dwells with every believer and is a witness to Jesus Christ and His members; therefore also You sent Him [the Holy Spirit] to His [Christ's] disciples visibly as a comfort and counselor of the Christian church, by which comfort and counsel the saints and children of God have fellowship with each other [cf. Jn 14:16–17, 26; 16:7ff]. As the key and treasure of Christ in His blood, there is the forgiveness and remission of sins, being purified through the Holy Spirit, the Spirit who also appeared over Christ (in His baptism) and awakened Him from death, and who will also gather all of us together with Him again. In and through the Holy Spirit You signal the dawn (provide a sign) that we will all be resurrected alive in our flesh and will live with You eternally. Then You will be all in all, when our Lord Your Christ hands over the kingdom to You [cf. Job 19:25–26; 1 Cor 15:28]. In such a life-giving Spirit, who proceeds from You and Your Son, we pray and further call upon You, in Your name and through Your dear and holy child Jesus, as He Himself also taught us. And we say from the heart:

"Our Father in Heaven"

Have mercy on us, Your poor children on earth. You are in heaven, which is Your footstool, high and powerful over all authority; also Your child Jesus is set at Your right hand, and all His enemies are cast under His feet. We, however, are on this earth, which is a stool for Your feet: we are Your poor abandoned orphans, scattered in exile on an unhealthy pasture like sheep without a shepherd [cf. Is 66:1; Ps 110:1; Jn 14:18; Mt 9:36]. Weak and sor-

---

149. Here and below the language echoes the Nicene Creed: "I believe in the Holy Spirit, the Lord and Giver of life, Who proceeds from the Father and the Son . . ."

rowing, we are also in the power of the wicked, under their rods and all kinds of abuse. Yes, dear Father, have mercy on us, remember us, do not leave us as orphans who are so far from You, our Father, and our fatherland, in a foreign land under many enemies of our souls and bodies.

But You are our Father and the true Father above all who are called father; therefore we cry, groan, and beg to come to You and ask You to ward off such enemies as prevent us from coming to You. You are heavenly and spiritual, but we are earthly and carnal, sold under sin with our wicked appetites and whole person, since we are by nature children of wrath [cf. Rm 7:14; Eph 2:3]. O dear Father, destroy all of that in us by Your Holy Spirit, and make us children of grace. Take from us the earth, give us heaven, that we may nevermore be earthly but heavenly and perfect, as You, dear Father, are heavenly and perfect; that You may thus truly be our dear Father, as You are the Father of Christ Jesus, and that we may be Your dear obedient children, as Christ Jesus was Your child and obedient to You even to death on the cross [cf. Mt 5:48; Phil 2:8]. Do this so that the lament in Your holy prophet may not come upon us, where You say, "A son should honor his father, and a servant his master; if I am your Father, where is my honor? If I am your Lord, where is the fear of me? There is no one among you who has any cause or means to close me out, yet you despise my name" [Mal 1:6, 10]. You also complain, "I have brought up and reared children, and they have despised me; an ox knows its master, and a donkey the manger of its lord, but my people do not want to acknowledge me" [Is 1:2–3]. Therefore, O God, make it so! That we may in truth acknowledge You as our Father and Lord and may again raise up Your covenant, which we have broken, that we may turn back to You and love You not with words of the tongue but in deed and in truth [cf. 1 Jn 3:18].

"That Your Name May Be Hallowed"

Grant, O dear Father, that we may be new people, and obedient to You, with our evil appetites destroyed so they may not break out in word or deed and we may not increase Your wrath, but that we may live according to Your commands, customs, and just ways. By that everyone may see and acknowledge that we are Your people and children and You are our God and Father; so Your holy name will be honored among us and through us it will also be highly praised and widely confessed among others.

"Your name be hallowed."[150] It will also be holy in us, that is, Your (only) natural (*geborner*) Son Jesus Christ, who is the true name, image, and being of Your hidden Godhead, through whom You have revealed Yourself to the world

---

150. Here the hallowing of God's name is focused on Jesus, probably with a polemical intent since Protestants maintained that the Roman church did not really honor Christ properly

and have allowed Your mercy to be seen and made Your will known to us [cf. Col 1:15]. You have also given Him a name above all names, that in His name we might pray to You and the Holy Spirit would be given to us and that through faith in His name all people might benefit and become children of God. That name is also holy: in it the nations hope and receive forgiveness of sins; everyone must kneel to that name, and there is no other name given to human beings (*den menschen*) by which we may be saved [cf. Phil 2:9–10; Acts 4:12]. O God and Father, help us to hallow this name, to magnify and honor it, to set it apart and distinguish it from others, to call on it, love, and confess it above all names, that name which is Jesus Christ, who saves His people from their sins [cf. Mt 1:21]. Grant also, dear Father, that we may not boast of Your name without cause (in a false hypocritical folly and show of praising Your grace and righteousness); grant that we may not enjoy being called by the name of Your Christ while still conducting our whole life contrary to it and sinning against the other words of Your commandments. If we did that our name would be struck from the book of life [cf. Rv 3:5]. Even if we said, "Have we not done many deeds in Your name?" You would answer, "I do not know you, depart from me" [Mt 7:22–23]. But grant us to acknowledge Your holy name, to honor it, to call upon it and confess it in truth, that we may be saved.

Grant also, O Lord and Father, that we may not swear by Your holy name falsely, in lying fashion, or unnecessarily [cf. Ex 20:7; Dt 5:11].[151] Let us not speak or conduct ourselves in a mocking or scandalous way toward You or Your name, word, and work, or also Your whole kingdom, so that we may not cause anyone to be scandalized against You and Your child Jesus or Your name to be slandered through us. But grant that we may conduct our lives so that Your name may be acknowledged and praised in us, that people may see our conduct and repent [amend their lives (*sich bessern*)] and You, Father in heaven, may be praised by that [cf. Mt 18:6; Mal 1:11–12]. Grant that we may thus overcome the world with its desires, that our names may not be struck from Your book of life but may stand written in heaven and also be confessed by Christ our Lord before You and Your angels [cf. 1 Jn 2:15–16, 4:4; Rv 3:5].

"Your Kingdom Come to Us"

O dear Father, grant that all that the enemy has in us may be killed and driven out; that we may be the children of Your kingdom and not cast out;

---

because they did not pray in His name alone but linked many other names of saints with His in their prayers; see "Hymnbook" at nn. 53 and 55.

151. Here there is no absolute rejection of swearing, that is, Schütz Zell does not suggest prohibiting all oaths, as many Anabaptists did, but only that they be made according to God's will.

that we may not fail to hear because we do not pay attention, when today we hear Your voice through Jesus Christ as He says, "Repent [make amends for your sins (*bessert eüch*)], the kingdom of God has come near" [Mt 4:17].[152] O God, help us to recognize and flee from the kingdom of the devil, to recognize and let go of the perishable kingdom of the world, for both are enemies that oppose You. But may we seek with seriousness and not hypocrisy and find Your good, enduring, imperishable kingdom and its righteousness [cf. Mt 6:33], that we may be admitted to it and become citizens and receive wisdom and all that we need from You.

O dear God, help us: we are so far from Your kingdom! Grant that we may not be so casual and stiff-necked toward You and Your kingdom, so that when You come again You may not judge us to be Your enemies who would not allow You to rule over us [cf. Lk 19:27]. But grant that we may receive and obey You from the heart and be the folk of Your kingdom; that through Your Holy Spirit You may rule and be Lord in our hearts, souls, bodies, and consciences; that Your word and commandment may live in us. For You are the King of honored lords, and Lord of the true kingdom, whom we all must acknowledge, seek, honor, fear, and love, to whom alone we should pray and to whom we should adhere as our true Lord, Ruler, and King.

"Your Will Be Done on Earth As in Heaven"

Oh, dear Father, grant that with our whole heart we may give ourselves to full obedience to Your will and confess that Your will is best of all so that we may break and hinder our evil will, which is still only inclined toward the flesh—which is why it also does not bring forth children of God. Help us to put off the old person who is born from the will of the flesh and put on the new person who is born (*geboren*) from God, according to Your image, the way You first created us [cf. Jn 1:13; Gn 1:27].

Grant us also, O God and Father, a pure heart and willing spirit so we may hear what You say to us and may obey it and not turn away from You and to wickedness. But write Your law in our hearts and grant us to acknowledge Your will and pay heed to Your wisdom, which otherwise is hidden. By that will and wisdom may we direct our life so that You may be pleased

---

152. The traditional Vulgate of this text said "do penance"; the Greek is *metanoeite*, "turn around/change your mind." The Vulgate translation supported the Roman sacrament of penance, but all Protestants rejected that meaning. Luther's German Bible kept the older language (*thut busse*), but the Zurich translation used *besserend euch*, which could mean "repent" or "make amends." Although Schütz Zell clearly knew Luther's translation and used it (see "Apologia" at n. 16), the fact that here (and above) she follows the more ethically oriented Zurich wording is an indication of her Reformed stance with its greater emphasis on sanctification. For references, see McKee, *Writings*, 352, n. 161.

with us—as You are pleased with all the blessed ones in heaven. There Your will alone pleases all of them and it is done in them [cf. Ps 51:10; Jer 31:33; 1 Cor 27; Ps 147:11]. Yes, dear Father, grant that Your will may also be done in us on earth as it is in heaven that we may live according to Your will and commandments, according to the way of the Spirit and not of the flesh. Yes, may we not strive against and wound Your Holy Spirit, but may we humble ourselves and give ourselves over into Your mighty hand [cf. Mt 12:31–32].

Grant us help also, O God and Father, that we may turn to You with our whole heart and give ourselves obediently to Your will, even to the cross if (through Your holy counsel and providence) You allow that to come upon us. If You strike us down because of our sins, may we not separate ourselves from You, deny, murmur, and wound You, like Judas, the children of Israel, and the thief on the left hand [cf. Mt 26:14–16; Ex 15:24; Lk 23:39]. But may we, with Peter, suffer the rod of discipline from You, reflecting on our sins, and may we weep for them from the heart and henceforth live in Your will [cf. Mt 26:75]. With the thief on the right side, may we acknowledge and confess our sin and Your just judgment and with him call to Christ on the cross and say, "Lord, I am guilty, but You are righteous; remember me in Your Kingdom" [Lk 23:40–42].

"And Give Us Our Daily Bread Today"

O dear Father, we call to You as Your children to their faithful Father who wills them good, who has in His hand food and nourishment for soul and body, who cannot deny His children who earnestly seek this from Him. We are now hungry in our souls, and so from the heart we pray You to feed us without ceasing and without delay, today and always, with Your holy word through which we learn Your will and may come to the true knowledge of You and of Him whom You sent, Jesus Christ, and may be strengthened in faith toward You [cf. Jn 17:3]. You say, "Man (*mensch*) does not live by bread alone but by every word that comes from the mouth of God" [Dt 8:3; Mt 4:4]; so do not deprive us of such food but satisfy our hunger.[153]

---

153. The discussion of "daily bread" tended to reveal Protestant views more than the other parts of the Prayer. The Roman tradition commonly read "daily bread" as the Mass, although some reformers like Erasmus identified it as "heavenly doctrine" or "spiritual bread"; all, however, agreed that it was not ordinary physical food. Luther's mark was a strong emphasis on the word and preaching, but at first he also continued the idea of spiritual food and made a brief reference to ordinary food. In 1527, Bucer followed the late fourth-century church father Chrysostom in identifying "daily bread" as ordinary food and all necessities of daily life. By 1529 Luther had dropped the reference to "spiritual bread" and put more emphasis on ordinary food. (For an overview see Elsie Anne McKee, "John Calvin's Teaching on the Lord's Prayer," in *The Lord's Prayer: Perspectives for Reclaiming Christian Prayer*, ed. Daniel L. Migliore [Grand

The Lay Reformer, Teacher, and Pastor 163

Dear Father, grant to us also wise, faithful preachers, who are faithful stewards [cf. Mt 24:45], who will not preach to us their own inclinations but will proclaim Your word, revealed from Your mouth through Jesus Christ, and who at the right time will spread forth that same appropriate food. Oh, dear Father, give them also a willing spirit and strong faith so they may not become listless, dull, and tired in their work and then, because of that, their work comes to be reviled and ungratefully received on earth. Grant that they may not therefore give up and think to go away and abandon us, as if they were working to no purpose.[154] But rather let them be like faithful servants to whom the householder earnestly commended his children and relatives, and to whom he gave command to direct the children and relatives and correct all disobedience [cf. Mt 24:45]. Let them bear abuse and suffering patiently to the end in the certain hope for holy perseverance, and let them conquer in faith.

Grant them also to maintain peace and unity among themselves and a common understanding of Your truth.[155] Take all pride, tendency to division, quarreling, and brawling from them, things that serve to harm their souls and ours, and bind them together in the bonds of peace and godly unity [cf. Eph 4:3], as also our Lord Jesus Christ Your dear Son prayed and said, "Father, I will that they may be one, as You and I are one, You in me

---

Rapids, Mich.: William B. Eerdmans Press, 1993], 88–106 at 100ff.) In her general distribution of emphasis Schütz Zell follows the revised exposition of Luther. The first and greatest weight falls on preaching; Luther discusses preachers but the lay theologian also gives significant attention to the hearers. When she treats the Supper, however, Schütz Zell focuses on the prior fellowship necessary for right celebration and the love that should flow out of the Supper, concerns that are characteristic of the Reformed tradition, and her language about the communion is also Reformed.

154. The description of ministers makes it clear that their primary role is as preachers and pastors. The main liturgy of the Roman church, the Mass, did not require either a sermon or even the presence of parishioners (see "Hymnbook" at n. 45). The Protestant liturgy was necessarily corporate, and clergy could indeed be discouraged if no one listened to them distributing the word by preaching.

155. Schütz Zell may well have had in mind the divisions between Luther and his followers and Zwingli and his. The latter had met in 1529 at Marburg for a colloquy sponsored by Philip of Hesse (with Bucer's help) to seek to reconcile the two groups' different views of the Lord's Supper, at least enough for them to make common cause against Roman opponents. Although the participants agreed on fourteen of the fifteen points at issue, their disagreement on the fifteenth separated the two parties even further. Schütz Zell wrote to Luther when she heard of the dispute, rebuking his lack of love. Her letter is lost, but Luther's actions and his polite acknowledgment of her letter, written in January 1531 (only about a year before this exposition of the Prayer), indicate that for him in this case doctrine took precedence over love. It is apparent below (see n. 158) that Schütz Zell's view of the Supper was closer to Zwingli's than to the (developed) Lutheran teaching, but her complaint to Luther was about the lack of love between the two parties, not the doctrine. See McKee, *Life and Thought*, 79–81.

and I in You, that they also may thus be one in us" [Jn 17:21]. Grant that to them for our good, O dear Father.

Grant that they may not be found to be shepherds of useless idols, but much rather may they be wise, scripture-learned and faithful stewards, who distribute appropriate food at the right time [Mt 24:45].[156] Thereby they themselves lead an honorable, disciplined, responsible life, ornamented with faith, humility, patience, chastity, mercy, peace, and all godliness, so that they do not hide their faith, teaching, and life under a bushel, but set them openly in the house as a light by which we all can see. Thus they may be the salt of the earth and may salt all things and make them healthy with sound teaching and keep them alive [cf. Gal 5:22; Mt 5:13, 15–16].

Grant also that we poor people may not despise that teaching but that, with hungry souls and great thanks, from our hearts we may seek, hear, and receive it and thus be taught, fed, and satisfied by Your grace and wholly given to Your will, so that we may be able to recognize and eat the right living Word and bread that came from heaven from You, that is, the Word of Your power who was with You from the beginning and has given life to all creatures.[157] That bread and word is Jesus Christ Your holy Son [cf. Jn 6:35, 1:1, 4, 14; Mt 26:45], whom You have given and sent to us, who came in the flesh for our sake and whom You gave over into the hands of sinners, even to death, for us. O dear Father, grant that we may learn to recognize that same Jesus Christ, the living Word and bread who rightly feeds, and that we may grow into full knowledge. Grant also that, with a lively spirit and faith, we may truly eat His flesh, which is the true bread given by You from heaven, which strengthens human hearts, and may truly drink His blood, which is the true drink and makes the human heart glad. Do this that He may abide in us and we may abide in Him and not die, but may eat this

---

156. This is an implicit polemic against Roman priests. Protestants considered the Mass idolatrous because it was understood as a sacrifice offered to God by the priest (something no human being could do) and efficacious without faith simply by being enacted (*opus operatum*). Protestants also insisted that no celebration of the Lord's Supper could take place without preaching (plus the presence and participation of at least a number of parishioners: the Reformed normally said that every adult believer in attendance should commune), so here the "appropriate food" would be the preaching of the word, or both preaching and the Supper together.

157. Schütz Zell's language of eating and drinking Christ's flesh and blood here could in principle apply either to preaching or to the Lord's Supper. Since she moves on below to talk of sharing in the Supper, the intent here is apparently spiritual eating (through preaching). Following a famous interpretation of John 6 by the fourth- and fifth-century church father Augustine, which Schütz Zell later cites in her argument with Rabus, Protestants generally (particularly Reformed) could speak of feeding on Christ by faith, that is, apart from the Supper. For exact references see McKee, *Life and Thought*, 293–94.

bread and through it may be raised up at the last day and live forever [cf. Jn 6:54–56; Ps 104:15; Jn 17:23, 11:24].

Grant that in this way we may be assured of Your grace and kingdom through the pledge and seal of Your Spirit, who also assures our spirit that we are Your children, fed and satisfied by You, that no other food may give us joy than Your Christ, grace, and eternal heir. Grant that we also may no longer hunger or thirst for the inconstant, unsatisfying world, with all its goods, joys, and honors, which are all a delusion and evil in comparison with Your wisdom, but that we may only hunger for Your wisdom, righteousness, sanctification, and redemption, hunger that You also will satisfy in Christ alone [cf. 2 Cor 1:22; Rm 8:15–16; 1 Cor 1:30].

Grant also, O holy Father, that as we acknowledge You and Him whom You sent, Jesus Christ [cf. Jn 17:3], and as we have received Him in faith and through Him have given ourselves to You in obedience as also being Your children and have offered You our bodies, and as we have found our life in His death and His death truly lives in our hearts—grant then that we also may be worthy to come together to celebrate the memorial of Your love and the obedience of Jesus Christ, to break the bread and to drink the cup of thanksgiving, to be fed in remembrance of Him, that it may be the communion of the body and blood of Jesus Christ for the forgiveness of our sins, in the communion of the saints. And so we may celebrate a living memorial of His death and proclaim it until He comes again, and in the Supper we may truly confess that His body is there given and broken for us and the record of our sins is wiped out and hung on the cross [cf. 1 Cor 11:17, 24–27, 10:16; Col 2:14].[158]

---

158. After some changes from Luther's first anti-Roman teachings in the early 1520s, the Lutheran view of the Supper was established in the Augsburg Confession of 1530; this states that (to receive grace) one must commune in the actual body and blood of Jesus Christ, which are "in, with, and under" the bread and wine. The theological reasoning was that because His humanity and divinity share their characteristics ("communication of idioms"), Christ's body is able to be everywhere that the sacrament is celebrated (the doctrine of "ubiquity"). Although Zwingli's earliest anti-Roman statements were not too dissimilar from Luther's, the Zwinglian position on the presence of Christ in the Supper developed in a very different direction. For Zwingli, the body of Jesus Christ is in heaven and the Lord's Supper is a memorial of Christ's Passion ("Do this in remembrance of me"), a thanksgiving for that salvation, and a pledge that Christians share together as a witness to their faith. Real feeding on Jesus the bread from heaven is spiritual, by faith, and not physical, by mouth. To the Lutheran mind this view of the Supper was a denial of the reality of the eating and thus endangered grace/salvation. To the Zwinglian mind, the Lutheran idea that Christ's two natures shared characteristics ("mixed" the two natures) so that the humanity could be everywhere at once compromised the nature of His humanity (because a human being can only be in one place at a time) and thus endangered grace/salvation. Schütz Zell does not deal explicitly with the argument, but her language of memorial and thanksgiving and fellowship of love is close to that of Zwingli—or the Luther of 1520—and elsewhere she sharply rejects the developed Lutheran view; see "Schwenckfeld" at nn. 45–47.

So burning love will also be kindled in us, and we will celebrate the living memorial and communion in Jesus Christ with our fellow believers. We will also willingly give ourselves obediently to bear the cross, to suffer with Christ all kinds of abuse, exile, poverty, and death. As Christ gave up Himself on the cross to pay for us and wagered His soul in death for us, so also may we offer ourselves for all people and brothers, Your disciples, our brothers and sisters, in their accidents, exile, poverty, sickness, and all need: to stand by them, to counsel and help them in the face of sin, poverty, exile, and all affliction, with our goods, honor, body, and life. So we may show and prove that we believe that Jesus Christ did this for us and that (as His deed was for us) so also ours should be for others as He commanded. So we may show that we are all one body, like many grains of corn in one loaf of bread, and Christ the head of us all [cf. Jn 15:12; Eph 4:15].[159]

O dear Father, grant that we may also be truly fed and strengthened with this bread so that we may not eat the bread of the Lord unworthily, to our judgment, and be guilty of the body and blood of Jesus Christ, but that we may be able to discern His body [cf. 1 Cor 11:27, 29] and not abandon or despise His members, but forgive, love, build up, help, and give them food and drink, as Christ has done for us.[160] O dear Father, grant that we may well prove whether we have faith in the Son of God and the bond of a good conscience through the resurrection of Jesus Christ. Grant that we may make our election firm by showing whether the death of Christ Jesus lives in us and we are dead to sin; whether we also want to drink the cup with Christ and with Him be baptized in the cross, in His death; and whether we love our neighbors as He loved us [cf. 1 Pt 3:21; 2 Pt 1:10; Rm 6:2–3; Mt 20:22, 26:39; Jn 15:12]. That way we may show whether we have fellowship with all God's children in the blood of Christ and they have fellowship with us for Christ's sake: fellowship in our goods, assistance, counsel, teaching, honor, and life. That way we show that we discern the body of the Lord, we show what the power and nature of His fellowship are, and

---

159. Christians' work is modeled on Christ's, but His is for human salvation and the work of Christians is an expression of love: it cannot contribute to anyone's salvation. See a similar distinction of Holy Spirit and human work above at n. 116.

160. Schütz Zell puts great emphasis on love of neighbors, and here she infers that this is a necessary prerequisite for sharing in the Supper, as well as its fruit (see following discussion of physical bread). First Corinthians 11:28 warns believers to examine themselves before eating the Supper; then verse 29 says that those who do not "discern the body" eat and drink damnation on themselves. Usually "discerning the body" was interpreted as recognizing Christ's body in the sacrament, and treating the body/blood (elements) with appropriate reverence. Schütz Zell, however, identifies all the people whom believers are called to love and serve as the body that Christians must discern, a characteristically Reformed ethical note.

then we eat the fellowship of this bread. By that we confess and witness that we will all be fed eternally through Him in the Holy Spirit, and so we sing the hymn of praise here, and with Your angels before Your throne eternally [cf. 1 Cor 11:29; Rv 5:11–12].

Feed us, also, O Lord, with the daily physical bread of our body's work, according to Your word.[161] Do not feed us with excess, that our flesh, desire, and wantonness may not proudly rise up against You and You be despised and forgotten in Your members. Also do not let us lack what we need, so that we fall into impatience and revile You, but supply our need like a faithful Father, as Solomon asked you [Prv 30:8–9]. Grant that we may not defraud and strangle the poor with greed, usury, cheating, and unfair money dealings against Your command or seek to abuse neighbors and bring them to the brink of ruin. If we ate our bread at their expense we would—with a curse from Your wrath—eat it to our eternal destruction and punishment [Ex 22:25ff; 1 Cor 11:29]. Therefore, O God and Father, grant Your blessing and benediction on the work of our hands, that through it we may nourish ourselves according to Your command, acknowledge and praise You in it, and according to Your command may remember our neighbors in their need and feed them, so that they also may be protected from impatience and from denying You. And grant that we may always enjoy our food with thanks, discipline, and hallowing of Your name, to the building up of Your kingdom and fulfilling of Your will [cf. Mt 6:9–10] and that we may never enjoy it to the increase of Your wrath, the corruption of our souls and illness of our bodies, and the injury of neighbors—as has very often happened. May You keep that away from us and protect us henceforth as a Father.

"And Forgive Us Our Debts As We Forgive Our Debtors"
O dear Father, we have sinned greatly against You, and our guilt is great! Our whole life may not stand in Your judgment but is completely shamed before You and also corrupts our whole nature that was conceived (*empfangen*) and born (*geboren*) in sin and always desires only what is wrong [cf. Ps 51:5]. Therefore also Your holy Word Christ Jesus had to take on the weak garb of the likeness of our flesh and suffer for us in it: that same Word through whom You created all people, and on the cross brought them back

---

161. To identify "daily bread" with ordinary material food was characteristic of Protestants (especially Reformed) but seemed "unspiritual" to many others; see above, n. 153. The priesthood of believers taught that ordinary work is good, a part of people's religious vocation (see "Hymnbook" before n. 49 and at n. 65); thus Schütz Zell can speak of people working to nourish themselves and to help their neighbors—both "according to Your commandment."

to Yourself through His blood and the anguish of His death, the cross by which He became the mediator between You and us and where He said, "Father, forgive them" [Lk 23:34; cf. Rm 8:3; 1 Tm 2:5]. Through that same living Word who came forth from You and returned to You through the cross and is at Your right hand, through Him we pray to You from the heart that in the Holy Spirit You may forgive us and all people our sins, and receive us in grace into the communion of Your saints, and, considering our groaning, may remember our sins no more, according to Your promise [cf. Jer 31:34; Heb 8:12].

May we be granted to sin no more, but henceforth to lead a new life according to Your will, so that we may willingly come to You out of this world, comforted and happy, as a pilgrim out of exile and a foreign place comes home to the fatherland, as children whose accounts have been settled come to their Father who wills them good. And so may we come to a blessed resurrection: not to the severe judgment of those on the left side, but that we may arise with the righteous to everlasting life and nothing may hinder us from that [cf. Rm 6:4; Heb 11:13–14; Mt 25:41, 46].

So, dear Father, for Your sake we also want to forgive all our debtors from the heart for all the harm and injury that they have done to us, all of which is indeed small and insignificant by comparison with how we have sinned against You and Your Son. But, dear Father, because we can do nothing without You and are only inclined to wrath, we ask You, long-suffering God, send and give us Your Holy Spirit, who will transform our hearts and gift us with His fruit: love, peace, long suffering, kindness, joy, so that we may be able to love our enemies and all people and feed and forgive them from the heart [cf. Gal 5:22; Mt 5:44, 18:35]. O God of all good, grant that we may thus forgive from the heart and that, as You also have commanded, we may be reconciled with our opponents on the way before we come to make our offering and to the judge, so that we also may obtain from You the forgiveness of our sins as You have promised [Mt 5:24–25; 6:14–15].

"And Lead Us Not into Temptation"

O righteous God and Father, save us from the temptation of becoming hardened in our hearts so that we come into Your just judgment through our debt (as happened to Pharaoh)—hardened so that we do not want to forgive and let our debtors go free, as Pharaoh did to Your people and as the servant in the Gospel strangled his fellow servant [cf. Ex 7:3; Mt 18:28ff]. You do not lead us into temptation—we do that ourselves! For You are not a tempter but the truth and the way through the revealed Word. Therefore without Your will (for You desire that all people should be saved and do right [cf. Jas 1:13–14; Jn 14:6]), but through our own sufficient deserts and self-chosen blindness, we are led from one sin into another. As we do not forgive people their faults, so You do not forgive our faults and so You let us go to ruin because no sacrifice pleases You unless mercy and unity with the neighbor go before it [cf. Mt 6:15; Ps 51:16].

Yes, dear Father, let us not because of our guilt be led by Your wrath into darkness and the temptation of our flesh, but let us overcome them through the love of Jesus Christ. "Lead us also not into temptation": that is, do not let us relax into a false, wicked, hypocritical conscience by which we persuade ourselves that we have forgiven our debtors and that we wish them well and so we only cloak our hearts and consciences with a false show when there is actually nothing there—like the drunken grave digger (who thinks he has done his job but is too drunk to realize he has not buried the body!—*trans.*).[162] O Father, help us! Grant that such a counterfeit grave and the temptation of this severe affliction, this concealed jealousy and wrath, may fall away from us and that we may forgive our debtors from the heart [cf. Mt 23:27; 18:35]. May we bear with all their lack of understanding, rudeness, and imperfections and have a heartfelt compassion for them— as You bear ten thousand times more and greater faults in us—and even beyond that, You "punish" us by doing us good! By that You teach us abundantly how to make the reckoning and comparison of our debts to You and the debts our neighbors owe us. Indeed You show that we should demonstrate a true love with all friendship toward them, with deeds as a pledge, and should also give our goods, honor, body, and life for them—as You have loved us and as Your Christ, our Lord and Master, gave His life for us when were still enemies; He prayed for His enemies on the cross, so that we also might be united with each other as children of one Father and members of one body in Christ, whom You have given us as the one and only head [cf. Rm 5:8; Lk 23:34; 1 Cor 12:27; Eph 4:15–16].

"Lead us not into temptation," that is, do not abandon us in the affliction that comes to us in life or death on account of our sins. Even though we must once descend into hell with Christ and become fainthearted [cf. 1 Pt 3:18–19], You want to lead us out with Christ through the gift of a living faith. But if You did not do that (though Your power is able to do it), You would still deserve to be respected, even if You had led us into this for

---

162. Schütz Zell uses a humorous image to express the way people may deceive themselves. The pretense of forgiving is likened to a counterfeit grave that someone drunk with hypocrisy, jealousy, and anger shows to the public but that does not deceive God that the fault has really been forgiven and enmity buried.

our destruction. Therefore, O dear Father, help us! In the lament and afflictions of our conscience let us not become exhausted in battle and fall away like Judas and with him bear forever the gnawing undying worm. But with Peter and Mary Magdalene let us weep for our sins, come to repentance, and achieve much love and so be received by You through Jesus Christ, comforted and strengthened, our faith increased and our unbelief helped [cf. Mt 26:47ff, 75; Jn 18:2ff; Mk 9:24, 48; Lk 7:15, 38, 47].[163]

O righteous Father, also help us to be strengthened and made sure by You, to break through the afflictions of this flesh and be able to enter through the narrow gate. Grant us Your Spirit of knowledge and strength, that we may not deny You [in this temptation of the enemy—*trans.*] because of the sin that sticks in our flesh with evil desires and unceasingly stirs it up [cf. Mt 7:13–14; Gal 5:17]. Therefore the flesh struggles against the spirit and the spirit against the flesh and its evil fruits. So there is a great conflict and struggle in us: we have the will but we do not have the ability to fulfill it, yet both of these are Yours. O holy Father, grant us help that in this affliction we may not be servants of sin but may overcome sin and be free children of Your grace through Jesus Christ—Who, being without sin, became sin for us that He might make us free [cf. Rm 7:18, 6:17; Heb 4:15; 2 Cor 5:21]. However, so long as there is this great struggle in us and we are weak and fleshly, strengthen us, dear Father. Grant us weapons to fight against such affliction and sins so that we may put on Your yoke against the cunning assault of the devil and, with our loins girded with truth and the breastplate of righteousness and the shield of faith, we can extinguish all the arrows of the devil and our flesh [cf. Eph 6:11, 14, 16]. By that, dear Father, through Your help we may not deny You in the afflictions and temptations of this world, even though poverty, sickness, insult, exile, prison, torment, and death come upon us. O God, we could not pass through these dangers if we were abandoned and if You did not bring us out of them; therefore help us and grant that we may from the heart entrust ourselves to You and set ourselves willingly to obey You through the crucified Jesus.[164]

---

163. Judas betrayed Jesus and did not seek (or trust?) forgiveness. Peter denied Jesus three times, and when he realized this he repented and wept (Schütz Zell might say "God helped his unbelief.") The reference to Mary Magdalene follows the common tradition (contested by some sixteenth-century scholars but still widely popular) that Mary Magdalene (Mk 16:1, 9), Mary the sister of Martha and Lazarus (Jn 11:1–2), and the sinful woman who came weeping to anoint Jesus's feet with ointment and wipe them with her hair (and received Jesus's forgiveness; Lk 7:38), were the same person.

164. This and the following meditation on the imitation of Christ and its tone are some of the strikingly medieval notes in Schütz Zell's exposition.

The Lay Reformer, Teacher, and Pastor 171

1. In poverty give us patience—as He was patient in the poverty of His whole life, since He did not have a place to lay His head, that His humility and poverty may be an eradication of our pride and arrogant superfluity; since, although He was the richest and most honorable of all, yet He emptied Himself and came down to us and took on Himself the form of a servant [cf. Mt 18:20; Phil 2:6–7].
2. Grant also that in our sickness we may remember His pains and sickness when He suffered for us on the cross in great weakness and thirst, drinking the gall and vinegar, with wounded body and sick members so that all His bones could be counted. Grant that we also may gladly suffer in the flesh with all patience, so that we may cease to sin and henceforth live in Your will [cf. Jn 19:28–29, 33–34; Mt 27:34, 48; Ps 22:17; 1 Pt 4:1–2].
3. Also when we are insulted and ill is spoken against us, let us diligently consider all the insults, the false witness and complaints, scoffing, derision, reproaches, and such like that He bore, that we may also bear such things with patience and not seek to respond with reproaches or wrath but may do good in return for evil. For the servant is not greater than the Lord who encountered this before; and with Him we also gladly bear such things, when we are taken out of the world and our kingdom is hidden in Christ and is not of this world. Grant that, if people speak evil of us and indeed lie about us, we may diligently remember and believe that our reward will be great in heaven; let us be glad and rejoice in that [cf. Mt 5:11–12, 10:24–25; Rm 12:12, 17; Jn 15:18–19].
4. Also when we are in exile may we remember that Your own people drove out from them Your best loved Son Jesus Christ, when He freed the possessed man from the evil spirit and made him well. Also how His own disciples fled and hid when His enemies wanted to stone Him and put Him out of the city, although He had done them great good with many wonders and signs and also fed and nourished them with physical food and He was the most innocent and kind of all [cf. Mt 8:28–34, 14:17ff; Jn 10:31–39; Lk 4:29]. Also in our imprisonment may we consider the bonds and imprisonment of the one who freed us from everlasting imprisonment and for our sake underwent it Himself, namely, Jesus Christ, Your dear Son; through Him and His Spirit we can have much room and knowledge for our spirit and faith. Grant, dear Father, that in our pain and experience of martyrdom we may not forget His great pain and His demeanor when He suffered in the judge's house: binding, crowning, scourging, and many pains, that such insolence and pain may not be foreign to us but we may gladly be participants of the suffering of Christ. When He was chastised and weak, He did not open His mouth, but like a sheep before His shearers He kept silent [cf. Mt 27:26–31; Jn 19:1–3; Is 53:7].

Grant that in our death and dying we may remember and weigh the gentle-spirited and holy death of the one who committed and entrusted His spirit into Your hands on the cross.[165] Through that death we have

---

165. Medieval instructions for dying (*ars moriendi*) frequently included exhortations to meditate on Christ's death. Such themes sometimes continue in Protestant books of counsel, but

inherited life, and in and through Him the everlasting death, sin, and hell have been conquered—so that in our physical death we may not truly die or come into the judgment, but that by faith in Jesus Christ we may enter into life through death, along with our friends and relatives, husband, wife, and children [cf. Lk 23:46; Jn 5:24]: so that we and all of them may be found again in joy at the last resurrection, through the Spirit of the Lord Jesus Christ. Lord God and Father, help us poor people to overcome all these temptations and afflictions through the power, assistance, and succor of Your Holy Spirit so that they may not defeat and so destroy us.

"But Deliver Us from Evil"

That evil [destruction] would follow us with an everlasting gnawing worm if we did not keep ourselves as proper children in obedience to You, if we did not hallow Your name, if You did not rule in us and we did not live according to Your will and commandments, if You also did not feed us and forgive our sins and unite us with all people, and if You did not save us from affliction. Then all evil would follow—indeed, the everlasting evil, where there is darkness, weeping, and gnashing of teeth: protect us from that, Lord and dear Father! [cf. Mk 9:48; Mt 8:12].

Protect us also from evil that comes to our bodies, that we may not fall into the power of our enemies and they may not be able to carry out their desires against us and then say, "Where is your God?" [Ps 42:3, 10]. Save us from their appetites and fury! Free us also from hunger, war, scarcity, and sickness, but yet only in such a way that in all things Your name may be hallowed, Your kingdom come and Your will be done, as also Christ Jesus said. With Him we want not our will but Yours to be done, for You alone know what real evil is and what is for our harm or use [Mt 26:39]. Therefore we do not ask You to take us out of the world, that is, we do not ask You to free us from the cross (as if we did not want to suffer with our Christ, for that is why we have come to this hour). But we ask that You protect us from evil and sanctify us in the truth, that we may not fall away from You but may remain in You and be kept in Your name [cf. Jn 17:11, 15, 17; 12:27].

"Amen"[166]

May You will to make all this certain and true through Jesus Christ Your holy Word, our anointed Lord and King, who lives with You in the Holy

---

usually (as Schütz Zell does here) the emphasis is on faith and confident trust that death, sin, and hell are conquered and resurrection and life are sure; see "Lament" at n. 87.

166. Schütz Zell probably puts the "Amen" before the doxological conclusion because traditionally the priest added the doxology after the corporate recitation of the Prayer.

Spirit eternally. Through Him we also have full hope without doubt that You will not allow our prayer to offend You but will grant all this to us poor people and to those who are Yours, for the honor of Your name, the increase of Your kingdom, and our salvation, and that You will always hear us according to His promise [cf. Jn 14:14].

"For Yours Is the Kingdom"

You may give it to whom You will, as also You gave to Christ Jesus all power in heaven and on earth, and You will put all His enemies under His feet. Grant also to us poor people as His members that the devil and the world may not reign in us but that Your kingdom may be in us [cf. Mt 28:18; Ps 110:1; 1 Cor 12:27].

"And Yours Is the Power"

Which no one can stand against: You can bring all counsel to nothing and hold the hearts of kings and all people in Your hand. Through Your power, by many signs You struck down the firstborn of Egypt and brought Your people out with Your mighty arm and saved them from their enemies at the great sea. Do that for us, dear Father, and help us in all our needs so that our enemy may not rejoice over us; for when You are with us, who can be against us? [cf. Ps 33:10, 30:1; Prv 21:1; Ex 11:4–10, 14:21ff; Rm 8:31].

"And Yours Is the Glory Forever"

All people should voice their praise to You, thank and serve You—yes, all creatures! And they should be glad in Your house and give You alone the praise: for You alone have made all things without anyone's counsel, and without anyone's wisdom You also preserve and increase them; You give food and clothing to all living things, and without You nothing lives. Therefore Your name and glory are widely known, and Your honor has no end, and You give it to no other [cf. Ps 104:27; Is 42:8].

II

AUTOBIOGRAPHY AND POLEMIC: A LAY THEOLOGIAN AMID THE CONFLICTS OF CONFESSIONAL DIVISIONS

INTRODUCTION

In the 1550s, the widowed Katharina Schütz Zell felt compelled to defend her own religious integrity and that of the first-generation reformers both privately and publicly in writings that have shaped the way she has been remembered ever since. The writings of these years, a personal letter to Caspar Schwenckfeld in October 1553 and a compilation of correspondence with Ludwig Rabus dedicated to the citizens of Strasbourg and published in December 1557, can be understood as the lay theologian's response to the period when the divisions in the reform movement had become institutionalized. It was now fellow followers of "the Gospel" with whom she must argue as she tried to maintain the original vision.[1]

Across western Europe, the religious and political scene had been gradually changing. After the first commonly shared reactions against Rome in the early 1520s, internal differences among those who had broken away began to develop; increasingly, each city or territory had to choose for one confession and therefore against another. This process not only reflected development in both theology and practical ecclesiastical structures, but it also sometimes required reinterpreting—or changing—what the first reformers had intended. At least, that was how it appeared to those like Schütz Zell, who had participated in the break with Rome from the first and still believed in the shape of the reform as they had known it in the 1520s. Now they no longer fitted into the scheme of things. Beyond finding themselves in an uncomfortable, shifting world, if they refused—as Schütz Zell did—to take sides, they often endured criticism and worse from the varied parties who were determined to label them one way or another and make

---

1. For a fuller account of Schütz Zell, Rabus, and Schwenckfeld from the beginning of the Interim up to the conflicts described in these writings, see McKee, *Life and Thought*, 130–55.

them fit the new confessions or suffer the consequences. The broad picture is well known, but it is important to sketch the specific situation in Strasbourg in order to understand Schütz Zell's writings against fellow "protesters."

The introduction of the Interim had forced Strasbourg's most vocal clerical opponents of compromise, Martin Bucer and Paul Fagius, into exile. The ministers who now became the dominant leaders had already begun to move toward an increasingly strict Lutheran theology, and they wished to drop Strasbourg's own Tetrapolitan Confession and use exclusively the 1530 Augsburg Confession as the standard of church teaching. This was particularly significant because of the rather different sacramental theology of the Lutheran confession, which emphasized the efficaciousness of the rites far more than had been true in Strasbourg in the 1520s.[2] Most laity were much slower to modify the theological ideas taught to them by the first-generation reformers. However, after Protestant forces defeated Charles V in 1552, the political reversal led to a new religious settlement in 1555 and the Augsburg Confession became legal in the Empire, so there was more political incentive for Strasbourg to adopt it officially.

One of the most strident voices promoting this change was Ludwig Rabus, a young minister who had been Matthew's assistant and lived with the Zells as a student before his marriage. When Zell died in January 1548 Rabus had been quite young to become the pastor of the cathedral parish, one of the most important in the city. However, after another candidate refused, he was chosen as Matthew's successor with the support of the old pastor's widow, which certainly reassured the parishioners if not the clerical authorities.

For several years Rabus and Schütz Zell worked together well, but gradually personal and confessional problems developed. Rabus was a

---

2. According to the traditional Roman teaching called *opus operatum*, sacramental effectiveness is not dependent on the faith or understanding of the minister or the recipient and normally their morality also does not prevent its effectiveness. A priest who does not maintain his vows of celibacy can still convey the grace of the Mass by doing the ritual properly; unconfessed mortal sin would prevent a person from receiving the host to his salvation but not interfere with its consecration. Protestants rejected this doctrine on several grounds. First, grace is given only by God: it cannot be achieved by human or ritual action. Grace is a relationship or state and not a quantitative thing to be conveyed mechanically. Second, grace can only be received by faith: trust in God. Over time, the Lutheran position on the second point shifted somewhat; in order to assure the reality of the grace, the efficaciousness of the ritual was stressed, until by the 1550s many clergy insisted that the rite of baptism was essential for salvation and the body and blood of Christ are actually "in, with, and under" the elements (therefore present everywhere, the doctrine of "ubiquity"). See "Schwenckfeld" at n. 46 and "Psalms/Prayer" at n. 158.

bright young man, and he wanted to be more than just a pastor. He was appointed professor of theology in Strasbourg's Academy, pursued a doctorate in theology, and began to write for publication. In 1552 he produced the first installment of what became a two-volume folio set on the Christian martyrs, in which he wished to include his predecessor and "father" Matthew Zell (although he would exclude those he considered heretics, such as Anabaptists and Zwinglians). For this book Rabus needed what Zell's widow could tell him about that first Protestant pastor of Strasbourg whom he was proud to succeed, but she would not cooperate with a project, which seemed to her to be motivated chiefly by self-interest on Rabus's part.[3] The young man's pride in his doctorate and his demand that Matthew's widow help him with his martyrology provided the first bones of contention between Zell's two "heirs." Schütz Zell said that the first-generation preachers had been right to abandon worldly titles such as "doctor," and she objected to her husband being used in a book that she believed was prompted more by Rabus's desire for extra income than by a concern to serve the church. The well-intended but very blunt maternal criticism of both of his key ambitions by his former foster mother undoubtedly contributed to souring the relationship between Rabus and Schütz Zell.

However, there were other, less obviously personal issues. Over time Rabus began to alter Zell's liturgies, teachings, and ways of handling pastoral responsibilities. These theologically based changes in worship, by which his young successor reshaped Zell's teaching on the Lord's Supper

---

3. Zell eventually appeared in book 8 of the *Historien der Martyrer* (History of the Martyrs), by Ludwig Rabus (*Historien der Martyrer: Erste Theil Darinn von den Heyligen / Ausserwölten Gottes Zeügen / Bekennern unnd Martyrern... Ander Theil*... [Strassburg: Josiah Rihel, 1571, 1572]), first published in 1558, but Rabus had to make do without the details that Schütz Zell could have provided. Technically Zell was not a martyr: he suffered but did not die for his faith. In fact, most of the sixteenth-century figures in Rabus's book were not killed for their faith, since he included only those who accepted a Lutheran confession and most of those who died for their beliefs (e.g., Anabaptists, Reformed, English) were heretics in Rabus's view and therefore not martyrs. When it appeared, Rabus's text on Zell provided a brief introduction and then reprinted the *Christeliche Verantwortung* (Christian Response; *Christeliche Verantwortung M. Matthes Zell... uber Artikel im vom Bischöfflichern Fiscal daselbs entgegengesetzt...* [Strassburg: Wolffgang Köpffel, 1523]), which Zell had written in 1523 to defend himself against the bishop's charges. In effect, Rabus interpreted Zell's lifelong admiration for Luther as evidence that the agreement with the latter expressed in 1523 remained equally unchanged. Rabus (born in 1523) had come of age in a world quite different from the Wittenberg where Luther had first taught and the Strasbourg where Zell had first preached, but his treatment of Zell appears not to take into account the generation of changes. Rabus understood Luther's faith according to the strict interpretation of the Augsburg Confession as it was read in the 1550s rather than through the treatises of the early 1520s, so he also read his Zell through that temporal and confessional filter.

to accord with the Augsburg Confession, and Rabus's increasingly sharp attacks on anyone who did not accept that Confession as the sole standard of faith, greatly upset Schütz Zell. And she said so frankly. Although she spoke to him in private, Dr. Rabus was naturally furious that an uneducated old woman presumed to correct him. The fact that one of the people whom he detested and criticized from the pulpit was a long-time friend of the Zells, Caspar Schwenckfeld, only added fuel to the fire. Indeed, this became the central issue: Rabus believed Schwenckfeld was a heretic, while Schütz Zell insisted that Schwenckfeld was a friend of Strasbourg's own first-generation reformers and taught essentially the same thing they had.

The Zells had become acquainted with Schwenckfeld during his years in Strasbourg (1529–33), and Schütz Zell had remained in intermittent contact with him for some years. Their correspondence was sporadic; with one exception, the only extant letters are those from him to her. Schwenckfeld wrote Katharina a letter of consolation when Matthew died, but their contact seems to have stopped completely some time after that, probably in late 1551. In November of that year, without her prior knowledge, Schwenckfeld published an open letter to Schütz Zell claiming her support for himself. Far from endearing him to her, Schwenckfeld's letter angered its addressee, although she later denied that it had caused her to break off their correspondence.[4] Besides unintentionally distancing Schütz Zell from its writer, Schwenckfeld's public letter functioned as part of the growing demand that everyone must take sides and no doubt fueled Rabus's belief that Zell's widow was not only an irritating and ignorant old woman but also an apostate from her husband's faith.

In the early 1550s then, Schütz Zell was being publicly claimed by Schwenckfeld and his Strasbourg circle as their partisan and being vilified by Rabus and some of his colleagues as an associate of heretics and herself suspect, also in an increasingly public way. With considerable skill, Schütz Zell asserted her autonomy from any human control, while affirming her desire for Christian fellowship with everyone; she would be friends with all who followed the Gospel, but she would not belong to any party. Since she

---

4. The only extant letter from Schütz Zell to Schwenckfeld is the one translated here. His letters to her are found in the *Corpus Schwenckfeldianorum*, annotated by his editors with a firm conviction that she was Schwenckfeld's disciple; this is evident in their interpretation of the public letter of November 1551 (see "Schwenckfeld" nn. 18 and 23, which also include her denial that anger caused the break but suggest that his friends thought otherwise). For references see McKee, *Writings*, 115–18 and passim; a full discussion is forthcoming in McKee, "Katharina Schütz Zell and Caspar Schwenckfeld: A Reassessment of Their Relationship," in *Archiv für Reformationsgeschichte*.

understood Rabus's accusations to implicate the whole first generation as well as herself, this early convert to "the Gospel" and widow of Strasbourg's first Protestant preacher felt compelled to defend her husband and herself (and their colleagues) from charges of heresy. When Rabus added Ulrich Zwingli to his list of heretics, Schütz Zell concluded that Dr. Rabus was more ignorant than even the simplest peasants. She could and did acknowledge that there were differences among the first-generation Strasbourg clergy with regard to Schwenckfeld, but she knew that they had ranked Zwingli with Luther in everything except the credit for initiating the reform. Of course, Rabus had not been there to see this. She had. Obedience to scriptural teachings about fraternal admonition, defending the truth and the innocent against lies, and Christian love for both the deceived and the deceivers required that Zell's partner in faith and ministry set the record straight.

The arguments between Schütz Zell and Schwenckfeld and his circle remained private—thanks perhaps to the cogency of her letter in October 1553. Having expressed herself firmly, she did not make the disagreement public property, which suggests that the Schwenckfelders tempered their demands for her allegiance. They certainly were not going to publish her criticisms and tell the world that she refused to number herself among them, and she would not bring any disagreement to the attention of "the church" (community) if it could be resolved appropriately in private. However, Schütz Zell's arguments with Rabus eventually became public knowledge precisely because he refused to allow any discussion, much less correction of, his behavior, even in private. The combination of Rabus's accusations with her defense of Schwenckfeld (and Zwingli and the Anabaptists) and the fact that her differences with Schwenckfeld were not known led to Zell's widow being permanently—although inaccurately—identified as a Schwenckfelder.

Schütz Zell's articulate and detailed defenses of Zell and herself are recorded in two extensive writings, which she produced in the 1550s to deal with and define her relationship to both Schwenckfeld(ers) and Rabus. Written in letter form, these texts include significant autobiographical statements, as well as the fuller development of a number of important theological teachings, and significant evidence of Schütz Zell's gifts as historian and controversialist. Although it has not been feasible to include the whole of the correspondence with Rabus, this chapter gives a good picture of the lay theologian making her way through the conflicts among those who had broken with Rome, defending her faith and integrity with intelligence, confidence, and considerable humor!

TO SIR CASPAR SCHWENCKFELD
Introduction

The only extant letter from Katharina Schütz Zell to Caspar Schwenckfeld, a fascinating autograph dated October 19, 1553, has recently been published for the first time. The text is quite long, twelve folio sheets written on both sides—virtually a short treatise. Although it took considerable time to produce (Schütz Zell says she was interrupted more than thirty times while working on it), the neatness of the extant autograph shows that it is the fair copy the writer made for herself after she arranged her ideas.[5]

The content of the letter is the remarkable thing, however. It is a very finely crafted set of arguments expressed with courtesy but clear independence by a strong, intelligent, and very articulate woman. The first part of the text and the very end form a personal letter from Schütz Zell to Schwenckfeld. In between there are extended presentations of the writer's positions vis-à-vis the two parties with whom she had to do: the city preachers, especially Rabus, on the one hand, and the Schwenckfelder party in Strasbourg and its leader on the other. To understand the text and appreciate her skill, it is necessary to pay careful attention to the audience Schütz Zell has in view in each case.

The beginning of the letter addresses the break in contact between the writer and the recipient. Schütz Zell assures Schwenckfeld that the silence was not a sign of bad feeling on her part, lists the responsibilities that fill her time, and explains that she has now addressed him again at the request of a mutual friend. She then moves directly to describe the situation as she sees it, indicating that she is being pulled between two parties. Each of these would gladly claim her if she would abdicate her independence and agree with (submit to!) them, but since she will not approve everything they do, both criticize her. Having set the scene, Schütz Zell then gives a full outline of each party's views and her responses to them. First she details her relationship and differences with the (Lutheran) Strasbourg city clergy in the person of Rabus, who has essentially decided that she is a heretic, and tells how she has answered him. Then she explains the accusations made by the Strasbourg Schwenckfelders and her responses to them. In the course of this second exposition Schütz Zell politely but quite clearly implicates Schwenckfeld himself in some of her criticisms of his party. She also offers

---

5. See McKee, *Writings*, 122–53, for the German text of this letter and notes on specific details; an example of her handwriting is found as the frontispiece of *Writings*, which gives the text of her letter of January 4, 1549, to Conrad Pellican.

a rather full autobiographical sketch of her spiritual journey. The text concludes in epistolary form with final greetings expressed in the cordial tone of fellowship restored.

Whether Schwenckfeld was as happy to receive this letter as Schütz Zell was to write it may be doubted. It was certainly not included in his collected correspondence, and when his editors mention Zell's wife they take care to present her as Schwenckfeld's disciple.[6] However, since her own copy of the letter has survived in the Strasbourg archives, it is clear that some person(s) close to Schütz Zell thought her communication to Schwenckfeld was valuable. After her death the letter was apparently forgotten. Most of the few later historians who knew of its existence have assumed it was an earlier form of the correspondence with Rabus, while others have expressed uncertainty about the addressee. None has really understood the structure of the argument.[7]

In terms of the light it casts on Katharina Schütz Zell, however, this letter is among her most significant writings. It clarifies a number of personal facts about her youth, her sense of vocation, conversion, and education. It also sets out her views on some very important theological ideas. Some of these, such as the means of revelation or sources of religious authority and the relationship between the church universal and the visible church, mark Schütz Zell's differences from both Rabus and Schwenckfeld, explicitly or implicitly. Others, such as the relationship of God and human ministers in salvation, the nature and qualifications for Christian ministry, the responsibilities of believers to the corporate body of the church, and women's roles in religious leadership, are more directed to one or the other opponent.

Schütz Zell sharply rejects any idea of direct or continuing revelation and stands in firm agreement with the Protestant teaching on revelation only through the Bible. Most obvious in this letter is her rejection of any alterna-

---

6. For full discussion see McKee, *Life and Thought*, 155–70, and "Katharina Schütz Zell and Caspar Schwenckfeld."

7. Some scholars have debated for whom the letter was written: was it for Rabus with a copy to Schwenckfeld? The similarity of the first part to the later published letters to Rabus ("Letter to the Citizens of Strasbourg Concerning Mr. Ludwig Rabus") and the general consensus that Schütz Zell was a follower of Schwenckfeld have led some to think that this was simply an earlier letter to Rabus. See Marc Lienhard, "Catherine Zell, née Schütz," *Bibliotheca Dissidentium: Répertoire des non-conformistes religieux des seizième et dix-septième siècles*, ed. A. Séguenny, vol. 1 (Baden-Baden: Valentin Koerner, 1980), 124–25; Roland H. Bainton, "Katherine Zell," *Medievalia et Humanistica* n.s. 1 (1970): 143–68. However, it is clear from internal evidence that it was written for Schwenckfeld, not for Rabus. Liebenau, *Catherine Zell*, 74ff, recognizes that the letter includes criticism of the Schwenckfelders but still believes that it was sent to Rabus and does not see the criticism of Schwenckfeld himself. See McKee, *Life and Thought*, 155, n. 21.

tive source of knowledge of God through the visions of an inspired individual. With a kind of popular humor borrowed from Luther she laughs at the idea that either she or the Schwenckfelder who claimed immediate revelation had ever received "a feather of the Holy Spirit" (who was often pictured as a dove). On the other hand, Schütz Zell also sharply rejects the need for worldly wisdom either as preparation for or supplement to scripture. In this letter, that worldly wisdom is a university course, which included such teachers as Plato, Aristotle, Cicero, and other "pagans"; some of that may be tolerable, but it is certainly not necessary and it can be dangerous, as she bluntly tells young Rabus. (Following other Protestants, in 1524 a younger Schütz Zell had already disproved to her own satisfaction the Roman argument for the necessity of unwritten church traditions not found in the Bible.) Religious authority among Christians must be grounded on knowledge of and obedience to scripture, which is summarized in the Nicene and Apostles' Creeds and Chalcedonian definition. Scripture is rightly explained by the preaching of the reformers like Luther and Zell, and one may also use the early church fathers, but none of these interpretations—much less the additions made by Roman church traditions or pagan philosophy or individual visions—has the unique and final status of the Biblical content itself.[8]

This Protestant view of the Bible as the locus of all necessary revelation is related to several other distinctively Protestant issues. Everyone agreed that knowledge of God is central for salvation, but that does not answer all questions. What is the relationship of God and human beings in salvation? Do specific people contribute to human salvation and thus in some measure share that honor with God, as the Roman priesthood was necessary for the sacramental means of grace (a position Rabus also seemed to be developing)? Or can everyone reach for immediate contact with God by himself, by herself, as the extreme Schwenckfelder (Spiritualist) position maintained? Schütz Zell adamantly insists that God in Christ, made known by the work of the Holy Spirit who gives Christians the gift of faith, is the sole source and means of election and salvation. No one but God is intrinsically necessary; the Roman "false teaching" about the need for or even the possibility of any kind of human intercessor or sacramental act (in Rabus's version) is flatly denied. However, God has also not left human beings without any task. God can freely choose to use human beings for His own purposes, but it is God who determines what those tasks are and what contribution

---

8. For objections to immediate revelation see below at nn. 26 and 67; pagan education at n. 33. Although she does not actually name Roman tradition in the "Apologia," the clerical celibacy she rejects is one manifestation of it, and her whole argument there is based on scripture as the sole authority; see at n. 24 et passim.

they can make to His purposes. The Bible shows that God both commands and practices employing human instruments, therefore God's children know that that is the right way and they must not seek another means of illumination or a different role for themselves. Again drawing on scripture, Schütz Zell affirms that the purpose for which God uses human instruments in human salvation is primarily preaching, announcing His judgment on sin, proclaiming His promises of forgiveness and reconciliation, and calling sinners to repentance and new life. So the Protestant lay theologian argues against the Schwenckfelder who rejects a human ministry of biblical preaching. God has chosen not only to put knowledge of Himself and the way to salvation in the Bible, but also to teach that knowledge through human voices, and no human being can choose otherwise.[9]

As the human means to fulfill the two great commandments to love God and each other, the chief ministry (function) of God's people is to learn and make known what God's word reveals. Access to the Bible must be available to everyone, women as well as men, and as Schütz Zell had already demonstrated in her hymnbook foreword, even the least important person is both able and expected to listen and learn. In fact, everyone ought to study diligently because faith and thus salvation comes through knowledge of God's grace in the Bible, not by some contented ignorance. The description of her own religious education that Schütz Zell presents in this letter demonstrates that she regarded laziness as reprehensible, and the extent of the religious knowledge she herself acquired is remarkable. However, even if everyone should learn as much as possible, there are still differences of gifts, both for learning and especially for teaching. Rote memorization of scripture itself, without real understanding, is not sufficient to make a good teacher. By God's choice, the gifts He gives to some make them better qualified to teach than others are.[10]

---

9. See below, at nn. 65ff.

10. See "Hymnbook" at n. 57 et passim for Schütz Zell's study; see below at nn. 37–38, 61–63; no mindless conformity or rote memorization, at n. 56; recognition of differences of gifts, see n. 11. The medieval church had taught that, although understanding of the faith was the goal, as a last resort a person could be saved by affirming that he/she believed "what the church believes." Neither Roman nor Protestant reformers were satisfied with this, but for the latter it was a much more urgent matter because knowing God's promises in Christ was necessary for personally trusting as well as confessing and teaching them. Reading the Bible became one of the marks of Protestants, women as well as men (cf. after n. 23), artisans and even peasants as well as social elites, "assimilating" women to men and lower ranks to higher ones, somewhat elevating "the subordinate group . . . by making it like the superior group," as Natalie Zemon Davis points out for French Reformed women and lower social ranks; see "City Women and Religious Change," in her *Society and Culture in Early Modern France* (Stanford: Stanford University Press, 1975), 93 and note. For extent of Schütz Zell's study and knowledge, see McKee, *Life and Thought*, 288–94.

As one necessary qualification for a public ministry, for teaching others, Schütz Zell clearly recognizes the importance of an inward call. However, she emphasizes much more the visible gifts by which other people can recognize someone as fit for public ministry. These include a (very) good knowledge of the Bible plus the faithful practice of that teaching, since words without deeds are hypocrisy and not true ministry. God's gifts of knowledge and faithfulness as well as God's call are not limited by sex or social condition or other similar factors. Schütz Zell does not believe that a woman who is rightly learned in God's word and truly practices that faith is excluded from any aspect of church service or ministry except ordination. That, she (reluctantly but clearly) concedes, is prohibited by Saint Paul. Zell's wife and widow clearly affirms the validity and appropriateness of an outward, official call for the ordained ministry of preaching and administering the sacraments, including a call supported (if not issued by) civil authorities within the Christian church.[11]

Schütz Zell's understanding of the church is strongly shaped by the doctrine of the priesthood of believers, and thus the recognition and calling of qualified ministers by the community of the faithful plays an important role. Laity are obligated to attend to their clergy with both receptive and critical minds and ears and eyes. They are to honor the office of preacher and to make good use of their teachers in the faith. However, they are also to maintain their own judgment, based on their own biblical knowledge. If lay Christians become convinced that the ordained ministers are offering wrong teaching or contradicting what they teach by their behavior, they should not follow them. In certain circumstances they may even have the duty to rebuke the clergy and perhaps also identify—again by the qualities of faith, biblical learning, and life—true preachers/teachers, even ones whom human institutions do not recognize. However, if recognition by the institutional church is no guarantee that a teacher is right, not being so established is also no such

---

11. The character of ministerial gifts and qualifications is especially seen in descriptions of Zell, below at nn. 43–45 and before n. 57; for inward call, see at n. 67. Another description is found in "Psalms/Prayer" at nn. 154–156. The insistence on the importance of learned teachers is evident in repeated references to the fact that she consulted them, for example, at n. 37, before n. 61 ("learned and God-fearing people"), at n. 62 ("God's learned ones"), and at n. 63 (will not "deny the offices of such servants of God"), but it is also clear that these are not only ordained clergy. For women's equality in this learning but not in ordination, see below at nn. 36–39. For a full discussion of Schütz Zell's understanding of women's roles in religious leadership, see McKee, *Life and Thought*, chap. 13, esp. 398–418. In rebuking Rabus for abandoning his parish, Schütz Zell expresses her clear conviction that his formal call by the city of Strasbourg was valid and his departure without permission calls into question his pastoral vocation; see "Strasbourg Citizens" after n. 76.

guarantee; Schütz Zell subjects Schwenckfeld and his followers to the same tests she applies to Rabus and the Strasbourg clergy.[12]

Unlike the Schwenckfelders, Schütz Zell clearly affirms her commitment to the church visible on earth and to its structured ministry and sacraments. She had participated entirely willingly in the corporate worship and work of the church led by her husband and his colleagues. Although that view is implicit here, elsewhere she not only accepts that the visible church may be rightly established by a civil government but also worries a great deal about the failure of the city's rulers to protect the Strasbourg church as they should. However, in her argument against Rabus, the lay theologian distinguishes clearly between the universal church of all the elect, which no Christian denied, and the visible institution, which was a matter of controversy. The universal church she will never leave, but Schütz Zell insists that the Bible does not bind her absolutely to the outward parish; she does not reject the visible church in principle, but she repeats the biblical justification for her claim that God may be worshiped anywhere and everywhere. Thus she will not abandon the parish as such—much to the dismay of the Schwenckfelders—but she will exercise her own informed judgment and refrain from participating in Rabus's errors, to his extreme annoyance.[13]

Besides providing rich insight into her personal faith and her theological convictions, Schütz Zell's letter to Schwenckfeld is significant for what it reveals of her mature character. It demonstrates her combination of independence and interdependence; her determination to study for herself along with her willingness to be taught; her capacity to recognize with gratitude the teachers God provides coupled with an insistence on maintaining her duty to critique as well as support them; her commitment to the corporate life of church and society along with an insistence on individual

---

12. Right humility of clergy (Zell as example) before n. 32; right attention to clergy at nn. 61–63; lay judgment at nn. 24, 27–28, 32–33, 34, 39, 55–56, and 71. Schütz Zell applies her (lay) right to correct the learned to both Rabus (at n. 39) and Schwenckfeld himself (at n. 55)—in effect following the latter's own advice (at n. 34) but applying it to him as well as Rabus—and summarizing by refusing to bow to anyone when all appear to be wrong (at n. 71). In "Strasbourg Citizens" before n. 96 Schütz Zell says that she needed to rebuke Rabus because his fellow clergy did not, but she can also apply her obligation to judge clerical teaching to Zell himself and indicate that she follows what he said because she knows for herself that it comes from God/is in accord with His will ("Strasbourg Citizens" at n. 89). See McKee, *Life and Thought*, 45, 51, 184, 403–7.

13. See universal-local at n. 35. For implicit acceptance of an established church (Roman and Protestant clergy) and Rabus's failures that disqualify him, see below at nn. 37, 39, and 43. The problem is the character of the ministers, not their established or nonestablished status, as Schütz Zell's critique of both makes clear (e.g., at n. 71). For civil rulers' obligations to protect the church, see "Psalms/Prayer" at n. 133.

186 *Two*

conscience; her confident voice as a woman along with her recognition that both women and men have varying gifts. This letter also provides the clearest example of Schütz Zell's remarkable ability to conduct a strong but civil argument with someone who seemed to have every advantage over her: a woman of artisan background and vernacular education speaking to a nobleman with a Latin education about a subject on which she felt obliged to criticize even himself and his friends—armed only with her own wits and integrity.

TO SIR CASPAR SCHWENCKFELD, MY GRACIOUS DEAR SIR AND OLD FRIEND: TO HIS OWN HANDS

My very dear sir (and as I hope) still my long-time friend: I wish for you, as also for myself and for all who know and call upon the name of the Lord, the grace and power of God the Holy Spirit for a holy, perfect, and finally blessed consummation of the pure faith in our Lord Jesus Christ, the true and excellent Son of the living God. May the one who is to come, come soon, and may He finally redeem us from this wicked world [cf. Rm 15:13; Joel 2:32; Rv 22:20].

I do not know whether the fault is mine, or yours, or theirs who perhaps sometimes have complained about me to you, that we now so seldom—or not at all—correspond as we used to do[14]: now when I especially need it, in my sorrowful and vexed time on earth, when I am alone, without comfort, laden with many cares and tasks, and also a great many crosses and afflictions, which God daily lays upon me. Among these also (and how appropriately) the greatest is my evil life as it lies open before God, which is that I have never rightly known His fatherly love nor been grateful for it. For this reason therefore my heart is also fittingly in constant fear and, with David, I worry about forgiveness of my sins and always need comfort [cf. Ps 51:1–2].[15]

---

14. Although she knows that some think she has broken off the correspondence, here she politely suggests that it is not really a break but rather a period of silence, and there is doubt about who stopped writing whom. Below she graciously takes this responsibility on herself, on the grounds that Schwenckfeld is too busy with (more) important things to write to her (!).

15. Schütz Zell identifies her greatest trouble as not knowing and being rightly grateful for God's fatherly love, an idea of sin in accord with the view that God causes her suffering (crosses) in order to lead her to repent. Her sincere awareness of her sins is, however, balanced by a very strong sense of God's forgiveness. In some ways, this sentence is a theological statement about what really matters, intended to put in perspective all the other temporal crosses that she bears; it also intends to identify what she *is* guilty of as opposed to what the clergy and the Schwenckfelders say (she makes a similar point in 1524 against different lies; "Apologia" at

However, I am glad to take on myself the fault for my failure toward you [the break in correspondence—trans.], excuse you, and consider rightly that you have much better things to do, in which I would also partly participate and for which I also thank the Lord Christ. Heartily I pray Him to bless His work in you and to add still more to the ten pounds that you have received. And I pray Him not to take back from miserable (*armen*) me the one given to me—as I have well deserved—but to be gracious to me and indeed to add only three pounds to the one (which I cannot deny that I have received) and to give me the strength to use these to gain others, that I may not be ashamed on the day of reckoning and the handing over of the pounds [cf. Lk 19:11–27 with Mt 25:14ff].[16]

Ah, may the good and faithful Joseph [Christ], distributor of the heavenly goods, take hold of me and further the good![17] He who received from the great king Pharaoh, His almighty Father, all power in the fullness of time

---

n. 21). A sincere expression of conviction, this does not have the degree of anguish found in her meditations on the Psalms. The writings of her last years (this letter and those to Rabus and Sir Felix), even when they recount temporal suffering and speak of sinfulness, carry a strong note of confidence in God's grace and her own salvation.

16. The parable of the pounds was a favorite metaphor for God's gifts and the concomitant responsibility for their profitable use (see "Lament" at nn. 90 and 93). In the Lukan version, ten people each received 1 pound; one made a profit of 10 pounds, another a profit of 5 pounds, and a third made none; when the day of reckoning came the lazy third was punished by having his one pound taken away from him and given to the person who had made ten pounds. Schütz Zell adds to this an idea from the Matthean parable of the talents in which different individuals initially received different numbers of talents; the ones who received five and two talents doubled their talents and were rewarded, but the one who received one talent made no profit and then his talent itself was taken away and given to the person who now had ten talents. The obvious point is that those who do not use their gifts will lose them. Schütz Zell says that Schwenckfeld received 10 pounds and she herself 1, which may express the natural distance between the two: man-woman, noble-artisan rank, Latin educated–vernacular girls' school. This praise serves to reassure Schwenckfeld of her respect, since he has reason to think the contrary—and since she will later criticize him.

17. The metaphors in this section are among the most mixed in Schütz Zell's whole corpus. The basic story is that of Joseph, who explains to Pharaoh his dream about the seven fat cows followed by seven lean cows and the seven good ears of corn and the seven withered ones, which represent seven years of good harvests and seven of bad times (Gn 41). For his wisdom Joseph is made second in command in Egypt to gather the grain of the seven good years and save it for the bad years. Here Christ is Joseph, God's second in command, who feeds people and is also Himself the heavenly food that they eat (for a similar idea, see "Psalms/Prayer" at n. 135). The final section of the mixed metaphors combines the Matthean parables of the wedding feast and the wheat and tares, along with the good steward (Mt 24:45), which Schütz Zell often applied to Zell and other clergy (see "Psalms/Prayer" before and after n. 154; "Lament" before n. 90). She anticipates sharing in the wedding banquet wearing the robe of a guest, and, along with the good householder (minister) whom God set over His house to teach His word (Zell), she will be taken into heaven at the final harvest when angels will gather the good grain and burn the weeds.

and years of grace: therefore may He also draw to Himself all my goods, soul, body, feelings, all strength, heart, and understanding, make them His own, and give to me, thirsty and hungry as I am, nourishment out of His grain bin and treasury of produce of the grace of David, the true heavenly bread and food of the angels (that is, give me Himself). May He bestow upon me, a miserable, sick, and wounded person, power, strength, and eternal health, that finally (after I have long been vexed and seen the world through tears) I may again be comforted and may bring my robe with joy, enjoy myself with and in Him, and at the great harvest be brought with the good wise one by the reaping of the holy angels into the harvest of eternal life [cf. Mt 28:18, 22:11, 13:30, 37–43, 24:45; Is 11:1; Jn 6:32; Ps 78:25, 23:2].

My very dear sir, the dear woman Elsbeth Hecklin, whom you know well (praise God), has often urged me to write to you yet again, so that you would not think that I have cast you out of my heart and Christian love.[18] However, although I myself would like and am inclined to have much conversation, verbal and written, with you (as sometimes occurred during my dear husband's blessed life), yet I have always pointed out to her my many cares, crosses, and inability now to write as much as I did previously.

On account of my sins (but for his [Zell's] good), God has taken away my simple, good, upright husband. As you also well know, my husband denied me nothing. He did not rule over or compel my faith; he also never put any obstacles in the way of my faith but rather much more he actively furthered and helped me.[19] He granted and allowed me space and will to read, hear, pray, study, and be active in all good things, early and late, day and night: indeed, he took great joy in that—even when it meant less attention to or neglect in looking after his physical needs and running his household. He also never kept me from talking with you or visiting you or you from visiting me; he never kept me from hearing you or showing you kindness while

---

18. Elizabeth Scher Hecklin was a member of a high-ranking family who had settled in Strasbourg and who were strong supporters of Schwenckfeld. Although of lower social status than they, Schütz Zell had come to know the Scher family well, and among her last public acts would be preaching at the burials of Felicitas and then Elizabeth because their family did not want the city clergy to call the women heretics. Schütz Zell's association with the Schers was one reason she was considered a Schwenckfelder herself. She recognizes that at least Strasbourg Schwenckfelders, if not Schwenckfeld himself, believed that she had rejected him; they would have been the ones to hear her comments on his open letter in 1551.

19. The description of Zell here and later (see at nn. 31ff) emphasizes his support for her independent judgment in faith and friends and for her religious activities such as study, even at the expense of the usual religious duties of the good Protestant housewife. Even if this description is remembered through a haze of years, the sheer extent of Schütz Zell's reading and knowledge witness to its basic truth; cf. McKee, *Life and Thought*, 288–94.

you were in Strasbourg; also thereafter (when you had left Strasbourg) he did not keep me from writing to you. He never rebuked or disliked me because of that. But rather he much loved me and held me in great honor (not because of my beauty or wealth: I never had much of either), but because of my zeal, deeds, and faith, which were all he sought for in me at the beginning of our marriage.[20] I was never worthy of this love and honor. All that I have failed to do toward you or others was never his fault but mine because of my self-satisfaction, sin, wickedness, and lack of understanding. But I lamented all that before God and still confess it before Him and hope for forgiveness for all of it through the blood of His Son [cf. Eph 1:7].

Now, however, the Lord has not only robbed me of my husband, as my great help, but also after his death He has sent me so many crosses and afflictions that almost all my strength is crushed; and in addition to all these He has laid a great burden on my shoulders with my brother's son.[21] It would be too long to write what marvelous and difficult exchanges (as high as the cross) God has had with me! If you, dear sir, knew it, you would be amazed how I have kept "bonnet and bones," indeed, any strength. But the Lord has laid such rods on me because of my sins, as it is written, "The fool deserves the rod on his back" [Prv 26:3]. O dear sir, if you knew or saw what business I have with my nephew day and night, you would be moved to pity for me and say it is a wonder that I could read a page or write a single letter of the alphabet, indeed, that I could keep my senses.

But while I have borne such a cross, all friends and the whole city of Strasbourg left me suspended and floundering: those for whom I devoted the strength of my body and our substance, day and night! I must keep house with great expense on account of my poor sick boy and disburse everything I have—as if I were richer than the city of Strasbourg, with all its welfare agencies, agencies that I helped to establish and make rich! But I thank my God that in these and other crosses He teaches me many things and gives me strength and in that way makes me wiser than my (so-called) relatives; by this He also teaches me to acknowledge my sins, to confess and pray for them.[22] Indeed, if God did not take me into His sanctuary to

---

20. From beginning to end, Schütz Zell affirmed that it was not her worldly gifts but her faith that attracted her husband; see "Apologia" after n. 39; also "Strasbourg Citizens" at n. 87.

21. Lux Schütz was handicapped, probably mentally as well as physically; Schütz Zell had adopted him, and his care consumed most of her time and money in her later years; see below at nn. 22 and 40.

22. Schütz Zell had been a major support to the first administrator of the city poor relief organization after it was reorganized in 1523 and helped him establish a separate fund for refugees during the Peasants' War because they were not covered by the city welfare. As the

look on the purpose of it all, I could not bear it. But by His grace I will (I hope) with Him leap over the walls [Ps 73:17; 18:29]. Now then, I ask you, for the Lord's sake to forgive me this foolishness; I would rather have written something better and wiser instead of this, but you should indulge my foolishness in this, recognize my timidity, and pray to God for me.

I have also written so that you would not think that I stopped writing to you for so long either from unwillingness on account of what you did or because I was afraid of what people would say or think, or for other such reasons.[23] But believe me that I have little or no time, and when I do have some, I would rather read your books and others (especially the Holy Scriptures), to increase my comfort, understanding, service, and advancement (the only thing that is necessary) [cf. Lk 10:42]. I have been interrupted more than thirty times in writing this letter before I finished it; advancing years and weaknesses also contribute so that I no longer like to do so much at night as I used to do. Finally now I will let this apology stand, close it, and henceforth commend it to your Christian love and judgment. (Even now I would rather write to you about many other things, but I do not have time at present; I would also much rather talk with you and say more in one hour than in ten quires of paper.)

I had much to say to/against (*gegen*) you and your opponents:[24] I have been troubled in many things on all sides, and not entirely and in all things

---

child of a citizen her nephew could have been cared for by the welfare system, but for some years Schütz Zell took care of him herself, apparently at considerable expense. In 1555, when her health was worse, aunt and nephew both lived in one of the city hospices for a time; Schütz Zell was not satisfied with the conditions, physical or religious, and got reforms going but also moved out. The "relatives" who neglect this pastor's widow are the Strasbourg clergy.

23. Schütz Zell names (and dismisses) two things that might have caused her to break off the correspondence. It is quite probable that both of these possibilities were being voiced by Schwenckfelders. (1) "[W]hat you did" (*zuokumendem* indicates something influenced by a prior act) probably refers to Schwenckfeld's open letter of November 1551, which was ostensibly a letter of consolation for Schütz Zell because of an illness, but clearly claimed her as his follower. In introducing this piece, the editors of the *Corpus Schwenckfeldianorum* say that Schütz Zell became ill because of the attacks on Schwenckfeld and so he wrote to comfort and encourage her (references in McKee, *Writings*, 118, n. 9). On the contrary, although she would have appreciated a private letter of consolation, it is clear that Schütz Zell did not welcome Schwenckfeld's public claims; see McKee, "Katharina Schütz Zell and Caspar Schwenckfeld." There is also evidence in the Strasbourg archives (dated September 1553) that Schwenckfeld's letter had brought Schütz Zell to unfavorable attention so she had good reason to be angry with him (see McKee, *Life and Thought*, 159). (2) "[W]hat people would say or think" refers to the Strasbourg clergy's view of Schütz Zell as heretical for following Schwenckfeld, something his public letter certainly appeared to support.

24. The German here can mean "to" but also "(over) against"; the former sense is dominant when referring to Schwenckfeld, but the latter is also at least implied, especially in view of

content. However, I must say, as my good upright husband Matthew Zell often said to me, "God will take the capacity for speech away from me." Why? Because he knew that the world no longer deserved it. Oh this great word, that I did not then understand, but now understand very well! Yes, I could say that and more: but why should I do so much, or bestir myself? I am now a poor solitary (*armes einiges*) woman, fit only (as some say!) to spin or wait on the sick. But no matter which side I were on, if I were pleased with everything about them, those who say these things would speak differently about me, indeed they would idolize me.[25] I well believe that if I agreed that everything said on the preachers' side was right and pleased me, they would count me the most devout and learned woman in Germany. But since I do not do that, they regard me instead as a presumptuous spirit and (as some mockingly say) "doctor Kathrina." Also, those who love your [Schwenckfeld's] faith and understanding (however little they themselves resemble such!): if I agreed to be pleased with all their swollen heads and foolish behavior, they would do the same as the preachers—but I would have to possess the whole Spirit of God, though I have never seen a single one of the Spirit's feathers, much less received one![26]

But what else should I say about all this except that I thank my God that, from my youth on, He has given me good judgment, without love or hate, and at the age of discretion He made me completely free from all others in Christ my spouse.[27] Yes, He, the same Lord Christ Himself as the true Son, has freed me and taught me through His apostles that I should no

---

Schütz Zell's later criticisms of him as well as of his followers. The "(over) against" is dominant for Rabus, although Schütz Zell had also spoken her criticism of him to Rabus himself.

25. Schütz Zell ironically cites the condescending attitude of her critics (probably from both sides), who count her fit only for what (old) women were stereotypically supposed to do. However, she also knows that she is of enough importance in Strasbourg that her approval would enhance either the clergy's or the Schwenckfelders' position. Zell's widow, one of the most charitable and morally upright women of the city, was still a person of considerable influence because of her popularity with ordinary citizens, as even the city council recognized (and treated her carefully when they were obliged to rebuke her). Cf. McKee, *Life and Thought*, 191–93, 201–9, 226.

26. Schütz Zell refers to the claim for direct inspiration by the Holy Spirit, which at least some of the Schwenckfelders boasted as their authority (below she details a conversation with one of them). Here and below at n. 67 she alludes to Luther's sarcastic comment in *Against the Heavenly Prophets* about the "enthusiasts" who swallow the Holy Spirit "feathers and all." See McKee, *Writings*, 128, n. 22 for reference.

27. At the "age of discretion" usually meant the time of the sacrament of confirmation (seven being the youngest age for this). It might be the "ten years old" to which Schütz Zell refers in her other autobiographical statement (see "Strasbourg Citizens" at n. 91, "Psalms/Prayer" at n. 121) or perhaps when she was about seven (see below at n. 37). Bridal imagery for Christ and

longer be a servant of any person [human being], nor allow a halter to be laid on my neck. With His help that is what I will do: I will demonstrate my love and service everywhere to whoever seeks it, but I will not give myself as a prisoner to anyone. I will also not liken any element or creature to my spouse Christ, nor give to them the throne in my heart that He Himself once took through His grace.[28] I will never cast Him from that same throne, and so He will also not abandon me or allow me to be torn out of His hand [cf. Jn 8:36; 1 Cor 7:23; Acts 15:10; Eph 3:17].

Since, however, there are many complaints about me from both parties, I must nevertheless here briefly name the issues; please pardon me this. The one party [the preachers] says that I should not shame my good husband by being so "Schwenckfeldian" and withdrawing from and despising the church's preaching and sacraments (which indeed my good husband practiced as a minister of the church). The other [Schwenckfelder] party says that I am not willing to forsake the preachers and move wholly to the truth on the right side [theirs], although I already know and understand it, because I was a preacher's wife, in order that my husband's behavior may not be impugned. Also they say that I am motivated by pride, that I want my own ideas and understanding and do not want to confess to being taught by others, and more such things. All that I leave aside as useless and foolish sayings and commend to the one who knows and judges all hearts [cf. Lk 16:15; Acts 15:8; 1 Pt 2:23].

However, I must nevertheless answer a little about these points: not to you, whom I know to be wiser and more upright, but to the fools who have spoken them and the naïve who receive and believe such foolish talk.[29] For the first: I have said that no one can or should say that I do anything to shame

---

the soul or the Christian was common in medieval piety, although Schütz Zell's use is infrequent and very restrained; see below after n. 69 and after n. 70 (quotation of Psalm 45, a wedding psalm); "Women" at n. 7 and "Psalms/Prayer" at n. 123.

28. Schütz Zell considers mindless submission to any person a kind of imprisonment. Protestants rejected the Roman teaching of transubstantiation as a similar kind of imprisonment; Christ is not in bread, wine, or any other "creature," so to adore the host is to dethrone him. Below where she describes Rabus's teaching (at n. 46) it is clear that Schütz Zell considers (and condemns) the Lutheran doctrine of ubiquity as a form of transubstantiation, so it is probable that Rabus is her primary object here. In the 1550s, despite the Interim, Schütz Zell was much more concerned about the insidious danger of "Roman" teaching among Protestants than the long recognized danger of Rome itself; she also felt betrayed by such teaching on the part of Protestants.

29. Although she explicitly distinguishes Schwenckfeld from the foolish, there may be implicit criticism here (see below at nn. 52 and 58, explicit after n. 68). Schütz Zell outlines for Schwenckfeld what she has said to Rabus (her response to the preachers' accusations). A rather more diffuse but similar form of this is found in her letters to Rabus, which is why the present text (not being carefully read) has often mistakenly been considered an earlier letter addressed

my upright and now blessed husband.[30] I do not tell them [the preachers] that they should think I am right; I do not ask them to approve my expression of my faith and deeds. If, however, they regard it as a shame to my honorable husband that I read Schwenckfeld's books and consider these as in part better and closer to the honor of Christ than their own, then I say "You are wrong [I am not shaming him]." I read these books twenty-four years ago, not in secret, books including one in which the blessed upright Dr. Capito wrote a fine preface in which he gave witness to Schwenckfeld's spirit and good gifts.[31] I have also never had anything secret or hidden from my dear husband, especially in spiritual matters; for we always had, for the most part, a like understanding and judgment in the Holy Scriptures, in the beginning, middle, and end, as long as we were together. He himself also at times read Schwenckfeld's books, gladly heard me read them, and never allowed evil to be spoken of him [Schwenckfeld] in his house. He loved Schwenckfeld and allowed me to hear his lectures on the two epistles of Saint Peter and other books, which he gave in the house of the dear blessed Dr. Capito, who also allowed his own wife to hear these lectures when Schwenckfeld was his houseguest. Schwenckfeld was also dear to Capito.

Also when I wrote to Sir Caspar Schwenckfeld (something I never did without my husband's knowledge), it was rare that my husband did not tell me to put in a greeting from him. Though he did not understand or accept everything that Schwenckfeld wrote, he never insulted him or condemned him because he thought of what Saint Peter says: "They insult and condemn what they have never known or understood" [2 Pt 2:12]. My husband always stood in holy fear of God in his judgment and said he would seek to be taught by a child; he did not stand in such pride and mischief in his old age as you [Rabus] do now in your youth. In sum, he died not as an enemy

---

to Rabus. It would be wholly out of character for Schütz Zell to criticize one person to another behind the offender's back, so although there is no written form of her rebuke to Rabus at this date, she had certainly said this to him verbally (as she explains in her letters to Rabus himself later). Note her distinction between the deceived and the deceivers, where she feels obliged (in love) to set both straight (as she explicitly does in the "Apologia" at n. 16 and before n. 21).

30. Defending Zell is one of his wife's key concerns. Rabus accuses her of dishonoring Zell by associating with Schwenckfeld and reading his books, so she vindicates Zell's support for both. Later she also has to defend Zell against the Schwenckfelders' slander (at nn. 57–59).

31. Wolfgang Capito was one of the four leading reformers of Strasbourg, very learned and of higher social status than the others; in 1524 he married Agnes Roettel, daughter of a prestigious Strasbourg family. Schwenckfeld lived with the Capitos 1529–31. The book was Schwenckfeld's "Apologia," published in 1529; one edition includes Capito's preface in which he describes the author as a *lieben* or *beiländige* brother and approves his teaching on the Lord's Supper (for references see McKee, *Writings*, 129, n. 29). Here and repeatedly Schütz Zell the historian refers to numbers: years, times, etc., as part of her proof.

but as a friend of Schwenckfeld; you should not speak otherwise of him or I will oppose you. In the last night before his death he earnestly said to me that I should tell his assistant ministers (of whom you also were one) that when they were preaching they should leave Schwenckfeld and the [Ana]Baptists alone and learn to preach Christ.[32]

Therefore I do not shame my dear husband or defy or disrespect him when I read Schwenckfeld's books, and I have and keep my free judgment about them and test them by the touchstone of Holy Scripture. The reason is that when he [Zell] was alive he never hindered or forbade that but always told me (as he himself also did) to read and listen, and so, after testing (as they do with the stone that is used to try gold), to hold to the good [cf. 1 Thes 5:21]. That I should therefore be considered "Schwenckfeldian," to this I say "no." For St. Paul said, "Why is one an 'Apolloian,' the other a 'Paulian' or a 'Peterian'? Were these men crucified for you? Was not Christ crucified for you?" [cf. 1 Cor 1:12–13]. Neither Schwenckfeld nor the dear Dr. Luther nor any devout minister, none of them ever sought that; I also will not do it. I do not want to be theirs [e.g., *Luther*ian], but with them I want to be Christ's [*Christ*ian]. However, the teachers who know much about righteousness will shine on that day of judgment like the sun and stars of the heaven. Such shining and reward, which Paul commended [Dn 12:3; 1 Thes 2:6], I do not want. Nor can I attribute it to them, but I want and ought to take it from them and give it to Christ. If we should count disciples according to whose teaching one hears and whose books one reads, that is, if a person is a disciple of a teacher or writer and should be called by his name if he reads his books—then all of you [Rabus and friends] must be called by the names of Aristotle, Virgil, Plato, Cicero, and many such heathens, also papist and all heathen poets and hypocrites, and be their disciples! Yes, also Turk and Mohammed, whose Koran and all whose books you still always read, and more than is sometimes good.[33] I could indeed give many examples of this.

---

32. Schütz Zell always uses "Baptists" for those usually called Anabaptists (rebaptizers) because of their rejection of infant baptism in favor of adult or believer's baptism. Here she cites Zell's deathbed instructions to his assistant Rabus, which the latter has ignored—a very serious fault.

33. The first "academic joke"; Schütz Zell had certainly heard the names of these classical writers from the clergy, although the way she lists them suggests that she did not know much about them. "Turk" was commonly used for all Muslims, who were prominent in German minds because of the Ottoman Turk conquests and wars in eastern Europe in the 1520s, especially the siege of Vienna in 1529. In 1540–42 there was a new surge of the military struggle and with it more attention to Islam, and it is to this that Schütz Zell refers. A Latin translation of the Koran was published by Theodor Bibliander in 1540 in Zurich, and Luther presented his own German version in 1542.

Why then should I not read the books of a Christian, in which he exhibits Christ my Lord and God as a mighty redeemer of the human race?

You say, however, that Schwenckfeld despises and does not observe the preaching, church service, and sacraments, but I will gather an answer out of his teaching to refute this. I have never understood from him, as long as I have known him (more than twenty-four years) that he despised all these things, but that he spoke of them entirely spiritually and gloriously to the honor of Christ and would gladly have helped to bring them out of error into the truth and right command and practice of Christ. He would teach people how to distinguish between the body and the shadow, as also his published books in part confess and exhibit; whoever would like to know about these matters, let him read for himself. Therefore he [Schwenckfeld] does not need my answering for him; he can (praise God) do it himself. But inasmuch as I nevertheless must witness to the truth and confess it before God, without any love or hate caused by attachment to him or anyone, I can truthfully say that he never has told me to remain away from the preaching. Rather he has counseled me to go, but then with a right and spiritual judgment to distinguish among teachings.[34] He also himself preached and heard preaching: yes, from the heart he sought to hear my dear husband and often attended his sermons.

You do me wrong to think that I would then leave church, preaching, and sacraments out of disregard for them: wherever I am or whatever I do, I would never leave the church (*kurch*) of Christ, in whose communion I always seek to remain (according to the saying of David in the eighth letter of the 119th Psalm) [Ps 119:63].[35] However, that I leave the outward church gathering and preaching, and cannot always visit it (as you think I should do), for that I will not lay a halter on my neck or allow myself to be

---

34. Rabus's second complaint about Zell's widow, that is, that she does not come regularly to worship, may be the more important one. Reading Schwenckfeld's books was not necessarily a public matter, although Schütz Zell also made these available to others who inquired about "the heretic," and that was an annoyance. Not attending public worship was more serious because that was very visible and others might follow Schütz Zell's example. Her answer: Schwenckfeld is not opposed to public worship but teaches a right (critical) judgment about it—something she believes is exactly contrary to what Rabus wants.

35. Schütz Zell distinguishes between the universal church/*kurch* and the local church/*gemeyn*, here translated "parish" because she is referring to the established church structures. Psalm 119 is a long acrostic text in which each of the twenty-two sections begins with a successive letter of the Hebrew alphabet, letters that also have the value of numbers. Schütz Zell could have learned this from Luther's exposition of the Psalm, which also says that the use of "thine" or an equivalent in every verse is intended to draw people away from human teaching and keep them in God's. This fits Schütz Zell's purpose of affirming her allegiance to the church but not to Rabus's outward forms.

bound to place and time [cf. Acts 15:10; Gal 4:10]. But for the sake of the prayer of the parish (*gemeyn*) (which at this time is still weak) I am always willing to join in crying to heaven in prayer and to go with the crowd to the temple, as David says [Ps 42:4 with echo of 18:29]. And—God willing—I would like often to pray with the parish and to hear preaching (although the church of Christ is not bound to that, for prayer does not have to be done either on this mountain or temple but in spirit and in truth [cf. Jn 4:21, 23]). Still I would gladly do this if you preached Christ rightly and did not hatefully abuse those who love Him.

For I also am no longer a young schoolchild who is still drinking milk and learning the ABCs; but I am an old student who has studied a long time, when you [Rabus and friends] were still children and played in the sand. I ought now to be a Master, while you would be a student who lights the fires. (Please accept this little joke well.)[36] I have exercised myself in the Holy Scriptures and godly matters for more than forty-eight years now and never abandoned the grace of God; I have heard the old teachers and let them be my counselors and made the wine new (to put in new skins) since I was ten years old [Mt 9:16, 17; Mk 2:22]. I never got bogged down hearing, learning, and following until the day (sad to me but happy to him) of the death of my dear and good husband.[37] I could now teach others and with the elderly Anna prophesy about Christ to those who are waiting for redemption and praise the Lord [cf. Lk 2:36–38]. But considering that I must appropriately be submissive under the man's office, according to the teaching of Saint Paul [cf. 1 Cor 14:34; 1 Tm 2:12], I myself seek to hear others and to be exhorted[38] as far as they speak the truth! But where that is

---

36. Rabus, born in 1523, is still much less experienced in the faith than Schütz Zell. This is the second "academic joke"; "Master" was the title for an advanced university degree but could also be used for other professions in which practical apprenticeship was the preparation. The irony is apparent: Rabus was not only a university graduate but had just that spring received his doctorate, while Schütz Zell had only a vernacular education. However, she outranks him in knowledge of the faith, as she shows by outlining her study and describing *her* teachers.

37. The dates are important for Schütz Zell's understanding of her lifelong religious study and commitment as well as her affirmation of human teachers, including those of her Roman childhood. (1) In October 1553 "more than 48 years" would be mid-1505, meaning she began her serious religious education when she was about seven and a half. (2) "[S]ince I was ten years old" refers to her dedication to God (see "Psalms/Prayer" at n. 121; "Strasbourg Citizens" at n. 91). The biblical image is Jesus's instruction: if you put new wine into old wineskins they will break and you will lose both the wine and the skins, so you must put new wine into new wineskins; in effect, this means putting the new life of dedication to God into new patterns of living.

38. Schütz Zell claims her authority to teach on the basis of what the elderly Anna did when Jesus's parents brought the baby to the temple to offer the sacrifices prescribed by the law; see "Strasbourg Citizens" at n. 85. "Prophesy" here does not mean to foretell but to proclaim.

Autobiography and Polemic 197

not so, then I would tell you and not keep silent, but speak, point out, and answer your wrong preaching and insulting words about the innocent.[39]

Against my will, however, I cannot hear many sermons. God has laid on me a great marvelous cross with my sick boy, which you all know well. What should I do with him? I wish that you preachers with your wives and "gracious ladies," together with many hypocritical people who attend sermons,[40] sometimes had to do what I sometimes must do during the sermon time! To undertake such great work and horror, to wash filth and urine night and day, so that I use up all my strength. How gladly I would during that same time sit in the sermon, speculate, and have the book lie open on my lap and then go out to be a "gracious lady." And then when the church is closed, leave in it what I have heard there and let it remain just words and lie about my profit, desire, and pride—but yet highly praise the sermon, count all the others, and see which ones were present and which were not! What is that except to make hearing sermons like the Jewish hypocrites?! who said to the Lord that He was a master and spoke the truth. But they did not ask Him sincerely about the way of truth as Nicodemus did— Nicodemus who did not come to the Lord with officiousness in the temple (as the Jews did), but with fear, secretly and by night. The hypocrites also did not ask about the way of truth as Nicodemus did; they asked Him about temporal matters, whether they should give the emperor money for the tax or withhold it [cf. Mk 12:13–15; Jn 3:1–2].

Oh, how many have listened to you preachers, and still do, on account of this tax money! They have greeted you and spoken well to you as if they were sincere, but have used their craft to see if they could get from you a

---

In the previous verses (Lk 2:25–35), Simeon has recognized the Christ; then the 84-year-old widow Anna, who has spent most of her life in prayer in the temple, "preaches" about Christ to the gathered people. Devout and learned, Anna is the elderly Schütz Zell's favorite biblical model of the woman preacher, but because of her strong focus on biblical authority Schütz Zell feels bound by Paul's words in 1 Corinthians 14:34 against women's speaking. However, she interprets this verse narrowly as a ban on official access to a pulpit ("ordination," although she does not use that word), not as a general prohibition on women speaking in public. See McKee, *Life and Thought*, 407–18.

39. The limits of the obligation to listen to ordained men ministers are clear: the preacher must speak the Gospel and not insult other Christians. Schütz Zell has two justifications: she has been taught by Luther, Zell, and her own reading of scripture to know what the Gospel is, so she is qualified to judge; and she also recognizes the character of the insults as untrue because she has long been acquainted with the people Rabus ignorantly defames. See McKee, *Life and Thought*, 398–407.

40. She suggests that Rabus's hearers are people of leisure who go to church for show; there they speculate (not meditate) on what they hear but do not practice it—instead they gossip about absentees, such as Schütz Zell herself.

conscience big enough that a cart could drive through it. You are not wise and understanding like Christ, however, to recognize such hearts and imposture [cf. Jn 2:24–25 or 13:11]. If people only do not accuse you of wrongdoing, but say "amen" to all your teaching and deeds, do not miss any sermon, take the Lord's Supper every time, etc., then you think that you have a fine tablecloth or vessel when it is outwardly clean, even if inwardly it is still a cat's dish [cf. Mt 23:25–26].[41] It is also the same with receiving the sacraments, which you say that I denigrate and avoid. I say "no," I do not denigrate them. Indeed, considering how you believe, teach, and behave, it would not be surprising if a great disrespect fell on the sacraments, as it did in the papacy! However, whenever you wish me to show you all my reasons for remaining away from the sacraments for a long time I will be happy to do so; I will show you that it is your own fault that drives me and others away, as I also once wrote to the blessed Dr. Luther.[42]

That you bring an action against me and say that my dear blessed husband practiced the sacraments in the church service, I say, yes, I know it well, I practiced them with him. But I did not make them a daily flea market or hypocrisy. He believed, taught, and behaved differently in these things than you. He was also different in his vocation, teaching, and life than you are. He did not—with deathly hate—make into an enemy any upright person who honored, loved, and taught Christ; he did not reproach such a person or seek to bring him into the hands of the magistracy and hangman, as you do. For I knew his good upright heart, faith, and life, his complete understanding of the Holy Scriptures and love toward those who believe and love Christ. He never sought to harm anyone or cast out or condemn anyone, except those whom Christ and His apostles cast out and condemned, but rather he sought for Christ's sake to gather together all who confess Christ [cf. Lk 13:34].[43]

---

41. Schütz Zell uses a vivid metaphor for an elastic conscience (big enough to let a wagon through), as she points out that the parishioners who flatter the ministers are manipulating them and the ministers like Rabus who lap up this superficial piety are quite happy to make no stringent demands as long as appearances are fine.

42. Schütz Zell tacitly agrees that she is staying away from the sacraments but blames Rabus's own behavior. Her analysis of the latter is the most devastating accusation possible: Rabus is leading the church in the direction of the medieval/Roman sins, for example, wrong understanding and use of the sacraments. Given her other criticisms of Rabus and Rome (see below at n. 46), she probably means that the sacraments are being used as magical rites (*opus operatum*), which are considered effective without faith or repentance (appropriate love of the neighbor) on the part of priest or people. The letter to Luther was written after the Marburg debate; see "Psalms/Prayer" n. 155.

43. Schütz Zell first describes Zell's pastoral behavior. He never persecuted or brought civil coercion to bear on those who did not agree with him on secondary matters provided they

Autobiography and Polemic 199

He also confessed and taught how to seek salvation, peace, and righteousness, his own and everyone's—not in creatures or elements, but only in the blood and death of Jesus Christ, His resurrection from the dead, and now His being at the right hand of God His Father in like honor, might, authority, and divine majesty. We are not to look for it stuck in bread, as you do! How many times and often did he say that he spoke to the heart so that the words of Christ might be received and grasped with true faith and that he did not speak to the bread?![44] Therefore it was fitting that I broke with him the bread of unity, remembrance, and fellowship of our Lord Jesus Christ, to confess to him and to others my like faith [cf. 1 Cor 10:16, 11:24–26]. How can I then break bread with you? You do not behave in his fashion or walk in his footsteps. Matthew Zell, who loved and sheltered pilgrims who had been driven out of their homes, who was a comforter and protector of the innocent—he never practiced the pastoral office as you do! With him I have exhibited and confessed the true and free faith sufficiently to prove that I hold it and have not yet become disloyal to his and my faith and confession.[45]

Ah, how often did he say, to me and from the pulpit, "It will happen after this that you will make a work, *opus opperatus* [*opus operatum*], out of taking the Lord's Supper and hearing sermons, as they did in the papacy out of the Mass and indulgences."[46] Such prophecies I have (I fear) experienced. You young preachers sit now in Moses's seat, but you are not his [Zell's] successors as he was Saint Paul's. You ate out of his plate, received his teaching

---

shared the fundamental point of Christ as sole savior. The only ones Zell excluded were ones who rejected Christ (refused to believe and allow Him to save them), which for the Zells meant people who followed Roman teaching. For the Zells' theological distinctions, see McKee, *Life and Thought*, chap. 10, esp. 273ff.

44. Next she defends Zell's teaching: justification only through trust in Christ, not through trust in anything created, especially not the bread and wine of the sacrament. She insists that Zell addressed Christ's promises to people to be believed. He did not say "this is my body" to the bread to make Christ's body present "under" the bread, as in the Lutheran teaching of ubiquity which Rabus shared (see introduction to chapter 2 at n. 2 and below at n. 46).

45. The language here, "breaking the bread of unity, remembrance, fellowship, . . . to confess to him and to others" echoes clearly the Zwinglian view of the Lord's Supper (see "Psalms/Prayer" at n. 158). In particular, the emphasis on the Supper as a pledge of faith was characteristic of the communal orientation of Zwingli and the Reformed tradition (and not of Luther). Schütz Zell takes it for granted that fellowship in the Supper should be based not only on right teaching (the words of consecration spoken to the people to be received with faith, not to the bread to change it into something else), but also on appropriate respect for other Christians ("discerning the body" as she calls it in "Psalms/Prayer" at n. 160).

46. In Roman teaching the mechanical enactment of the sacrament (*opus operatum*) was efficacious as a "good work," that is, meritorious in God's sight simply by being done (see above at n. 2). In her letters to Rabus Schütz Zell cites his agreement with a colleague's sermon in which

and work, but now you trample him in the ground [Mt 23:2, 26:23; Heb 10:29; Rm 10:9ff]. The words of his teaching and confession in the breaking of bread you have thrown out, and those people whom he loved and never hated or scolded you now condemn so terribly and revile and abuse so slanderously—with so many untrue and detestable sayings by which you shamelessly hand them over to the devil as much as you are able [1 Cor 5:5]. I pleaded with you in a very friendly way, also showed you writings and books to give you a better understanding of Schwenckfeld, but nothing helped.

How then can I break and eat the bread of love and unity with such deathly enemies, and make myself a participant with them, when the wise man warns not to eat physical bread with the envious, and much more Saint Paul forbids doing so with this bread, the Lord's Supper, and John says that the one who hates his brother is a murderer [2 Jn 11; Prv 23:6; 1 Cor 10:16–21; 1 Jn 3:15].[47] But you hate him [Schwenckfeld] with full and furious hate, he who confessed Christ with us, indeed in many ways did so much better than you. Where did the old Matthew Zell do this? He into whose field and work you all have come. He also was zealous against false teaching—but in a very different way! Also his fellow preachers: Capito, Hedio, and others of the old ones did so; those clergy loved the church and worked for her fully as much as you. Which one among them—even Bucer himself, who was otherwise indeed very hard and strong against him [Schwenckfeld]—which one ever talked about him so horribly from the pulpit before the people? Yes, not one of them ever publicly and shamelessly so dishonored him as you do. And neither did you, in the time before your position was secure: but now you and your young fools, when you are well set [you change your coats for your own advantage]![48]

However, you are truly not the folk to knock down one to whom you do not measure up: you do not come up to his waist. You do not have the

---

the family of a little girl (who had not been baptized as an infant) was in essence told that if she had died before baptism she would have been lost (cf. McKee, *Writings*, 248 at n. 292; 246, n. 284 for Rabus himself). Her use of the phrase *opus operatum* indicates Schütz Zell's clear understanding of the doctrine but since she misspells the words (writing *opus opperatus*), it is apparent that she did not really know it as Latin.

47. It was agreed that eating and drinking unworthily would bring damnation (1 Cor 11:29), but ideas of what constituted unworthiness varied. Following 1 Corinthians 10:16–21 Schütz Zell insists that one requirement for table fellowship is being at peace with the community; those who hate others cannot eat the meal rightly, and sharing it with those who hate or teach hate is equally wrong.

48. Capito and Caspar Hedio were, with Bucer and Zell, the four leading reformers of Strasbourg. Their relations with Schwenckfeld ranged from friendly to combative; Capito and

sling and spirit of David, nor do you have a Philistine in front of you [1 Sm 17:40ff]. You should think better of abusing a man who, in all the gifts of God, spiritual and bodily, is so far above you; who is also of such an honorable age and name (a family whom also the heathens sometimes spared and held in honor). Also you should follow what the wise man teaches: to rise up before gray heads, and Saint John: to rebuke the elders like fathers (and not like devils and blasphemers, which they indeed are not) [Lv 19:32; 1 Tm 5:1].[49]

These are, among others, my reasons for withdrawing from the fellowship of your sacraments and why I have till now avoided them. The other reasons I will gladly show you and tell you, when you wish. Also I will gladly hear all that you have against me, explain my views with simplicity and truth, and make my free confession, which I know is not contrary to my faith and confession during my dear husband's life—it was also his own! I hope that you will allow me to abide by this. If you do not, then I must commend it to God, to whom I have given soul and body, and not to any human person: no person should have any more power over such matters as faith than what God allows, which is to kill the body or cast it into prison. Otherwise I want always to be one of God's freed ones [cf. 1 Pt 4:19; Jn 19:11; 1 Cor 7:22].[50]

Now, dear sir [Schwenckfeld], this is what, among other words, I have answered Rabus and his clerical friends. I will not say more until I am driven further, for I think it does not become me to step out further before I am called and forced to speak. Thus I want to allow God to give me what I should say and do [cf. Mt 10:19–20].[51]

Zell were the most welcoming, Bucer the least. The latter strongly opposed Schwenckfeld from 1533 on and won Capito's cooperation, but the arguments were conducted in church synods, not from the pulpit, and they never included physical harm. Rabus himself changed his stance between the time he was an assistant without his own pulpit and his later secure place in the cathedral parish with all the first generation gone. (Hedio, who died in 1552, was the last of the four "fathers.")

49. Schütz Zell may be citing a story Schwenckfeld had told her. According to his biographer, his family coat of arms may signify that they fought against the Tartars at Liegnitz, 1241 (reference, McKee, *Writings*, 138, n. 71). Here she makes a rare mistake in biblical attribution; the text is Pauline (1 Tm), not "Saint John."

50. Schütz Zell concludes the account of her defense to Rabus and politely asks him to accept her confession, but if he does not she will not change. She adds an implied criticism: the only power he has over her is to kill or harm her body (he can persecute her as he has others), but he has no authority to change her faith.

51. The condition for saying more was for the sake of "the honor of Christ and of God" (see below after n. 56). Eventually she published what she had said, when Rabus paid no attention to anything she said or wrote (see "Strasbourg Citizens" at nn. 96–100); each time she gives

How should I answer the other party? The ones who highly praise your faith (which you have in Christ), who say that I am not willing to break with the preachers and will not side with the truth on account of my husband; and that it hurts my pride since I want to live by my own understanding and do not wish to confess to being taught by others, as I have said above. I cannot go over the whole business here, but nevertheless I must answer a little so that you may not think it is really the way they say. For I have seen in some of your letters written to (mutual) good friends that all kinds of sayings about me come to you; that is why I once wrote to you appealing to your love, that if people sometimes complain about me to you, I would like (to know so as) to respond.[52]

Now regarding the first complaint, that I am unwilling to avoid the preachers, etc., I must ask those same fools how I am supposed to avoid them.[53] Should I do what they [the Schwenckfelders] so much complain about the preachers doing to them? That is, should I hate and despise and abuse the preachers and cry out against and scold everyone—people who (I know) nevertheless in many things gladly do their best. [Besides the gratuitous attacks by the preachers], we also know that many people fail from lack of understanding; should I not consider the example of Saint Paul? He was an enemy of Christ, a great persecutor of His church and one who took pleasure in the death of Stephen, and yet nevertheless he obtained mercy and thereafter became a pillar of the same church he had persecuted and then worked and suffered more for it than all the others did [cf. Acts 8:1, 9:1ff; 1 Tm 1:13; Gal 2:9; 2 Cor 11:23]. Along with that there is the example of the Samaritan who did good to one who was a foreigner to his faith. Yes, also much more, there is the command of Christ to pray for our enemies, to speak

---

biblical grounds for her action—not simply to justify it to Rabus but also probably to justify it to her own conscience. The basis is here: she responds when compelled by her conscience and trusts that in that circumstance God will supply the words, according to His promise in Matthew 10:19–20.

52. Schütz Zell begins her answer to the Schwenckfelders by briefly listing again their charges, but goes on to chide Schwenckfeld. He repeated the charges in letters to their mutual friends, including Elizabeth Scher Hecklin who had persuaded her to write this letter, without first checking with her as she had specifically requested in case of misunderstanding. This also suggests that the criticisms by the Schwenckfelders had been going on for some time, since they antedated Schütz Zell's last letter to Schwenckfeld, which was probably at least several years earlier than this one.

53. What does "avoidance" mean? (1) Is it attacking the clergy the way they attack others, especially the Schwenckfelders and herself? Schütz Zell is discriminating; she does not make a blanket accusation of all the clergy but recognizes both human failings and repentance and further she offers grounds for being forbearing with those who do wrong, in hopes that they will repent.

and do good to those who speak evil, and He Himself did not revile others in return when He was reviled [cf. Lk 10:30–35, 6:27–28; 1 Pt 2:23].

Besides, I must ask them [the Schwenckfelders], What fellowship do I still have with the preachers that I should break off? Since they scarcely know me nor I them anymore—indeed, they have forgotten all my good deeds to them.[54] Do I count it as just when they act unjustly? Or do I help them increase, gather, and keep together their goods, pleasure, nobility? Are they fornicators, tyrants, drunkards, and such like folk, and I with them, eating of their unjust bread? Do I bestir myself for them to gain the favor of the emperor with all kinds of effort, in all kinds of worldly activities and business by which they abandon their spirituality? Do I make myself in such matters like the others, the world's children, and not keep my house in order [cf. Lk 16:8; 1 Tm 3:4]? Where I have fellowship with them in such matters, there will I break with them and gladly suffer rebuke!

I would like, however, to say this and more about those who defame me. I have also said some of it *to* them, and they know that I do not lie, although they persuade you—as you have written to the dear woman [Elizabeth Hecklin]: "The good Kathrina should not be so hasty to believe (that we are defaming her)." I would also ask the same of you, very dear sir. Besides, I do not need to believe hastily, when I know it for a fact and they must also acknowledge it to me.[55]

---

54. Is avoidance (2) tolerating or helping the clergy in the pursuit of worldly gain? She does not help them with such matters and would gladly be punished if it were so. Schütz Zell rejects not only visible immorality but also worldly behavior (they "abandon their spirituality"). Although Protestants made an explicit distinction between the person and the office in principle, they expected clergy to maintain a higher standard of behavior than laity because of the importance and visibility of their office. One of Schütz Zell's most devastating critiques of Ludwig Rabus was that he was just an ordinary Christian, not fit for his ministerial task. "I do not deny that he is as devout as any worldly 'worthy' is; I readily believe that he does not steal, he has not stained himself with other crude offenses; he also prays and gives alms, punishes crude offenses, and has other good virtues . . . But all this is still not the right piety which is appropriate to and necessary for a wise scripture-learned and prudent steward of God, a rightly faithful shepherd and servant of Christ and His church . . ." For fuller discussion, see McKee, *Life and Thought*, 280–84 (quotation on 283 is cited from her response to Rabus's accusations). Note that Schütz Zell applies to herself a phrase describing a minister/bishop as one who rules his house well (1 Tm 3:4); she is in fact head of her household, but the allusion suggests that she sets the same standard for every mature Christian, even if it means applying a term used for a man and bishop to herself, a woman (!).

55. Schütz Zell has spoken to the Schwenckfelders who accuse her of being quick to believe gossip/take offense: she is not going behind their backs as they—and Schwenckfeld himself—have done. She turns the tables on Schwenckfeld, who has cited this charge (gossip) to Hecklin: he should not be so quick to believe the tales (or go behind her back)! She herself does not have to rely on gossip because she has personally heard the Schwenckfelder charges.

Now further [the second complaint], they say that I will not side with the truth on the right side, that is, I cannot and will not spin to suit everyone—although the one who says this does not himself act in all things in right faith and judgment of love. God allows me daily to see so much! Because of that I thank Him and will not allow anyone to bind me. Nor will I, without foundation and the understanding of my heart, copy them like a monkey putting on shoes or like a child copying the mother in praying the "Our Father in Heaven" who still knows only the earthly father.[56] I have sided with Christ, who is the truth itself, the way, and the life, at the right hand of God His Father, and I seek every day to come to Him, the longer I live, the more; I hope, too, that He will not deny me or cast me from Him. Also I have not (I hope) practiced any hypocrisy toward anyone of high or low estate, and I have made my confession (so much as my conscience has received and is convinced of) in health and in sickness and never been ashamed of it [cf. Jn 14:6, 6:37; Ps 110:1; Mt 10:33; Rm 1:16]. I am not afraid also to confess my faith before many people, when the advancement of the honor of Christ and of God requires that.

As for the third complaint, they say that I do not change because of my dear husband. Why should I abandon what I profess on his account? When was he ever so contrary to me or the honor and knowledge of Christ? Did he behave and teach so badly, or know Christ so little—Christ whom he indeed preached with such great faithfulness and effort and prepared the field for others with his plow and at his expense and did not seek his own interest in this; to that I can give witness before God! He proclaimed Christ as the perfect and true Son of God, held Him for his Lord and God, loved, honored, and prayed to Him [cf. Jn 4:38, 5:30, 20:28]. Also, in the last night before his death he said in great pain, "O my Lord and God, Jesus Christ! I have preached You wholly faithfully according to my small ability, which You have given to me; You know that. I confess You still, against all the gates of hell. To You, to You, I give up my spirit and my office; You remain the chief shepherd over Your poor people." Besides this he said many other such beautiful words and prayers, on his knees, with great earnestness [cf. Mt 16:18; Ps 31:5; 1 Pt 5:4].

---

56. The charge of not agreeing with them although she knows they are right Schütz Zell interprets as demanding mindless conformity and rote learning without comprehension—a complaint Protestants made against the traditional Roman church (!). The first example suggests that the act being imitated is foolish; the second example does not intend disrespect to the content of the Prayer but emphasizes that rote memorization is the childish act of someone who does not actually know the person she is addressing. Schütz Zell goes on to affirm that her confession is based on conscience and conviction combined with sincere behavior.

Then how dare the foolish blockhead say that he was "a good heathen" and did not know Christ![57] Ach! Did he [Zell] not know the one to whom, in such a mighty battle (to put off the mortal and to put on the immortal), he commended and entrusted his spirit [cf. 1 Cor 15:53; Ps 31:5]—not for a time but for eternity! And at the last, with great earnestness, he commended to me that I should serve that same one my whole life long. Therefore, these people really lie about him. Let the one who accuses Zell ask God that it be forgiven him, and let him check whether he is lying when he says his confession comes from right knowledge and truthful faith and finally brings such a truce with the devil at the end! When you must speak with the enemy [devil] before the door of death—then it will be serious!—it will not matter anymore to mix in all worldly business and to talk a lot about the Spirit. Your "follower" should also not have said this to dishonor you, to rebuke your holy witness as a lie, since what he says contradicts what you so movingly wrote me to comfort me in my cross (after my dear husband's death), and I believe what you wrote was not hypocritical.[58]

I hope and do not doubt that the Lord has received from him [Zell] his pound with interest and told him to enter into the joy of his Lord and so now he rests in Christ from all his work [cf. Lk 19:13ff with Mt 25:21, 23; Heb 4:10]. How should I be ashamed to hide something on his account, something that I know in truth and am obligated to confess? He was not ashamed to confess his faults in his life here on earth, after he came to know them. Then should I now consider it a shame to confess our faults (where I know them) for him and myself? If we did not acknowledge that we had been wrong, if we did not want to be shamed or disgraced by recognizing our fault, we would have had to remain in all our former error and lack of understanding. Also Paul would have had to remain in his legal zeal, and Matthew and Zacheus in their unjust gain, in order not to be shamed by confessing that they had been wrong [cf. Phil 3:5–6; Mt 9:9; Lk 19:2–10].

---

57. Occasionally Christian humanists proposed including among the saved some of the pre-Christian philosophers like Socrates who were famous for their piety. Zwingli did so; Luther once accepted but then attacked the idea (for references cf. McKee, *Writings*, 142, n. 91). Although apparently not all Schwenckfelders accused Zell of being a "good heathen" (not knowing Christ), this lie probably angered his widow more than Rabus's view of Zell.

58. Schütz Zell points to the deathbed with the devil at the door as the point where one recognizes the seriousness of faith and tells the Schwenckfelder that his worldly claims and babbling of being inspired by the Holy Spirit will not matter then. She presents the Schwenckfelder's slander of Zell as dishonor to Schwenckfeld himself, but in effect she catches the latter in a dilemma: he can deny his letter of consolation or disown what has actually been said by his follower.

No. I am not so foolish that, where I know his faults, I would want to keep silent and not confess the truth (of which I am convinced in my heart). Here on earth, in his weakness, he never asked that of me; how would I serve him now by denying his sins, when he is in the state of peace, where he and all the blessed no longer are burdened by any faults? On the contrary, after he came to recognize the truth, he so gladly, freely, and openly, with no shame, confessed his faults, errors, and ignorance, which he (like all of us) had while under the papacy.[59] Yes, it is a much greater source of praise and joy to turn from what is recognized as error to the truth; all the angels rejoice over that [cf. Lk 15:10]. Therefore, I also would not be at all ashamed to break with something bad or turn from ignorance, if I knew of it; for the apostle teaches us always to grow in understanding, and in His humanity the child Jesus also increased in wisdom, age, and grace with God and people. Of these things [acknowledging our sins, growing in knowledge] my good husband and I have also never been ashamed, and I do not pride myself that I have (even) yet learned everything or understood everything, but I still pursue this [cf. 2 Pt 3:18; Lk 2:52; Phil 3:12].

Now for the fourth criticism: that (as they say) pride makes me so set on remaining in my own ideas and understanding and unwilling to be taught by someone else.[60] God knows that this is a blind and presumptuous judgment! My pride, glory, and boast is only in my Lord Jesus Christ, as the prophet says, "The one who wants to glory, let him glory in the Lord" [cf. 1 Cor 1:31; Jer 9:23–24]. I have always listened in my heart to the saying of God: "Hear, O Israel; in yourself is your destruction, but in Me is your salvation" [cf. Dt 6:4; Hos 13:9]. And again, "The one who wants to be taught must be taught by God (not by himself)"; and Saint Paul says, "No one is wise of himself"; and the dear James says, "The one who wants wisdom, let him ask it of God" [cf. Is 54:13; Rm 12:16; Jas 1:5]. That I have done from my youth on.

From my youth on I have zealously sought and prayed for God's wisdom, which He has also given to me. From a child in my dear father's

---

59. For his widow, Zell's acknowledged faults were what they had all been taught as Roman doctrine and recognizing the truth was knowing the Gospel. The Schwenckfelder apparently considered everything short of direct personal revelation by the Holy Spirit as "good heathenism." Note the implicit denial that Zell is in purgatory, one of the Roman doctrines they had wrongly believed and rightly rejected.

60. Schütz Zell's response to the fourth accusation is the longest and has two parts. First is an account of her religious experience from childhood, a confession that she is a sinner, and her joy in God's grace of conversion. The second part is a dialogue with a Schwenckfelder who denied being taught by any human, where Schütz Zell explains the relationship of God's grace and human teachers as God's instruments.

house onward He laid the foundation stone in my heart to despise the world and exercise myself in His religion [cf. 1 Pt 2:6]. That I did under the papacy with great earnestness. In that time of ignorance I very zealously, with great pain of body and anxiety of heart, sought out so many clergy and God-fearing people to experience the way to heaven; about that I will say no more. How very wonderfully the Lord led me then! And afterward He did not leave me in my distress. He sent to me, and to many poor afflicted consciences, the dear and (I hope) now blessed Martin Luther, who showed me my error and pointed me to Christ, in whom I would find rest. Then God opened my understanding to comprehend the Holy Scriptures, which I had previously read as a closed book and had not understood; then the Lamb opened the book of the seven seals and took away my lack of understanding and gave comfort in my heart [Mt 11:29; Rv 5:1, 8–9].[61] So it happened to me as to one lost and benighted in a wild forest where many murderers lived: God sent that person an angel who led him out of the forest and showed him the right path. So I have not (as these relate) chosen my own ideas, but I have let the will of God be more pleasing to me than my own. God has sent His Holy Spirit in my heart and allowed the messengers He has sent to teach me with outward writings and words so that the longer the time the more I have come to the knowledge of Christ. I have not been passive and lazy in that but have sought out, loved, and listened to you [Schwenckfeld] and others of God's learned ones and never closed my heart to anyone's teaching and exhortation.[62]

That I still do and also want to continue to do: to pray to the Lord Christ and thank Him for His gifts which He gave to people after He ascended into heaven; praying daily and (with David) in the night [Ps 68:16, 119:62; Eph 4:8]; also thanking Him for the holy teaching that He gave me through Luther, my dear husband, you [Schwenckfeld], and many other dear men. Yes, I thank Him all the time in my heart for the true

---

61. Schütz Zell's account of her conversion (from anxiety to trust) is modeled on Luther's, but that does not invalidate the accuracy of the basic outline; here she is addressing it to someone who was most certainly no longer a fan of Luther's, for whom being like Luther would not necessarily be a recommendation (see "Strasbourg Citizens" at n. 92). Roman clergy did not encourage laity to read the Bible for themselves. However, some printed vernacular Bibles were available in Schütz Zell's childhood and she obviously read one but claims she did not have the key to understand it without God's human messenger Luther. She appears to interpret the heavenly "book with seven seals" (Rv 5:1) as the Bible.

62. Here in brief is the theme later developed: knowledge of Christ through God's teaching enabled by the Holy Spirit, proclaimed by messengers with outward words taught them by the Bible, accompanied by active effort by the student.

knowledge of Christ the sole savior, which the longer I know it the more I love it, in which I also have great joy and wonder; I seek to grow and increase in it while I live, and I labor at that and will sing praises to my God because of it as long as I live [Ps 104:33]. To this I have been greatly motivated also through your service and earnestness; that I cannot deny. Why then would I, out of pride, want not to be taught by anyone and to deny the offices of such servants of God and be so ungrateful for their work, which God laid upon them in order to serve human beings?[63]

However, I heard from one among those companions of your faith. He said to me, "I received nothing from Luther, I had it from God."[64] I said, "You are lying that you have nothing from Luther. We know that all is from God, but Saint Paul says that he and Apollos have planted and watered, but God is the one who has given the increase [cf. 1 Cor 3:6]. However, if Paul and Apollos together with Peter, John, and other apostles did nothing, why would God have chosen Paul and sent him out to bear and confess His name before the heathen, kings, and Jews? And also sent Ananias to Paul, and Peter to Cornelius, and Philip to the circumcised Moor [Ethiopian] on the chariot when he was reading the scripture but could not understand it until Philip explained it to him [cf. Acts 9:1ff, 10:17ff, 8:26ff]? There are many examples of this, how He has used human beings.

"In the work of redemption God and Christ do not want to have anyone alongside (as some kind of co-redeemer); God does not allow His own glory to anyone.[65] But in the work of calling, like a great king He wants to have many servants and messengers, according to the prediction of David in the Psalm [68:18] and the saying of Paul to the Ephesians [4:8]. Therefore, He also sent out the apostles to preach repentance and forgiveness of sins (not, however, in their own name, but in His name). As also He gives a lovely parable in the Gospel: the householder sent out his servant

---

63. Schütz Zell speaks of being taught by ministers and insists that she would be ungrateful to God to deny the good work, the offices, of God's servants; the function is the key thing, but in second place there is the recognition of the ministers who carry out the task using the gifts that God has given. See above before n. 57 where Zell uses this same language for her ministry.

64. For clarity in Schütz Zell's conversation with a Schwenckfelder, his words in the third person have been changed to first person to match hers.

65. In the medieval Roman tradition the Virgin Mary was not only regarded as the chief of the saints but also sometimes called mediatrix or "comediator" with her Son. Immediately below is one of Schütz Zell's few references to Mary, and it is (typically) very restrained, limited essentially to credal statements. In fact, it is rather remarkable that she gives virtually no attention to Mary; in the "Hymnbook" at n. 55 she clearly denies any redemptive role for Mary, and her references to Anna (Lk 2:36–38) are far warmer and more fully developed. See McKee, *Life and Thought*, 381–85.

(as he had already planned) to invite guests to the marriage [cf. Acts 5:31, 10:43; Mt 22:2ff]. The choosing, beginning, and preparation or drawing of the heart is the work of God and His Spirit alone, but the outward calling He does through people.[66] Otherwise how would Christ have ventured to choose and send out the apostles? Therefore He also said to them, 'You have not chosen me, but I have chosen you that you should go and bring forth fruit.' Therefore also Paul so earnestly commanded his dear sons Timothy and Titus and also told them to establish others to pasture the community of God and said that they should not neglect the gifts of God [cf. Jn 15:16; 1 Tm 1:2, 4:14; Tit 1:4–5].

"Did not God the Father also decree from eternity to allow His Word to become Man (*mensch*) for us? Did He not also choose and sanctify Mary to be the mother? Did He not, however, manage all this through the angel as His messenger (according to His predetermined counsel) [cf. Jn 1:14; Lk 1:26ff; Acts 2:23, 4:28]? Did He not make you know it through outward speech and voice, yet inwardly Himself prepare your heart through His Spirit to believe and be obedient to it? This is what God has done through His servant Moses with the people of Israel, thereafter through the prophets; also, Christ at His coming did it through the apostles and will continue doing so until the end of the world [cf. Acts 3:18ff; Lk 10:1ff; Jn 17:18, 20:21; 1 Cor 1:17]. I am not talking about just any puppy, or any learned one sent by the world: neither of them knows or is acquainted with a feather—much less the power—of the Spirit! But I am speaking of right-minded folk who are God's learned ones, who find in their hearts a call and gifts of faith—of these there are few in the world (I know well). However, God also uses those whom we count as the least, of whom I could give many examples, also scriptural ones [cf. Rm 15:15; 1 Thes 4:9; Eph 2:8].[67]

---

66. Here and below Schütz Zell makes her clearest statements about Protestant views of ministry. Salvation is by God alone, who by the Holy Spirit prepares the heart to trust in Christ the Word made flesh. People can do nothing to earn their salvation, but they are God's chosen instruments for proclaiming the Gospel. The latter is revealed only in the Bible, which teaches the content of what must be believed; faith is both trust effected by the Holy Spirit and knowledge conveyed by the Bible, which the Holy Spirit gave. However, the human agents are vital precisely because they are God's choice, and denying them is refusing God and choosing one's own ideas. Schütz Zell thus turns the tables on the Schwenckfelder accusation.

67. For feather of the Spirit, see above at n. 26. Visible signs of the Holy Spirit (like the ironic "feather") are subordinated to the power of the Spirit, which is what matters. Those who are learned in a worldly sense, or other fools claiming inspiration, do not have even the signs of being sent by God, but Schütz Zell points out that God uses not only ones people recognize (like Zell), but also those the world despises as having no value (including herself?!).

"How could you [this Strasbourg Schwenckfelder—trans.] say without qualification that you got nothing from Luther? Why did you become a monk and renounce sin, except that you thought that was the means to serve God and obtain eternal life? Now who taught you that? The pope was your teacher for that—you cannot deny it. Who told you nevertheless to leave the monastic life, as a useless and unfounded human law, and to seek and find your salvation only in Christ—against the previous papal teaching? Did you become so wise yourself? Why then did you become a monk? Did you want for a little while to play carnival and carry on a mockery between God and yourself? You would certainly not say that. You are then foolish. So you must confess with me and with others that Luther said, 'You have gone astray; you do not serve God by being a monk.'[68] You know his books and once read them with diligence, believed him, and took him for a blessed messenger sent by God. You then searched the Holy Scriptures, to which Luther also pointed you and me; and God's Spirit (who also, I well know, had laid the foundation stone in your heart) led you further [cf. Is 28:16; 1 Pt 2:6]. So you also went further and came to Schwenckfeld; you heard him and read his writings and so received good from God through him also."

But this man then said to me, "I got nothing from Schwenckfeld." Then I answered him, "You lie once again. All that you know, perform, and do, you have from him, yes, all your speech and words. You do not know your mother tongue anymore; all the words that he [Schwenckfeld] speaks and writes as his [Silesian] form of German, you follow him in speaking and writing—against your own nature and native form of German! How can you so presumptuously say that you got nothing from him? Everyone knows that I said, 'Schwenckfeld is more upright and learned than you and ten others, and he acknowledges in his writings that he also received good through Luther's service.'" The man answered once again, "I learned nothing from Luther or from Schwenckfeld." Then I said, "Were you taught by the devil? Or who then taught you? God did not use some special revelation with you anymore than with me." Then he left me in anger.

I think, dear sir [Schwenckfeld], that you are also implicated in this complaint. How could I do otherwise with him? I heartily wish that you yourself had heard by degrees (bit by bit) this and other things or that I were present

---

68. Schütz Zell apparently knew this man well; she reminds him of his own life, following first the pope, then Luther, then Schwenckfeld, but now denying everything, against the evidence of his own spoken German. Her speech has a slapstick quality: "You learned the value of celibacy from the pope. If you were already so wise that you knew monastic vows were wrong, then you were mocking God by taking them. However, if you learned their worthlessness from Luther, then . . . !"

when many things were shown to you. I say all this now only because this man and many others accuse me that, out of pride, I do not want to be taught by anyone, when instead I always confess more than all of them and give God thanks for all that I learned and received from Luther, my dear husband, you, and all other learned ones. But I give God the glory, who looked on me with mercy and called me according to His gracious election and allowed me to come to understanding, faith, righteousness, and His glory. He did all that because of His everlasting grace and loving mercy, through which also, coming down out of the heavens, He sought me who sat in darkness and the shadow of death and directed my feet in the path of peace [Rm 8:28ff; Ps 107:10; Lk 1:79]. How then could I object to being taught by you and all those who have right love for Christ, and how could I take pride in my own understanding, as they say of me (but unjustly)?

Ah, God, my "pride" when I regard myself as a child of fallen Adam [cf. Gn 3:1ff] is this: that on account of my "wisdom" (gained by the Fall), I am not only a companion but also a member of the household, footstool, and filthy rag of the wicked, dark, damned, worthless serpent head and devil, in the lowest place of hell, on account of my inherited sins and those I have done, yes, on account of the true chief sin of unbelief. Also by nature I am a child of wrath and have a great fear of God and enmity toward Him. Therefore I hide myself in the obscurity or cover as Adam did, and like Cain I flee before God, but His countenance finds me and He speaks to me with His angry voice [cf. Eph 2:3; Rm 8:7; Gn 3:8, 4:8ff]. From that comes my eternal anxiety (and not my pride).[69]

However, when in faith I look on my Lord Jesus Christ, who is not merely equal to the blessed angels but a Son of God who is above all the heavens, received into the height and adored by many thousands of thousands of angels and saints; when I consider that He was sent to me by the Father, crowned through suffering, made Lord and Christ after He gave Himself as a sin offering and reconciled me with Him (God the Father) through Himself; when I consider that God raised Him, set Him at His right hand, and sent Him to His people as a glorious gift and gain from His great struggle and effective victory and triumph over the devil and eternal death [cf. Heb 1:2ff, 9:12ff; Acts 2:36; Ex 29:14; Ps 110:1]; when I look on Christ in faith and consider all He has done for me—then this is my pride, that I am

---

69. The serpent tempted Adam and Eve to eat the forbidden fruit by saying it would make them wise, knowing good and evil. Schütz Zell lists her sins, original (inherited from the Fall) and actual (ones she has done), and names unbelief as "the true chief sin" (see "Lament" at n. 85; "Psalms/Prayer" at n. 125). For her Protestant prayer for God to help their unbelief, see "Women" at n. 10, "Psalms/Prayer" at n. 163.

a daughter of Sarah who believed, one blessed of the Lord, a child of God, a bride and fellow-heir of His Son Jesus Christ, a purified shrine and temple of God the Holy Spirit, a companion who shares with all the saints the good things of heaven in eternal life [cf. Heb 11:11; Rm. 8:16–17; 1 Cor 6:19].

That is my glory, honor, joy, heavenly pride, and glorying in God and Christ, not in myself. I glory that God the Father gave me the gift of faith in His Son (which is not given to everyone), solely out of His gracious love, without any ability or merit on my part [cf. Eph 2:19, 4–8]. In view of this great gift of faith, all the world with its ornaments, desires, and wantonness is to me (and certainly to God) a filthy, unclean, stinking pig stall, and all its children (for whom the Lord Christ did not pray) are bastards and not God's children; they belong in eternal darkness, excluded from the inheritance and kingdom of Christ [cf. 1 Jn 2:16, 3:10; Jn 17:9; Mt 22:13].[70] Like the wife of King Ahasuerus [Vashti], instead of whom Esther was chosen; and Ishmael (born of the maid Hagar), who was counted out of the succession with a gift, instead of whom Isaac (born of Sarah) was blessed in faith and remained the true heir [cf. Est 1:19, 2:16–17; Gn 16:15, 17:15, 21:1ff, 25:5–6]. They [Vashti, Ishmael] are also not temples of God but an eternal dwelling place of the devil. From this, however (I hope without doubting), my Lord and God Jesus Christ has freed me—to Him be the glory!

From my mother's womb He has chosen me and said to me through His Spirit, "Hear, daughter, look on this; forget your father's people and house, so the king will desire your beauty, for He is your Lord and you should adore Him" [cf. Ps 45:10–11]. Oh, these words! I have thought about them so much, and because of that I have forgotten the whole world and adored Jesus Christ my Lord and God [cf. Jn 20:28]. By His grace I hope to do that to the end. So I am also not ashamed to learn through your [Schwenckfeld's] service and help; moreover, I confess with thanks before God and you that I have learned from you, and I do not insist on following my own head and ideas out of pride—as these [Schwenckfelders] say I do.

However, I daily see and experience so much that I am afraid of people and would not so readily give myself as anyone's prisoner to confess a pretended faith that is not at all rooted in my heart.[71] But I allow God to

---

70. Schütz Zell clearly expresses her own sense of election and salvation by faith alone, which is purely a gift (grace alone). Some are elect, some are excluded and damned; Schütz Zell names several biblical examples: Esther chosen in place of Vashti, Isaac in place of Ishmael (see "Women," paragraph 4). The reference to Jesus's prayer is John 17:9, where Jesus says "I am praying for them; I am not praying for the world but for those whom You gave me."

71. Following her confession of God's grace and her expression of appreciation for God's instruments like Schwenckfeld, Schütz Zell implicitly reiterates her obligation to judge for

teach me, and not human beings (yes, especially such people as I see—and indeed, even more, experience these to be). However, my work, with praying, reading, listening, and doing what remains for me to do, before God, that I will not hold back [cf. 1 Cor 7:23; Eph 3:17]. Such, dear sir, I had to show to/against you (*gegen*) and to answer a part (not all) of the foolish sayings that are said hin and yon about me. During his life my dear husband often talked with me about this, and also at the end, and comforted me about this. Also in the last night and hour before his death he said to me when we were alone, "You will remain a while after me, and see much— also lies against yourself. Do your best and be comforted, God will be with you; you have been till now the wife of Master Mathis [Zell]; he will now be taken from you. If you do not sing to please everyone, things will change. However, do not fear, God has given you enough, more than any other woman; that He will not take from you." And quickly it was the end [cf. Is 41:10, 14; Lk 10:42]. Oh, how these words went into me like a knife!

They have already in part come true. I am as little valued by our clergy as if I had never served the church. I am left without any love and comfort in my crosses because (as my dear husband expressed it) I do not sing to please them. I am given so little comfort by all of them that I thank God, who through this has taught me a great deal and also humbled me and put me in His school. Further, He will have mercy on me as a poor solitary woman who has nevertheless always earnestly sought Him and now continues to do so as I sorrow, weep, and lament. The angel Uriel of the Most High, who came to the sorrowing Ezra in the wilderness, will also comfort me and teach the secrets of the wisdom of God to me as to the dear Ezra, with whom also I mourn the destruction of the temple, the people, and the city of Jerusalem [cf. 2 Esd 4:1; 1 Cor 2:7; Ezr 9:5–15].[72]

With that I will close for this time and send you this letter as a beginning (to refresh again our former love and acquaintance), with hearty thanks for all the good in teaching and comfort that I have received from you. Also I thank you for the glorious, Christian, and good testimony about my blessed husband that you sent to me in my cross, with such great con-

---

herself. Practical experience makes it clear that she cannot trust the kinds of messengers she presently sees (clergy or Schwenckfelders), but she will continue to be faithful to her Christian duties without regard to the inadequate leaders.

72. The reference to Esdras is one of the very few explicit citations of the Apocrypha in Schütz Zell's writings; the others are 2 Maccabees (once), Judith (three times), part of the Greek addition to Daniel (once). For the Apocrypha see, "Apologia" at n. 30. Here and elsewhere Schütz Zell's distress about the Interim is heard; see "Lament" at nn. 76, 92, and 97; "Psalms/Prayer" at n. 133.

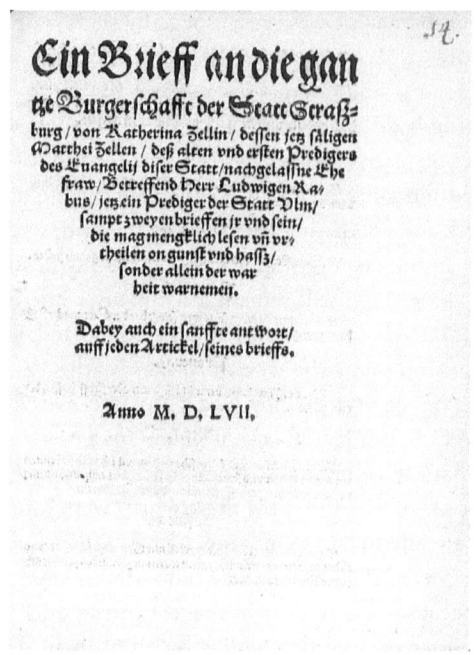

Figure 4 Title page of Katharina Zellin's "Ein Brieff." This comes from Katharina Schütz Zell's 1557 publication, which assembled her correspondence with Rabus under the title *A Letter to the Whole Citizenship of the City of Strasbourg*. Note that in this book she signs her name using the feminine form of her husband's name, "Zellin," since that was the way she was known *outside* Strasbourg. Although she did in fact adopt Zellin for earlier, nonpolemical writings such as the hymnbook, the use here emphasizes her claim to represent her husband Matthew. Photograph courtesy of Zentralbibliothek, Zurich.

fidence of his faith and now his blessedness, peace, and rest in Christ—the letter that also exhorted me about the sole savior whom he confessed. For that, may our Lord and God repay you and never leave you without comfort. I also ask you to receive this letter from me in Christian love (which bears and suffers all things) [cf. Rm 2:6–7; Jn 14:18; 1 Cor 13:7]. Henceforth I will take other matters in hand, with publication of some writings and also the confession of my faith and questioning where I am not satisfied with all the writings and sayings.[73]

Also I commend you to the grace of our Lord Jesus Christ, a hero, one Person from two natures, true God and true Man in the indivisible being of

---

73. The gracefully crafted conclusion thanks Schwenckfeld for his teaching and his beautiful letter of consolation and ends with a warm biblical blessing that includes a reference to the Chalcedonian definition of Christ's two natures.

the holy trinity, reigning king of His people forever, a Prince of Peace and eternal Father of all who trust in Him and call upon Him, who saves His people from their sins: to Him be praise, with the Father and the Holy Spirit, one God, forever, amen [cf. Acts 20:32; Rm 16:20; Mt 1:21; Is 9:6]. Pray to him earnestly for me.

Dated at Strasbourg at night (in the day I have crosses to bear, I do not want to write), the 19th of October 1553.

Katharina Zell,
the sorrowing widow of the blessed Matthew Zell; yours in the Lord Christ and willing to serve you in whatever ways I am able

A LETTER TO THE WHOLE CITIZENSHIP OF THE CITY OF STRASBOURG FROM KATHARINA ZELL, . . . CONCERNING MR. LUDWIG RABUS

Introduction

The argument between Katharina Schütz Zell and Ludwig Rabus remained mostly out of the public eye for some years. Although they had worked together after Matthew's death, contact decreased rapidly about 1552–53. Schütz Zell continued to try, however; she attempted unsuccessfully to talk with Rabus, first alone, then perhaps with the presence or at least the knowledge of a mutual friend. Finally she resorted to writing; at the end of December 1555 she drafted a letter objecting to the way Rabus was attacking Schwenckfeld from the pulpit. Over the next few days she had second thoughts about sending this, however, and decided that she would leave the correcting of Rabus to God. Nonetheless, some weeks later Matthew's widow felt compelled to do something because she thought her silence was unfaithful to her husband's deathbed charge to see that his successor did not preach against Schwenckfeld and the [Ana]Baptists. In fact, Rabus had now added the Zells' old colleague Zwingli to his list of heretics! So on February 6, 1556, Schütz Zell added a postscript and sent the letter.[74] Rabus returned the letter without reading it, and his foster mother gave up the effort to bring him to a sense of his errors—until something further happened that she felt she could not ignore.

In November 1556, Rabus accepted a position as the chief pastor of the city of Ulm and quietly left Strasbourg. The difficulty was that he had not

---

74. For Schütz Zell's response to Rabus's attacks, see McKee, "The Defense of Zwingli, Schwenckfeld, and the Baptists, by Katharina Schütz Zell."

received permission from the city of Strasbourg, of which he was an employee. From the viewpoint of the government, Rabus had walked off the job; from the viewpoint of his parishioners, he had abandoned them without even saying farewell.[75] The Ulm council, however, was unaware that Rabus had not told his current employers about his wish to leave; since they operated on the same principles as their counterparts in Strasbourg, it was natural for them to write to the Strasbourg council to make the official arrangements for Rabus's move. Their letter of December 1, 1556, said that they had heard from a third party (possibly Rabus himself) that he wanted a change of scene for health reasons and they wanted to employ him. The letter was a shock to the council and people of Strasbourg, and the former answered by offering Rabus better material conditions and a leave for his health but telling both him and the Ulm council that they did not want to lose Rabus because they were short of ministers. (The council did not add that they had helped pay for his education and supported him for many years, but others in Strasbourg would point this out.) If Rabus chose to leave anyway, his Strasbourg employers would not stop him but they would commit the reckoning to the judgment of God (and his conscience).

Rabus refused to change his mind, and Ulm persisted in wanting him, so in January 1557 he returned to Strasbourg to collect his family. He also spoke to the council and asked for a certificate of his good service in Strasbourg, which the authorities at Ulm wanted. When he was called upon to explain himself, Rabus took the high ground. He said that, although (as the council knew) he had long wanted a situation where he would have better remuneration and improved health, his primary concern was to seek a place where the government did not tolerate Roman Catholic worship, which he called "idolatry." He was referring to the situation produced in Strasbourg as a result of the Interim. Early in 1550, when Roman worship was reintroduced in the city, Rabus's parish had been forced to cede the cathedral to the Roman clergy and move to another building. At the time, the recently chosen young minister appeared to accept this with good grace, however reluctant he might have been; now, nearly seven years later, he claimed that Strasbourg's toleration of Roman worship was against his conscience.

The arguments between Rabus and the Strasbourg council dragged on for almost two years, in fact, until November 1558. Rabus vigorously justified his acts and repeatedly demanded a certificate of his good service in Strasbourg and blamed the city for defaming him or allowing him to be

---

75. For details from city archives, see McKee, *Writings*, 157–63. For a complete story of "the Rabus affaire" see McKee, *Life and Thought*, 174–88, 193–210.

defamed. News filtered back to Strasbourg about uncomplimentary or even libelous things that Rabus and his friends in Ulm were saying about Strasbourg and its council members. Eventually, on his last visit (in November 1558) Rabus claimed that the Strasbourg offer of better conditions had been a temptation of the devil since his quarrel with the city was their toleration of heretics, not his desire for material gain. Over the course of this long though intermittently pursued controversy, Rabus's abandoned flock became ever more irate and the city council (which felt maligned) listened to Rabus's pleas but consistently refused to grant what he wanted.

Schütz Zell had been ill when Rabus left Strasbourg. However, friends told her of his departure, so in late March 1557, when she was well enough to write, she sent her former foster son a very pained letter, asking him to explain and justify his actions. This letter offers some of the most pointed—and humorous—writing from Schütz Zell's pen, so a brief synopsis is worth including.[76]

As his former foster mother saw it, Rabus had been called by the church in Strasbourg, through its leaders (both civil and ecclesiastical), and he had accepted the call. Now he had left, without permission and even without the knowledge of those leaders. Would he please provide his justification for this behavior, which looked to her like a denial of his pastoral vocation? Schütz Zell indicates that she wishes to understand how he could be right, but she is dubious. As always, her standard of measurement is the Bible. The Gospel [Mt 10:5ff] records Jesus's commission to His disciples, which says that when they enter a town to preach they are to take nothing for their own support but to stay with the household that welcomes them. If people refuse to listen to their preaching, then the disciples should "shake off the dust" as they leave, as a testimony against the town. But Rabus has done the opposite! He was welcomed and given a good place, and the magistracy had even offered him more money and free time and begged him to come back—yet nonetheless he had left Strasbourg. He had done everything contrary to Jesus's teaching about leaving a ministry. His departure called into question the validity of his ordination: either his call to Strasbourg had been true and his departure was wrong; or if he justified his departure, then he had never rightly been a pastor in Strasbourg.

Since there was no biblical justification for his departure, Schütz Zell considered other, less admirable, possibilities, and she thought it looked

---

76. For a summary of Schütz Zell's criticisms of Rabus and defense of Strasbourg in March 1557, see McKee, *Life and Thought*, 184–88.

like ambition. In Ulm he was head of the church, in Strasbourg he had been a parish pastor; the facts spoke for themselves. If he had been serious about objecting to Strasbourg's toleration of Roman worship, why had he not protested when the Interim was introduced? And now, if he truly could not bear the Roman worship, why had he gone to Ulm rather than to the poor peasants in the countryside where the Interim had not really been felt? There he could have escaped this "idolatry," which Strasbourgers did not like any better than he did. But in fact, as Schütz Zell pointed out, Ulm also had Roman worship because of the Interim. So what was his excuse?

> You say that in Ulm the idolatry is an old monk who does not dare preach [while the Roman clergy in the Strasbourg cathedral do preach—trans.]. Ach, God! Is that better? I would rather they preached than read Mass . . . Suppose one says that the Mass in Ulm is in a corner and cloister, and no one pays attention to it and they hope that it will also soon go away. (If only they had stuck the Mass in a cloister in Strasbourg and left the cathedral free!) O dear sir, I perceive clearly that you think our Lord God is old and no longer sees well and that what happens in a corner does not bother Him: He only looks at the great high temple [cathedral]![77]

Rabus might well be infuriated by such humor! (In fact, his blunt old foster mother was not the only person in Strasbourg who thought that ambition was his motivation.)

Then Schütz Zell also addresses another similar issue. According to a report (independently confirmed by various Strasbourg sources), which she had at first refused to believe, Zell's widow heard that in Ulm Rabus himself was wearing the "Roman" surplice: he was even imitating what he had claimed to despise and leave behind. How can he explain himself?! Having caught Rabus on the horns of the dilemma of his own inconsistent behavior, Schütz Zell then defends Strasbourg by recounting the teaching of Strasbourg's first-generation leaders and their relations to Zwingli,

---

77. From her letter to Rabus, March 1557, in McKee, *Writings*, 193–94. Comparison of Schütz Zell's text with completely independent evidence in the city archives and other people's correspondence, dated January 1557 (before her letter of rebuke), makes it clear that she was a good observer and did not exaggerate the charges circulating in Strasbourg; for example, the report on Rabus's wearing the surplice in Ulm, the accusation of ambition, the suspicion of his hypocrisy in claiming the "high ground" of not tolerating "idolatry," the departure without knowledge or permission of the council or even other clergy; cf. McKee, *Writings*, 196, n. 106; 191, n. 84; 188, n. 75; 179 n. 48.

Schwenckfeld, and the [Ana]Baptists and concludes by criticizing Rabus's own intolerance.

Schütz Zell's letter was dated March 24, 1557. Unlike the one sent in 1556, this letter got a quick and very sharp response from Rabus. (His answer is found below as an appendix.) In effect, his short note called Schütz Zell an apostate and heretic, a false witness, and one inspired by the devil, who had caused trouble for the church and her husband from the beginning. It was a comprehensive indictment of her and a blanket denial of any wrongdoing on his own part, but it did not answer any of her specific questions except the one about giving the Strasbourg magistrates a deadline for getting rid of the Mass—which he blamed on the other clergy. Rabus also told Schütz Zell henceforth to leave him alone.

Having pondered Rabus's letter and his refusal to explain himself, Schütz Zell concluded that she must reply publicly, and she gives two overlapping justifications.[78] One is explicit in the letter to her fellow Strasbourgers, the other is implicit here but explicit in her response to Rabus's accusation of attacking him without first giving him a hearing. Before explaining why she is presenting this matter in print, however, Schütz Zell indicates why she regarded Rabus's behavior as any of her business. Clergy are supposed to rebuke each other, as Paul did Peter for withdrawing from table fellowship with gentiles because he feared what other Jews would say [Gal 2:11–14]. Since the Strasbourg ministers have failed to call Rabus to account, Matthew's widow (his "rib") had to do so for the sake of Rabus as well as his abandoned flock. Having demonstrated that her former pastor's behavior is her business, Schütz Zell then justifies her publication on the same grounds she had used for the "Apologia for Matthew Zell," that is, Christ teaches His people to suffer others' wrongdoing but not to keep silence and He exemplifies this Himself. Rabus has spread the word publicly that Schütz Zell is an apostate, and while she promises to do him good, she also is obliged to speak out because silence would seem to confirm his lies. The other justification for her decision to bring the whole matter out in the open is Schütz Zell's conviction that she had reached the third stage of church discipline described in Matthew 18:15–17. She had tried three times: in person, by letter to him in Strasbourg, and then by letter to Ulm; Rabus had not listened to her when she brought his fault to his attention, and he refused to answer any further. In fact, he had previously spo-

---

78. For her involvement in rebuking Rabus, appealing to Strasbourg as the church, and acting on Christ's example, see below at nn. 96–98 and 103; see discussion in McKee, *Life and Thought*, 400–7. The explicit locus of the Matthew 18:15–17 example is in McKee, *Writings*, 260.

ken outrageously about her to a mutual friend, refusing to talk with her again except in the presence of the magistrate (although he never carried through on this threat to cite her before the council). From Schütz Zell's viewpoint, she had done everything possible to keep matters private, but he refused. Now it was necessary to bring the whole matter to the church, the public forum of the whole religious community.

And so the elderly but sharp-witted witness for the first generation set about writing a refutation of Rabus's letter, a very long and full reply to every word of his short note, including a number of bitingly humorous demonstrations of the young man's self-contradictions. In the course of this response to Rabus's claims that Schütz Zell had been a troublemaker from the beginning, Zell's widow also provides a remarkable history of the early Reformation in Strasbourg, as she proves (to her satisfaction if not Rabus's) that she had been faithful to the first reformers and that he had defamed them so that she must defend them. At the end of 1557 Schütz Zell gathered up her various letters to Rabus and his to her and published them, together with a dedicatory letter to her fellow Christians ("the church" of Matthew 18:17) and citizens in Strasbourg.[79] Besides an appeal for a fair hearing, which expresses her trust in her fellow lay Christians as competent judges, Schütz Zell's dedication includes an impassioned autobiographical sketch to justify her response to Rabus. The basic outline is much like what she recounted in the letter to Schwenckfeld, although some of the emphases naturally differ, particularly the weight this daughter of the city and partner of their beloved pastor gives to her relationship with Strasbourg.

One of the most interesting facets is the way Schütz Zell names or alludes to the key ways that she understood herself. Some of these are specifically related to her husband and their partnership. The first to be

---

79. McKee, *Writings*, 213-303, gives Schütz Zell's very long response to Rabus's very short note; for summary, see McKee, *Life and Thought*, 195-200. Near the end of her response to Rabus, Schütz Zell adds a note to her fellow citizens and offers her book as a "Christmas gift," which she may have planned to sell at the Strasbourg winter fair. This was held around the time of Saint Nicholas Day, December 6, until 1570, when it was moved closer to Christmas to eliminate reference to the saint, since preaching had not been sufficiently effective for that. Schütz Zell certainly knew the late medieval tradition of clergy giving "New Year's" gifts to their people in their sermons, since Geiler von Kayserberg, the cathedral preacher when she was a child, had preached on a different virtue ("spiritual gem") each year as his "gift"; cf. Douglass, *Justification in Late Medieval Preaching*, 35. Since Christmas was the turning point of the year in Strasbourg, as in much of German-speaking Europe (e.g., December 26, 1555, would be called December 26, 1556), a Christmas gift would be virtually a New Year's gift, which as Davis indicates was "the most important public gift day of the year," *The Gift*, 23. For notes, see McKee, *Writings*, 264, n. 343; 299 n. 462.

named is her role as Matthew's "wedded companion," (1) which describes the character of their marriage. This is followed by an allusion to being his "faithful help in his office," (2) which Schütz Zell more explicitly defines and asserts in her letters to Rabus, where she says that she was Zell's assistant minister (like Rabus, only better!). The phrase "mother of the poor and exiled" (3) is not found here but its substance is, as Katharina describes her service to the needy of Strasbourg and to refugees. To these should be added the reference to herself as "Matthew's rib" (4), meaning that parishioners continued to regard her as part of the pastoral unit that had always been ready to help them. Another way she refers to herself is "fellow worker" (5) of Strasbourg's first-generation Protestant ministers, Zell's colleagues, and although the phrase is not here, some of the substance appears in her description of the common service with "many fine learned men." All of these titles are predicated on Christ's call to be a "fisher of people" (6), the fruit of her conversion that focused her life on teaching and preaching. By calling herself a "church mother" (7) in Strasbourg Schütz Zell seems to comprehend particularly her active engagement in Christian nurture and dedication to the church, which she claims began in her youth at age ten. The final role she ascribes to herself is restricted to her old age. Again, although she does not use the word, her identification with Anna (8) may constitute a kind of claim for the Biblical "office" of "widow," which enrolled women of age sixty in a kind of teaching/mentoring office [cf. 1 Tm 5:9].[80] (In the following translation, the numbers 1–8 are inserted by the editor to identify these self-designations.) Altogether Schütz Zell clearly possessed and came to express a remarkably full understanding of herself as a woman reformer, theologian, pastor, and faithful Christian citizen. Her voice in this letter is very emotional but also confident, as she appeals to fellow Christians and neighbors to read and judge. Many she could expect to be friendly; some (like the city council) would no doubt also be critical, but she was prepared for that. There is assurance in the way she sets out her own identity and character and lifelong service to God and her people.

Schütz Zell's book, written to vindicate Zell and herself and to set straight the story of Strasbourg's early Reformation, appeared without the name of place or publisher. Rabus and his friends in Ulm blamed the Strasbourg council for permitting this publication, which defamed him, but the council denied that Schütz Zell's work had been printed in their city. In fact, it probably had been; there were enough of her fellow citizens who

---

80. For each of these names or allusions, see below at nn. 85ff. For full discussion, see McKee, *Life and Thought*, 439–76.

agreed with Schütz Zell's opinion of Rabus, and later even expressed approval of her book, that she could fairly easily have found a printer. Evidently the author herself sold the book from her home; there were reports of school boys coming to buy as many as five at a time, apparently to sell to family, friends, and others. Late in March 1558 the city council called Schütz Zell to account for this, ordering her to hand over whatever she had left and not to sell any more. By this point, however, she probably retained only two or three copies and did not want to sell them anyway, and the council seems to have dropped the matter. Zell's widow was too much loved, and there were too many people in sympathy with her, for anything more stringent than slapping her hands as a public warning and/or political hand washing.[81] Her book was reprinted in the eighteenth century by a Swiss editor collecting information about the history of the early Reformation, and modern study confirms that Schütz Zell was a remarkably careful and detailed historian.[82]

A LETTER TO THE WHOLE CITIZENSHIP OF THE CITY
OF STRASBOURG FROM KATHARINA ZELL, WIDOW
OF THE (NOW BLESSED) MATTHEW ZELL, THE FORMER
AND FIRST PREACHER OF THE GOSPEL IN THIS CITY,
CONCERNING MR. LUDWIG RABUS, NOW A PREACHER
OF THE CITY OF ULM, TOGETHER WITH TWO LETTERS:
HERS AND HIS. MAY MANY READ THESE AND JUDGE WITHOUT
FAVOR OR HATE BUT ALONE TAKE TO HEART THE TRUTH.
ALSO A HEALTHY ANSWER TO EACH ARTICLE OF HIS LETTER

Dear Reader, I ask you not to be annoyed by the following foreword. It should show you why this book was written: not for my glory but for the praise of God and clarification of the conflict. Have patience and do not take this amiss.

---

81. For her sales and the council's and Rabus's responses to her book, see McKee, *Life and Thought*, 201–10. Among those Strasbourgers who approved it was Sébald Büheler, a moderate Roman Catholic about Rabus's age. That Büheler did so suggests that he preferred a woman who was outspoken against the Interim and Roman idolatry but did not believe in coercion to a man who had even adopted the Roman surplice but was willing to coerce those not of his faith. Rabus's friends attacked Schütz Zell in print; if the importance of the writer is measured by the intensity of the response, they thought she was a significant nuisance!

82. Reprinted by Füsslin with an interesting alteration in the title, where he calls Rabus "superintendent" while Schütz Zell's original names him "preacher" of the church at Ulm, a small but significant change; see the appendix at n. 4 for Rabus's own claim and the bibliography for Füsslin's full title. For appreciation of Schütz Zell as historian, see McKee, *Life and Thought*, 343–61.

Lord, You are my God, I will honor You and praise Your name, for You do marvelous things.[83]

Isaiah 25[:1]

It is well with the one whom You discipline, Lord, and to whom You teach patience.

Psalms 94[:12–13]

Each one thinks his own way is good, but the Lord makes the heart certain.

Proverbs 16[:2]

The one who accepts rebuke will be wise; but whoever hates rebuke will die.

Proverbs 15[:10]

Christ says, "Whoever confesses me before people I will also confess before my Father and His angels; but whoever is shamed of me and my truth, of that one I will also be ashamed."

Matthew 10[:32–33], Mark 8[:38]; Luke 9[:26], 12[:8–9]

Oh how happily will I speak, because God has and does rebuke; therefore I will be thankful all my life long for my afflictions.

Isaiah 38[:19, 17, 20]

Foreword

I, Katharina Zell, the respectable widow of Matthew Zell, the blessed departed preacher of Strasbourg, wish you, dear Church and Citizenship of Strasbourg (in which I was born, brought up, and still live), peace and increase of the grace of God, through true faith in the resurrected Son of God, our Lord Jesus Christ, who is preached to you with such great faithfulness and diligence [cf. Rm 1:7].

Through His special grace and undeserved love, this Christ called me, a poor (*armes*) woman,[84] to the holy and true knowledge of Him. Yes, from

---

83. The scripture she cites actually begins Schütz Zell's argument. Here she submits to God's discipline for her own good (Rabus's defamation is an affliction from which she can learn patience), but she is not willing to keep silence about lies, and she is obliged to witness to Christ publicly no matter what the cost. That is, she is willing to suffer abuse but not to stop speaking out to confess God's truth. See "Apologia" at n. 14; "Hymnbook," title page; "Psalms/Prayer" at n. 113.

84. Occasionally, Schütz Zell uses what appears self-deprecating language; context indicates whether it is sincere (as here) or ironic (see "Schwenckfeld" at n. 25). In relationship to God or when as a widow she refers to her grief, *arme* expresses humility and vulnerability (e.g., below at n. 101). With people, it may express social inferiority but often, especially with Rabus, it is ironic; cf. McKee, *Life and Thought*, 396–97.

my youth on He drew me to Him, and so it is fitting that I extol and praise His holy name and always speak of His love and goodness. I hope I have done that till now, and I ought and wish to do so to the end, in this weak struggling church on earth. And then, in the victorious triumphant church of the communion of all the angels and saints, I will eternally honor and confess the Lamb of God who is the lion of the race of Judah and branch of the root of David [cf. Gal 1:15; Ps 103:1; Rv 5:5]. With the holy old Anna (8) in the temple of God, I praise the Lord and speak of His Son Christ to all who wait with me for redemption and the coming of His glorious appearing [Lk 2:36–38].[85]

Since then the Lord drew me from my mother's womb and taught me from my youth, I have diligently busied myself with His church and its household affairs, working gladly and constantly. I have dealt faithfully according to the measure of my understanding and the graces given to me, without deception, and I have earnestly sought what is of the Lord Jesus [Rm 12:6; Eph 4:7]. So when I was still young all the parish priests and those related to the church loved and feared me. Therefore also my devout husband Matthew Zell, at the beginning of his preaching of the Gospel, sought me for his wedded companion (1). I was also a faithful help to him in his (ecclesiastical) office (2) and household management, to the honor of Christ, who will also bear witness to this before all believers and unbelievers on the great day of His judgment, when all will be revealed. It will be seen that I have not acted according to the measure of a woman but have done faithfully and simply according to the measure of the gift that God through His Spirit has given to me, with great joy and effort, day and night.[86] So, constantly, joyously, and strongly, with all good will have I given my body, strength, honor, and goods for you, dear Strasbourg; I have made them a footstool for you [cf. Mt 25:31ff; Rv 20:12; Eph 4:7; Ps

---

85. In Schütz Zell's later years, Anna was her favorite biblical ideal for herself; see "Schwenckfeld" at n. 38. See McKee, *Life and Thought*, 434–39 for Anna; 378–85 for other biblical women.

86. Here Schütz Zell is not claiming authority on the basis of special inspiration by the Holy Spirit but empowerment and gifts that are not gender specific. The phrase is not meant to denigrate women's abilities but to insist that the gifts of the Spirit are given without regard to sex. Implicit is Schütz Zell's recognition that her society considered women's abilities less than men's and she may have shared this. However, on the basis of the priesthood of believers that transcends human categories of measurement, she claims that her actions are those of a Christian gifted by the Spirit and thus greater than what was usually conceded to women. Although clearly affected by the cultural views of gender, Schütz Zell is remarkably not dominated by them and comes closer to transcending gender stereotypes in favor of what she regarded as the "real" criteria of human worth, that is, faith and faithfulness, than do most of her contemporaries. See McKee, *Life and Thought*, 390–97.

110:1]. My devout husband too was very heartily glad to allow this, and he also loved me very much for it; he often allowed there to be something lacking in his own physical and household needs because of my absence and gladly sent me as a gift to the community; also, at his death he commended me to continue such activity—not with a command, but with a friendly request.[87]

Also I hope that I have faithfully followed that. For I remained in the pastor's house still two years and eleven weeks after his death. I received refugees and the poor (3), helped to maintain the church, and did good to them all at my own expense without anyone's financial support; I harbored faithful and upright preachers as guests. Among others, namely, there was the dear man Marx Heilandt from Kalb in Württemberg when he was put out of his pulpit; I maintained and recommended him and, against the will of some of the clergy (who were beginning to be overly irritable), he came again to the pulpit of a church and also served there until the end of his life.[88] So up till now, besides bearing my own great crosses and severe illnesses, I have gladly served many with counsel and deed, according to my ability (as much as God has bestowed on me)—as I was also obligated before God to do, and as my husband commended to me at the end. I have gladly followed his behest since I know that it is godly and came out of God's behest [Mt 25:31ff].[89]

Meanwhile, then, O Strasbourg, my good husband, who served you for thirty years in the office of preacher, who loved you so much and cared for you so faithfully (you know that, don't you?), also at his end, when he was in great difficulty and misery, he did not forget you; he faithfully prayed to God for you and with great earnestness commended you to the chief shepherd Christ Himself [cf. 1 Pt 5:4]. And I also have loved and served you, Strasbourg, from my youth, as I still also do in my old age and almost sixty years (8). And I seek to serve you until the end, while I am able, and also to defend you with mind

---

87. Repeatedly, from beginning to end, Schütz Zell emphasizes the cooperative character of her marriage, based on both partners following God first; see "Apologia" after n. 39; "Lament" after nn. 81 and 94; "Schwenckfeld" at nn. 19 and 20 and after nn. 31 and 42.

88. Schütz Zell frequently gives exact historical details; in polemic these serve as evidence for her being a faithful witness, but she also documents times, places, writings, etc., when the only purpose seems to be full description. Here she alludes to hiding Bucer and Fagius when they were exiled in 1549 and needed a little more time to prepare their departures. Marx Heilandt, who was forced out of his church by the Interim, came to Strasbourg in 1548, and Schütz Zell helped him find a place in Saint Nicolas parish. Because he was Zwinglian, he was not welcomed by the increasingly Lutheran Strasbourg clergy.

89. Schütz Zell subjects her husband to the same criteria as other teachers: she obeys him because she knows (judges for herself) that what he commends is according to God's will.

and body.⁹⁰ So I must also tell you what has now happened to me—not for the sake of getting your help, and also not so that you should be provoked to anger with anyone, but only that you may pray to God for me, that He may give me patience, joy, and a sure conscience in this matter.

Since I was ten years old I have been a church mother (7), a nurturer of the pulpit and school. I have loved all the clergy, visited many, and had conversations with them—not about dances, worldly pleasures, riches, or carnival, but about the kingdom of God. Therefore also my father, mother, friends, and fellow citizens, and also many clergy (whom I have much questioned in order to learn) have held me in great love, honor, and fear.⁹¹ Since, however, my distress about the kingdom of heaven grew great and in all my hard works, worship, and great pain of body I could not find or obtain from all the clergy any comfort or certainty of the love and grace of God, I became weak and sick to death in soul and body [Lk 7:2, Phil 2:27]. I was like the poor little woman in the Gospel who spent all her property and strength with doctors but lost yet more. However, when she heard of Christ and came to Him, then she was helped and healed by Him [Mk 5:25–34].

So it was for me also and for many afflicted hearts who were then in great distress along with me: many honorable old women and virgins who sought out my company and were glad to be my companions. We were in such anxiety and worry about the grace of God, but we could never find any peace in all our many works, practices, and sacraments of that [Roman] church. Then God had mercy on us and many people. He awakened and sent out by tongue and writings the dear and now blessed Dr. Martin Luther, who described the Lord Jesus Christ for me and others in such a lovely way that I thought I had been drawn up out of the depths of the earth, yes, out of grim bitter hell, into the sweet lovely kingdom of heaven. So I thought of the word that the Lord Christ said to Peter, "I will make you a fisher of people (6) and henceforth you

---

90. The number here is a bit looser than the precision Schütz Zell usually offers; Zell came in the summer of 1518 and died in January 1548. She counts his whole Strasbourg ministry, not just his Protestant pastorate—and refers to this as the office of preacher, emphasizing the function. The reference to her own age as "almost sixty" allows her to claim the office of "widow" (1 Tm 5:9). The promise to defend the city with her mind may also refer to the present book because setting the record straight is something she owes her deceived fellow citizens as an act of Christian love.

91. Schütz Zell says this, the oldest of her vocations, began at age ten (see "Psalms/Prayer" at n. 121 and "Schwenckfeld" at n. 37 for similar claim without the title). Exactly what is meant by "church mother" must be gathered from context; it appears to be renunciation of the world, dedication to God, and, in consequence of that religious vocation, a role in nurturing others by supporting preaching and teaching and leading in devotion. Above she describes it as "busied myself with His church and its household affairs."

shall catch people" [Lk 5:10]. And I have striven day and night that I might grasp the way of the truth of God, which is Christ the Son of God [Jn 14:6]. What distress I have drawn upon myself because I have here learned (*lernen*) to know and helped to confess the Gospel (5) that I commit to God.⁹² Then when I married my good husband, that was counted as a disgrace, outrage, calumny, and falsehood. God knows it all! And the work that fell on me, in the house and out, those who now rest in God and those who still live can well testify to it, and to how I have helped build up the Gospel, received refugees (3), comforted the sorrowing, and loved and furthered the church, pulpit, and school (5 and 7). All those things will console my good conscience before God [cf. 1 Pt 3:16] (even if the world has forgotten or disregarded them): how I have honored, loved, sheltered so many fine learned men with my dear husband⁹³ and with him—and with much work and expense—I have visited many dear men in cities and lands far and near. I did not cease to persevere: I heard their sayings and sermons, read their books, received their letters with joy, and they received mine with joy.⁹⁴ All this will be known after my death, what I left behind.

---

92. In sixteenth-century German *lernen* can mean "to learn" or "to teach"; here it is translated according to her normal usage, but the context suggests that both meanings are possible. Schütz Zell's account of her conversion is modeled on that of Luther but, although the formulation was shaped by the reformer she praised all her life, it is probable that the substance is her own since she tells a very similar story in "Schwenckfeld" (at n. 61). Even if here the reference is partly intended to demonstrate to Strasbourg (yet again) that she honors Luther at least as much as Rabus does, lauding Luther would not particularly recommend her faith to Schwenckfeld and thus it is likely that this is indeed the way Schütz Zell remembered her own experience of fearful anxiety relieved by God's grace.

93. The German *gelerter menner* is literally "learned men" and is usually used for those who had a Latin or university education; in the later Middle Ages the connotation was often a negative contrast to the unlearned "common people" who had a vernacular education and were considered the "true proponents of religious reform" (see Scribner, "Heterodoxy, Literacy, and Print," 246–50, quotation on p. 246). For Schütz Zell, however, the connotation is positive; the majority of those she intends were Protestant ministers, although she also obviously includes Schwenckfeld, whom some would not consider a minister because he and his community did not believe in the institutional structure of the church and its ministry.

94. Schütz Zell alludes to the Zells' visit to Luther and others in northern Germany in 1538, as well as her own travels, for example, to Bullinger and the Pellicans in Zurich in the summer of 1548. Her letters have mostly been lost, but a number of Luther's, Schwenckfeld's, and others' letters to her are extant in their collected works. Schütz Zell read extensively, but there were also limits, both linguistic (naturally she read only German) and theological; she explicitly indicates that she honors the reformers' "first and best books." The most notable example of what she means is the fact that she cites many of Luther's works but essentially only those of the 1520s and a few from the very early 1530s. See McKee, *Life and Thought*, 289–91. (Virtually the only later work by Luther to which Schütz Zell alludes, his *Malediction* against Schwenckfeld in 1543, is given a negative connotation. See McKee, *Life and Thought*, 112.)

In summary, I am writing all this because I must show how in my younger days I was so dear to the fine old learned men and architects of the church of Christ (5)—those who now rest in the Lord from their work and some who are still alive.[95] They never withheld from me their conversation about holy matters and they gladly (from the heart) heard mine [cf. Heb 4:10]. I devoted myself to that conversation about holy matters and gave no place to any worldly foolishness. Since I was waiting for the kingdom of God, my desire, longing, and joy was always only to speak of and be busy with these same (holy) things. Therefore also the dear saintly men sought my company and took pleasure in it—to God be all the glory.

Now, however, in my old age, this is all forgotten and disregarded by these [new] clergy, as well as all the honor, faithfulness, love, and motherly heart that I have shown to them themselves. Yes, it is not only forgotten, but reckoned as disgrace and outrage, although not by all, but only by some, and namely one, whom you, dear church in Strasbourg, received in his youth, loved and honored. But he has ungratefully turned his back on you, on account of which unworthy act I could not keep silence. I wrote to him in an admonishing and rebuking way—for I have seen that all the world practices hypocrisy with each other, including brothers in the faith with each other; no one calls another to account (to his face) as Saint Paul did with dear Peter over a lesser matter [cf. Gal 2:11–14]. I was also grieved for and motivated by many dear people who have been so greatly scandalized by him, who have come to me, weeping and afflicted, as one to whom they can still come for refuge, as still a little piece of the rib (4) of the blessed Matthew Zell [cf. Gn 2:21–22].[96]

This one is namely Mr. Ludwig Rabus, now preacher in the city of Ulm. Dear Strasbourg, I must let you read what disrespect this man has shown me and what he has written in answer to my faithful writing, which I sent to him on account of his injudicious departure. Since, however, I cannot carry it from house to house, to each one individually, I have permitted it to be published so that all may read and judge for themselves. For I think

---

95. Among the dead were Strasbourg's four main reformers: Capito (d. 1541), Zell (d. 1548), Bucer (d. 1551), and Hedio (d. 1552). Others included Fagius, Zwingli, Oecolampadius, and Urbanus Rhegius. Among the living from the first generation were Conrad Hubert in Strasbourg, probably Ambrose Blaurer (driven out of Constance by the Interim and at this time pastor in Biel, Switzerland), and Schwenckfeld.

96. Among Strasbourg's benefits to Rabus were a large loan by the city to finance his doctorate and various fine presents from citizens (e.g., a fur coat). Schütz Zell criticizes the Strasbourg clergy for not rebuking Rabus as was their duty. That failure, combined with the evident grief of parishioners who still regarded Zell's widow as a pastor—an extension of Zell ("his rib")—led her to believe she had to act; cf. McKee, *Life and Thought*, 403–407, for justification.

he may well suffer this, and perhaps think that it is ostensibly an honor (to have his name in print, since he was so eager to publish his martyrology). So I also am not ashamed of letting what he said to me be known, because of the words of Christ: "They will malign you for the sake of the truth and my name; rejoice when they speak evil of you and lie about you, your reward is great in heaven" [Mt 5:11–12]. Therefore I do not seek to have him injured by a sharp word said to him on my account; I am not at all distressed by a letter like his and quite at peace with it because my heart and conscience are right before God. Yes, his letter gives me more reason to thank God that I am not as Rabus describes me and to ask God also to continue to protect me from such. Furthermore, if I could do Mr. Ludwig good in soul or body, I would, despite this wicked letter and other brutality that he has done to me verbally, and also despite the wicked and false reputation about me that he has spread in city and country: that I have fallen away from the Gospel (apostatized) and am no longer of the faith and teaching of my dear husband and of other Christians.[97]

All of that (abuse and lies) would not hinder me from doing good to him and his, according to the saying and teaching of the Lord Christ [cf. Mt 5:44]. He encountered greater insults than I, but as Saint Peter said, "He did not strike back when He was struck" [cf. 1 Pt 2:23]. If God wills, that is also what I want to do toward Rabus: he should not make me upset or angry with his wicked letter; as the wise man teaches me and says, "When someone stronger than you goes against your will, do not let yourself be provoked" [cf. Eccl 6:10]. That is what I want to do, as much as I am able. What I wrote to him, which motivated him and gave him reason to write me such an injudicious wicked letter, I have also permitted to be put here so that you can read both letters, mine and his, and can recognize with Christian judgment who has behaved in a less heated, more friendly, more Christian fashion toward the other. I also wrote to him alone in private, so that he might consider his injustice in private and pray to God for it, and I wanted to let what I wrote remain between him and me. Since, however, he has sent me such an insulting letter as answer, I cannot leave the matter as if he were in

---

97. The promise to do him good applied only to what Schütz Zell thought was for Rabus's true good and did not include whatever he might ask. Later in 1557, after writing Schütz Zell the short nasty note in April, Rabus did not hesitate to send a message to her by a third person asking her again for information for his martyrology! Apostasy is the worst accusation of Schütz Zell and the first major lie about her. It leads into one of her biblical defenses for writing: to bear witness to the truth while suffering injustice and not to keep silence as if the lies were true. She then presents the written letter of lies and a point-by-point, word-by-word, refutation.

the right and keep silence as if I were the way he describes me. For that I take an example from our Lord Christ, when He spoke to the bishop's servant: "If I have spoken evil, give witness to that; but if I have spoken rightly, why then do you strike me?" [Jn 18:(22–)23]. So I say also to Mr. Ludwig. If what I have spoken and written is evil, then he should give truthful witness to it and tell me what is wrong with it; but if it is not wrong, why then does he insult and condemn me this way?[98] Otherwise, according to the teaching of Christ our Lord, I will gladly do good to my enemy, and according to the saying of Saint Paul, put burning coals on his head [cf. Mt 5:44, Rm 12:20].

So that you, dear Strasbourg, may know why I have first introduced this long speech about how I was loved in my youth and marriage (a speech that should be unnecessary!), so read now also what disrespect and judgment I have received in my old age. Therefore I have put here the letter that Mr. Ludwig sent to me. See how he ascribes to me insult, dishonor, and godlessness together with all errors and heresies before God and human beings. He hands me over to the devil, with whom (God be praised) I have nothing to do forever; but I belong to my Lord Jesus Christ, who with His own blood redeemed me from the devil. So besides showing Rabus's letter, I also seek to give a full accounting of my faith to anyone who wants it [cf. 1 Cor 5:5; Rv 1:5; 1 Pt 3:15].[99] In this account you may see whether my good husband's faith and mine are alike or unlike or whether my confidence and faith in the Lord Jesus have changed or not. However, I will clearly show Rabus that he and others have not kept to the pure knowledge of Jesus Christ as the old architects of our church taught us, in the sacraments and other matters.[100] But I know what the Holy Spirit and the old ones through Him have taught me, when at the beginning of the Gospel we were still in fear, great zeal, and under the cross. If God wills, I shall remain with that to the end, when I wish to say with joy the prayer of the dear Simeon: "Now, O Lord, let me, a poor woman (*armes weib*), go hence in peace and rest, for

---

98. The defense is similar to the one she uses in the "Apologia" at nn. 16ff, but it also follows another biblical example, the pattern of discipline in Matthew 18:15–18; see below at n. 103. See above n. 78 and in text after n. 78 and "Lament" at n. 79.

99. In "Schwenckfeld" at n. 51, Schütz Zell had indicated that she would not speak further until compelled to do so; now she experiences that obligation and therefore trusts that God is leading her in what she says.

100. Here is the second major lie: regarding the actual character of Zell's faith. His widow intends to show positively that her confession is like Zell's (she has not changed and she knows what Zell taught). She follows this, however, by reversing the charges with a demonstration that Rabus and his friends are the ones who have in fact changed Zell's teaching so that what they say about him is lies.

the eye of my faith has seen Your savior in my heart and held Him in the arms of my desire" [cf. Lk 2:28–30].[101]

Well then, this is now enough. However, if Mr. Ludwig is not satisfied with his injudicious condemnation of me, a poor solitary (*armes einiges*) woman, then I want to take God as my helper and further recount my dear husband's and my faith, teaching, and life, and let anyone who wants to do so judge who has fallen away or climbed out of the right way! Now, dear Strasbourg, read this letter that Mr. Ludwig Rabus sent to me and judge without any favor and ill humor toward him or me. If I am owed this and have behaved as he describes, then I will gladly bear my punishment. But I believe that no Jew would give me such a testimony and bring such a judgment on me![102] I am also assured in my heart that I stand before my Lord Christ and His heavenly Father in a fitting way through the power of His Spirit; I stand before Him through the great and high merit of Christ in whom I believe, who also will bring to light this wicked letter or witness by Mr. Ludwig (which lies about me) on the great day of His glorious appearance, when all the books of the conscience will stand open [cf. Tit 2:13; Rv 20:12]. Yes, here I stand also before many people who know me, who know my life story and have seen me from youth: as a young woman in my father's house, in my marriage, and now in my grieving widowhood—let them also judge this matter between Mr. Ludwig and me.[103]

To God alone be all honor and glory in His Son Jesus Christ who, with His Father and the Holy Spirit, lives and reigns in the same honor and divine majesty, in the indivisible being of God, true God and true Man (*mensch*), our God and Lord, now and forever. Amen.

---

101. This paraphrase has a Protestant emphasis on seeing with faith—perhaps implicitly criticizing the Roman practice of making visual representations of biblical figures ("idols"). Here Schütz Zell's language expresses Christian humility; below it probably expresses her social position as one not only experiencing the grief of loss but also less socially secure than Rabus. A good pastor ought to have special compassion for an elderly widow, but Rabus does the opposite: he attacks her.

102. Rabus is not only not a good pastor, but he is worse than a Jew. Among the most negative criticisms possible was comparison to a Jew. Schütz Zell shares the prejudice typical in her day, but elsewhere she clearly insists that Jews must not be persecuted because faith is a gift not given to everyone; cf. McKee, *Writings*, 205.

103. With a trinitarian emphasis on Father, Son, and Holy Spirit, Schütz Zell reiterates her trust in Christ's merit and appeals also to the human witnesses of her entire life: "the church" of Matthew 18:17. In the concluding prayer here as elsewhere ("Schwenckfeld"n. 73) the trinitarian doxology includes a reference to the Chalcedonian definition of Christ's two natures in one Person.

APPENDIX
LETTER OF LUDWIG RABUS TO
KATHARINA SCHÜTZ ZELL (APRIL 1557)

My glory, honor, and comfort are in the crucified Christ.

Your heathen, unchristian, stinking, lying letter reached me on April 16, Good Friday, when I was busy and much laden with preaching. I find in the same poisonous, envious, stinking, and lying writing that, although God has wonderfully visited you, yet there is no improvement left to hope for you—you are more and more hardened in your frightful error of false witness and devilish gossip about devout people. So I commit you to the just judgment of God and have no doubt that He will some day give you the well-deserved reward for your pharisaic arrogance.[1]

Your letter was produced not from the Spirit of God, who is a Spirit of truth, but from the devil's spirit, who was a liar from the beginning; this I will diligently hold up as witness of your shameless mouth, since you dare boldly to slander and revile a servant of Christ, unheard, without inquiry, accusing him of all devilishness, so that one well may see the beautiful little fruit of the stinking Schwenckfelder weed and other such heretical hearts and spirits. And you say (as your shameless mouth spews forth and as you previously accused me) that I wanted to quarrel with and provoke the magistrates [of Strasbourg] with a three-day limit.[2] That is a stinking, lying saying from the devil without any truth. Also you shamelessly and dishonorably lie about me in your other writing.

---

1. The "visitation" by God that Rabus means here is an affliction sent to lead the sinner to repentance—but he thinks it has had no such salutary effect on Schütz Zell. Rabus considers himself a devout person and what Schütz Zell has said is "false witness and devilish gossip," and he is confident that God has (already) judged Schütz Zell (harshly) for it.

2. The phrase refers to the comment in Schütz Zell's letter about Rabus and the other Strasbourg clergy setting a deadline by which time the city council must have evicted Roman clergy and worship. When Rabus came before the Strasbourg government in January 1557 to account for himself, he blamed the deadline on other Strasbourg clergy and said that he had opposed them, but in view of the way he acted (i.e., walking off the job because the council did not act quickly), Schütz Zell thinks he was supporting the deadline; cf. McKee, *Writings*, 180–81, n. 51.

Are you to be prayed for that God may forgive you?[3] You made such trouble in the church in Strasbourg from the beginning, and also for your devout husband himself, that I believe God's judgment will some day catch up with you. From now on leave me alone with your lying and slanderous writing.

If you think this letter is too harsh, remember that one must answer the fool as he deserves. April 19, 1557.

> Ludwig Rabus, Doctor in the Holy Scriptures and Superintendent of the Church at Ulm, against all Zwinglian, Stenckfelder, Anabaptist spirits. But besides that a poor weak servant of the crucified Christ and of His poor church.[4]

---

3. Rabus alludes to 1 John 5:16, which instructs Christians to pray for fellow believers who sin, as long as their sins are not mortal; by questioning whether it is appropriate to pray for her, he implies that Schütz Zell's sin is the worst kind.

4. In her response Schütz Zell ironically plays with Rabus's titles: both "Doctor in the Holy Scriptures and Superintendent of the Church" and then "poor weak servant": how can he be both at once?! See "Strasbourg Citizens" at and after n. 82.

SERIES EDITORS' BIBLIOGRAPHY

PRIMARY SOURCES

Alberti, Leon Battista (1404–72). *The Family in Renaissance Florence*. Trans. Renée Neu Watkins. Columbia, SC: University of South Carolina Press, 1969.

Arenal, Electa and Stacey Schlau, eds. *Untold Sisters: Hispanic Nuns in Their Own Works*. Trans. Amanda Powell. Albuquerque, NM: University of New Mexico Press, 1989.

Astell, Mary (1666–1731). *The First English Feminist: Reflections on Marriage and Other Writings*. Ed. and Introd. Bridget Hill. New York: St. Martin's Press, 1986.

Atherton, Margaret, ed. *Women Philosophers of the Early Modern Period*. Indianapolis, IN: Hackett Publishing Co., 1994.

Aughterson, Kate, ed. *Renaissance Woman: Constructions of Femininity in England: A Source Book*. London and New York: Routledge, 1995.

Barbaro, Francesco (1390–1454). *On Wifely Duties*. Trans. Benjamin Kohl in Kohl and R. G. Witt, eds., *The Earthly Republic*. Philadelphia: University of Pennsylvania Press, 1978, 179–228. Translation of the Preface and Book 2.

Behn, Aphra. *The Works of Aphra Behn*. 7 vols. Ed. Janet Todd. Columbus, OH: Ohio State University Press, 1992–96.

Boccaccio, Giovanni (1313–75). *Famous Women*. Ed. and trans. Virginia Brown. The I Tatti Renaissance Library. Cambridge, MA: Harvard University Press, 2001.

——. *Corbaccio or the Labyrinth of Love*. Trans. Anthony K. Cassell. Second revised edition. Binghamton, NY: Medieval and Renaissance Texts and Studies, 1993.

Booy, David, ed. *Autobiographical Writings by Early Quaker Women*. Aldershot and Brookfield: Ashgate Publishing Co., 2004.

Brown, Sylvia. *Women's Writing in Stuart England: The Mother's Legacies of Dorothy Leigh, Elizabeth Joscelin and Elizabeth Richardson*. Thrupp, Stroud, Gloceter: Sutton, 1999.

Bruni, Leonardo (1370–1444). "On the Study of Literature (1405) to Lady Battista Malatesta of Moltefeltro." In *The Humanism of Leonardo Bruni: Selected Texts*. Trans. and Introd. Gordon Griffiths, James Hankins, and David Thompson. Binghamton, NY: Medieval and Renaissance Studies and Texts, 1987, 240–51.

Castiglione, Baldassare (1478–1529). *The Book of the Courtier*. Trans. George Bull. New York: Penguin, 1967; *The Book of the Courtier*. Ed. Daniel Javitch. New York: W. W. Norton and Co., 2002.

Christine de Pizan (1365–1431). *The Book of the City of Ladies.* Trans. Earl Jeffrey Richards. Foreward Marina Warner. New York: Persea Books, 1982.

———. *The Treasure of the City of Ladies.* Trans. Sarah Lawson. New York: Viking Penguin, 1985. Also trans. and introd. Charity Cannon Willard. Ed. and introd. Madeleine P. Cosman. New York: Persea Books, 1989.

Clarke, Danielle, ed. *Isabella Whitney, Mary Sidney and Aemilia Lanyer: Renaissance Women Poets.* New York: Penguin Books, 2000.

Crawford, Patricia and Laura Gowing, eds. *Women's Worlds in Seventeenth-Century England: A Source Book.* London and New York: Routledge, 2000.

"Custome Is an Idiot": Jcobean Pamphlet Literature on Women. Ed. Susan Gushee O'Malley. Afterword Ann Rosalind Jones. Chicago and Urbana: University of Illinois Press, 2004.

Daybell, James, ed. *Early Modern Women's Letter Writing, 1450–1700.* Houndmills, England and New York: Palgrave, 2001.

Elizabeth I: Collected Works. Ed. Leah S. Marcus, Janel Mueller, and Mary Beth Rose. Chicago: University of Chicago Press, 2000.

Elyot, Thomas (1490–1546). *Defence of Good Women: The Feminist Controversy of the Renaissance.* Facsimile Reproductions. Ed. Diane Bornstein. New York: Delmar, 1980.

Erasmus, Desiderius (1467–1536). *Erasmus on Women.* Ed. Erika Rummel. Toronto: University of Toronto Press, 1996.

Female and Male Voices in Early Modern England: An Anthology of Renaissance Writing. Ed. Betty S. Travitsky and Anne Lake Prescott. New York: Columbia University Press, 2000.

Ferguson, Moira, ed. *First Feminists: British Women Writers 1578–1799.* Bloomington, IN: Indiana University Press, 1985.

Galilei, Maria Celeste. *Sister Maria Celeste's Letters to her father, Galileo.* Ed. and trans. Rinaldina Russell. Lincoln, NE and New York: Writers Club Press of Universe.com, 2000; *To Father: The Letters of Sister Maria Celeste to Galileo, 1623–1633.* Trans. Dava Sobel. London: Fourth Estate, 2001.

Gethner, Perry, ed. *The Lunatic Lover and Other Plays by French Women of the 17th and 18th Centuries.* Portsmouth, NH: Heinemann, 1994.

Glückel of Hameln (1646–1724). *The Memoirs of Glückel of Hameln.* Trans. Marvin Lowenthal. New Introd. Robert Rosen. New York: Schocken Books, 1977.

Harline, Craig, ed. *The Burdens of Sister Margaret: Inside a Seventeenth-Century Convent.* New Haven: Yale University Press, abr. ed., 2000.

Henderson, Katherine Usher and Barbara F. McManus, eds. *Half Humankind: Contexts and Texts of the Controversy about Women in England, 1540–1640.* Urbana, IL: Indiana University Press, 1985.

Hoby, Margaret. *The Private Life of an Elizabethan Lady: The Diary of Lady Margaret Hoby 1599–1605.* Phoenix Mill, Great Britain: Sutton Publishing, 1998.

Humanist Educational Treatises. Ed. and trans. Craig W. Kallendorf. The I Tatti Renaissance Library. Cambridge, MA: Harvard University Press, 2002.

Hunter, Lynette, ed. *The Letters of Dorothy Moore, 1612–64.* Aldershot and Brookfield: Ashgate Publishing Co., 2004.

Joscelin, Elizabeth. *The Mothers Legacy to her Unborn Childe.* Ed. Jean leDrew Metcalfe. Toronto: University of Toronto Press, 2000.

Kaminsky, Amy Katz, ed. *Water Lilies, Flores del agua: An Anthology of Spanish Women Writers from the Fifteenth Through the Nineteenth Century.* Minneapolis, MN: University of Minnesota Press, 1996.

Kempe, Margery (1373–1439). *The Book of Margery Kempe.* Trans. and ed. Lynn Staley. A Norton Critical Edition. New York: W.W. Norton, 2001.

King, Margaret L., and Albert Rabil, Jr., eds. *Her Immaculate Hand: Selected Works by and about the Women Humanists of Quattrocento Italy.* Binghamton, NY: Medieval and Renaissance Texts and Studies, 1983; second revised paperback edition, 1991.

Klein, Joan Larsen, ed. *Daughters, Wives, and Widows: Writings by Men about Women and Marriage in England, 1500–1640.* Urbana, IL: University of Illinois Press, 1992.

Knox, John (1505–72). *The Political Writings of John Knox: The First Blast of the Trumpet against the Monstrous Regiment of Women and Other Selected Works.* Ed. Marvin A. Breslow. Washington: Folger Shakespeare Library, 1985.

Kors, Alan C., and Edward Peters, eds. *Witchcraft in Europe, 400–1700: A Documentary History.* Philadelphia: University of Pennsylvania Press, 2000.

Krämer, Heinrich, and Jacob Sprenger. *Malleus Maleficarum* (ca. 1487). Trans. Montague Summers. London: Pushkin Press, 1928; reprinted New York: Dover, 1971.

Larsen, Anne R. and Colette H. Winn, eds. *Writings by Pre-Revolutionary French Women: From Marie de France to Elizabeth Vigée-Le Brun.* New York and London: Garland Publishing Co., 2000.

de Lorris, William, and Jean de Meun. *The Romance of the Rose.* Trans. Charles Dahlbert. Princeton: Princeton University Press, 1971; reprinted University Press of New England, 1983.

Marguerite d'Angoulême, Queen of Navarre (1492–1549). *The Heptameron.* Trans. P. A. Chilton. New York: Viking Penguin, 1984.

Mary of Agreda. *The Divine Life of the Most Holy Virgin.* Abridgment of *The Mystical City of God.* Abr. by Fr. Bonaventure Amedeo de Caesarea, M.C. Trans. from French by Abbé Joseph A. Boullan. Rockford, IL: Tan Books, 1997.

Mullan, David George. *Women's Life Writing in Early Modern Scotland: Writing the Evangelical Self, c. 1670–c. 1730.* Aldershot and Brookfield: Ashgate Publishing Co., 2003.

Myers, Kathleen A. and Amanda Powell, eds. *A Wild Country Out in the Garden: The Spiritual Journals of a Colonial Mexican Nun.* Bloomington: Indiana University Press, 1999.

Russell, Rinaldina, ed. *Sister Maria Celeste's Letters to Her Father, Galileo.* San Jose and New York: Writers Club Press, 2000.

Teresa of Avila, Saint (1515–82). *The Life of Saint Teresa of Avila by Herself.* Trans. J. M. Cohen. New York: Viking Penguin, 1957.

Travitsky, Betty, ed. *The Paradise of Women: Writings by Englishwomen of the Renaissance.* Westport, CT: Greenwood Press, 1981.

Weyer, Johann (1515–88). *Witches, Devils, and Doctors in the Renaissance: Johann Weyer, De praestigiis daemonum.* Ed. George Mora with Benjamin G. Kohl, Erik Midelfort, and Helen Bacon. Trans. John Shea. Binghamton, NY: Medieval and Renaissance Texts and Studies, 1991.

Wilson, Katharina M., ed. *Medieval Women Writers.* Athens, GA: University of Georgia Press, 1984.

———, ed. *Women Writers of the Renaissance and Reformation*. Athens, GA: University of Georgia Press, 1987.

———, and Frank J. Warnke, eds. *Women Writers of the Seventeenth Century*. Athens, GA: University of Georgia Press, 1989.

Wollstonecraft, Mary. *A Vindication of the Rights of Men and a Vindication of the Rights of Women*. Ed. Sylvana Tomaselli. Cambridge: Cambridge University Press, 1995. Also *The Vindications of the Rights of Men, The Rights of Women*. Ed. D. L. Macdonald and Kathleen Scherf. Peterborough, Ontario, Canada: Broadview Press, 1997.

Women Critics 1660–1820: An Anthology. Edited by the Folger Collective on Early Women Critics. Bloomington, IN: Indiana University Press, 1995.

Women Writers in English 1350–1850: 15 published through 1999 (projected 30-volume series suspended). Oxford University Press.

Wroth, Lady Mary. *The Countess of Montgomery's Urania*. 2 parts. Ed. Josephine A. Roberts. Tempe, AZ: MRTS, 1995, 1999.

———. *Lady Mary Wroth's "Love's Victory": The Penshurst Manuscript*. Ed. Michael G. Brennan. London: The Roxburghe Club, 1988.

———. *The Poems of Lady Mary Wroth*. Ed. Josephine A. Roberts. Baton Rouge, LA: Louisiana State University Press, 1983.

de Zayas Maria. *The Disenchantments of Love*. Trans. H. Patsy Boyer. Albany, NY: State University of New York Press, 1997.

———. *The Enchantments of Love: Amorous and Exemplary Novels*. Trans. H. Patsy Boyer. Berkeley, CA: University of California Press, 1990.

SECONDARY SOURCES

Abate, Corinne S., ed. *Privacy, Domesticity, and Women in Early Modern England*. Aldershot and Brookfield: Ashgate Publishing Co., 2003.

Ahlgren, Gillian. *Teresa of Avila and the Politics of Sanctity*. Ithaca: Cornell University Press, 1996.

Akkerman, Tjitske and Siep Sturman, eds. *Feminist Thought in European History, 1400–2000*. London and New York: Routledge, 1997.

Allen, Sister Prudence, R.S.M. *The Concept of Woman: The Aristotelian Revolution, 750 B.C.—A.D. 1250*. Grand Rapids, MI: William B. Eerdmans Publishing Company, 1997.

———. *The Concept of Woman: Volume II: The Early Humanist Reformation, 1250–1500*. Grand Rapids, MI: William B. Eerdmans Publishing Company, 2002.

Amussen, Susan D. And Adele Seeff, eds. *Attending to Early Modern Women*. Newark: University of Delaware Press, 1998.

Andreadis, Harriette. *Sappho in Early Modern England: Female Same-Sex Literary Erotics 1550–1714*. Chicago: University of Chicago Press, 2001.

Armon, Shifra. *Picking Wedlock: Women and the Courtship Novel in Spain*. New York: Rowman and Littlefield Publishers, Inc., 2002.

Backer, Anne Liot Backer. *Precious Women*. New York: Basic Books, 1974.

Ballaster, Ros. *Seductive Forms*. New York: Oxford University Press, 1992.

Barash, Carol. *English Women's Poetry, 1649–1714: Politics, Community, and Linguistic Authority*. New York and Oxford: Oxford University Press, 1996.

Battigelli, Anna. *Margaret Cavendish and the Exiles of the Mind*. Lexington, KY: University of Kentucky Press, 1998.

Beasley, Faith. *Revising Memory: Women's Fiction and Memoirs in Seventeenth-Century France*. New Brunswick: Rutgers University Press, 1990.

Becker, Lucinda M. *Death and the Early Modern Englishwoman*. Aldershot and Brookfield: Ashgate Publishing Co., 2003.

Beilin, Elaine V. *Redeeming Eve: Women Writers of the English Renaissance*. Princeton: Princeton University Press, 1987.

Benson, Pamela Joseph. *The Invention of Renaissance Woman: The Challenge of Female Independence in the Literature and Thought of Italy and England*. University Park, PA: Pennsylvania State University Press, 1992.

_____ and Victoria Kirkham, eds. *Strong Voices, Weak History? Medieval and Renaissance Women in their Literary Canons: England, France, Italy*. Ann Arbor: University of Michigan Press, 2003.

Berry, Helen. *Gender, Society and Print Culture in Late-Stuart England*. Aldershot and Brookfield: Ashgate Publishing Co., 2003.

Bicks, Caroline. *Midwiving Subjects in Shakespeare's England*. Aldershot and Brookfield: Ashgate Publishing Co., 2003.

Bilinkoff, Jodi. *The Avila of Saint Teresa: Religious Reform in a Sixteenth-Century City*. Ithaca: Cornell University Press, 1989.

Bissell, R. Ward. *Artemisia Gentileschi and the Authority of Art*. University Park, PA: Pennsylvania State University Press, 2000.

Blain, Virginia, Isobel Grundy, and Patricia Clements, eds. *The Feminist Companion to Literature in English: Women Writers from the Middle Ages to the Present*. New Haven: Yale University Press, 1990.

Bloch, R. Howard. *Medieval Misogyny and the Invention of Western Romantic Love*. Chicago: University of Chicago Press, 1991.

Bogucka, Maria. *Women in Early Modern Polish Society, Against the European Background*. Aldershot and Brookfield: Ashgate Publishing Co., 2004.

Bornstein, Daniel and Roberto Rusconi, eds. *Women and Religion in Medieval and Renaissance Italy*. Trans. Margery J. Schneider. Chicago: University of Chicago Press, 1996.

Brant, Clare and Diane Purkiss, eds. *Women, Texts and Histories, 1575–1760*. London and New York: Routledge, 1992.

Briggs, Robin. *Witches and Neighbours: The Social and Cultural Context of European Witchcraft*. New York: HarperCollins, 1995; Viking Penguin, 1996.

Brink, Jean R., ed. *Female Scholars: A Traditioin of Learned Women before 1800*. Montréal: Eden Press Women's Publications, 1980.

_____, Allison Coudert, and Maryanne Cline Horowitz. *The Politics of Gender in Early Modern Europe*. Sixteenth Century Essays and Studies, V.12. Kirksville, MO: Sixteenth Century Journal Publishers, 1989.

Broude, Norma and Mary D. Garrard, eds. *The Expanding Discourse: Feminism and Art History*. New York: HarperCollins, 1992.

Brown, Judith C. *Immodest Acts: The Life of a Lesbian Nun in Renaissance Italy*. New York: Oxford University Press, 1986.

_____ and Robert C. Davis, eds. *Gender and Society in Renaisance Italy*. London: Addison Wesley Longman, 1998.

Burke, Victoria E. Burke, ed. *Early Modern Women's Manuscript Writing*. Aldershot and Brookfield: Ashgate Publishing Co., 2004.

Bynum, Carolyn Walker. *Fragmentation and Redemption: Essays on Gender and the Human Body in Medieval Religion*. New York: Zone Books, 1992.

———. *Holy Feast and Holy Fast: The Religious Significance of Food to Medieval Women*. Berkeley: University of California Press, 1987.

Cambridge Guide to Women's Writing in English. Edited by Lorna Sage. Cambridge: University Press, 1999.

Cavallo, Sandra, and Lyndan Warner. *Widowhood in Medieval and Early Modern Europe*. New York: Longman, 1999.

Cavanagh, Sheila T. *Cherished Torment: The Emotional Geography of Lady Mary Wroth's Urania*. Pittsburgh: Duquesne University Press, 2001.

Cerasano, S. P. and Marion Wynne-Davies, eds. *Readings in Renaissance Women's Drama: Criticism, History, and Performance 1594–1998*. London and New York: Routledge, 1998.

Cervigni, Dino S., ed. *Women Mystic Writers*. Annali d'Italianistica 13 (1995) (entire issue).

——— and Rebecca West, eds. *Women's Voices in Italian Literature*. Annali d'Italianistica 7 (1989) (entire issue).

Charlton, Kenneth. *Women, Religion and Education in Early Modern England*. London and New York: Routledge, 1999.

Chojnacka, Monica. *Working Women in Early Modern Venice*. Baltimore: Johns Hopkins University Press, 2001.

Chojnacki, Stanley. *Women and Men in Renaissance Venice: Twelve Essays on Patrician Society*. Baltimore: Johns Hopkins University Press, 2000.

Cholakian, Patricia Francis. *Rape and Writing in the Heptameron of Marguerite de Navarre*. Carbondale and Edwardsville, IL: Southern Illinois University Press, 1991.

———. *Women and the Politics of Self-Representation in Seventeenth-Century France*. Newark: University of Delaware Press, 2000.

Christine de Pizan: A Casebook. Edited by Barbara K. Altmann and Deborah L. McGrady. New York: Routledge, 2003.

Clogan, Paul Maruice, ed. *Medievali et Humanistica: Literacy and the Lay Reader*. Lanham, MD: Rowman and Littlefield, 2000.

Clubb, Louise George (1989). *Italian Drama in Shakespeare's Time*. New Haven: Yale University Press

Clucas, Stephen, ed. *A Princely Brave Woman: Essays on Margaret Cavendish, Duchess of Newcastle*. Aldershot and Brookfield: Ashgate Publishing Co., 2003.

Conley, John J., S.J. *The Suspicion of Virtue: Women Philosophers in Neoclassical France*. Ithaca, NY: Cornell University Press, 2002.

Crabb, Ann. *The Strozzi of Florence: Widowhood and Family Solidarity in the Renaissance*. Ann Arbor: University of Michigan Press, 2000.

Crowston, Clare Haru. *Fabricating Women: The Seamstresses of Old Regime France, 1675–1791*. Durham, NC: Duke University Press, 2001.

Cruz, Anne J. and Mary Elizabeth Perry, eds. *Culture and Control in Counter-Reformation Spain*. Minneapolis: University of Minnesota Press, 1992.

Datta, Satya. *Women and Men in Early Modern Venice*. Aldershot and Brookfield: Ashgate Publishing Co., 2003.

Davis, Natalie Zemon. *Society and Culture in Early Modern France*. Stanford: Stanford University Press, 1975. Especially chapters 3 and 5.
———. *Women on the Margins: Three Seventeenth-Century Lives*. Cambridge, MA: Harvard University Press, 1995.
DeJean, Joan. *Ancients Against Moderns: Culture Wars and the Making of a Fin de Siècle*. Chicago: University of Chicago Press, 1997.
———. *Fictions of Sappho, 1546–1937*. Chicago: University of Chicago Press, 1989.
———. *The Reinvention of Obscenity: Sex, Lies, and Tabloids in Early Modern France*. Chicago: University of Chicago Press, 2002.
———. *Tender Geographies: Women and the Origins of the Novel in France*. New York: Columbia University Press, 1991.
Dictionary of Russian Women Writers. Edited by Marina Ledkovsky, Charlotte Rosenthal, and Mary Zirin. Westport, CT: Greenwood Press, 1994.
Dixon, Laurinda S. *Perilous Chastity: Women and Illness in Pre-Enlightenment Art and Medicine*. Ithaca: Cornell Universitiy Press, 1995.
Dolan, Frances, E. *Whores of Babylon: Catholicism, Gender and Seventeenth-Century Print Culture*. Ithaca: Cornell University Press, 1999.
Donovan, Josephine. *Women and the Rise of the Novel, 1405–1726*. New York: St. Martin's Press, 1999.
Encyclopedia of Continental Women Writers. 2 vols. Edited by Katharina Wilson. New York: Garland, 1991.
De Erauso, Catalina. *Lieutenant Nun: Memoir of a Basque Transvestite in the New World*. Trans. Michele Ttepto and Gabriel Stepto; foreword by Marjorie Garber. Boston: Beacon Press, 1995.
Erdmann, Axel. *My Gracious Silence: Women in the Mirror of Sixteenth-Century Printing in Western Europe*. Luzern: Gilhofer and Rauschberg, 1999.
Erickson, Amy Louise. *Women and Property in Early Modern England*. London and New York: Routledge, 1993.
Ezell, Margaret J. M. *The Patriarch's Wife: Literary Evidence and the History of the Family*. Chapel Hill: University of North Carolina Press, 1987.
———. *Social Authorship and the Advent of Print*. Baltimore: Johns Hopkins University Press, 1999.
———. *Writing Women's Literary History*. Baltimore: Johns Hopkins University Press, 1993.
Farrell, Michèle Longino. *Performing Motherhood: The Sévigné Correspondence*. Hanover, NH and London: University Press of New England, 1991.
The Feminist Companion to Literature in English: Women Writers from the Middle Ages to the Present. Edited by Virginia Blain, Isobel Grundy, and Patricia Clements. New Haven, CT: Yale University Press, 1990.
The Feminist Encyclopedia of German Literature. Edited by Friederike Eigler and Susanne Kord. Westport, CT: Greenwood Press, 1997.
Feminist Encyclopedia of Italian Literature. Edited by Rinaldina Russell. Westport, CT: Greenwood Press, 1997.
Ferguson, Margaret W. *Dido's Daughters: Literacy, Gender, and Empire in Early Modern England and France*. Chicago: University of Chicago Press, 2003.
———, Maureen Quilligan, and Nancy J. Vickers, eds. *Rewriting the Renaissance: The Discourses of Sexual Difference in Early Modern Europe*. Chicago: University of Chicago Press, 1987.

Ferraro, Joanne M. *Marriage Wars in Late Renaissance Venice*. Oxford: Oxford University Press, 2001.
Fletcher, Anthony. *Gender, Sex and Subordination in England 1500–1800*. New Haven: Yale University Press, 1995.
French Women Writers: A Bio-Bibliographical Source Book. Edited by Eva Martin Sartori and Dorothy Wynne Zimmerman. Westport, CT: Greenwood Press, 1991.
Frye, Susan and Karen Robertson, eds. *Maids and Mistresses, Cousins and Queens: Women's Alliances in Early Modern England*. Oxford: Oxford University Press, 1999.
Gallagher, Catherine. *Nobody's Story: The Vanishing Acts of Women Writers in the Marketplace, 1670–1820*. Berkeley: University of California Press, 1994.
Garrard, Mary D. *Artemisia Gentileschi: The Image of the Female Hero in Italian Baroque Art*. Princeton: Princeton University Press, 1989.
Gelbart, Nina Rattner. *The King's Midwife: A History and Mystery of Madame du Coudray*. Berkeley: University of California Press, 1998.
Glenn, Cheryl. *Rhetoric Retold: Regendering the Tradition from Antiquity Through the Renaissance*. Carbondale and Edwardsville, IL: Southern Illinois University Press, 1997.
Goffen, Rona. *Titian's Women*. New Haven: Yale University Press, 1997.
Goldberg, Jonathan. *Desiring Women Writing: English Renaissance Examples*. Stanford: Stanford University Press, 1997.
Goldsmith, Elizabeth C. *Exclusive Conversations: The Art of Interaction in Seventeenth-Century France*. Philadelphia: University of Pennsylvania Press, 1988.
_____, ed. *Writing the Female Voice*. Boston: Northeastern University Press, 1989.
_____ and Dena Goodman, eds. *Going Public: Women and Publishing in Early Modern France*. Ithaca: Cornell University Press, 1995.
Grafton, Anthony, and Lisa Jardine. *From Humanism to the Humanities: Education and the Liberal Arts in Fifteenth- and Sixteenth-Century Europe*. London: Duckworth, 1986.
Grassby, Richard. *Kinship and Capitalism: Marriage, Family, and Business in the English-Speaking World, 1580–1740*. Cambridge: Cambridge University Press, 2001.
Greer, Margaret Rich. *Maria de Zayas Tells Baroque Tales of Love and the Cruelty of Men*. University Park, PA: Pennsylvania State University Press, 2000.
Gutierrez, Nancy A. *"Shall She Famish Then?" Female Food Refusal in Early Modern England*. Aldershot and Brookfield: Ashgate Publishing Co., 2003.
Habermann, Ina. *Staging Slander and Gender in Early Modern England*. Aldershot and Brookfield: Ashgate Publishing Co., 2003.
Hackett, Helen. *Women and Romance Fiction in the English Renaissance*. Cambridge: Cambridge University Press, 2000.
Hall, Kim F. *Things of Darkness: Economies of Race and Gender in Early Modern England*. Ithaca, NY: Cornell University Press, 1995.
Hampton, Timothy. *Literature and the Nation in the Sixteenth Century: Inventing Renaissance France*. Ithaca, NY: Cornell University Press, 2001.
Hannay, Margaret, ed. *Silent But for the Word*. Kent, OH: Kent State University Press, 1985.
Hardwick, Julie. *The Practice of Patriarchy: Gender and the Politics of Household Authority in Early Modern France*. University Park, PA: Pennsylvania State University Press, 1998.

Harris, Barbara J. *English Aristocratic Women, 1450–1550: Marriage and Family, Property and Careers*. New York: Oxford University Press, 2002.
Harth, Erica. *Ideology and Culture in Seventeenth-Century France*. Ithaca: Cornell University Press, 1983.
———. *Cartesian Women. Versions and Subversions of Rational Discourse in the Old Regime*. Ithaca: Cornell University Press, 1992.
Harvey, Elizabeth D. *Ventriloquized Voices: Feminist Theory andEnglish Renaissance Texts*. London and New York: Routledge, 1992.
Haselkorn, Anne M. and Betty Travitsky, eds. *The Renaissance Englishwoman in Print: Counterbalancing the Canon*. Amherst: University of Massachusetts Press, 1990.
Hendricks, Margo and Patricia Parker, eds. *Women, "Race," and Writing in the Early Modern Period*. London and New York: Routledge, 1994.
Herlihy, David. "Did Women Have a Renaissance? A Reconsideration." *Medievalia et Humanistica*, NS 13 (1985): 1–22.
Hill, Bridget. *The Republican Virago: The Life and Times of Catharine Macaulay, Historian*. New York: Oxford University Press, 1992.
Hills, Helen, ed. *Architecture and the Politics of Gender in Early Modern Europe*. Aldershot and Brookfield: Ashgate Publishing Co., 2003.
A History of Central European Women's Writing. Edited by Celia Hawkesworth. New York: Palgrave Press, 2001.
A History of Women in the West.
   Volume 1: *From Ancient Goddesses to Christian Saints*. Ed. Pauline Schmitt Pantel. Cambridge, MA: Harvard University Press, 1992.
   Volume 2: *Silences of the Middle Ages*. Ed. Christiane Klapisch-Zuber. Cambridge, MA: Harvard University Press, 1992.
   Volume 3: *Renaissance and Enlightenment Paradoxes*. Ed. Natalie Zemon Davis and Arlette Farge. Cambridge, MA: Harvard University Press, 1993.
A History of Women Philosophers. Ed. Mary Ellen Waithe. 3 vols. Dordrecht: Martinus Nijhoff, 1987.
A History of Women's Writing in France. Ed. Sonya Stephens. Cambridge: Cambridge University Press, 2000.
A History of Women's Writing in Germany, Austria and Switzerland. Ed. Jo Catling. Cambridge: Cambridge University Press, 2000.
A History of Women's Writing in Italy. Ed. Letizia Panizza and Sharon Wood. Cambridge: University Press, 2000.
A History of Women's Writing in Russia. Edited by Alele Marie Barker and Jehanne M. Gheith. Cambridge: Cambridge University Press, 2002.
Hobby, Elaine. *Virtue of Necessity: English Women's Writing 1646–1688*. London: Virago Press, 1988.
Horowitz, Maryanne Cline. "Aristotle and Women." *Journal of the History of Biology* 9 (1976): 183–213.
Howell, Martha. *The Marriage Exchange: Property, Social Place, and Gender in Cities of the Low Countries, 1300–1550*. Chicago: University of Chicago Press, 1998.
Hufton, Olwen H. *The Prospect Before Her: A History of Women in Western Europe, 1: 1500–1800*. New York: HarperCollins, 1996.
Hull, Suzanne W. *Chaste, Silent, and Obedient: English Books for Women, 1475–1640*. San Marino, CA: The Huntington Library, 1982.

Hunt, Lynn, ed. *The Invention of Pornography: Obscenity and the Origins of Modernity, 1500–1800*. New York: Zone Books, 1996.

Hutner, Heidi, ed. *Rereading Aphra Behn: History, Theory, and Criticism*. Charlottesville, VA: University Press of Virginia, 1993.

Hutson, Lorna, ed. *Feminism and Renaissance Studies*. New York: Oxford University Press, 1999.

Italian Women Writers: A Bio-Bibliographical Sourcebook. Edited by Rinaldina Russell. Westport, CT: Greenwood Press, 1994.

Jaffe, Irma B. with Gernando Colombardo. *Shining Eyes, Cruel Fortune: The Lives and Loves of Italian Renaissance Women Poets*. New York: Fordham University Press, 2002.

James, Susan E. *Kateryn Parr: The Making of a Queen*. Aldershot and Brookfield: Ashgate Publishing Co., 1999.

Jankowski, Theodora A. *Women in Power in the Early Modern Drama*. Urbana, IL: University of Illinois Press, 1992.

Jansen, Katherine Ludwig. *The Making of the Magdalen: Preaching and Popular Devotion in the Later Middle Ages*. Princeton: Princeton University Press, 2000.

Jed, Stephanie H. *Chaste Thinking: The Rape of Lucretia and the Birth of Humanism*. Bloomington, IN: Indiana University Press, 1989.

Jones, Ann Rosalind and Peter Stallybrass. *Renaissance Clothing and the Materials of Memory*. Cambridge, UK: Cambridge University Press, 2000.

Jordan, Constance. *Renaissance Feminism: Literary Texts and Political Models*. Ithaca: Cornell University Press, 1990.

Kagan, Richard L. *Lucrecia's Dreams: Politics and Prophecy in Sixteenth-Century Spain*. Berkeley: University of California Press, 1990.

Kehler, Dorothea and Laurel Amtower, eds. *The Single Woman in Medieval and Early Modern England: Her Life and Representation*. Tempe, AZ: MRTS, 2002.

Kelly, Joan. "Did Women Have a Renaissance?" In *Women, History, and Theory*. Chicago: University of Chicago Press, 1984. Also in Renate Bridenthal, Claudia Koonz, and Susan M. Stuard, eds., *Becoming Visible: Women in European History*. Third edition. Boston: Houghton Mifflin, 1998.

———. "Early Feminist Theory and the *Querelle des Femmes*." In *Women, History, and Theory*.

Kelso, Ruth. *Doctrine for the Lady of the Renaissance*. Foreword by Katharine M. Rogers. Urbana, IL: University of Illinois Press, 1956, 1978.

Kendrick, Robert L. *Celestical Sirens: Nuns and their Music in Early Modern Milan*. New York: Oxford University Press, 1996.

Kermode, Jenny and Garthine Walker, eds. *Women, Crime and the Courts in Early Modern England*. Chapel Hill: University of North Carolina Press, 1994.

King, Catherine E. *Renaissance Women Patrons: Wives and Widows in Italy, c. 1300–1550*. New York and Manchester: Manchester University Press (distributed in the U.S. by St. Martin's Press), 1998.

King, Margaret L. *Women of the Renaissance*. Foreword by Catharine R. Stimpson. Chicago: University of Chicago Press, 1991.

Krontiris, Tina. *Oppositional Voices: Women as Writers and Translators of Literature in the English Renaissance*. London and New York: Routledge, 1992.

Kuehn, Thomas. *Law, Family, and Women: Toward a Legal Anthropology of Renaissance Italy*. Chicago: University of Chicago Press, 1991.

Kunze, Bonnelyn Young. *Margaret Fell and the Rise of Quakerism*. Stanford: Stanford University Press, 1994.
Labalme, Patricia A., ed. *Beyond Their Sex: Learned Women of the European Past*. New York: New York University Press, 1980.
Lalande, Roxanne Decker, ed. *A Labor of Love: Critical Reflections on the Writings of Marie-Catherine Desjardina (Mme de Villedieu)*. Madison, NJ: Fairleigh Dickinson University Press, 2000.
Lamb, Mary Ellen. *Gender and Authorship in the Sidney Circle*. Madison: University of Wisconsin Press, 1990.
Laqueur, Thomas. *Making Sex: Body and Gender from the Greeks to Freud*. Cambridge, MA: Harvard University Press, 1990.
Larsen, Anne R. and Colette H. Winn, eds. *Renaissance Women Writers: French Texts/American Contexts*. Detroit, MI: Wayne State University Press, 1994.
Laven, Mary. *Virgins of Venus: Enclosed Lives and Broken Vows in the Renaissance Convent*. London: Viking, 2002.
Lerner, Gerda. *The Creation of Patriarchy and Creation of Feminist Consciousness, 1000–1870*. New York: Oxford University Press, 1986, 1994.
Levin, Carole and Jeanie Watson, eds. *Ambiguous Realities: Women in the Middle Ages and Renaissance*. Detroit: Wayne State University Press, 1987.
Levin, Carole, Jo Eldridge Carney, and Debra Barrett-Graves. *Elizabeth I: Always Her Own Free Woman*. Aldershot and Brookfield: Ashgate Publishing Co., 2003.
Levin, Carole, et al. *Extraordinary Women of the Medieval and Renaissance World: A Biographical Dictionary*. Westport, CT: Greenwood Press, 2000.
Levy, Allison, ed. *Widowhood and Visual Culture in Early Modern Europe*. Aldershot and Brookfield: Ashgate Publishing Co., 2003.
Lewalsky, Barbara Kiefer. *Writing Women in Jacobean England*. Cambridge, MA: Harvard University Press, 1993.
Lewis, Jayne Elizabeth. *Mary Queen of Scots: Romance and Nation*. London: Routledge, 1998.
Lindenauer, Leslie J. *Piety and Power: Gender and Religious Culture in the American Colonies, 1630–1700*. London and New York: Routledge, 2002.
Lindsey, Karen. *Divorced Beheaded Survived: A Feminist Reinterpretation of the Wives of Henry VIII*. Reading, MA: Addison-Wesley Publishing Co., 1995.
Lochrie, Karma. *Margery Kempe and Translations of the Flesh*. Philadelphia: University of Pennsylvania Press, 1992.
Longino Farrell, Michèle. *Performing Motherhood: The Sévigné Correspondence*. Hanover, NH: University Press of New England, 1991.
Lougee, Carolyn C. *Le Paradis des Femmes: Women, Salons, and Social Stratification in Seventeenth-Century France*. Princeton: Princeton University Press, 1976.
Love, Harold. *The Culture and Commerce of Texts: Scribal Publication in Seventeenth-Century England*. Amherst, MA: University of Massachusetts Press, 1993.
Lowe, K. J. P. *Nuns' Chronicles and Convent Culture in Renaissance and Counter-Reformation Italy*. New York: Cambridge University Press, 2003.
MacCarthy, Bridget G. *The Female Pen: Women Writers and Novelists 1621–1818*. Preface by Janet Todd. New York: New York University Press, 1994. (Originally published by Cork University Press, 1946–47).
Maclean, Ian. *Woman Triumphant: Feminism in French Literature, 1610–1652*. Oxford: Clarendon Press, 1977.

———. *The Renaissance Notion of Woman: A Study of the Fortunes of Scholasticism and Medical Science in European Intellectual Life.* Cambridge: Cambridge University Press, 1980.

MacNeil, Anne. *Music and Women of the Commedia dell'Arte in the Late Sixteenth Century.* New York: Oxford University Press, 2003.

Maggi, Armando. *Uttering the Word: The Mystical Performances of Maria Maddalena de' Pazzi, a Renaissance Visionary.* Albany: State University of New York Press, 1998.

Marshall, Sherrin. *Women in Reformation and Counter-Reformation Europe: Public and Private Worlds.* Bloomington, IN: Indiana University Press, 1989.

Masten, Jeffrey. *Textual Intercourse: Collaboration, Authorship, and Sexualities in Renaissance Drama.* Cambridge: Cambridge University Press, 1997.

Matter, E. Ann, and John Coakley, eds. *Creative Women in Medieval and Early Modern Italy.* Philadelphia: University of Pennsylvania Press, 1994. (sequel to the Monson collection, below)

McGrath, Lynette. *Subjectivity and Women's Poetry in Early Modern England.* Burlington, VT: Ashgate, 2002.

McLeod, Glenda. *Virtue and Venom: Catalogs of Women from Antiquity to the Renaissance.* Ann Arbor: University of Michigan Press, 1991.

Medwick, Cathleen. *Teresa of Avila: The Progress of a Soul.* New York: Alfred A. Knopf, 2000.

Meek, Christine, ed. *Women in Renaissance and Early Modern Europe.* Dublin-Portland: Four Courts Press, 2000.

Mendelson, Sara and Patricia Crawford. *Women in Early Modern England, 1550–1720.* Oxford: Clarendon Press, 1998.

Merchant, Carolyn. *The Death of Nature: Women, Ecology and the Scientific Revolution.* New York: HarperCollins, 1980.

Merrim, Stephanie. *Early Modern Women's Writing and Sor Juana Inés de la Cruz.* Nashville, TN: Vanderbilt University Press, 1999.

Messbarger, Rebecca. *The Century of Women: The Representations of Women in Eighteenth-Century Italian Public Discourse.* Toronto: University of Toronto Press, 2002.

Miller, Nancy K. *The Heroine's Text: Readings in the French and English Novel, 1722–1782.* New York: Columbia University Press, 1980.

Miller, Naomi J. *Changing the Subject: Mary Wroth and Figurations of Gender in Early Modern England.* Lexington, KY: University Press of Kentucky, 1996.

——— and Gary Waller, eds. *Reading Mary Wroth: Representing Alternatives in Early Modern England.* Knoxville, TN: University of Tennessee Press, 1991.

Monson, Craig A., ed. *The Crannied Wall: Women, Religion, and the Arts in Early Modern Europe.* Ann Arbor: University of Michigan Press, 1992.

Moore, Cornelia Niekus. *The Maiden's Mirror: Reading Material for German Girls in the Sixteenth and Seventeenth Centuries.* Wiesbaden: Otto Harrassowitz, 1987.

Musacchio, Jacqueline Marie. *The Art and Ritual of Childbirth in Renaissance Italy.* New Haven: Yale University Press, 1999.

Newman, Barbara. *God and the Goddesses: Vision, Poetry, and Belief in the Middle Ages.* Philadelphia: University of Pennsylvania Press, 2003.

Newman, Karen. *Fashioning Femininity and English Renaissance Drama.* Chicago and London: University of Chicago Press, 1991.

O'Donnell, Mary Ann. *Aphra Behn: An Annotated Bibliography of Primary and Secondary Sources.* Aldershot and Brookfield: Ashgate Publishing Co., 2nd ed., 2004.

Okin, Susan Moller. *Women in Western Political Thought*. Princeton: Princeton University Press, 1979.

Ozment, Steven. *The Bürgermeister's Daughter: Scandal in a Sixteenth-Century German Town*. New York: St. Martin's Press, 1995.

———. *Flesh and Spirit: Private Life in Early Modern Germany*. New York: Penguin Putnam, 1999.

———. *When Fathers Ruled: Family Life in Reformation Europe*. Cambridge, MA: Harvard University Press, 1983.

Pacheco, Anita, ed. *Early [English] Women Writers: 1600–1720*. New York and London: Longman, 1998.

Pagels, Elaine. *Adam, Eve, and the Serpent*. New York: Harper Collins, 1988.

Panizza, Letizia, ed. *Women in Italian Renaissance Culture and Society*. Oxford: European Humanities Research Centre, 2000.

Parker, Patricia. *Literary Fat Ladies: Rhetoric, Gender and Property*. London and New York: Methuen, 1987.

Pernoud, Regine and Marie-Veronique Clin. *Joan of Arc: Her Story*. Rev. and trans. Jeremy DuQuesnay Adams. New York: St. Martin's Press, 1998 (French original, 1986).

Perry, Mary Elizabeth. *Crime and Society in Early Modern Seville*. Hanover, NH: University Press of New England, 1980.

———. *Gender and Disorder in Early Modern Seville*. Princeton: Princeton University Press, 1990.

Petroff, Elizabeth Alvilda, ed. *Medieval Women's Visionary Literature*. New York: Oxford University Press, 1986.

Perry, Ruth. *The Celebrated Mary Astell: An Early English Feminist*. Chicago: University of Chicago Press, 1986.

Rabil, Albert. *Laura Cereta: Quattrocento Humanist*. Binghamton, NY: MRTS, 1981.

Ranft, Patricia. *Women in Western Intellectual Culture, 600–1500*. New York: Palgrave, 2002.

Rapley, Elizabeth. *A Social History of the Cloister: Daily Life in the Teaching Monasteries of the Old Regime*. Montreal: McGill-Queen's University Press, 2001.

Raven, James, Helen Small and Naomi Tadmor, eds. *The Practice and Representation of Reading in England*. Cambridge: University Press, 1996.

Reardon, Colleen. *Holy Concord within Sacred Walls: Nuns and Music in Siena, 1575–1700*. Oxford: Oxford University Press, 2001.

Reiss, Sheryl E. and David G. Wilkins, ed. *Beyond Isabella: Secular Women Patrons of Art in Renaissance Italy*. Kirksville, MO: Turman State University Press, 2001.

Rheubottom, David. *Age, Marriage, and Politics in Fifteenth-Century Ragusa*. Oxford: Oxford University Press, 2000.

Richardson, Brian. *Printing, Writers and Readers in Renaissance Italy*. Cambridge: University Press, 1999.

Riddle, John M. *Contraception and Abortion from the Ancient World to the Renaissance*. Cambridge, MA: Harvard University Press, 1992.

———. *Eve's Herbs: A History of Contraception and Abortion in the West*. Cambridge, MA: Harvard University Press, 1997.

Roper, Lyndal. *The Holy Household: Women and Morals in Reformation Augsburg*. New York: Oxford University Press, 1989.

Rose, Mary Beth. *The Expense of Spirit: Love and Sexuality in English Renaissance Drama.* Ithaca, NY: Cornell University Press, 1988.

———. *Gender and Heroism in Early Modern English Literature.* Chicago: University of Chicago Press, 2002.

———, ed. *Women in the Middle Ages and the Renaissance: Literary and Historical Perspectives.* Syracuse: Syracuse University Press, 1986.

Rosenthal, Margaret F. *The Honest Courtesan: Veronica Franco, Citizen and Writer in Sixteenth-Century Venice.* Foreword by Catharine R. Stimpson. Chicago: University of Chicago Press, 1992.

Rublack, Ulinka, ed. *Gender in Early Modern German History.* Cambridge: Cambridge University Press, 2002.

Sackville-West, Vita. *Daughter of France: The Life of La Grande Mademoiselle.* Garden City, NY: Doubleday, 1959.

Sánchez, Magdalena S. *The Empress, the Queen, and the Nun: Women and Power at the Court of Philip III of Spain.* Baltimore: Johns Hopkins University Press, 1998.

Scaraffia, Lucetta and Gabriella Zarri. *Women and Faith: Catholic Religious Life in Italy from Late Antiquity to the Present.* Cambridge, MA: Harvard University Press, 1999.

Schiebinger, Londa. *The Mind Has no Sex?: Women in the Origins of Modern Science.* Cambridge, MA: Harvard University Press, 1991.

———. *Nature's Body: Gender in the Making of Modern Science.* Boston: Beacon Press, 1993.

Schutte, Anne Jacobson, Thomas Kuehn, and Silvana Seidel Menchi, eds. *Time, Space, and Women's Lives in Early Modern Europe.* Kirksville, MO: Truman State University Press, 2001.

Schofield, Mary Anne and Cecilia Macheski, eds. *Fetter'd or Free? British Women Novelists, 1670–1815.* Athens, OH: Ohio University Press, 1986.

Schutte, Anne Jacobson. *Aspiring Saints: pretense of Holiness, Inquisition, and Gender in the Republic of Venice, 1618–1750.* Baltimore: Johns Hopkins University Press, 2001.

———, Thomas Kuehn, and Silvana Seidel Menchi, eds. *Time, Space, and Women's Lives in Early Modern Europe.* Kirksville, MO: Truman State University Press, 2001.

Seifert, Lewis C. *Fairy Tales, Sexuality and Gender in France 1690–1715: Nostalgic Utopias.* Cambridge, UK: Cambridge University Press, 1996.

Shannon, Laurie. *Sovereign Amity: Figures of Friendship in Shakespearean Contexts.* Chicago: University of Chicago Press, 2002.

Shemek, Deanna. *Ladies Errant: Wayward Women and Social Order in Early Modern Italy.* Durham, NC: Duke University Press, 1998.

Smith, Hilda L. *Reason's Disciples: Seventeenth-Century English Feminists.* Urbana, IL: University of Illinois Press, 1982.

———. *Women Writers and the Early Modern British Political Tradition.* Cambridge: Cambridge University Press, 1998.

Sobel, Dava. *Galileo's Daughter: A Historical Memoir of Science, Faith, and Love.* New York: Penguin Books, 2000.

Sommerville, Margaret R. *Sex and Subjection: Attitudes to Women in Early-Modern Society.* London: Arnold, 1995.

Soufas, Teresa Scott. *Dramas of Distinction: A Study of Plays by Golden Age Women.* Lexington, KY: The University Press of Kentucky, 1997.

Spencer, Jane. *The Rise of the Woman Novelist: From Aphra Behn to Jane Austen.* Oxford: Basil Blackwell, 1986.

Spender, Dale. *Mothers of the Novel: 100 Good Women Writers Before Jane Austen*. London and New York: Routledge, 1986.
Sperling, Jutta Gisela. *Convents and the Body Politic in Late Renaissance Venice*. Foreword by Catharine R. Stimpson. Chicago: University of Chicago Press, 1999.
Steinbrügge, Lieselotte. *The Moral Sex: Woman's Nature in the French Enlightenment*. Trans. Pamela E. Selwyn. New York: Oxford University Press, 1995.
Stephenson, Barbara. *The Power and Patronage of Marguerite de Navarre*. Aldershot and Brookfield: Ashgate Publishing Co., 2004.
Stocker, Margarita. *Judith, Sexual Warrior: Women and Power in Western Culture*. New Haven: Yale University Press, 1998.
Stretton, Timothy. *Women Waging Law in Elizabethan England*. Cambridge: Cambridge University Press, 1998.
Stuard, Susan M. "The Dominion of Gender: Women's Fortunes in the High Middle Ages." In Renate Bridenthal, Claudia Koonz, and Susan M. Stuard, eds. *Becoming Visible: Women in European History*. Third edition. Boston: Houghton Mifflin, 1998.
Summit, Jennifer. *Lost Property: The Woman Writer and English Literary History, 1380–1589*. Chicago: University of Chicago Press, 2000.
Surtz, Ronald E. *The Guitar of God: Gender, Power, and Authority in the Visionary World of Mother Juana de la Cruz (1481–1534)*. Philadelphia: University of Pennsylvania Press, 1991.
———. *Writing Women in Late Medieval and Early Modern Spain: The Mothers of Saint Teresa of Avila*. Philadelphia: University of Pennsylvania Press, 1995.
Suzuki, Mihoko. *Subordinate Subjects: Gender, the Political Nation, and Literary Form in England, 1588–1688*. Aldershot and Brookfield: Ashgate Publishing Co., 2003.
Teague, Frances. *Bathsua Makin, Woman of Learning*. Lewisburg, PA: Bucknell University Press, 1999.
Thomas, Anabel. *Art and Piety in the Female Religious Communities of Renaissance Italy: Iconography, Space, and the Religious Woman's Perspective*. New York: Cambridge University Press, 2003.
Tinagli, Paola. *Women in Italian Renaissance Art: Gender, Representation, Identity*. Manchester: Manchester University Press, 1997.
Todd, Janet. *The Secret Life of Aphra Behn*. London, New York, and Sydney: Pandora, 2000.
———. *The Sign of Angelica: Women, Writing and Fiction, 1660–1800*. New York: Columbia University Press, 1989.
Tomas, Natalie R. *The Medici Women: Gender and Power in Renaissance Florence*. Aldershot and Brookfield: Ashgate Publishing Co., 2004.
Traub, Valerie. *The Renaissance of Lesbianism in Early Modern England*. Cambridge: Cambridge University Press, 2002.
Valenze, Deborah. *The First Industrial Woman*. New York: Oxford University Press, 1995.
Van Dijk, Susan, Lia van Gemert and Sheila Ottway, eds. *Writing the History of Women's Writing: Toward an International Approach*. Proceedings of the Colloquium, Amsterdam, 9–11 September. Amsterdam: Royal Netherlands Academy of Arts and Sciences, 2001.
Vickery, Amanda. *The Gentleman's Daughter: Women's Lives in Georgian England*. New Haven: Yale University Press, 1998.

Vollendorf, Lisa, ed. *Recovering Spain's Feminist Tradition.* New York: MLA, 2001.
Walker, Claire. *Gender and Politics in Early Modern Europe: English Convents in France and the Low Countries.* New York: Palgrave, 2003.
Wall, Wendy. *The Imprint of Gender: Authorship and Publication in the English Renaissance.* Ithaca, NY: Cornell University Press, 1993.
Walsh, William T. *St. Teresa of Avila: A Biography.* Rockford, IL: TAN Books and Publications, 1987.
Warner, Marina. *Alone of All Her Sex: The Myth and Cult of the Virgin Mary.* New York: Knopf, 1976.
Warnicke, Retha M. *The Marrying of Anne of Cleves: Royal Protocol in Tudor England.* Cambridge: Cambridge University Press, 2000.
Watt, Diane. *Secretaries of God: Women Prophets in Late Medieval and Early Modern England.* Cambridge, England: D. S. Brewer, 1997.
Weaver, Elissa. *Convent Theatre in Early Modern Italy.* New York: Cambridge University Press, 2002.
Weber, Alison. *Teresa of Avila and the Rhetoric of Femininity.* Princeton: Princeton University Press, 1990.
Welles, Marcia L. *Persephone's Girdle: Narratives of Rape in Seventeenth-Century Spanish Literature.* Nashville: Vanderbilt University Press, 2000.
Whitehead, Barbara J., ed. *Women's Education in Early Modern Europe: A History, 1500–1800.* New York and London: Garland Publishing Co., 1999.
Wiesner, Merry E. *Working Women in Renaissance Germany.* New Brunswick, NJ: Rutgers University Press, 1986.
Wiesner-Hanks, Merry E. *Christianity and Sexuality in the Early Modern World: Regulating Desire, Reforming Practice.* New York: Routledge, 2000.
———. *Gender, Church, and State in Early Modern Germany: Essays.* New York: Longman, 1998.
———. *Gender in History.* Malden, MA: Blackwell, 2001.
———. *Women and Gender in Early Modern Europe.* Cambridge, UK: Cambridge University Press, 1993.
———. *Working Women in Renaissance Germany.* New Brunswick, NJ: Rutgers University Press, 1986.
Willard, Charity Cannon. *Christine de Pizan: Her Life and Works.* New York: Persea Books, 1984.
Winn, Colette and Donna Kuizenga, eds. *Women Writers in Pre-Revolutionary France.* New York: Garland Publishing, 1997.
Woodbridge, Linda. *Women and the English Renaissance: Literature and the Nature of Womankind, 1540–1620.* Urbana: University of Illinois Press, 1984.
Woodford, Charlotte. *Nuns as Historians in Early Modern Germany.* Oxford: Clarendon Press, 2002.
Woods, Susanne. *Lanyer: A Renaissance Woman Poet.* New York: Oxford University Press, 1999.
———, and Margaret P. Hannay, eds. *Teaching Tudor and Stuart Women Writers.* New York: MLA, 2000.

INDEX

Aaron (high priest of Israel), 113n92
Abraham, 47–49, 51, 53, 55, 149, 157
Abray, Lorna Jane, 4n6, 9n11
Acciaiuoli, Andrea, xxiii
Adam (first man), xiii, xiv, xxi, xxvi, 106, 112n88, 137, 138n, 153, 157, 157n, 158, 211, 211n
Agatha, Saint, 136n123
Agnes, Saint, 136n123
Agnetha (possibly Agnes or Agatha), 136, 136n123
Agrippa, Henricus Cornelius, xxi–xxiii
Ahasuerus, King of Persia, 212
Alberti, Leon Battista, xxi
almsgiving, 11–12, 90n
Alsace, 4, 31, 18, 113n91, 135n121; Alsatian (person, language), 18, 30, 40
Alvaro de Luna, xxiii
Amazon (title given to women), xxv–xxvi
Ambrose, Saint, 104, 104n77, 135, 135n121
Anabaptism, 15n21, 22–23, 85n, 88, 93n59, 127, 145, 160n151, 177, 177n, 179, 194, 194n32, 200n46, 215, 215n, 234
Ananias (servant of high priest), 66
Anna (prophetess in Jerusalem temple), 196, 196n38, 208n65, 224, 224n85
Anne of Brittany, Queen, xxiii
Anne of Denmark, Princess, xxiii

Annunciation, 95n62. *See also* times of worship
antichrist, 79, 109n, 121
Apocrypha, 72n30, 213n72
Apollos (preacher), 194, 208
Aquinas, Thomas, xii, xiv
Ariosto, Ludovico, xxvi
Aristotle, x, xn, xi, xin, 182, 194
Armbruster, Sir Felix, 10, 24, 27, 33, 46, 124–26, 131–32, 133n, 134–35, 187n15; in title 33, 40, 123
Armstrong, Brian G., 32n38
ars moriendi, 100, 171n
Artemisia (ancient warrior-heroine), xxv
artisans and "common people," 1–2, 6, 10, 18, 26, 27n, 28–30, 40, 46, 96, 124, 126, 183n10, 186, 187n16, 227n93
Ascension, 95. *See also* times of worship
asceticism, 47
assurance of salvation, 100–1, 125–26, 154–55, 212–13, 221, 230–31
Assyria, king of, 113n92
Assyrians, 120, 120n103
Astell, Mary, xxiii, xxv, xxvii
Augsburg, 9, 18n23, 46, 49, 55n8, 97, 99n68
Augsburg Confession, 10, 15n21, 165n, 176, 177n, 178

Index

Augsburg Interim, 22, 24, 31, 33, 97, 99, 102, 104n76, 111, 116, 124, 127, 129, 143n, 175n, 176, 213n72, 222n81, 228n95
Augustine, Saint, xiv, 164n157
Augustinians (religious order), 7, 62, 69–70
Austria, xxiii
authority, religious. *See under* Bible; inspiration and special revelation; tradition, Roman source of doctrine; university

Babylon, 143n
Bainton, Roland H.
Balaam, 81n43, 82
baptism, 72n29, 158, 176n, 200n46; infant or believer's, 194n32
Baptists. *See* Anabaptism
Barbaro, Francesco, xxi, xxvi
Barnes, Jonathan, xn
Bathsheba (mother of Solomon), 140n130, 141n130, 152n142
Beelzebub, 52
beggers and begging, 11–12
beguines, 3
Bible, x, xiii, xix, 16, 22, 25–26, 29–30, 45, 52n, 67, 69n23, 80n, 83, 87–88, 90, 92n, 93, 107n83, 127–28, 130n114, 135n121, 139n127, 144n, 154, 161n, 181–83, 183n, 184–85, 190, 193–94, 196, 198, 207, 207n, 210, 217, 234n; authority of (*sola scriptura*), 20, 25, 43, 45–46, 57–62, 67, 73–74, 93n, 179, 181–82, 184, 196n, 216; contrasting Old and New Testaments, 154–55; in German, 14, 15, 207n61; New Testament, x, xiii–xiv, 14, 17, 47, 63n, 73, 93n59, 94n, 152n142; Old Testament, 47, 63n, 72n30, 73, 93n59, 139n128, 144n, 147, 148n139, 152n142; preaching, 21, 30, 82–85, 162n, 183; reading (devotional, educational), 183n10, 190, 207n61, 208; Word of God, 50, 65, 69n24, 84–85, 88, 118, 162, 184; Zurich translation, 65n, 161n

Bibliander, Theodor, 194n33
Bierma, Lyle, 18n23
birth, 138–39, 161; pain of childbirth, 152; rebirth in Christ (God), 152n143, 154, 156, 161
Blaurer, Ambrose, 33, 228n95
Boccacio, Giovanni, xv–xvi, xvin, xix, xxiii
Bodin, Jean, xxii
Bohemia, 92
Bohemian Brethren, 21, 83, 86, 88–90, 100; Bohemian "heresy," 71n27
Bomer, Elizabeth, 150
Brady, Thomas A., Jr., 4n, 7, 9, 10n12, 13n16
Brant, Sebastian, 13
Brantôme, Pierre de, xx
Bruni, Leonardo, xxvi
Bucer, Martin, 9–10, 17, 19, 21–22, 24, 26, 30n, 71n27, 82n, 98, 103, 104n76, 106n81, 112n89, 113n90, 143n, 162n, 163n155, 176, 200n48, 201n48, 225n88, 228n95
Büheler, Sébald, 18n23, 222n81
Bullinger, Heinrich, 227n94
Bynum, Carolyn Walker, 153n

Cain (son of Adam), 211
Caleb, 60, 67, 93
call (by God), 206–210, 212, 221, 224
Calvin, John, 26, 86n47, 102, 162n
Calvinism, 9n11, 12
canon law, 17, 57, 58, 106n81
Cantelma, Margherita, xxiii
Capito, Wolfgang, 21, 30n, 70n26, 71n27, 106n81, 193, 193n31, 200, 200n48, 201n48, 228n95
carnival, 210, 226
Cassell, Anthony K., xviii
Castiglione, Baldassare, xx
catechism, 30, 91, 93n58, 113n, 118
cathedral of Strasbourg, 5, 8, 97, 103–4, 215, 218, 220n; cathedral parish, 6, 18, 104n78, 176, 184n, 201n48, 215
Catherine of Aragon, xxiii
Catherine de Medici, xxv

celibacy, 3, 16, 57–58, 60–61, 65n20, 72n29, 176n, 182n, 210n
Cereta, Laura, xxiii
Chalcedonian definition, 45, 107n83, 182, 214n, 231n103
Charles V (king of France), xxiii
Charles V (Hapsburg, holy Roman emperor), 9–10, 21, 97, 104n76, 109n, 114, 150n, 176. *See also* king of Assyria
Charles VIII (king of France), xxiii
children, 20, 93–96, 151–152, 193, 196, 200n46, 204, 206, 220n. *See also under* Schütz Zell
Chrisman, Miriam U., 4n, 13n17, 28, 29, 62n13, 71n28
Christ, xiv, 15–17, 22, 26, 40, 43–46, 48–54, 56, 59, 63–65, 68, 70, 72, 73n31, 77n38, 79–84, 87, 89–91, 94–96, 99–101, 104–110, 111, 113, 114, 114n, 115, 116, 117, 118–20, 121–23, 127–37, 139, 142n, 144n, 145, 145n135, 146, 146n, 147–53, 153n, 154, 154n, 155–57, 157n, 158–64, 164n, 165, 165n, 166, 166n, 167–68, 170, 170n, 171–73, 183n10, 186–87, 187n17, 189, 191–96, 196n37, 197n38, 198–99, 199n, 200, 201n51, 202, 203n54, 204–7, 207n62, 208–12, 214, 219, 221, 223–31, 233–34; as chief shepherd, 111, 116, 204, 225; Christ's merit, 134, 231; comforter, 152, 154, 207, 232; imitation of, 170n164, 171; as sole savior, 26, 48, 77n38, 101, 105n80, 107, 109, 113–15, 199n43, 208, 210, 214; trust in creature as betrayal of, 107, 192, 199
Christian life and Protestants, 29, 46, 87, 96, 101, 122, 127, 144–47, 156, 160, 165–70, 184, 203n54; hypocritical behavior, 197–98; mutuality as siblings, 156; relationship to faith, 29, 127; standards of morality, 203. *See also* forgiveness; love of neighbor / brotherly love; persecution of Protestants; *and under* Zell

Christmas, 89, 94, 220n. *See also* times of worship
Chrysostom, John (archbishop of Constantinople), 162n
church, 57, 179, 181, 184–85, 196, 198n42, 203n54, 217–21, 224, 226–28, 231n103, 234; definitions of, 63–64, 82, 111, 119, 135, 142–43, 151, 156, 158, 166–70, 173, 185, 209, 211–13, 224; and early church fathers, 45, 93n59, 135n121; established by civil law, 185, 195n35, 196, 217; "household" structure in, 224, 226n91; militant ("struggling") or triumphant, 224; parish structure in, 185, 216, 218; synod, 201n48 (*see also* Strasbourg clergy); universal or visible, 185, 195–96
Cicero, Marcus Tullius, 182, 194
Cisterians, 153n
clergy, ordained: bishop, 203; call (*see under* vocation); character, 185n13, 193, 231n101, 197–198, 203, 209, 231 (*see also under* Rabus, Ludwig); education (*see* university); as good steward, 113, 163, 187n17, 203n54 (*see also under* Zell); mutual censure, 219, 228; pastor (*see under* "offices"; vocation); ranks of ordained, 194, 201n48
clergy, Strasbourg Protestant: "architects of church," 228, 230; first generation, 7, 10, 19, 21–22, 26–27, 29, 30n, 31, 57, 70, 82, 89, 99, 104, 106n81, 118, 127, 143n, 175–79, 185, 194n33, 200, 201n48, 217, 220–221, 225, 227–28, 230; as citizens, 87 (*see also under* "offices"; vocation; Zell); conducting theological arguments, 200, 201n48; second generation / Lutheran, 10, 19, 23–24, 30, 98, 176, 178, 180, 185, 190n22, 191–94, 197, 199–203, 212, 218n, 219, 225n88, 228, 230, 233n2; wives, 17, 19–20, 58, 188n19, 193, 197

clergy, Roman, 11, 15–16, 60–62, 65, 67, 69, 73–74, 79, 83–86, 97, 99, 105n69, 143n, 164n156, 172n166, 198n42, 207, 207n61, 215, 218, 233n2; immoral lives, 16, 43, 45, 58, 61, 65, 73, 75, 77; reformers, 20, 84n, 86, 90n, 113n90, 183n10; sexual mores of, 18, 73–75; women and children of priests, 16, 18, 58, 75n, 76
Cochlaeus, Johannes, 61–62, 70
coercion, religious, 30n, 222n81, 231n102
Col, Gontier, xx
Cologne (city) 112n89
confessions, Protestant, 177n, 178; Augsburg Confession, 10, 15n21, 165n, 176, 177n, 178; confessional conflict, 21–22, 41, 175–79; Tetrapolitan, 176
confirmation, sacrament, 191n27
conscience, 121, 124, 161, 166, 169, 186, 198, 202n51, 215, 231; good / peace of, 44, 64, 131, 150, 204, 226–27, 229; troubled, 129, 133–34, 170, 207, 226
Constance (city), 9, 33, 228n95
Cornelius, 208
covenant (God's with people), 54, 141, 151, 159; human covenants, 74
Cranmer, Thomas, 112n89
creeds, 44, 45, 88, 99, 107n83, 128, 131n114, 208n65; Apostles, 88, 118n, 128, 131n114, 151, 156, 182; Chalcedonian definition, 45, 107n83, 182, 214n, 231n103; Nicene, 88, 107n83, 118n, 119n100, 131n114, 135n122, 158n, 182
crucifix, 100

dances, 95, 226
Daniel (prophet), 71, 117; additions to book of Daniel, 72n30
David (biblical king), 53, 55, 68, 79–80, 93, 115, 119, 123, 129, 133, 136, 137n, 140n130, 141n130, 145, 146n136, 149, 152n142, 154, 157, 186, 188, 195, 196, 201, 207–8, 216
Davis, Natalie Zemon, 125, 183, 220n10
death and dying, 45, 79, 89, 99–103, 104n76, 109, 110n, 111–12, 120, 126, 135, 150, 155, 166–67, 170–72, 189, 194n32, 202, 205, 210, 226–27; Jewish burial practice, 134n118. *See also under* Zell
devil, xxii, xxiv, 60, 66–67, 69, 77–78, 81, 94, 96, 100–1, 107, 112, 114–16, 121, 155, 161, 170, 173, 200–1, 205, 210–12, 217, 219, 230, 233
diaconate, Reformed, 12
discipline, church, 9, 10, 179, 219–20; right attitude, 201; stages, 105n79, 229–30. *See also* excommunication
disobedience, 136–38, 141, 152, 157
Dominicans, xxii, 71
Dona María (wife of Juan II of Castile), xxiii
Douglas, Jane Dempsey, 84n, 220n
Doumergue, Emile, 5
Drenss, Agnes, 7; Andreas, 7; Margaret, 7

Easter, 83, 95; Easter lamb, 106. *See also* times of worship
education, religious. *See under* Schütz Zell
Egypt, 67, 114n92, 120, 139n128, 173
Eleanora of Aragon, xxiii
election (doctrine of), 47, 140n129, 166, 182, 209, 211–12, 212n70; damnation, 107, 212
Elijah (prophet), 119
Elizabeth (mother of John the Baptist), 82
Elizabeth I (queen of England), xxv
Elyot, Sir Thomas, xxv
Emmaus, 52
Empfinger, Simeon, 32

England, xxiii, xxv, xxvii, 112n79, 177n
Equicola, Maria, xxi, xxiii
Erasmus, Desiderius, xxi, 92n, 162n
Erb, Sebastian, 13. *See under* poor relief
Ercole I d'Este, xxiii
Esdras, 72n30, 213
Esther (queen), 72, 212
Eucharist, 10n11. *See also* Lord's Supper; Mass
Europe, ix, xii–xiii, xvi–xviii, xxiii–xxv, 1, 4, 8–13, 175, 220n
Eve (first woman), xiii–xiv, xix, xxi, xxiv, xxvi, 112n, 138n, 157n, 211n
excommunication, 105n79
exegesis, exegetical practices, 127, 146n136
exile, 47, 79, 104n76, 105, 143, 157, 158, 166, 168, 170–71, 176, 225n88
extreme unction, 100–1
Ezekiel (prophet), 81–82, 117
Ezra, 213

Fagius, Paul, 104n76, 143n, 176, 225n88, 228n95
fair, Strasbourg, 53, 220n; Frankfurt book fair, 70–71
faith, 15–16, 26, 46–47, 49, 50–51, 54–55, 61, 65, 80, 87, 90, 92, 95–97, 101–2, 107–10, 113, 117, 122, 124–26, 134n118, 138, 142, 150, 162–64, 169–70, 172, 176n, 177n, 182, 184, 186, 189, 193, 198–99, 201, 204–5, 209, 211–13, 223, 224n86, 228–30; belief-unbelief, 46, 48, 50, 55, 108–9, 115, 120, 137, 138n, 170, 180, 211; believing as spiritual, 47, 50; gift of faith, 209, 212; justification by, 16, 20, 29, 44, 61, 62n, 83, 90, 101, 107, 108n, 114n93, 127–28, 172, 199n, 212n70; preaching, relationship of faith to, 65; sin of unbelief, 137, 137n, 211
fall into sin, 112n88, 138, 152, 157, 211
farmers, 96

fasts, 117n, 144
Fedele, Cassandra, xxii
Ferrara, xxiii
Ferdinand Hapsburg, 9
Filippo da Bergamo, xx
Flanders, xvii
flesh and spirit, conflict, 47–48, 50, 55, 170
Florence (city), xxiii
Fonte, Moderata, xxv
forgiveness, 82, 105, 111, 156, 166, 168–69. *See also under* God
France, xv, xxii–xxiii, xxv, xxvii, 86n47, 125n106, 183n10
Franciscans (religious order), 69, 72n31
Franco-Prussian War, 33
Frankfurt book fair, 70–71
Frederick the Wise, Elector of Saxony, 7
freedom, Christian, 192, 201, 204
free will, 100; bound will, 101, 127, 137, 137n, 161, 167, 170
Freiburg, University of, 18
Freybe, P, 62n13
Frölich, Jacob, 91
Fullneck, Moravia, 92
Füsslin, J. C., 28, 33n41, 222n82

Galeazzo Flavio Capra (or Capella), xxi
Galen, x
Galilee, 104
Geiler of Kaysersberg, Doctor Johann, 13, 20, 84n, 220n
gemeinen nutz, 29, 71
gemeynen mann, 26n31, 27n
gender language: begetting, 130, 138–39, 149, 153–54, 156–57, 159, 161, 167; bridal, 136, 191–92, 212; maternal for God or Christ, 44, 49, 54–55, 129, 153–55, 156n147; masculine for women, 48–49; stereotypes for women, 191, 224n86 (*see also under* women); Schütz Zell's use, 25n, 135n120, 224n86 (*see also under* Schütz Zell)

German (language) Bible. *See under* Bible; Protestants
Germany, xxii, 4, 14, 18, 20n, 33, 49, 70, 113, 191, 194n, 227n94
Gerson, Johannes, 100n71
Gerster family, 3; Elisabeth, 2, 226
gift giving, 124, 125n106, 220n
Giuliano de Medici, xx
God, xiii, 16, 40, 44–55, [56], 58, 60, 63–70, 72, 74–75, 77–85, 87–88, 93, 95–96, 99–101, 104–110–14, 116, 118, 121–25, 125n107, 126–30, 130n, 131–133, 134–46, 148–50, 152–62, 164n156, 166–68, 169n, 170, 172, 181–87–90, 195–97, 199, 201, 202n51, 203n54, 204–16, 222–31, 233–34; comforter, 54–56, 121–22, 130, 132–34, 138–40, 155–56, 168, 188, 213 (*see also under* Christ; Holy Spirit); discipline (relationship of sin and affliction), 112, 119n101, 121, 126, 132–33, 139–40, 186n15, 223n83, 233n1; as Father, 151–52, 154–55, 159–60, 164, 167–69, 172; forgiveness / mercy, 16, 66, 82–83, 100–1, 111, 116, 121, 123, 125n, 127, 130n113, 134, 137–38, 141, 144, 148–49, 158, 160, 165, 168–69, 170n163, 172, 183, 186, 189, 205, 208, 226; love (divine), 48–51, 53, 55, 94, 130–33, 135, 141–44, 151–53, 155, 169, 186, 212, 223–24, 226; promises 45, 47, 51, 55–56, 138, 140–41, 143, 145, 148, 155, 157, 168, 173, 183, 202n51; as grandfather, 154
godparents, 19n26
Goggio, Bartolommeo, xxi, xxiii
Golden Legend, The, 104n121
Gomorrah, 76
Good Friday, 233. *See also* times of worship
"good heathen," 205–6
good works: almsgiving, 11–12, 90n; denial of meritorious works and polemic vs. Roman teaching, 115, 117, 137, 141–42, 145; indulgences, 199; merit, 15–16, Protestant understanding, 114, 117, 208n63 (*see also* love of neighbor / brotherly love); and Rabus, 199, 209n66, 212; Roman understanding, 3, 11, 15, 48, 55n9, 61, 92, 107, 115, 226; 45, 143n, 144n; sacraments, 199n46, 226
Gospel as Biblical teaching, 6, 7, 9, 15, 18, 20, 22, 26, 43, 47–49, 59, 69, 73, 83, 85–86, 95n63, 99, 105, 106n81, 13n90, 133n, 143n, 147, 168, 175, 178, 197n38, 208, 209n66, 217, 226–27, 229–30
Gottesheim, Jacques von, 30n
Gournay, Marie de, xxvii
government / council / magistracy, Strasbourg, 1, 7, 9n11, 10, 13, 31–33, 90n, 124, 129, 132, 143n, 191n25, 215–16, 220–22, 233; Ammeister, 78; city secretary, 32; constitution of, 4, 6; "Politiques," 9–10; "Zealots," 7, 9–10, 12n15, 13
grace (divine), 45, 60, 63, 79, 81–83, 87–88, 100–101, 108, 116, 120–23, 127–28, 133–35, 137–41, 143n, 144, 147n, 148–50, 153–54, 158–60, 164–65, 170, 176n, 183, 187n15, 188, 190, 192, 206, 211, 212n71, 214, 223, 226, 227n92; relationship of God's grace to human trust, 140
Gregory the Pfennigmaister, 150, 150n
Grosse, Sven, 100n71
Guazzo, Stephano, xxii
guilds, 2, 6–7, 10; fishermen, 6; gardeners, 6–7; shoemakers, 6
Guillame de Lorris, xv
Gutenberg, Johann, 13

Hackfurt, Lukas, 12
Hagar, 47, 51, 212
Hagenau (city), 7n8
Haman, 72
Hannah, 93

Hapsburgs, 47. *See also* Charles V (king of France); Ferdinand Hapsburg; Margaret Hapsburg; Maximilian (emperor)
heathen, 208. *See also* "good heathen" *and under* university
Hecklin, Elsbeth (Elizabeth Scher), 24, 188, 202n52, 203, 203n55
Hedio, Caspar, 7, 71n, 200, 200n48, 201n48, 228n95
Heidnischwerck (woven tapestry), 3
Heilandt, Marx, 225, 225n88
hell, 52, 106–107, 110, 155, 158, 169, 172, 204, 211, 226
Henry VIII (king of England), xxiii
Herlin, Martin, 7
Hermann von Wied, Bishop, 112n89
Herminjard, Aimé Louis, 86n47
Herod, King, 76n36
Herodias (wife of Herod), 76n36
Hesse. *See* Philip
Holland, xxvii
Holofernes, 72
Holt, Mack, 32n38
Holy Roman Empire, 4–7, 9, 12, 97, 97, 150n, 176; Diets, 5; emperor, 5, 53, 150n, 203; Imperial Judicial Court, 5, 150, 150n
Holy Spirit, 16, 40, 45, 52n, 53, 56, 62, 74–75, 80, 83, 85n47, 88, 91n55, 94, 101n72, 104–109, 113, 116–22, 125, 127–29, 131, 132n, 135–37, 139n, 140, 141n131, 144–45, 149, 150–51, 154, 156–58, 158n, 159–62, 165–68, 170–71, 173, 182, 186, 191, 191n26, 205, 206n60, 207, 20–10, 212, 215, 224, 230, 231, 233; comforter, 56, 125, 127, 131, 134n, 135, 150, 158; power of, 209, 231; teaching through inspiration of and learning from Holy Spirit, 109, 116. *See also under* "offices"
Horning, W., 31n37, 98n68, 103n
Hubert, Conrad, 9n11, 10n11, 24, 228n95

human nature, created and fallen, 138, 167, 211
humanism, humanists, xviii, xxi–xxii, xxvi, 4, 11, 13, 93n59, 127, 145n136, 146n136, 205n57
hunger (physical), 166–67, 172
Hur (Moses' assistant), 113n92

ignorance, 183, 204–7. *See also* knowledge of and teaching about God (Christ)
image of God, 119, 140, 152, 161
indulgences. *See under* good works
inspiration and special revelation, 62, 181–82, 205n58, 206n59, 209n67, 210, 224n86; "feather of the Holy Spirit," 191, 209
Isaac (son of Abraham and Sarah), 47–48, 51, 53, 212
Isaiah (prophet), 54–55, 72, 75, 80, 82, 107, 107
Ishmael (son of Abraham and Hagar), 47, 51, 212
Islam, 194n33
Israel, people of, 54, 67, 80, 114n92, 115, 135n120, 139n128, 148, 151, 152, 197, 206, 219. *See also* Jews
Italy, xvii–xviii, xx–xxii, xxvi

Jacob (son of Isaac), 53, 148
James, Saint, 94
Jancke, Gabrielle, 62n13
Jeremiah (prophet), 112
Jerome, Saint, xiv, 86n47
Jerusalem, 113, 114n92, 143, 143n, 144, 213
Jesse (father of David), 91n55
Jesus Christ. *See* Christ
Jews, xiv, xx, 30n, 231, 231n102
Job, 55, 105, 130, 147
Joel (prophet), 82
John, Saint, 115, 152, 200–1, 208
John the Baptist, 76, 82, 95, 119; Saint John's Eve bonfire (*see under* times of worship)
Joseph (son of Jacob), 187, 187n17
Joshua, 60, 67, 93, 113, 114n92

258 *Index*

Juan II (king), xxiii
Juan Rodríguez de la Camara (Juan Rodríguez del Padron), xx
Judah, 224
Judas, 162, 170, 170n
judgment (divine), judgment day, 68, 77, 79–81, 114–16, 109, 131–32, 137–40, 162, 166, 168, 172, 183, 215, 224, 231, 233–34
justification. *See under* faith

Kalb, 225
Kappel, battle of, 9
Kaufmann, Thomas, 62n13
Kaysersberg, 6. *See also under* Geiler of Kaysersberg, Doctor Johann
Kentzingen, 17, 27, 43, 47–50, 105n1, 125–26; in title 30, 40, 46, 63, 98n68, 99n68, 125
Kessler, Johannes, 49
king of Assyria, 113, 114n92
King, Margaret L., ix
Kniebis, Claude, 7, 9
knowledge of and teaching about God (Christ), 132, 183, 206–9, 226–27, 230; comforting, 207; communicated by human instruments, 183, 203n54, 207–9, 211–12; enabled by Holy Spirit, 136, 170–71, 182, 207, 209; necessary for salvation, 65, 121, 127–28, 134–40, 139n127, 143, 147n, 162, 182–83, 206, 223, 227; not mindless submission, 192, 212; not rote memorization, 183, 206; motivated by teachers, 208; obligation to study, 207, 226. *See also under* Bible; call (by God)
Knox, John, xxv
Koerner, Valentin, 181n7
Köpffel, Wolfgang, 46, 49, 62
Koran, 194, 194n33
Krämmer, Heinrich, xxii

laity, 11–12, 25n, 26–27, 29, 43–45, 57–61, 72n29, 81, 83–85, 87–91, 95, 96n64–65, 99n69, 102, 105, 113n90, 124, 163n154, 203n54, 207n61 (*see also* religious activity among laity; Strasbourg laity); households, 21, 88, 90–92; pamphleteers, 3, 28; popular immorality, 44. *See also* gender language; women; *and under* Schütz Zell
Landskron, Bohemia, 92
Landskron, Stephan von, 100n71
law, divine, 45, 82, 127, 141, 145–46, 149, 151, 154–55, 159–62, 167; Christian use of, 9, 45, 127, 144n, 145–46, 167–68, 172; damnation by, 106, 154
law, human, 210. *See also* canon law; Roman law
Lazarus, 170n163
Le Franc, Martin, xx
Le Moyne, Pierre, xx
Lent, 117n
lepers and leprosy, 11, 24, 124
Leser, Master Hans the, 150, 150n
Liebenau, Ulrike, 181n7
Liegnitz, 201n49
Lienhard, Marc, 181n7
liturgical year, 89–90, 94, 95n62. *See also* times of worship
Locher, Gottfried W., 23n
Lord's Prayer, 20, 24, 40, 43–44, 110, 119, 120–21, 123, 128, 134, 150, 151, 158–73.
Lord's Supper (Protestant), 44, 83, 128, 145n135, 163, 163n155, 164–66, 193n31, 198–99; "bread of unity," 199–200; as confession of faith, 165, 167, 199–200; language, 9, 165, 165n, 166n160, 199; polemic vs. Rome (and Rabus), 192n28, 198–200 (*see also under* Protestants, polemic against "false teaching / worship"); ubiquity, teaching of, 9, 165n, 176n, 192n28, 199n45; "worthiness" (love / unity), 166, 198n42, 199n45, 200n47 (*see also* unity, Christian, through love)
Löscher, Abraham, 20n, 98, 104n76, 116n96

Lot (Abraham's nephew), 76
love of neighbor / brotherly love, 29–30, 44, 56, 59, 63–64, 66, 87–88, 105, 124–25, 132, 133n, 134n, 144, 156, 166–69, 179, 188, 190, 192, 198, 202, 213–14, 226n90, 228; "judgment of love," 204, 228–30; "works of love," 53
lullaby, 95, 96n64
Luther, Martin, 9n11, 15–16, 22, 27–28, 29n, 31, 49, 61, 63n16, 65n19, 67, 69, 70n25, 73n31, 83, 101n72, 106, 110, 113, 114n92, 135n121, 144n, 161n, 162n, 163n153 & 155, 177n, 179, 182, 191n26, 194, 194n33, 197n39, 198, 198n42, 207, 207n61, 208, 210, 210n, 211, 226, 227n92
Lutheran tradition, 29, 95n, 102n, 163n155, 165n, 176, 176n, 177n, 180, 192n28, 194, 199n44. See also under clergy; Lord's Supper

Maccabees, 72n30
magistracy, 198; Christian magistracy (see under "offices")
maidservants, 78–79, 96, 152, 212
Malachi (prophet), 146
Mantura, xxiii
Marbach, Johann, 9n11
Marburg, 105n80, 163n155
Margaret the Virgin, 136, 136n123
Margaret Hapsburg, Duchess of Austria and regent of the Netherlands, xxiii
marriage, 74–75, 146–147; clerical, 16, 17, 1823n, 31, 43, 57–62, 73, 75, 77, 106; Protestant teaching on, 16–17, 18n23, 19; Roman teaching, 17; Zells' (see also under Zells, Matthew and Katharina)
Martha (sister of Mary and Lazarus), 115, 170n163
Martyr, Peter Martyr Vermigli, 104n76, 112n89
martyrs and martyrdom, 171, 177, 229

Mary Magdalene, 104, 104n, 115, 134, 170, 170n163
Marys in the New Testament, 134
Mary (mother of Jesus), 82, 90–91, 95n62, 104, 116n97, 134, 156, 157n, 208n65, 209; co-redeemer / mediatrix, 208n65; perpetual virginity, 157. See also times of worship
Mary (sister of Martha and Lazarus), 170n163
Mass, 7, 45, 55n9, 83–84, 96, 107n84, 109n, 118n, 122n104, 162n, 163n154, 176n: doctrine of, 84; Mass (time), 96
Mathéolus, xv, xviii
matins, 96. See also times of worship
Maximilian (emperor), 72n31
McKee, Elsie Anne, 1n, 2n, 3n, 5, 7n8, 8, 9n10, 12n15, 13n16, 14n18 & 20, 18n24, 23n, 25n, 26n31, 29n33, 30n, 31n, 32n, 33n, 39, 49n, 88n51, 89n, 90n, 91n55, 98n67, 103n, 110n, 113n92, 116n, 129n, 135n121, 147, 153n, 161n, 162n, 163n155, 175n, 180n, 181n, 183n10, 184n, 188n19, 190n23, 191n25–26, 193n31, 197n38–39, 199n43, 201n49, 203n54, 208n, 215n, 216n, 217n, 218n, 219n, 220n, 221n, 222n, 223n84, 224n, 227n94, 228n96, 231n102, 233n2
Medici. See Catherine de Medici; Giuliano de Medici
medieval period, ix, xiv, xvi–xvii, xix, 8, 15, 84, 91n54, 100, 135n121, 136n123, 146n136, 170n164, 171n, 183n10, 192n27, 198n42, 208n65, 220n, 227n93
merit. See under Christ; good works
Meun, Jean de, xv, xx
Meyer, Jacob, 7, 10
Mieg, Daniel, 7
Migliore, Daniel L., 162n
ministry. See under clergy, laity; vocation
Mohammed, founder of Islam, 194
Molitur, Ulrich, xxii

monasticism, 2, 44, 72n29, 87, 92, 96n64–65, 105n80, 142n136, 210, 218; music, 95, 96n; vows, 72n29, 210n. *See also* Augustinians (religious order); beguines; Dominicans; Franciscans (religious order); monks; nuns and convents
monks, 12, 87, 92, 95, 96n, 105n80, 210, 218
Montreuil, Jean de, xx
Morata, Olympia, xxiii
Moravia, 92
Mordecai (uncle of Queen Esther), 72
Moses, 67, 93, 113, 114n92, 115, 119–20, 120n102, 139, 152, 154–55, 199, 209
motherhood, 95–96, 129, 152–53; foster mothers, 204, 212, 215, 217–18, 228
Mount of Olives, 120
Mr. Ludwig (Rabus). *See* Rabus, Ludwig
Murner, Thomas, 14, 61–62, 69, 72–73, 73n31
music: modal-tonic, 91n54; popular (pre-Reformation), 86, 90, 92, 93n58, 94–96, 97n; Protestant hymns or singing, 21, 44, 85–96, 100, 102, 122, 167
Muslim, 194n33

Nathan (prophet), 82, 141, 141n130, 145
Netherlands, xxiii
New Testament. *See under* Bible
New Year's Day, 220n. *See also* times of worship
Nicholas, Saint, 220n79; Saint Nicolas parish, 225n88
Nicodemus, 197
Noah, 74
Nogarola, Isotta, xxiii, xxvi
nuns and convents, 3, 48, 85, 92, 95, 96n
Nuremberg, 9

oaths, 160
Oberman, Heiko A., 23n

Oecolampadius, Johannes, 105n80, 228n95
"offices": of Christians as love and compassion, 88n50, 125, 132, 134, 136; of Christian magistracy, 143, 185n13; of discipline, 105; of God, 125n107, 136–137; of Holy Spirit, 46, 125, 127–128, 131, 134; of pastor (care), 44, 46, 111, 134n119, 203n54, 204; of preachers and preaching, 46, 65, 88, 104, 128, 184, 203n54, 208, 225, 226n91 (*see also under* Bible); of widows, 221, 226; office theory, Protestant teaching, 125n107
Old Testament. *See under* Bible
ordination: "man's office," 196; Protestant clergy, 184, 217; Roman clergy, 87n; of women, 27, 184, 196n38
organ, organist, 95, 96n64
Orff, Carl, 86n48
orphans, 11, 90n, 122, 158–59
Otter, Jacob, 13, 14n18, 17
Ottoman Turks, 9, 194, 194n33

Pallavicino, Gasparo, xx
parents, advice to, 94–96
Passover, 139n128
"pastor's wife," 1, 17, 18, 19
Paul, Saint, xiv, 53, 55, 67–68, 70–71, 72–75, 77, 80, 82, 86n47, 94, 108–109, 113–14, 117, 133, 184, 194, 196–97, 199–202, 205–6, 208–9, 219, 228, 230
peasants, 11–12, 21, 92, 92n, 93n54, 179, 183n10, 218
Peasants War, 12, 189n22
Pelagius, 86n47
Pellikan, Conrad, 26n31, 32n38, 180n, 227n94
penance: attitude of repentance, 141, 150; Roman sacrament of, 101, 105n79, 161n
Penitential Psalms, 126
Pentecost, 95. *See also* times of worship

persecution of Protestants, 47–52, 54, 59, 64–65, 78–79, 112n89, 116–17, 120, 126, 171, 201n50, 213; of Anabaptists, 200n48. *See also* coercion, religious
perseverance, 163, 227
Peter, Saint, 55, 72, 77, 162, 170, 170n163, 193–94, 208, 219, 226, 228–29
Pfarrer, Mathis, 116n96
Pfennigmaister, Gregory, 150, 150n
pharaoh, 68, 168, 187, 187n17
Philip (deacon), 208
Philip of Hesse, 9, 163n155
Philistine, 201
philosophy and philosophers, 182, 205n57. *See also* Aristotle; Plato; Socrates
Pietro Paolo de Ribera, xx
pilgrims and pilgrimages: Protestant usage, 104, 168, 199; Roman, 107n84
piping (with musical instrument), 95
Pizan, Christine de, xv, xviii, xviiin, xix–xx, xxiii, xxv, xxvii
Plato, xi, 182, 194
poets, classical (pagan), 194
"Politiques," 9–10
Pontius Pilate, 156
poor, 11–13, 24, 94, 221, 225. *See also* sick, sickness
poor relief, 1, 4, 10–13, 32, 189, 189n22, 190n23; Blatterhaus (institution of Strasbourg city welfare system), 13, 24, 32, 190n23; pastoral care of, 13; Protestant practices and teaching, 12; Roman practices and teaching, 11–12
popes and the papacy, 74, 79n40, 97, 108–9, 114–17, 121, 198–99, 206–7, 210
poverty, 166, 170–71
prayer and prayers, 83–85, 87, 89, 96n65, 100–101, 110, 143–44, 148, 160n151, 173, 189–90, 196, 197n38; attitude of trust, 152, 155; daily, 207; for enemies, 202; kneeling, 204; teaching to pray, 204; "public prayers" (*see* Protestants, worship)
preaching. *See under* Bible; call (by God); clergy; laity; Protestant worship; Schütz Zell; Zell
priesthood of believers, 16, 18n23, 26–27, 45–46, 83–88, 90, 92, 95n64, 126–27, 167n, 184, 224n86
printing, in Strasbourg, 4, 13–14
prisons and imprisonment, 170–71, 192, 201, 212
promised land (of Canaan), 67, 93
Protestants, xvii, xx, 15, 17, 21–22, 30–31, 41, 47, 83, 85–88, 93n59, 97, 99, 101–102, 108n85, 109n, 110n, 112n89, 114n94, 116n97, 118n, 125n107, 126–28, 137n, 143n, 144n, 145, 146n136, 156n147, 157n, 159n, 162n, 164n156, 167n, 171n, 176, 176n, 177, 179, 181, 183, 185n13, 192n28, 203n54, 204n, 211n, 221, 226n90, 227n93, 231n101
  EDUCATION (NATURAL HUMAN), 88, 184, 184n; polemic against "false teaching / worship," 43, 58, 60, 70–71, 99n69, 107, 107n74 108–9, 112, 114n94, 115, 121, 200
  TEACHING, 44–45, 47–48, 57, 60, 65n19–20, 69, 74n, 83–88, 91, 99, 101–2, 107, 108n85, 114n94, 137n, 145n135, 157n, 159n, 162n, 164n156, 176n, 182 (*see also under* Bible; *see also* call (by God); church; faith; good works; grace; law; Lord's Supper; marriage; poor relief; saints; work)
  WORSHIP, PUBLIC, 20–21, 83–87, 192, 195–98; sacraments, 21, 89, 230;
Psalms, 14, 22, 24, 45, 69n, 111, 123, 126–27, 128–30, 136, 147, 149, 154, 155, 187n15, 195, 208
purgatory, 45, 106n81, 112n88, 115n, 141n131, 206n59

Rabil, Jr., Albert, ix
Rabus, Ludwig, 2n1, 3n, 9n11, 23–24, 26n31, 27–28, 30, 32–33, 41,

Rabus, Ludwig (*cont.*)
  135n120, 164n157, 175–77, 177n3, 178–81, 181n7, 182, 184n, 185, 185n12–13, 187n15, 191n24, 192n28, 193–94, 195n34–35, 196, 196n36, 197n39, 198n41–42, 199n 44 & 46, 201, 201n54, 203n55, 205n57, 214–15, 215n, 216–17, 217n, 218, 218n, 219, 219n, 220, 220n, 221–22, 222n81, 223n83, 227n92, 228, 228n96, 229, 229n, 230, 230n100, 231, 231n101–102, 233, 233n1–2, 234, 234n3–4; ambition, 218; character, 203n54, 231
Raemond, Florimond de, 86n47
Reformed tradition and teaching, 10n11, 12, 17, 26, 44–45, 85n, 86n47, 93n59, 102n73, 127–28, 144n, 161n, 163n153, 164n157, 166n160, 167n, 183n10, 199n45. *See also* discipline; law; *and under* Lord's Supper
refugees, 1, 17, 189n22, 199, 221, 225, 227
Reinburg, Virginia, 84
Reinis, Austra, 100n, 101n71 & 72
religious activity among laity: educators, 44, 88, 90; hearers of religious truth, 164, 184, 199; judges of truth, 27, 184, 185n12, 190, 195, 220–21, 228–29, 231; personal responsibility for faith, 80n; "preaching" / "speaking out," 16, 27, 44, 90, 92; rebuking clergy, 184, 185n12; religious vocation, 87, 167n
Rémy, Nicolas, xxii
Renaissance, ix, xv
resurrection from the dead, 112, 114–17, 120, 122–23, 129, 143, 148n139, 155, 158, 166, 168, 172, 199
revelation, sources. *See* inspiration; tradition; *under* Bible
Rhegius, Urbanus, 148, 228n95
Rhine River, 4
Rihel, Josiah, 177n
Richards, Earl Jeffrey, xviii
Roettel, Agnes, 193n31
Rome, ancient, xii, xviii, xxi
Rome and the Roman Church, x, xvii, xx, xxiv, 1, 4–5, 7, 9–10, 15n21, 17, 21–22, 26, 29, 41, 43, 57–58, 61, 83, 85n, 86, 90n, 96n66, 100, 102n73, 108n85, 114n94, 118, 127, 143n, 144n, 145, 156n147, 159n, 161n, 162n, 163n154, 164, 165n, 175, 176n, 179, 182, 182n, 185n13, 192n28, 198n42, 204n, 208, 216, 218, 222n81, 226. *See also* clergy, Roman; Strasbourg clergy; teaching, Roman; worship practices, Roman
Roman law, x, xii
Roper, Lyndal, 2n2, 18n23
Roussel, Gérard, 86n47

sacraments, 184–85, 192, 195, 198, 201. *See under* Protestants; Rome
Saint Gall, Switzerland, 49
saints: communion of saints (*see* church); saints as intercessors. Protestant objections to, 77, 77n38, 89, 91n55, 95, 101, 136n123, 208n65; Roman teaching and practice on, 44, 56n11, 77n38, 84, 86, 89, 90n, 91, 100, 107n84, 114n94, 135n, 136n, 160n151, 208n65, 220n. *See also* times of worship
salvation / rest in Christ, 42n, 57, 59–60, 63, 77, 83, 88, 94–96, 100–1, 107, 112–14, 118, 127–29, 132, 141–42, 145n135, 165n, 173, 181, 199, 206, 209n66, 210, 214. *See also* assurance
Samuel (judge), 93
Sarah, 47, 51
Saxer, E., 23n
Saxony, 7
Schadeaus, Oseas, 33
Scher family, 24; Elisabeth Scher Hecklin (*see* Hecklin, Elsbeth [Elizabeth Scher]); Felicitas Scher von Andernach, 24
Schindler, A., 23n
Schmalkald League, 9, 10, 21, 97

Schurman, Anna Maria von, xxvii
Schütz family, 2, 3, 18; Hans, Sr. (relative in Senate), 2, 6; Jacob (father), 2, 46, 78, 206, 226, 231; Jacob (brother), 131n115; Lux ("Meister," brother), 2; Lux (handicapped nephew), 24, 124, 131, 189, 190n22, 197; niece, 3. *See also* Schütz Zell
Schütz Zell, Katharina, 1–4, 7n, 8, 9n10, 10, 12–30, 40–41, 43–50, 52n, 53, 54n, 56, 58–62, 64–73, 74n, 76n35–36, 77–81, 83–84, 86–92, 94, 95n60–61, 96–100, 101n72, 102–7, 108n84–85, 110–25, 125n106, 126–29, 130n113–114, 131–45, 146n136–137, 147–73, 175, 175n, 176–78, 178n, 179–215, 217–31, 233, 234n3–4
  DEFENDING TRUTH: exercising personal judgment, 66, 184–85, 188n, 191, 193–95, 197n, 212–13, 225n89, 227n94; exercising personal responsibility, 80n, 192–93; study, 183n10, 188 (*see also under* religious education); giving reason for belief or action, 198, 201, 230; refuting opponents and liars, 59, 62–66, 194, 196–97, 219, 228–30 (*see also* confession of faith); service to Strasbourg, 213, 224–25 (*see also* love of neighbors)
  HUMAN AGENTS: clergy, 188–89, 191, 193, 196, 207–13, 227, 230; formal means 193, 196, 197n39, 207; informal means, 227–28
  LIFE: autobiography, 28, 131–35, 191–92, 196–97, 206–7, 211–12, 220, 223–31; children, 20, 24, 117, 129; education, 2–3, 15, 70n25, 124, 181, 200n46; experience of suffering, 103, 111, 119–21, 125, 133, 189, 213: as mother, 20; prayers of, 110–11, 119–23, 135, 156, 214–15, 230–31 (*see also* expositions of Psalms and Lord's Prayers); vow of celibacy (as young girl), 3, 61, 77n, 135n121, 226n91; unity with husband, 78–79, 106, 111, 114–16, 193, 204, 105n80, 224–25, 227–30
  LANGUAGE: for church work, 224; of disapproval: "fools and children," 73, "fools, naive" 192; of praise (for laity or Zell): "simple" / "honest," 59–61, 63–67, 69, 104, 112, 122, 188; "self-denigration," 25, 119n101, 122, 126–27, 131, 135, 135n130, 186, 188, 191, 213, 223n84, 230–31 (*see also* gender language); on social ranks, 3n, 197; on widows, 54, 123, 231
  PERSON: on appearance, 77, 189; on wealth, 77, 189
  PROTESTANTISM OF, 25n, 36, 47, 72n, 127–28, 137
  RELIGIOUS EXPERIENCE: anxiety, 207, 226, 227n92: assurance / confidence in salvation, 15–16, 125–26, 187n15, 221, 230–31; conversion, 181, 206n60, 207, 226, 227n92; conviction and maturity, 203n54, 204, 206, 212, 231; inward call by God, 206, 209, 212 (*see also* religious roles)
  RELIGIOUS EDUCATION: confidence in, 15, 27n, 90, 93, 194, 196, 207, 209n67, 227n94, 230, constantly growing in knowledge, 206–8, 224, 227; questioning, 226; private study, 95n62, 135, 190, 193–96, 197n, 207, 210, 213, 227; seeking out teachers, 226–27; source, 194, 210, 230
  RELIGIOUS PRACTICES, PROTESTANT: church attendance, 195–96, 198; confession of faith, 111, 114–19, 121, 130–31, 151, 156–57, 199, 201, 204, 214, 223–24, 227, 230 (*see also under* Lord's Supper); confession of sin, 25, 66, 116, 130n113, 149, 186n14, 189, 205–6; conversation with God, 133, 135; prayer, practice of, 63, 126–27, 130n,

Schütz Zell, Katharina (*cont.*)
132–33, 135, 139, 145, 206–7, 213
RELIGIOUS ROLES: educator, 30, 93n, 118, 127, 135, 140, 196, 227n94 (*see also* sermon at Zell's grave, 114–22); historian, 28, 105n78, 106n82, 117, 131n, 135, 179, 193n31, 222, 225n88; pastor, 30, 124–126, 128, 131–134, 228; "speaking out," 25, 27, 179, 196–97, 219, 223n, 228–30
TITLES: "Anna" / "widow's office," 196, 197n, 221, 224–25, 226n90; "assistant (minister)" / "helper," 19, 106, 203n54, 221, 224; "church mother," 1, 221, 226–27; "colleague of [first generation] Protestant clergy," 221, 227–28; "fisher of people," 16, 61, 221, 226; "Matthew's rib," 219, 221, 228; "mother of the afflicted," 19, 221, 225, 227; "pastor's wife" / "preacher's wife," 1, 192; "wedded companion," 19, 221, 224
AS WRITER: allegory / story forms, 65–67, 74–75, 109, 143, 151–52, 207–8; Biblical parables, 113–14, 117, 155, 186–87, 196, 205, 208–9; case for writing, 25, 59, 62, 66, 124–25, 219, 222, 228–30; dialogue, 65–66, 75, 94–95, 134, 207; humor / mockery, 25, 70, 169, 182, 191, 218; proverbs / plays on words, 65, 152, 157n, 189, 213; scriptural paraphrases, 47–48, 50, 52, 64, 113, 133, 146n137, 166, 231
Schwenckfeld, Caspar, 2n, 15n, 21, 22–24, 27–28, 30n, 32, 41, 89, 175, 178–81, 181n7, 185–93, 193n31, 194–95, 200–1, 201n49, 202, 202n52, 203, 203n55, 207–8, 210–14, 215n, 219–29; in title, 40
Schwenckfelders, 22, 23, 24, 127, 178, 181n7, 185–86, 188n18, 190n23, 191, 191n26, 192, 193n30, 202, 202n52, 203–6, 208, 209n66, 210, 212, 213n71, 227n92–94, 228n95, 233–34

Scribner, Robert, 2n2, 26n31, 29, 227n93
Séguenny, André, 181n7
Selderhuis, Herman, 18n23
Selmenitz, Felicitas von, 31, 49
Semler, Barbara, 150
Sheba, Queen of, 69
sickness, 166–67, 170–72, 189, 191, 197, 204, 226. *See also* lepers
Silbereisen, Elisabeth, 106n81
Silesia, 21, 210
Simeon, 116, 116n97, 197n38, 230
sin, 25, 45–46, 66, 101, 105–6, 110, 114, 123, 136–39, 141–42, 144–45, 147–50, 155, 158, 160–61, 165–67, 169–70, 172, 176n, 185–86, 189, 206, 211, 215, 234n3; actual, 211n; against the poor, 167; ignorance / wrong belief, 206n; mortal sin, 176n, 234n3; original, 138n, 138n; relationship to affliction (*see under* God); secret or outward, 145; spiritual interpretation of, 146–47; of unbelief, 137, 211
Socrates, 205n57
Sodom, 74, 76
Solomon, 69–70, 167
Specklin, Daniel, 98
Spenser, Edmund, xxvi
Speyer (city), 5, 20, 27, 128, 135, 150n
Spiritualists, 15n21, 182
Sprenger, Jacob, xxii
Saint Thomas. *See under* Strasbourg clergy
Stephen, 202
Stocker, Benedict, 33
Strasbourg, 1–7, 9–10, 12–14, 16–18, 20, 26–27, 29, 32, 40–41, 46–47, 49, 53, 56, 58, 62–63, 69, 70n25–26, 77–78, 82–83, 85n, 86n47, 89, 91, 94n60, 95n62, 97–99, 103–105, 112n89, 113, 116, 116n97, 118, 124, 126–29, 129n112, 136n123, 143n, 150n, 175–77, 177n3, 178–80, 184n, 185,

188n18, 189, 190n22–23, 191n25, 193n31, 200n48, 210, 214–17, 217n, 218–19, 219n, 220, 220n, 221–25, 225n88, 226n90, 227n92, 228, 230, 233–34; archives, 190n23, 216n, 218n; parishes and Saint Nicolas Parish, 225n88. *See also* cathedral of Strasbourg; clergy, Strasbourg Protestant; government, Strasbourg; Strasbourg clergy; Strasbourg laity
Strasbourg clergy, 196, 224, 226; bishop, 5, 16, 27, 58, 63n15, 64n18, 73, 105n79, 106, 119, 177n; cathedral clergy, 6, 216, 218; canons of Saint Thomas, 6
Strasbourg laity, 15, 23–24, 27–29, 59, 64, 89, 94, 98–99, 103, 109, 114, 116–18, 121–22, 124, 176, 197–200, 215–17, 219, 221–23, 226, 228, 230–31
Stucki, H., 23n
Sturm, Jacob, 9, 10
Sunday as resurrection day, 134n118. *See also* times of worship
surplice. *See under* worship practices, Roman
Swiss (Protestants), 9
Switzerland, 14, 18, 33, 49, 222; Biel, Switzerland, 33, 228n95; Confederation, 70, 71n27

Tatars, 201n49
teaching, Roman, 11–12, 16–17, 29–30, 43–45, 48, 57–58, 60–61, 65, 69n, 72n, 83–84, 99–102, 176n, 181–82, 199, 199n43, 199n46, 206n59, 208, 231n101. *See also* canon law; free will; tradition
Tertullian, Quintus Septimus Florens (church father), xiv
Tetrapolitan Confession, 176. *See also* confessions
thieves on crosses with Christ, 162
times of worship: Annunciation, 94; daily or weekly, 83, 85, 89, 95 96, 109; feast days of Christ, 89, 94; feast days of saints, 56, 89, 95, 95n; Nativity, 94. *See also* Annunciation; Ascension; Christmas; Easter; Good Friday; liturgical year; New Year's Day; Pentecost
Timothy (disciple of Paul), 68, 74, 209
Titus (disciple of Paul), 74, 209
tradition, Roman source of doctrine, 16, 57, 72n29, 182
Treger, Conrad, 7, 31, 61–62, 69–72
trinity, doctrine of, 44, 107n83, 118, 135n122, 215, 231n103
Turk. *See* Ottoman Turk

ubiquity. *See under* Lord's Supper
Ulhart, Philip, 46, 49
Ulm (city), 89, 112n89, 216–18, 218n, 219, 221–22, 222n82, 228, 234
Ulpianus, Domitius (classical jurist), xiii
United States, ix
unity, Christian, through love, 193. *See also under* Lord's Supper
university: degrees, 177, 196, 228n96; education, 182, 194, 227n93; scholastic philosophy / worldly learning, xviii, xxi, 209
Urbino, xx
Uriah (husband of Bathsheba), 140n130, 141
Uriel (angel), 213

Vashti (queen), 212
Vermigli, Peter Martyr. *See* Martyr, Peter
Vienna, 9, 194n33
vine dresser, 96
Virgil (classical poet), 194
Virgin Mary. *See* Mary (mother of Jesus)
virgins (devout women), 226
Viscal, bishop's official, 74
Vives, Juan Luis, xxi, xxiii, xxvi
vocation, 182–84; as Christians, 184; for clergy, 184, 216; inward / by God, 182, 184; outward / by church, 184, 216; by magistracy, 184–85,

vocation (cont.)
  216; for preaching / pastoral ministry, 183–84, 216. See also Christian life; laity; love of neighbor / brotherly love; see also under Schütz Zell; Zell
Vriend, J., 18n23
Vulgate (version of the Bible), 65n19, 68–69, 72n30, 81, 93n59, 161n

Wachernagel, Philip, 31n37
Wandel, Lee Palmer, 10n13
war, 21, 114n92, 172, 176
Weisse, Michael, 89–94
welfare. See poor relief
Weid, Bishop Herman von, 112n89
Weyer, Johann, xxii
Wimpfeling, Jacob, 13
Winckelmann, Otto, 12n14, 13n16
witch, xxi–xxii
Wittenberg (city), 177n
Wittenberg Concord, 9n17
Wolff, Anne, 91n54
women, 15, 17–18, 20, 25n, 27, 30, 43, 47–56, 62, 81, 85, 92, 93n58, 105n79–80, 126, 128, 135, 146n, 150, 183–84, 186, 187n16, 197, 213, 224, 226; abilities and gifts, 224; Biblical women, 129, 154–55, 211, 224n85 (see also Anna; Elizabeth; Esther; Hagar; Judith; Martha; Mary, Virgin; Mary; Mary Magdalene; Sarah; Vashti); devotional activities, corporate, 15, 95, 226; equality in Christian responsibility, 146–47; preaching / speaking out, 16, 43–45, 48, 52, 86n47, 90, 92, 104n77, 125, 129, 184, 197n; as religious leaders, 184n, 226; singing (in public worship), 85, 86n47. See also laity; under clergy, Roman, sexual mores of
work, women and: domestic, 92, 95–96, 188; nursing, 191, 197; money-earning, 3; as mothers, 92, 95–96; as widows, 54, 223n, 231; as wives, 48–49, 51–52, 54; as writers, 125n106

work, (Protestant) doctrine of, 12, 167n
worship. See under Protestants; worship practices, Roman
worship practices, Roman, 84, 97, 143n, 215, 218, 233n2; music, 86, 95; opus operatum, 114n94, 164n156, 176n, 198n42, 199, 199n46, 200n46; prayer, aids to (books of hours, rosaries), 84 (see also crucifix); sacraments, 15, 83, 87n, 97, 100–1, 161n, 176n, 182; transubstantiation, 192n28; surplice, 222n81. See also confirmation; extreme unction; Mass; penance; saints
Württemberg, 225

Zacheus, 205
Zanchi, Girolamo, 9n
Zechariah (father of John the Baptist), 82
Zell, Matthew, 1, 6–7, 15–20, 22–24, 26n, 27–28, 30–31, 40, 45, 56–61, 63–64, 66n, 67–69, 70n26, 71n27, 77–80, 96–100, 101n72, 102–20, 122, 125–26, 129, 135n121, 143n, 176–77, 177n, 182, 184n, 185n12, 187n17, 188, 191, 193, 193n39, 194n33, 197n39, 198, 198n43, 199, 199n44, 200n48, 201n48, 205, 205n57–58, 206n59, 209n67, 211, 213–15, 218, 221–25, 226n90, 227–28, 228n95, 230n100; confession of faith, 108; confession of sin, 110n; death, 110–11, 113, 118, 120, 194, 196, 204–5, 215, 225; good life, 77–78, 80, 102–5, 113, 115; humility, 193; knowledge of Christ / faith, 107–8, 204–6; as pastor / shepherd, 99, 103–5, 109, 111–14, 122, 198–200, 204–5, 225; as preacher / teacher, 6–7, 15, 18, 21–22, 69, 99, 102–9, 112–14, 118, 122, 199–200, 204; prayers (texts of), 110–11, 122, 204, 225; sermon text, 109; sin, 79n; in title, 48, 62
Zells, Matthew and Katharina, 19, 21, 102, 105n80, 125, 176, 178, 227n94;

marriage, 1, 16, 17, 18, 19, 20, 56, 58–59, 61, 64n, 77, 79–80, 106, 111, 121, 188–89, 204, 221, 224–25, 227, 230–31; servant girl, young, 78–79. *See also under* Schütz Zell, life

Zion, 111, 142, 142n, 143, 143n, 144

Zurich, 9, 33, 161, 194n33, 227n94. *See also under* Bible

Zürich Zentralbibliothek, 31, 33, 46

Zwingli, Ulrich, 22, 26, 85n, 105n80, 163n, 165n155, 167, 179, 199, 205n57, 215, 225n88, 228n95, 234

www.ingramcontent.com/pod-product-compliance
Lightning Source LLC
Chambersburg PA
CBHW050858300426
44111CB00010B/1297